Psychology of Learning

READINGS IN BEHAVIOR THEORY

Psychology of Learning

READINGS IN BEHAVIOR THEORY

EDITED BY

Barry Schwartz
Swarthmore College

W. W. Norton & Company
New York   London

Cover photograph by Bill Boyarsky. Used by permission.

Copyright © 1984 by W. W. Norton & Company, Inc.
ALL RIGHTS RESERVED.

This book is composed in Baskerville.
Composition by New England Typographic Service, Inc.
Manufacturing by The Murray Printing Company.
Book Design by Nancy Dale Muldoon.

Library of Congress Cataloging in Publication Data
Main entry under title:
Psychology of learning, readings in behavior theory.
    Includes bibliographical references.
    1. Learning, Psychology of—Addresses, essays,
studies. 2. Behaviorism (Psychology)—Addresses,
essays, studies. I. Schwartz, Barry, 1946-
LB1051.P72937   1983   370.15'23   82-24670

ISBN 0-393-95305-X

W.W. Norton & Company, Inc.
500 Fifth Avenue, New York, N.Y. 10110
W.W. Norton & Company, Ltd.
10 Coptic Street, London WC1A 1PU

    5 6 7 8 9 0

Contents

Psychology
of Learning
READINGS IN BEHAVIOR THEORY

Introduction

The discipline known as behavior theory has been at the heart of experimental psychology for most of this century. It has been concerned with exploring the determinants of certain kinds of learning and with studying the ways in which behavior can be controlled by environmental events. The principles of behavior theory have been derived primarily from laboratory experimentation with nonhuman animals; but many of these principles have been demonstrated to apply not only to animals in laboratories, but also to people in complex social environments.

This book contains a collection of articles that have contributed over the years to the development of behavior theory. The articles are organized into seven groups, each reflecting a major area of inquiry in behavior theory. Each group is further subdivided into sections and each of the sections is preceded by a brief introduction that previews the articles contained in the section and indicates why they are significant. With one exception (A Cognitive Theory of Avoidance Learning, by Seligman and Johnston), the articles have been reprinted without editing or abridgment. This decision was based on the view that an important component of one's education in psychology is in learning how to read and evaluate primary source material. In addition to their content, these articles convey the logic and subtleties of experimental design, execution, and analysis—in short, the process underlying the scientific endeavor.

Part I
Pavlovian Conditioning

At the turn of the century, Russian physiologist I. P. Pavlov (1849–1936) discovered what he called "psychic reflexes." When food was placed in a dog's mouth, the dog would salivate. This salivary response to food was wired into the dog's nervous system. It was a reflex that required no experience to be triggered by an appropriate stimulus. What Pavlov discovered was that other stimuli that bore no "wired-in" relation to salivation could also trigger the salivary response if they regularly preceded the delivery of food. These other stimuli came to be known as *conditioned stimuli* (CSs), because their ability to trigger reflexes was conditional upon the animal's experience. The CS had to be paired with an *unconditioned stimulus* (US), such as food, whose power to trigger salivation is independent of experience. The result of such pairing was the formation of an *association* between CS and US, so that the CS came to trigger a *conditioned response* (CR).

Pavlov devoted the rest of his life to the study of these "psychic reflexes," or *conditioned reflexes* as they came to be called (Pavlov, 1927).* He saw them as the building blocks of all learning by association and, indeed, perhaps all learning. In addition, he gave birth to a field of inquiry that has continued to be vigorously pursued to the present day. In the years since Pavlov's early work, the methods used to study Pavlovian conditioning, the phenomena discovered, and the accounts offered to explain these phenomena have broadened considerably. The articles included in Part I provide a glimpse of the range of concerns that occupy modern researchers.

Section A presents an article that demonstrates excitatory and inhibitory Pavlovian conditioning, using a method, quite different from Pavlov's, that has come to dominate research on Pavlovian conditioning. Section B presents an article that asks what it is an animal actually learns in Pavlovian conditioning, that is, what is conditioned. Section C explores the nature of the response conditioned to the CS, and its relation to the response triggered by the US. Section D is concerned with the kind of experience that is necessary for conditioning to occur. Is pairing of CS and US enough, as Pavlov thought, or is something more required? The evidence in Section D suggests that pairing of CS and US is not enough. This is buttressed by the article in Section E, which shows that organisms are sensitive to how informative a CS is about a coming US, and that they will learn to ignore CSs that are not informative. Finally, Section F presents an article that suggests that organisms may be pretuned to associate certain types of CSs with certain types of USs.

---

* For bibliographic information on all works cited in the introductions to the various sections of this book, see References to Introductions, beginning on p. 388.

A. EXCITATION AND INHIBITION

In studying conditioned salivation in dogs, Pavlov discovered two types of conditioning. One type, **conditioned excitation**, resulted when a CS was presented in conjunction with a US; the other type, **conditioned inhibition**, resulted when a CS was presented in the absence of a US. Pavlov showed that when, for example, a tone was presented in the absence of food, in a situation in which food was being delivered at other times, the tone did not remain neutral with respect to salivation; it actually inhibited the occurrence of salivation. Much of Pavlov's own research actually focused on the phenomenon of conditioned inhibition.

The article in this section, by Rescorla and LoLordo, demonstrates both conditioned inhibition and conditioned excitation using methods quite different from Pavlov's. Animals are first trained to avoid electric shock by running back and forth across a barrier. It is assumed that their continued avoidance responding is motivated by their fear of being shocked (see Part III). Then Pavlovian conditioning is introduced. One CS (the CS +) is followed by shock with the expectation that it will eventually trigger conditioned fear. Another CS (the CS −) is not followed by shock, with the expectation that it will eventually inhibit fear. Now what should happen when these two CSs are presented while the animal is responding to avoid shock? The CS + , if it makes the animal more afraid, should increase the rate of avoidance responding. The CS − , if it makes the animal less afraid, should decrease the rate of avoidance responding. Thus changes in the rate of avoidance responding are used to measure excitatory and inhibitory Pavlovian conditioning.

1 Inhibition of Avoidance Behavior

ROBERT A. RESCORLA AND VINCENT M. LOLORDO

Conditions for establishing stimuli which inhibit conditioned fear reactions are demonstrated in 3 experiments. Dogs, trained in a shuttle box to avoid shock on a Sidman avoidance schedule, received Pavlovian fear conditioning involving the presentation of tones and shock in various temporal relations. Subsequently, these tones were presented while S performed the avoidance response. Stimuli preceding shock in conditioning increased rate of avoidance; Pavlovian conditioned and discriminative inhibitors depressed it. Furthermore, a stimulus whose presentation was "contrasted" with that of shock depressed the avoidance rate. These findings imply that inhibitory as well as excitatory Pavlovian processes are involved in fear conditioning. Implications for pseudoconditioning control procedures and reinforcement of avoidance behavior are discussed.[1]

Although the establishment of conditioned fear by excitatory Pavlovian processes has been well accepted, the diminution of fear by inhibitory Pavlovian processes has received little attention. In salivary conditioning, some contingencies between a neutral stimulus and an US produce excitatory Pavlovian processes; other contingencies yield inhibitory processes (Pavlov, 1927). If the fear reaction follows the laws of Pavlovian conditioning, both excitatory and inhibitory processes should occur for it as well.

The three experiments reported here are based upon this reasoning: If avoidance behavior is maintained in part by a conditioned fear reaction, then any stimulus that increases this reaction should enhance the avoidance response and any stimulus which inhibits fear should weaken the avoidance response. Using avoidance responding as the index of fear, these experiments demonstrate that certain Pavlovian conditioning procedures produce elicitors of fear while others yield inhibitors of the fear reaction.

Experiment 1: Conditioned Inhibition

This experiment was designed to explore the possibility of inhibiting avoidance behavior by means of a Pavlovian conditioned inhibitor. We used a modification of one of Pavlov's (1927) conditioning procedures, employing two CSs, one of which warned S of the onset of shock and one of which informed S that no shock would follow.

Method

Subjects and Apparatus The Ss were 10 mongrel dogs obtained from a local supplier. They were maintained in individual cages on ad-lib food and water throughout the course of the experiment. Short exercise periods were given before and after the daily 1-hr. sessions.

The apparatus was a two-compartment shuttle box for dogs described

"Inhibition of Avoidance Behavior" by Robert A. Rescorla and Vincent M. LoLordo. *Journal of Comparative and Physiological Psychology,* 1965, *59,* 406-412. Copyright 1965 by the American Psychological Association. Reprinted by permission of the publisher and author.

in detail by Solomon and Wynne (1953). The two compartments were separated by a barrier of adjustable height and by a drop gate which, when lowered, prevented S from crossing from one compartment into the other. The floor was composed of stainless-steel grids which could be electrified through a scrambler. Speakers mounted above the hardware-cloth ceiling provided a continuous white noise background and permitted the presentation of tonal stimuli. The general noise level in the box, with the white noise and ventilating fans on, was about 80 db. re. .0002 dyne/sq cm; the tones added 10 db. to this level. Events were recorded on an Esterline-Angus operations recorder.

Procedure. Each S was trained to jump a barrier, separating the two sides of the shuttle box, to avoid electric shock. An unsignaled avoidance schedule similar to that described by Sidman (1953) was used. If S did not jump the barrier, a shock was delivered to the grid every 10 sec.; each jump postponed the next shock for 30 sec. Thus the shock–shock interval was 10 sec. and the response–shock interval was 30 sec. Shock duration was 0.25 sec.; the intensity was 6 ma. from a 550-v. ac source.

The S received 3 days of avoidance training. The height of the barrier separating the compartments of the shuttle box was 9, 12, and 15 in. on successive days. Beginning with the fourth experimental day, S was confined to one-half of the shuttle box and given five 1-hr. Pavlovian conditioning sessions on alternate days. On the days between Pavlovian conditioning sessions, S continued to receive 1-hr. sessions of avoidance training, with the barrier at 15 in. This particular order of events was adopted to prevent adventitious reinforcement of the avoidance response during Pavlovian conditioning. In preliminary experimentation, dogs given inescapable shock in the shuttle box had tended to have some difficulty in subsequent avoidance training; therefore, we established the avoidance behavior prior to Pavlovian conditioning and maintained the response by alternating avoidance training and conditioning sessions.

During the Pavlovian conditioning sessions, S received two kinds of conditioning trials: (a) CS_1 was presented for 5 sec.; either 2, 5, or 8 sec. following the termination of CS_1, a 5-sec. 3-ma. shock was presented; (b) CS_1 was presented for 5 sec.; either 2, 5, or 8 sec. following its termination, CS_2 was presented for 5 sec. but no shock was presented. Thus CS_1 was a trace CS with a variable gap between CS and US; the gaps of 2, 5, and 8 sec. were presented equally often for each kind of trial. In addition, CS_1 was followed by shock on only some trials, with CS_2 replacing shock on the remaining trials. Following CS_1, the onset of CS_2 was the only event which informed S that the particular presentation of CS_1 would not be followed by shock.

On each conditioning day, 18 of each of the two kinds of trials were presented in random order. The intertrial intervals were 1, 1.5, and 2 min., with a mean of 1.5 min. For five Ss, CS_1 was a 400-cps tone and CS_2 a 1,200-cps tone; for the other five Ss, the tones were interchanged.

After S had completed the sequence of five Pavlovian conditioning and seven avoidance sessions, a single test session was given. During this 1-hr. session, S performed the avoidance response under extinction conditions, i.e., no shocks were delivered. The 400- and 1,200-cps tones were presented in random order without respect to S's behavior. Sixty 5-sec. pre-

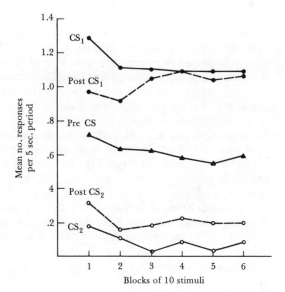

FIG. 1. *Mean number of responses during 5-sec. periods before, during, and following stimulus presentations in the test session (Experiment 1).*

sentations of each tone were given with a mean intertone interval of 25 sec. (range: 10–40 sec.).

Results

Nine Ss acquired the avoidance response, with distinct signs of learning appearing in the first 1-hr. session. One S was eliminated for failure to avoid one-half of the shocks programmed on Day 2. By the seventh day of avoidance training, the behavior of the nine Ss was stable. The mean number of shocks received on this day was 1.2; however, the response rate varied considerably among Ss. During the seventh avoidance training day, rates ranged from 6.5 to 12.7 jumps per minute, with a mean of 8.1. Even S with the lowest rate was responding at approximately three times the minimum rate necessary to avoid all shocks.

In order to evaluate the effects of the two CSs upon jumping during the test session, comparison was made with a base-line jumping rate. The rate of jumping during the 5-sec. periods immediately preceding the onset of the tones was taken as a base rate. Since the mean values of 0.61 and 0.63 jumps for the pre-CS_1 and pre-CS_2 periods did not differ significantly ($T = 18$, $p > .20$), a single base-rate score was computed by averaging the scores for these two periods. Figure 1 shows this base rate (pre-CS) together with the jumping rates both during and after the tones, all plotted in terms of the mean number of responses per presentation of each stimulus over blocks of 10 presentations.

The response rate was higher during the presentations of CS_1 than during the prestimulus periods for all Ss, yielding a $p < .01$ by the Wilcoxon signed-ranks test. In addition, the rate of responding in the 5-sec. period immediately following CS_1 was considerably higher than the base rate ($p < .01$). For some Ss, this period had a higher rate than the during-CS_1 period. But for every S the relation between response rates during CS_1 and during the 5 sec. following CS_1 was consistent throughout the session. Approximately 5–10 sec. after the termination of CS_1 (not shown), responding had returned to the base rate.

In striking contrast to the effects of CS_1, the response rate during CS_2 was well below the base rate for each S ($p < .01$). As in the case of CS_1, the effects of CS_2 continued after its termination. For both the period 0–5 sec. after CS_2 and the period 5–10 sec. after CS_2, the rate of responding was below the prestimulus rate ($p < .01$). However, response rate was higher during the 5 sec. following CS_2 than during CS_2 ($p < 05$). Even though these conclusions are based upon responding for the test session as a whole, the same relations obtain within each block of 10 stimulus presentations. Though Fig. 1 indicates a slight decline in responding during the test session, this was not statistically significant (Friedman two-way analysis of variance by ranks; $p > .20$).

To summarize, response rate suddenly increased upon presentation of the CS_1, remained high for the next few seconds, and then slowly returned to the prestimulus level. Upon presentation of CS_2, there was a sharp drop in response rate lasting about 15 sec., then responding returned to the base rate.

Discussion

The novel finding of this experiment was the capacity of CS_2 to depress avoidance responding. Observation of S during Pavlovian conditioning sessions confirmed the inference that CS_2 inhibited fear. Upon the onset of CS_1 S typically showed signs of fear and agitation—barking, crouching, running around with its ears back and its tail between its legs, etc. However, by the last conditioning session, CS_2 clearly produced termination of this behavior; during CS_2 S seemed to relax, cocking its head at the sound of the stimulus.

It is interesting to note that CS_2 had the same relation to shock in the present experiment that stimuli associated with the avoidance response have in the traditional signaled avoidance training procedure. In a (trace) avoidance situation, the CS occurs briefly; if S responds following the CS, shock does not occur, while failure to respond leads to the delivery of shock. In our Pavlovian conditioning procedure, CS_1 occurred briefly; if it was followed by CS_2, no shock occurred. The failure of CS_2 to occur led to the delivery of shock. Thus stimuli associated with an avoidance response might be expected to acquire properties similar to those of CS_2. The capacity of such stimuli to inhibit the fear previously aroused by the warning stimulus would mean rapid reinforcement for the avoidance response and might provide a mechanism for the "conservation of anxiety" suggested by Solomon and Wynne (1954).

However, before concluding that Pavlovian inhibition was the source of the depressed response rates, it is necessary to demonstrate similar effects from other Pavlovian conditioning paradigms known to yield inhibitors. The next experiment does this.

Experiment 2: Discriminative and Conditioned Inhibition

Pavlov (1927) reported the development of both discriminative and conditioned inhibitors of the salivary reflex. The present experiment explores these conditioning paradigms for the conditioning of fear. One group of Ss received discriminative Pavlovian conditioning in which one stimulus was always followed by shock and another never followed by shock. A second group received conditioning designed to establish a Pavlovian conditioned inhibitor; unlike the inhibitor in Experiment 1, this stimulus preceded CS_1 and bore a constant time relation to it.

Method.

Subjects and Apparatus. The apparatus was identical to that used in Experiment 1. The Ss were 10 mongrel dogs.

Procedure. The Ss first received 3 days of Sidman avoidance training. On Day 1, the barrier height was 9 in.; on all subsequent days the height was 15 in. Beginning with Day 4, each S received Pavlovian conditioning while confined to one-half of the shuttle box. The Ss received this treatment on alternate days, with avoidance days intervening, for five Pavlovian conditioning and seven avoidance training days. Each S was then tested in the manner described in Experiment 1.

For five Ss the Pavlovian conditioning was discriminative, involving two kinds of trials: (a) CS_1 came on for 5 sec., and coincident with its termination a 3-ma. shock was presented for 5 sec. (b) CS_2 was presented for 5 sec., and no shock was delivered. Another group of five Ss received a conditioned inhibition procedure involving two kinds of trials: (a) CS_1 came on for 5 sec., and a 5-sec. shock was presented coincident with its termination. (b) CS_2 was presented for 5 sec., and coincident with the termination of CS_2, CS_1 came on for 5 sec.; on these trials no shock was delivered.

Thus, the Pavlovian conditioning procedures for the two groups were identical with but one exception: On trials when the Discrimination group received CS_2 alone, the Conditioned Inhibition group received CS_2 alone, the Conditioned Inhibition group received CS_2 followed by CS_1. Half the Ss had the 400-cps tone and half the 1,200-cps tone as CS_2. Eighteen trials of each type were given per day in random order. The intertrial intervals were 1, 1.5, and 2 min. ($M = 1.5$ min.).

In addition to these two groups, a control group of seven Ss was run in order to check on the unconditioned properties of the 1,200- and 400 -cps tones. The treatment of these dogs was identical to that of the experimental Ss except that the Pavlovian conditioning days were omitted.

Results

Avoidance learning proceeded as in the previous experiment. Two Ss, however, had to be discarded because of ill health—one from each of the two experimental groups. On the last avoidance training day, the mean jumping rate for the Discrimination group was 8.0 responses per minute; for the Conditioned Inhibition group 9.3. The difference is not significant ($U = 7$, $p > .40$).

A three-way analysis of variance performed on the test-session scores of the two experimental groups revealed no significant effect involving groups. Therefore, for all subsequent analyses the results of these two groups have been combined. Fig. 2 shows the mean jumping rates for various 5-sec. periods of the test session as a function of blocks of 10 stimulus presentations. Because the analysis of variance indicated no reliable

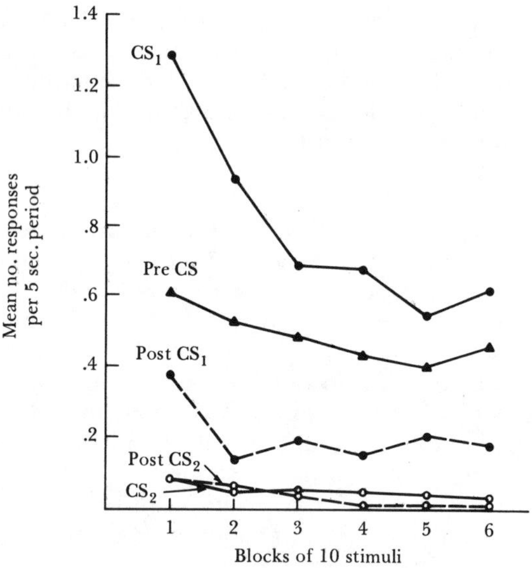

FIG. 2. *Mean number of responses during 5-sec. periods before, during, and following stimulus presentations in the test session (Experiment 2).*

difference between the response rates in the pre-CS$_1$ and pre-CS$_2$ periods, these rates were averaged to give a single base rate.

For the session as a whole, the rate during CS$_1$ was significantly greater than the base rate ($T = 4$, $p < .05$). However, it is clear from Fig. 2 that the main effect of CS$_1$ occurred during the first 10 stimulus presentations. The rate of jumping during the 5-sec. period following the termination of CS$_1$ also differed from the base rate ($p < .01$). However, unlike the post-CS$_1$ rate of Experiment 1, the rate following the fear-eliciting stimulus was considerably lower than the base rate. This depression appeared early, lasted throughout the test session, and extended into the period 5–10 sec. following CS$_1$ termination (not shown).

In both experimental groups jumping rate during CS$_2$ was depressed considerably below the prestimulus rate ($p < .01$). Depression of rate also appeared during the 5–10 sec. following CS$_2$ ($p < .01$). These depressed rates continued throughout the session, and were lower than the rate during the 5 sec. following CS$_1$ ($p < .05$).

The test session results for the seven control Ss showed no differences between the rates during the two tones. For the session as a whole the mean number of responses in the 5-sec. periods before, during, and after stimulus presentations were 0.51, 0.62, and 0.42, respectively. Both the higher rate during the tones and the lower rate following stimulus termination were significantly different from the prestimulus rate ($p < .05$). The effects of the tones occurred primarily early in the test session.

However, unconditioned effects of the tones were minor compared with the effects of CS$_1$ and CS$_2$ in the two experimental groups. Comparison was made between the control group and the combined experimental groups by means of suppression ratios (Annau & Kamin, 1961). This ratio of response rate during the CS to the sum of the rates during and pre-CS allows comparison among animals independently of their base rate. Using this ratio, the increase in rate during CS_1 was found to be greater in the experimental groups ($p < .05$). Similarly the ratios for the periods during CS_2, and following CS_1 and CS_2, in the experimental groups differed from the corresponding ratios for the control group ($p < .01$).

Discussion
The results confirm the hypothesis that Pavlovian conditioned inhibitors and discriminative inhibitors can depress the rate of avoidance responding. Though the effects of CS_2 in this experiment were consistent with the results obtained in Experiment 1, several findings about the properties of CS_1 were unexpected and somewhat puzzling. First, the fear reaction to CS_1 in the present experiment seemed to extinguish more rapidly than in Experiment 1. Perhaps the variable temporal gap between CS_1 and US in Experiment 1 retarded extinction in that experiment; such phenomena are well known in instrumental learning (e.g., McClelland & McGown, 1953).

Equally unexpected was the depression of response rate immediately following the unreinforced presentation of CS_1. This depression seems independent of the fear-eliciting properties of CS_1 since it remains relatively constant through the session in spite of the decreasing capacity of CS_1 to elicit fear. A possible explanation is that during Pavlovian conditioning CS_1 termination preceded the intertrial interval. The end of a conditioning trial was an event which reliably signaled a period free of shock. To the extent that the termination of CS_1 occurred near the end of a trial, that termination might become an inhibitory stimulus. The failure of the termination of CS_1 in Experiment 1 to produce the depression may be related to its favorable position for fear conditioning during the Pavlovian conditioning sessions. The next experiment explores the possibility that an event which precedes a long period without shock becomes inhibitory.

Experiment 3: Contrast
Experiments 1 and 2 have varied the relationship of CS_2 to CS_1, and the relationship of CS_1 to shock, without affecting the reliable depression in avoidance responding produced by CS_2. These experiments have held constant only the relationship of CS_2 to shock—CS_2 was always followed by a period free from shocks. It may be that for CS_2 to depress the rate of avoidance responding, it need only have preceded a period which is shock-free; differentiation or contrast between CSs may be unnecessary.

Method
Subjects and Apparatus. The apparatus was identical to that of the previous experiments. The Ss were 10 mongrel dogs.
Procedure. Two groups of five Ss each received treatment identical to that of Ss in Experiment 2 in all respects except that the procedure on Pavlovian conditioning days differed. For one group (Contrast) two kinds of conditioning trials occurred: (a) a 5-sec. 3-ma. shock occurred without any warning signal and (b) a 5-sec. presentation of a tone (CS_2) occurred without a shock. Thus, this group received exactly the same Pavlovian conditioning procedure as the Discrimination group of Experiment 2,

except that CS_1 was omitted entirely. For three Ss CS_2 was the 400-cps tone and for two Ss it was the 1,200-cps tone. A second group (Tones) of five Ss also received two kinds of "conditioning" trials: (a) a 5-sec. presentation of the 400-cps tone and (b) a 5-sec. presentation of the 1,200-cps tone. This group, then, had Pavlovian conditioning identical to that of the Discrimination group of Experiment 2, except that shock was omitted entirely. The Contrast group is an experimental group receiving the CS_2–shock relationship common to the groups of Experiments 1 and 2. The Tones group serves as a control for the number of stimulus events during Pavlovian conditioning, as well as for familiarity with the CS_2 tone. Both groups received 36 trials per session, with the two types of trials occurring in random order. The mean intertrial interval was 1.5 sec. For both groups, instrumental avoidance training and testing procedures were identical to those of Experiment 2.

Results

Avoidance learning proceeded as in the previous experiments. One S was eliminated from the Contrast group because of a procedural error and one from the Tones group because of illness. The mean rates of responding on the last training day were 8.2 responses per minute in the Contrast group and 7.2 for the Tones group ($U = 7$, $p > .40$).

For the Tones group, the mean number of responses in the 5-sec. periods before, during, and after stimulus presentations in the test session were 0.55, 0.54, and 0.49, respectively; clearly, the tones had little effect upon avoidance responding.

The results for the Contrast group are given in Fig. 3. Even though these Ss were presented only with CS_2 during Pavlovian conditioning sessions, they received both tones during the test session. The novel tone has been labeled CS_1. It is clear from Fig. 3 that CS_2 had a strong depressant effect, similar to that observed in earlier experiments. This effect persisted for the 5-sec. period following CS_2. In addition, the response rates during and just after CS_1 were depressed below base rate. This effect. presumably the result of generalization from CS_2, was less than the depression produced by CS_2; CS_2, CS_1, and the period 5 sec. following CS_2 showed greater depression in the Contrast group than in the Tones group ($p < .05$).

Discussion

This experiment demonstrates that in order for a stimulus to depress avoidance responding it is sufficient that it previously be explicitly paired with a period free of shock. However, the results of the Tones group make it evident that mere experience with the stimulus in the total absence of shock is not sufficient. Rather, for a stimulus to depress avoidance behavior, it must occur without shock against a background in which shock does in fact occur.

It is of some methodological importance that the simplest condition which produced the inhibitory effect is also one which is often used as a control for "pseudoconditioning" (e.g., Fromer, 1963). To rule out the possibility that simple, independent presentation of CS or US, or both, is a sufficient condition for the CRs under study, a group such as the Con-

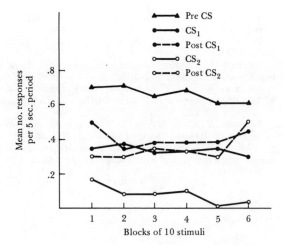

FIG. 3. *Mean number of responses during 5-sec. periods before, during, and following stimulus presentations in the test session (Experiment 3, Contrast group.)*

trast group from Experiment 3 is often used. An alternative procedure is that of discriminative conditioning, in which one compares the reaction to CS + with that to CS − (e.g., Solomon & Turner, 1962). The results of the present investigation bring into question the validity of both of these procedures as controls for nonassociative factors in conditioning. These procedures do far more than simply leave CS and US unpaired— they explicitly keep CS and US separate in such a way that the CS can become a signal for the *absence* of the US. As seen in Experiments 2 and 3, such procedures can endow the CS with inhibitory properties. Thus, though such procedures allow us to say that a CS paired with the US is different from a discriminated or "contrasted" stimulus, they do not permit a conclusion that the positive CS has acquired excitatory properties. Possibly presentations of CS and US which are truly random in time, as well as in order, would serve as a better control procedure for nonassociative factors in Pavlovian conditioning.

These experiments demonstrate that Pavlovian procedures, administered independently of instrumental responding, can control that responding. We consider the changes in response rate to be evidence for corresponding changes in the level of fear. Thus, inhibitors as well as elicitors of fear seem conditionable by Pavlovian procedures. This finding adds considerable support to the notion that the acquisition of fear follows the laws of Pavlovian conditioning.

Notes

[1] This research was supported by United States Public Health Service Grant MH-04202 and National Science Foundation Grant G-14438 to Richard L. Solomon. The authors are grateful to R. L. Solomon for his advice and criticism; we also thank Russell M. Church, Francis W. Irwin, Marged Lindner, and J. Bruce Overmier, for criticism of an earlier draft of this report.

References

Annau, Z., & Kamin, L. J. The conditioned emotional response as a function of intensity of the US. *J. Comp. Physiol. Psychol.*, 1961, **54**, 428–432.

Fromer, R. Conditioned vasomotor responses in the rabbit. *J. Comp. Physiol. Psychol.*, 1963, **56**, 1050–1055.

McClelland, D. C., & McGown, D. E. The effect of variable food reinforcement on the strength of a secondary reward. *J. Comp. Physiol. Psychol.,* 1953, **46,** 80–86.

Pavlov, I. P. *Conditioned reflexes.* (Trans. by G. V. Anrep.) London: Oxford University Press, 1927.

Sidman, M. Avoidance conditioning with brief shock and no exteroceptive warning signal. *Science,* 1953, **118,** 157–158.

Solomon, R. L., & Turner, L. H. Discriminative classical conditioning in dogs paralyzed by curare can later control discriminative avoidance responses in the normal state. *Psychol. Rev.,* 1962, **69,** 202–219.

Solomon, R. L., & Wynne, L. C. Traumatic avoidance learning: Acquisition in normal dogs. *Psychol. Monogr.,* 1953, **67** (4, Whole No. 354). 354.

Solomon, R. L., & Wynne, L. C. Traumatic avoidance learning: The principles of anxiety conservation and partial irreversibility. *Psychol. Rev.,* 1954. **61,** 353–385.

B. SECOND-ORDER CONDITIONING: WHAT IS LEARNED?

One of the persistent questions in studies of Pavlovian conditioning asks what organisms learn. When a CS like a tone is paired with a US like food, until animals start salivating to the tone, do the animals learn to associate the CS with salivation or do they learn to associate the CS with food? The first possibility suggests that conditioning involves the formation of stimulus–response (S–R) associations, whereas the second suggests that it involves stimulus–stimulus (S–S) associations.

There are a number of different ways to ask this question experimentally. Suppose we first pair a tone with a light. No conditioned responses develop, because the light produces no unconditioned responses. Then we pair the light with a US until the light is producing CRs. Finally, we present the tone in a test. Does the tone produce CRs? If it does, it must be because the animal associated the tone with the light before the light was itself producing CRs. This is known as a sensory preconditioning procedure.

Suppose we modify this procedure slightly. First we pair a light with food until it is producing CRs. Then we pair a tone with the light. Does the tone come to produce CRs also? This is known as a second-order conditioning procedure. The light, a first-order CS, comes to serve as a US for the tone, a second-order CS.

The article in this section by Rizley and Rescorla asks what is learned in Pavlovian conditioning using these two methods. It contrasts sensory preconditioning and second-order conditioning. Consider what should happen if after establishing second-order conditioning one presents the first-order CS without the US. This procedure, called extinction, is known to eliminate the CR. What is the effect of extinguishing the first-order CS on responding to the second-order CS? If second-order conditioning involves associating the CS with the CR, the animal should continue responding; however, if it involves associating the second-order CS with the first-order CS, the animal should stop responding, since the first-order CS is no longer associated with the US. Rizley and Rescorla show that extinction of the first-order CS has different effects in sensory preconditioning than it does in second-order conditioning, suggesting that the "what is learned" question may have more than one answer. It employs a method for studying Pavlovian conditioning that is similar to the method in Section A. Animals are trained to respond for food. Then Pavlovian conditioning with shock as a US is conducted. Finally the CS is presented while the animal is responding for food. If the CS has become associated with shock, and triggers fear, it will suppress responding for food. The degree of conditioned suppression or conditioned emotional response (CER) is a measure of the strength of Pavlovian conditioning.

This article, in addition to telling us something about what is learned, also provides a clear demonstration that second-order conditioning is a robust phenomenon. In recent years, second-order conditioning procedures have been used to investigate a wide range of interesting issues in the study of Pavlovian conditioning (see Rescorla, 1980).

2 Associations in Second-Order Conditioning and Sensory Preconditioning

ROSS C. RIZLEY AND ROBERT A. RESCORLA

A series of four experiments is reported using a CER procedure with rats as subjects. The first three experiments provide demonstrations of second-order fear conditioning and suggest that second-order conditioning is unaffected by extinction of the first-order stimulus upon which it was based. A fourth experiment indicates that in the analogous sensory preconditioning procedure, extinction of the first-order stimulus does affect responding to the secondary stimulus. The results are interpreted as inconsistent with an interpretation of second-order conditioning in terms of associations between the first- and second-order stimuli.[1]

Although second-order conditioning has often been accorded considerable responsibility in theoretical accounts of learning, it has not received commensurate empirical examination. After the initial demonstrations by Pavlov (1927) there were few studies of second-order conditioning until quite recently. Even more rare are studies which demonstrate such conditioning under adequately controlled conditions. To assert that a change in response to a CS results from second-order conditioning requires demonstration both (*a*) that the change results from the relation arranged between the CS and some reinforcer and (*b*) that the reinforcer has acquired its ability to condition as a result of a prior relation with a primary reinforcing event. Failure to satisfy the first requirement leaves the results open to interpretation in terms of nonassociative effects of presentation of the CS and reinforcer, while not satisfying the second leaves in question the "second-order" character of any changes in response to the CS. One purpose of the present series of experiments is to provide an experiment appropriate to demonstrate second-order conditioning and to rule out such alternatives.

A second aim of the present research is to provide some insight into the character of second-order conditioning. Consider a typical second-order conditioning situation in which S_1 is first paired with a US and then S_2 is regularly followed by S_1. As a consequence of the first stage, presentation of S_1 elicits a CR, while during the second-order conditioning stage S_2 also comes to elicit that CR. Three quite different conceptualizations have been suggested for interpreting the ability of S_2 to evoke a CR. One obvious alternative is that the second stage results in an association between S_2 and S_1, so that the presentation of S_2 evokes a CR because S_1 does so and S_2 is associated with S_1. A second plausible interpretation is that since S_1 reliably evokes a CR in the presence of S_2, a direct association is formed between S_2 and the CR (e.g., Hull, 1943). Finally, Konorski (1948) has suggested a third alternative according to which S_1 is initially associated with a neural representation of the US. When S_2 is followed by S_1, S_1 reactivates the US representation and S_2 also becomes associated with it.

One distinguishing feature of the first account is the assumption that a CR to S_2 is dependent upon the continued elicitation of the CR by S_1. Thus, S_2 evokes a CR following second-order conditioning only because S_1 continues to do so. Consequently, should extinction of the response to S_1 follow immediately upon the establishment of second-order conditioning of S_2, we would anticipate loss of the conditioned response to S_2 as well. Neither of the alternative interpretations makes that prediction. The first three experiments reported here examine that prediction in a conditioned suppression situation.

Experiment 1

Method

Subjects and Apparatus. The subjects were 32 Sprague-Dawley male rats about 100 days old at the start of the experiment. They were maintained throughout the experiment at 80% of their normal body weight.

The experimental chambers consisted of eight identical Skinner boxes $9 \times 8 \times 8$ in. Each chamber had a recessed food magazine in the center of the end wall and a bar to the left of the magazine. The floor of the chamber was composed of $\frac{3}{16}$-in. stainless-steel rods spaced $\frac{3}{4}$ in. apart. This grid could be electrified through a relay-sequence scrambler (Hoffman & Fleshler, 1962) from a high-voltage, high-resistance shock source. The two end walls of the chamber were aluminum, the side wall and top were clear Plexiglas. Each Skinner box was enclosed in a sound- and light-resistant shell. Mounted on the rear wall of this shell was a $6\frac{1}{2}$-w. light bulb and two speakers The speakers permitted the presentation of a 250- and a 1,800-Hz. tone CS. Experimental events were controlled and recorded automatically by relay equipment located in an adjoining room.

Procedure. In the first session, each rat was magazine trained automatically with food pellets (45 mg., P. J. Noyes Co.) delivered on a VI 1-min. schedule. In addition, each bar press yielded a food pellet. This session continued until the subject had emitted about 50 bar presses; shaping was used if necessary. Starting with the second experimental day, all sessions were 2 hr. long and the animal was placed on a VI schedule of reinforcement. For the first 20 min. of this session the schedule was VI 1 min.; throughout the remainder of the experiment a VI 2-min. schedule was in effect.

After 5 days of VI training, two pretest sessions were given during which the stimuli subsequently to be used in conditioning were presented. During each session two presentations each of a 30-sec. 1,800-Hz. tone and of a 10-sec. flashing of the houselight (2/sec) were superimposed on the bar-pressing behavior.

The next day began Phase I conditioning, designed to establish first-order conditioned fear to the light CS. The rats were divided into four groups of eight animals each, labeled to indicate their treatment in three successive phases. A "P" indicates paired presentation; a "U," unpaired presentation; an "N," no trials; and an "E," extinction. During Phase 1 Groups PPN, PPE, and PUE all received paired presentations of the 10-

sec. light and a 1-ma. $\frac{1}{2}$-sec. footshock; shock onset coincided with CS termination. Four such trials were given during each of the two 2-hr. sessions. Group UPE received explicitly unpaired presentations of the CS and shock. During each session they received four lights and four shocks.

For the next two sessions only the VI schedule was in effect. This permitted recovery of the base-line bar-press rate which had been depressed during first-order conditioning. The next day began Phase 2, designed to produce second-order conditioning in some groups. Groups PPN, PPE, and UPE each received trials consisting of a 30-sec. 1,800-Hz. tone followed immediately by a 10-sec. flashing of the houselight. Four such trials were administered on the first day of Phase 2; two additional trials were given during the first hour of the subsequent session. The second hour of that session began Phase 3. During Phase 2 Group PUE received the same number of presentations of each stimulus, but they were unpaired. By the end of Phase 2, Groups PPN and PPE had both received first pairing of the first-order CS with shock and then pairing of a second-order CS with the first-order CS. The remaining groups were controls designed to present the same number of events but to omit the pairing relation in one of the two phases.

Phase 3 was designed to manipulate the level of first-order conditioning to the light CS. Groups PPE, UPE, and PUE all received nonreinforced presentations of the 10-sec. light superimposed on VI responding for $2\frac{1}{2}$ sessions. During this time lights were presented at a rate of four per hour, for a total of 20 presentations. Group PPN simply continued bar pressing throughout Phase 3.

The next session assessed the conditioning of the second-order stimulus. During this session all groups continued to respond on the VI 2-min. schedule. Superimposed upon this performance were four nonreinforced presentations of the 30-sec. tone CS.

Throughout, the measure of conditioned fear was the amount of suppression of bar pressing produced by a stimulus presentation. In order to attenuate the effects of individual differences in overall rate of responding, the results are plotted in terms of a suppression ratio. This ratio has the form $A/(A+B)$, where A is the rate of responding during the CS and B is the rate of responding in a comparable period prior to CS onset. Thus, a suppression of 0 indicates no responding during the CS (good conditioning) while one of .5 indicates similar rates of responding during the CS and pre-CS periods (little conditioning).

Results and Discussion

First-order conditioning of fear to the light proceeded rapidly. By the final trial of Phase 1 all animals showed virtually complete suppression during the light presentation.

Figure 1 shows the results of Phase 2 second-order conditioning. Groups PPE and PPN both show marked and similar increases in suppression over the six trials of Phase 2. By the final block of two trials they were reliably more suppressed than either of the control groups ($Us < 2$, $ps < .01$). Thus, substantial second-order conditioning was observed. It is also of interest to note that Group UPE showed more suppression than

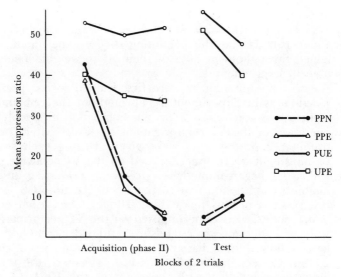

FIG. 1. *Mean suppression ratio during the second-order stimulus in Experiment 1. (Extinction of the first-order stimulus intervened between acquisition and test of the second-order stimulus.)*

did Group PUE ($U = 8$, $p < .01$). The former group received pairing of the tone and light during Phase 2, but no prior first-order conditioning of the light. This result may indicate that the light is a mildly aversive stimulus itself, capable of producing some first-order conditioning of the tone.

Figure 1 also shows the results of test presentations of the tone after intervening nonreinforced presentation of the light in Phase 3. Of most interest is the comparison of Groups PPE and PPN. Despite the intervening nonreinforcement of the light in Group PPE, the two groups showed virtually identical and substantial second-order fear of the tone. Both groups are reliably more suppressed than the controls, which continued to show little suppression ($Us < 2$, $ps < .01$).

However, the results of Phase 3 indicated that extinction of the first-order CS was incomplete in Group PPE; by the final four trials, the mean suppression ratio was .14, still substantially below .50. Furthermore, the absence of an assessment of fear of the light in Group PPN precludes the assertion of a difference in first-order responding in the two groups. Therefore, while this experiment may be taken as evidence that strong second-order conditioning of fear was obtained, it provides only weak evidence bearing on the effects of extinction of the first-order stimulus.

Experiment 2

This experiment was designed to provide a more powerful test of the effects of extinction of the first-order stimulus following second-order conditioning. It employed a procedure similar to that of Experiment 1 except that it included more substantial first-order extinction, together with assessment of the level of first-order conditioning in both groups.

Method

Subjects and Apparatus. The subjects were 16 male Sprague-Dawley rats about 100 days at the beginning of the experiment. They were maintained throughout at 80% of their ad-lib weight. The appratus was that used in Experiment 1.

Procedure. All subjects were first trained to bar press on a VI 2-min. schedule as in Experiment 1. Throughout the remainder of the experiment all sessions were 2 hr. in length and all involved the continued operation of the VI reinforcement schedule. After 5 days of simple VI training, 2 pretest days were given. During each session four 30-sec. flashing lights were superimposed on the VI behavior.

Phase 1 began immediately following pretesting and was designed to establish conditioned fear to the 1,800-Hz. tone CS. During each of the two sessions of this phase four 10-sec. tones, each ending in a .5-sec. .5-ma. shock, were superimposed on the VI performance.

Phase 2, designed to establish second-order conditioning to the flashing light, followed immediately after Phase 1. On each of the 2 days of Phase 2, four 30-sec. flashing lights were presented; the termination of each light was coincident with the onset of the 10-sec. 1,800-Hz. tone. No electric shock was delivered at any point during Phase 2 or during the remainder of the experiment.

Following Phase 2, subjects were divided into two groups of eight animals each to receive differential treatment during Phase 3. Group E (extinction) received 12 10-sec. presentations of the 1,800-Hz. tone on each of the 3 days of this phase. Group C (control) received only 3 days of continued VI bar-press training.

Following Phase 3, two test procedures were administered on successive days. On Test Day 1, each subject received four 30-sec. flashing light presentations superimposed upon the VI responding. No shocks or tones were delivered. This test was designed to detect differences in suppression to the second-order light CS. On Test Day 2, all subjects received 12 10-sec. tone presentations while bar pressing. This testing day was included to verify that Phase 3 had indeed established a difference between groups in conditioning to the tone. Throughout the experiment, suppression ratios were used as the measure of conditioning.

Results and Discussion

The first- and second-order conditioning of Phases 1 and 2 were similar to those of Experiment 1. Figure 2 shows the acquisition of second-order conditioning in the two groups; both groups showed substantial increases in suppression during Phase 2. At no point were the groups reliably different during this phase.

During Phase 3, Group E showed considerable extinction of fear to the tone first-order CS. Every subject in this group was less suppressed during the tone on Day 3 than on Day 1. The mean suppression ratio by the final day as .45, indicating near complete extinction of fear to the tone.

The data of primary interest, suppression to the second-order light CS during Test Day 1, are presented in the second panel of Fig. 2. As may be seen, there was a small but nonreliable difference between the groups during that test ($Us > 26$, $ps > .28$). Of equal interest is the result of test-

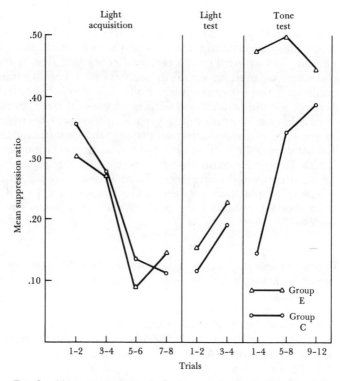

FIG. 2. *Mean suppression ratio during second-order conditioning of the light and final testing of the light and tone in Experiment 2. (Extinction of the first-order tone followed acquisition of suppression to the light.)*

ing the first-order conditioning responding to the tone on the following day, shown in the final panel of Fig. 2. Group C showed substantially greater suppression to the tone than did Group E ($U = 6$, $p < .01$).

These data indicate that despite substantial differences in the level of conditioning remaining to the first-order CSs following Phase 3, the two groups showed comparable fear of the second-order CS. Especially worth pointing out is that Group E showed no evidence of fear of the first-order CS while still showing substantial conditioning to its second-order CS. This indicates that continued maintenance of conditioned fear to the first-order CS is not necessary for continued control over behavior by the second-order CS.

Experiment 3

It seemed possible that in Experiment 2 the extinction of the first-order CS did affect the level of second-order conditioning but that the experiment was not sufficiently sensitive to detect that effect. Experiment 3 was designed to increase that sensitivity in three ways: by providing more extensive testing of the second-order stimulus, by producing even greater differences in the levels of first-order conditioning, and by employing a within-subject design. In this experiment fear was conditioned to two tone stimuli in the first phase, but only one of these was later used to establish second-order conditioning. The experimental group received both extinction of that fear elicitor which had been used to establish second-order conditioning and also continued conditioning of the other fear elicitor. The control group received continued first-order conditioning of the stimulus used to establish second-order conditioning and extinction trials with the other stimulus. Following this differential experience, the level of second-order conditioning was tested over several days.

In addition to establishing greater differences between the two groups in the level of first-order conditioning, this design equates the two groups for total number of first-order stimulus presentations and for experience with a first-order extinction procedure. Both groups receive the same set of treatments following second-order conditioning; they differ only in which treatments are applied to the first-order CS used to establish their second-order conditioning and which are applied to some other first-order CS.

Method

Subjects and Apparatus. The subjects were 32 male Sprague-Dawley rats about 110 days old at the start of the experiment, maintained at 80% of their ad-lib weight throughout the experiement. The apparatus was identical to that of Experiment 1.

Procedure. Initial magazine and bar-press training were conducted as in the previous experiments. Thereafter, all sessions were 2 hr. in duration and involved the maintenance of bar pressing on a VI 2-min. schedule. After 5 days of simple VI training, all animals received two pretest sessions, during each of which four 30-sec. flashing lights were presented.

Immediately following pretest, Phase 1 first-order conditioning was begun, designed to establish fear to the tonal stimuli. On each of the 3 days of this phase, four fear conditioning trials were superimposed on the VI behavior. On each trial a 10-sec. tone terminated in a 5-sec. 5-ma. footshock. For two randomly chosen trials the tone was 250 Hz. interrupted at a rate of 3/sec., while the remaining two trials it was 1,800 Hz. presented without interruption.

Following Phase 1, all subjects received 1 additional day of VI training to permit recovery of the slightly depressed base-line response rates. Phase 2, the second-order conditioning phase, began immediately following the recovery day. On each of the 2 days of Phase 2, all subjects received four conditioning trials consisting of a 30-sec. flashing light, the termination of which was coincident with the onset of a 20-sec. tone. For half of the animals the tone was 250 Hz. and for the remaining half it was 1,800 Hz.

Following Phase 2, subjects were given 7 days of Phase 3, designed to extinguish fear of one tone while maintaining it to the other. All animals received eight 10-sec. trials on each day, six of which were nonreinforced presentations of one tone and two of which were presentations of the other tone terminating in a .5 sec. .5ma. footshock. For the 16 animals of Group E the tone employed to condition the light in Phase 2 was nonreinforced and the other tone reinforced; for the 16 animals of Group C, the tone employed to condition the light in Phase 2 was reinforced and the other nonreinforced. For half the animals in each group

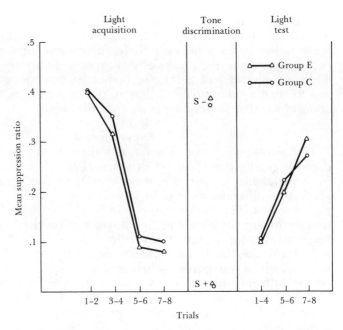

FIG. 3. *Mean suppression ratio from various stages of Experiment 3. (The first panel shows second-order conditioning of the light. The second panel shows discriminative performance to the two tones on the final day of Phase 3. The final panel shows the results of subsequent testing of the light second-order stimulus.)*

the 250-Hz. tone was the reinforced tone, while for the other half the 1,800 Hz. tone was reinforced.

The testing phase, which followed immediately upon Phase 3, was designed to assess fear to the second-order light stimulus. On each of 3 days, subjects received four 30-sec. presentations of the light while bar pressing on the VI schedule. The question of primary interest is whether suppression to the light is a function of the level of fear remaining conditioned to that tone which had previously been used to condition the light. As in previous experiments the data were converted into suppression ratios.

Results and Discussion

The first panel of Fig. 3 shows the acquisition of second-order conditioning separately for Groups C and E. For both groups suppression to the light increased over trials to a mean of about .10 on the final two trials. There were no reliable differences between the two groups.

During Phase 3, discrimination developed between the two tones. The second panel of Fig. 3 shows the mean suppression ratio for the reinforced stimulus (S+) and the nonreinforced stimulus (S−) on the final day of Phase 3. There were no reliable differences between the two groups in responding to either S+ or S−, but in both groups S+ evoked complete suppression while S− produced little interruption of bar pressing.

The final panel of Fig. 3 shows the results of testing the light, the second-order stimulus. Although both groups continued to show initial suppression to the light which extinguished with repeated nonreinforced presentation, at no point were there any reliable differences between the two groups. Thus, the results of this experiment are consistent with those of Experiments 1 and 2. The second-order conditioned stimulus continued to elicit a substantial CR despite the extinction of the first-order CS upon which that responding was originally based.

Experiment 4

The second-order conditioning paradigm is similar to a second paradigm originally described by Brogden (1939), sensory preconditioning. Both paradigms involve the same operations, but these operations are applied in different orders. In second-order conditioning, a CS is first paired with a US and then a second CS is paired with the original CS. In sensory preconditioning the two stages are reversed, with one CS first being paired with another and then the second CS being separately paired with the US. In both paradigms, a CR is eventually elicited by the stimulus which was never itself paired with the US. The procedural and behavioral similarities of the two paradigms suggest examination of the effects of extinction of the first-order CR following sensory preconditioning similar to that of the previous experiments following second-order conditioning.

The present experiment employs five groups, three of which are controls necessary for an adequate demonstration of sensory preconditioning. The two experimental groups both receive a standard sensory preconditioning treatment, following which one group receives extinction of the first-order CS. Final comparison of the response to the second preconditioned stimulus permits assessment of the effects of that extinction procedure.

Method

Subjects and Apparatus. The subjects were 40 male Sprague-Dawley rats about 100 days old at the start of the experiment. They were maintained throughout at 80% of their ad-lib weight. The apparatus was identical to that of previous experiments.

Procedure. The subjects were trained to bar press for food as in previous experiments. After initial training all sessions were 2 hr. in duration and all involved maintenance of behavior on a VI 2-min. schedule. After 5 days of VI training, Phase 1 preconditioning began. The subjects were divided into five groups of eight animals each and labeled according to the treatments received in each phase. A "P" designates paired presentation; a "U," unpaired presentation; an "E," nonreinforced presentation (extinction); and an "N," the omission of all trials. During Phase 1, three groups, PPE, PPN, and PUE, received trials during which a 30-sec. flashing light preceded and terminated with the onset of a 10-sec. 2,000-Hz. tone. Eight such trials were presented on each of the 2 successive days of Phase 1. The two remaining groups, UPN and UPE, received unpaired presentations of the tone and light. On each day these subjects received eight 30-sec. flashing lights and eight 10-sec. 2,000-Hz. tones, presented separately and in random order.

During Phase 2, the first-order conditioning, phase, subjects in Groups PPE, PPN, UPN, and UPE all received standard fear conditioning, designed to produce conditioned suppression to the 2,000-Hz. tone. On each of 2 days, these subjects received four presentations of the 10-sec. tone terminating in a .5-sec. .5-ma. footshock. The subjects in Group PUE received four 10-sec. tones and four .5-sec. .5-ma. shocks, unpaired and in random order, on each of the 2 Phase 2 days. By the end of this phase two groups, PPE and PPN, had received first light paired with the tone and then the tone paired with shock. These groups may be expected to show the effects of sensory preconditioning to the light. Groups UPN and UPE are included to demonstrate the importance of pairing during the preconditioning phase, while Group PUE is intended to show the importance of pairing the tone with shock.

Following Phase 2, subjects began Phase 3, designed to extinguish the conditioned suppression to the tone for subjects in Groups PPE, UPE, and PUE. On each of the 4 days of this phase, these subjects received 12 10-sec. nonreinforced presentations of the 2,000-Hz. tone superimposed on the VI performance. The subjects in Groups PPN and UPN received 4 days of the VI schedule, without tone presentation.

Following Phase 3, a 2-day test sequence was administered to assess sensory preconditioning to the light. All subjects received four 30-sec. flashing light presentations on each day; a random half of these trials terminated in a .5-sec. .5-ma. shock. The data of primary interest are the rate of acquisition of suppression to the light; presumably the effects of sensory preconditioning should appear as a facilitation of conditioning in this savings test.

Finally, following this test, subjects received a single test session during which 12 10-sec. tones were presented. This test was designed to verify that the treatment during Phase 3 reduced the suppression in Groups PPE, UPE, and PUE compared with that in Groups PPN and UPN.

Results and Discussion

Tone conditioning in Phase 2 resulted in virtually complete suppression to the tone for those groups in which the tone and shock were paired. Group PUE, for which tone and shock were unpaired, was reliably less suppressed than the remaining groups on the second conditioning day.

Throughout Phase 3, Group PUE continued to exhibit little suppression to the tone. Groups PPE and UPE showed considerable extinction over the course of Phase 3, with each subject being less suppressed on the final than on the first day of this phase. However, even by the final Phase 3 day, these groups exhibited a mean suppression ratio of .35 which was reliably below the .54 ratio of Group PUE (Mann–Whitney $z = 2.5$, $p < .01$).

The results of the light test phase are shown in the first panel of Fig. 4. Although no group showed substantial initial fear of the light, it is clear that Group PPN acquired conditioned suppression most rapidly. Mann–Whitney U tests for Test Day 1 indicate that Group PPN differed reliably from all other groups ($ps < .05$), whereas the other four groups did not differ among themselves. The superiority of Group PPN to Groups UPN and UPE indicates that the saving was not due to nonassociative processes

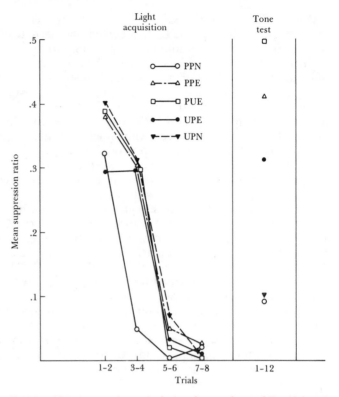

FIG. 4.   *Mean suppression ratio during the test phases of Experiment 4. (The left panel shows the acquisition of suppression to the light [preconditioned] stimulus. The right panel shows final level of suppression to the tone [first-order] stimulus.)*

but was a function of the pairing of stimuli during Phase 1. Similarly, comparison with Group PUE indicates that the savings in Group PPN depended upon first-order conditioning of the tone during Phase 2. These outcomes imply that Group PPN did show sensory preconditioning. The comparison between Groups PPN and PPE, on the other hand, indicates that extinction of conditioning to the tone in Phase 3 erased the savings effect. Such extinction effectively eliminated any evidence for sensory preconditioning in Group PPE. Furthermore, this elimination does not appear to be due to generalization of extinction from the tone to the light; Groups UPN and UPE did not differ during the light savings test.

The results of the tone test are shown in the second panel of Fig 4. These results confirm that Phase 3 did reduce suppression to the tone for the subjects in Groups PPE, UPE, and PUE. Individual Mann–Whitney U tests indicate that these groups, all of which received tone extinction, were reliably less suppressed than Groups PPN and UPN, which had received no extinction experience ($ps < .05$).

General Discussion

The experiments reported here provide reasonably well-controlled demonstrations of both second-order conditioning and sensory preconditioning. Furthermore, they provide some understanding of the similarities and differences in the learning involved in these two paradigms. The retention of conditioning to a second-order CS, despite the extinction of conditioning to a first-order CS upon which it was based, suggests that associations between the two stimuli do not provide the basis for second-order conditioning. Indeed, the absence of *any* measurable effect of extinction of the first-order CS raises the possibility that such inter-stimulus connections are entirely absent in second-order conditioning.

Konorski (1948) briefly reports an experiment by Lindberg which is conceptually similar to those reported here and supports this conclusion. Lindberg first used a CS previously paired with food to establish second-order salivary CRs to another CS. He then paired the first-order CS with shock. Subsequent presentations of the second-order CS were reported to produce only the original salivary CR, but not the CR appropriate to shock.

The present results, together with those of Lindberg, leave two major alternative interpretations for second-order conditioning. One possibility is that during the second-order phase the first-order CS rearouses a representation of the US which then becomes associated with the second-order stimulus. Alternatively, the second-order conditioning procedure may result in a connection between the second-order stimulus and the CR, which is evoked in its presence by the first-order stimulus. The present experiments do not distinguish between these possibilities.

The results of the sensory preconditioning experiment were quite different from those of the second-order experiments. First, although similar procedures were employed in Experiments 1 and 4, the magnitude of suppression was substantially less with sensory preconditioning than with second-order conditioning. Indeed, the effects of sensory preconditioning were only detectable with a savings measure. Apparently, the presence of first-order conditioning when the two stimuli are paired is an important determinant of the suppression accruing to the secondary stimulus.

Furthermore, in the case of sensory preconditioning, extinction of the first-order stimulus *did* completely eliminate responding to the secondary stimulus. Either of the theoretical accounts of second-order conditioning mentioned above can provide an explanation for this elimination. According to an interpretation in terms of associations with the US, inter-stimulus connections result from the preconditioning stage of the experiment, while associations between one stimulus and the US result from the second stage. When the secondary stimulus is then tested, it must employ the connection between the first-order stimulus and the US to evoke a response. Consequently, extinction of that connection should destroy sensory preconditioning. Notice that this account ascribes inter-stimulus associations to the sensory preconditioning, but not to the second-order conditioning, experiment. Furthermore, it appeals to a connection between the CS and the subsequent stimulus event when discussing first-order conditioning but not when discussing second-order conditioning.

The account provided for sensory preconditioning by the alternative S–R theory has been developed in some detail by Osgood (1953) and Coppock (1958). Briefly, this approach suggests the conditioning of covert responses from the to-be-conditioned stimulus to the secondary stimulus during preconditioning. During the subsequent stage, those same responses evoke stimulus consequences which are conditioned to the CR. Subsequent presentation of the secondary stimulus leads to the evocation of the (learned) covert responses and their stimuli, which in turn evoke the CR. On this account, sensory preconditioning depends upon the integrity of the conditioned response to the stimulus consequences of the covert responses of the first-order stimulus; intervening extinction of that stimulus would also extinguish that conditioning and thus be expected to eliminate sensory preconditioning. Similar associative structures would be expected to occur during second order conditioning; but these would be unnecessary for the evocation of the second-order response because in that procedure the CR becomes directly associated with the second-order stimulus.

Thus, these experiments eliminate only one of three contenders for explaining second-order conditioning, that involving associations between the two conditioned stimuli. They do suggest, however, that the S–R theory may provide a more consistent account of both second-order conditioning and sensory preconditioning than does a theory in terms of associations with the US.

One final implication of these studies may be mentioned. It is common to regard certain phobic behaviors as examples of Pavlovian fear conditioning (e.g., Bandura, 1969). And it seems plausible that in many cases the phobia may be based upon second-order conditioning. If that is so, the present experiments suggest that elimination of fear of the original first-order stimulus upon which the phobia was based will not eliminate the phobia. The origin of the fear may have long ago lost its effect while secondary stimuli continue to produce anxiety. This observation may help to account for some of the apparent irrationality of such fears as well as to indicate that procedures aimed at their removal should not involve a search for their origin.

Notes

[1] This research was supported by National Science Foundation Grants GB-6493 and GB-12897. Thanks are due to Karen Gould and Barbara Steinfeld for aid in data collection and analysis. R. C. Rizley is a National Science Foundation predoctoral fellow.

References

Bandura, A. *Principles of behavior modification.* New York: Holt, Rinehart and Winston, 1969.

Brodgen, W. J. Sensory preconditioning. *Journal of Experimental Psychology,* 1939, **25**, 323–332.

Coppock, W. J. Pre-extinction in sensory preconditioning. *Journal of Experimental Psychology,* 1958, **55**, 213–219.

Hoffman, H. S., & Fleshler, M. A. relay sequencing device for scrambling grid shock. *Journal of the Experimental Analysis of Behavior,* 1962, **5**, 329–330.

Hull, C. L. *Principles of Behavior.* New York: Appleton-Century-Crofts, 1943.

Konorski, J. *Conditioned reflexes and neuron organization.* Cambridge, England: University Press, 1948.

Osgood, C. E. *Method and theory in experimental psychology.* New York: Oxford University Press, 1953.

Pavlov, I. P. *Conditioned reflexes.* (Trans. by G. V. Anrep.) London: Oxford University Press, 1927.

C. THE NATURE OF THE CONDITIONED RESPONSE

Pavlov thought that the response produced by a CS—the conditioned re-sponse *(CR)—essentially mimicked the response produced by the US—the* un-conditioned response *(UR). While in many conditioning situations, this is true, we now know that it is not always true; often CRs and URs are quite different. Indeed, sometimes CRs may be the opposite of URs. The article by Siegel and co-workers provides a dramatic example of a CR that is opposite to the UR.*

The US is morphine, known to produce, among other things, analgesia or de-creased pain sensitivity. Siegel and co-workers demonstrate that the CR to a vari-ety of stimuli paired with morphine administration is an increase *in pain sensitivity. They go on to suggest that we may be able to understand the wide-spread phenomenon of drug tolerance (with repeated administration of some drugs, larger and larger doses are needed to produce the same effect) as the result of Pavlovian CRs that are antagonistic to the drug-produced URs. Indeed, we may be able to understand phenomena of habituation as resulting from these kinds of antagonistic CRs (see Solomon, 1980, for a general theory that follows these lines).*

3 The Role of Predrug Signals in Morphine Analgesic Tolerance: Support for a Pavlovian Conditioning Model of Tolerance

SHEPARD SIEGEL, RILEY E. HINSON, AND
MARVIN D. KRANK

According to a model of morphine tolerance, which emphasizes Pavlovian conditioning principles, tolerance results from an association between predrug environmental cues and the systemic effects of the drug. To assess this model, groups of rats were administered morphine on either three or nine occasions, with a complex environmental stimulus either paired or not paired with each injection. Control groups had equivalent experience with the environmental cue and injection procedure, but the injected substance was physiological saline. Subsequently, the analgesic effect of the opiate was tested in all subjects following administration of the drug in conjunction with the environmental cue. As expected on the basis of the conditioning model of tolerance, subjects with a pretest history of paired morphine administrations displayed analgesic tolerance, but subjects with a pretest history of unpaired administration displayed no evidence of such tolerance. The results suggest that prior demonstrations that the display of morphine tolerance is specific to the drug administration environment may be readily interpreted by a conditioning analysis of tolerance.[1]

Tolerance is said to have developed when an effect of a given dose of a drug decreases over the course of successive administrations. For example, morphine has a pronounced analgesic effect the first time it is administered, with the level of analgesia decreasing with subsequent experience with the opiate. It has recently been suggested that Pavlovian conditioning processes may be important in the development of such analgesic tolerance (Siegel, 1975b, 1976, 1977b, 1978; Wikler, 1973).

The learning analysis of tolerance is based on the suggestion by Pavlov (1927, pp. 35ff.) that the administration of a drug normally constitutes a classical conditioning trial because the pharmacological stimulation (the unconditional stimulus, UCS) is almost always signalled by a variety of cues (the conditional stimulus, CS) uniquely present when the drug is administered. These cues consist of the procedures, rituals, and other environmental stimuli that regularly precede the drug effect. The development of an association between the environmental CS and pharmacological UCS may be revealed by presenting the usual predrug cues not followed by the usual chemical stimulation; for such a conditional response (CR) test session, a placebo is administered (for a review of drug conditioning, see Siegel, 1977a). It has frequently been noted that pharmacological CRs revealed in this manner are opposite in direction to the drug-induced unconditional responses (UCRs). Thus, in response to a placebo, animals with a history of epinephrine administration (with its ensuing decreased gastric secretion, tachycardia, and hyperglycemia) display increased gastric secretion (Guha, Dutta, & Pradhan, 1974), bradycardia (Russek & Piña, 1962; Subkov & Zilov, 1937), and hypoglycemia (Russek & Piña, 1962). If the blood glucose level of rats is repeatedly decreased by injections of small doses of insulin, injection of physiological saline leads to a hyperglycemic response (Siegel, 1972; 1975a; Woods & Shogren, 1972). Many other examples of such compensatory type conditional drug responses have been summarized by Siegel (1978) and Wikler (1973). Since organisms frequently evidence CRs opposite to those induced by the drug when confronted with the usual administration cues without the usual pharmacological stimulation, it would be expected that when the drug *is* presented in conjunction with the usual predrug cues, the effect of the drug would be attenuated by these anticipatory compensatory responses. As the association between the drug administration procedure and the systemic effect of the drug is strengthened by repeated pairings, the drug's effect would be expected to become increasingly cancelled as the compensatory CR increases in magnitude. Such a decreased effect of a drug, as a function of repeated experiences with the drug, defines tolerance.

Of special relevance to the role of learning in morphine analgesic tolerance are demonstrations that the CR following training with morphine (with its analgesic consequences) is a heightened sensitivity to nociceptive stimulation (Siegel, 1975b). According to the conditioning model, morphine analgesic tolerance (in part) results from this drug-compensatory CR attenuating the analgesic effect of the opiate.

The learning analysis of tolerance may be contrasted with other interpretations of the phenomenon that do not acknowledge a role for associative processes. These alternative theories postulate physiological changes, induced by early drug administrations, which functionally reduce the effect of later drug administrations (see reviews by Hug, 1972; Kuschinsky, 1977). Such wholly systemic theories of tolerance are all similar in stipulating that repeated drug stimulation is a sufficient condition for tolerance development. There is considerable evidence, however, that tolerance does *not* result simply from the organism suffering repeated pharmacological insult. Instead, tolerance results from repeated application of the drug in the context of environmental cues that reliably signal the pharmacological stimulation. The importance of contextual signals in tolerance was demonstrated in a number of experiments by Mitchell and his colleagues, indicating that humans (Ferguson & Mitchell, 1969) and rats (e.g., Adams, Yeh, Woods, & Mitchell, 1969; Kayan, Woods, & Mitchell, 1969) responded in the expected tolerant manner to the last of a series of morphine injections only if the final injection was administered in the same environment as the prior injections in the series. Several recent investigations from our laboratory have replicated and extended these findings concerning the situation-specificity of tolerance (Siegel, 1975b, 1976, Note 1) and have interpreted them within the context of the conditioning model of tolerance. That is, subjects make a compensatory CR, which attenuates the drug effect only when the drug is administered in the context of situational cues that have, in the past, been paired with morphine. Some investigators, however, have indicated that these results concerning the situation-specificity of analgesic tolerance may be attributable to factors other than the acquisition of an association between predrug environmental cues and the pharmacological stimulation (Adams et al., 1969; Carder, 1978; Kayan et al., 1969). The basis for most of these alternative interpretations concerns the fact that the tolerance test procedure itself constituted part of the environmental cues paired with morphine. It has thus been suggested that the situation-specificity of tolerance is attributable to tolerant subjects having had more practice than nontolerant subjects in making the analgesia-indicant response (e.g., Kayan et al., 1969) and/or to tolerant subjects having sustained more stress in conjunction with each drug administration (e.g., Adams et al., 1969; Carder, 1978).

The purpose of the present experiment was to further assess the importance of predrug signals in the display of morphine analgesic tolerance. In contrast with the previous experiments, however, the analgesia assessment situation did not constitute part of the stimuli paired with the drug. Rather, rats were exposed both to a series of presentations of a complex visual/auditory stimulus and to a series of morphine administrations. For some subjects, the complex environmental stimulus was always paired with the drug, and for other subjects it was explicitly unpaired with the drug. Finally, all subjects were tested for the analgesic effects of morphine following administration of the opiate in the context of the visual/auditory stimulus (no subject having had any experience with the analgesia assessment situation prior to this test session). On the basis of the conditioning model of tolerance, tolerance should be more marked in the paired group than in the unpaired group. Since no subject had the opportunity to practice the analgesia-indicant response prior to the first test of the drug's analgesic effect, the results of this experiment cannot be due to such practice nor to an interaction between the effects of the opiate and the stress of the test procedure.

Method

Design

The experimental consisted of three phases: (a) acclimatization to the experimental environment, (b) tolerance development, and (c) tolerance testing. During acclimatization, all subjects were accustomed to the experimental environment in which they were maintained throughout the investigation. For the subsequent tolerance-development phase of the experiment, independent groups, each consisting of 8 rats, were assigned to each of the 8 cells of a complete $2 \times 2 \times 2$ factorial design. The groups differed with respect to the number of times they were injected (three or nine), the substance injected (morphine or physiological saline), and the relationship between the complex visual/auditory cue and the injection (paired or unpaired). During the final tolerance-test phase of the experiment, the analgesic responsivity of all subjects was measured following morphine administration in conjunction with the visual/auditory cue.

According to the conditioning model of morphine tolerance, subjects given either three or nine paired morphine injections should display more tolerance to the analgesic effect of the drug than subjects given the same number of unpaired morphine injections. Indeed, to the extent that morphine anticipatory responses are crucial for tolerance development, it might be expected that unpaired morphine subjects should show little evidence of tolerance during the tolerance-test phase of the experiment, regardless of the number of pretest tolerance-development trials they received. This is because the cue that signals the morphine during testing would not be expected to elicit the compensatory CR, which attenuates the analgesic effect of the opiate, for subjects that experienced no pretest cue–drug pairings. To evaluate the degree to which the unpaired administration procedure deleteriously affected the display of tolerance, the design of the experiment included groups that received morphine for the very first time during the tolerance-test phase of the experiment (all pretest injections consisting of physiological saline). To the extent that unpaired morphine administration does not promote the acquisition of tolerance, animals with a history of unpaired morphine administration should, during the tolerance-test phase of the experiment, evidence a drug-induced analgesic response resembling that seen in groups receiving the opiate for the first time during tolerance testing.

Procedure

Subjects and Apparatus. The subjects were 64 experimentally naive, male, 90–110-day-old, Wistarderived rats (obtained from Canadian Breeding Farms, St. Constant, Quebec, Canada). They participated in the experiment in squads of 4. Shortly after arrival in the laboratory, each member of a simultaneously run quartet was placed in a translucent cage (45 × 23 × 15 cm) located in one drawer of a fireproof (concrete encased), four-drawer filing cabinet. Each of the four independent compartments was vented with a centrifugal fan, which provided approximately 70 db (A) of background noise. There was no illumination in the cabinet, and it was assumed that the construction of the unit substantially attenuated sound transmission from outside.

Acclimatization Phase. When subjects were first placed in the cabinet, they were provided with food and water sufficient for the acclimatization phase of the experiment, which lasted for 5 days. Subjects were left undisturbed in the homogeneous environment during acclimatization.

Tolerance-Development Phase. During the tolerance-development phase of the experiment, which followed acclimatization, each subject (depending on its group assignment) received either three or nine injections and an equal number of presentations of the complex visual/auditory stimulus. This stimulus consisted of a 45-min period during which the four filing cabinet drawers were opened (exposing the rats to overhead room light) and the ventilation fans were turned off. Thus, when the filing cabinet was opened, illumination and relative quietness replaced the darkness and ambient noise of the environment in which the subjects were maintained. Additional stimulation was provided while this cue was presented by replenishing each rat's food and water and changing its bedding. The intervals between stimulus presentations ranged from 24 to 72 hr, with a mean of 48 hr. Within these constraints, the duration of the intervals was determined from a table of random numbers. All four rats in each squad received the same schedule of stimulus presentations, but different schedules were used for each squad.

Two of the subjects in a squad were randomly assigned to paired groups, and two to unpaired groups. Paired group subjects were injected 15 min after each drawer opening, the drawer being closed (and the vent fans turned on again) 30 min after the injection.

Unpaired group subjects received no injection in conjunction with the drawer openings; rather, injections for rats in unpaired groups were made in accordance with a schedule independent of that used to schedule the drawer-opening-stimuli presentations. The unpaired injection schedule (like the paired injection schedule) had a mean interinjection interval of 48 hr (range = 24–72 hr), with the additional constraint that no injection could occur less than 2 hr after a drawer-opening-stimulus presentation. An attempt was made to inject unpaired animals in a manner that would minimize preinjection stimulation. When a rat assigned to an unpaired group was injected, a dim red light provided the only illumination in the room in which the filing cabinet was located; the drawer was opened, the animal was injected, and the drawer was immediately closed. This treatment is termed "unpaired" to distinguish it from the alternative treatment, where the visual/auditory stimulus was explicitly paired with each morphine or saline administration. Strictly speaking, the effect of the injected substance for unpaired subjects was, in fact, paired with antecedent cues, since the drawer opening and injection occurred immediately prior to the systemic effects of the injected substance (the time from drawer opening to drawer closing for unpaired subjects was about 15 sec). The issues raised by the "unpaired" pharmacological UCS procedure in this experiment are similar to those encountered in virtually any conditioning preparation in which a nominally "unpredictable" UCS, although not signalled by the designated CS, is in fact signalled by a variety of other cues, such as the operation of the UCS delivery apparatus and/or the contextual cues of the experimental environment (see Pavlov, 1910, p. 91). The important distinction between the two contingency treatments in the present experiment is that although paired and unpaired subjects do not differ with respect to their exposure to the explicit visual/auditory stimulus and the pharmacological stimulation during the pretest tolerance-development phase of the experiment, only paired subjects were tested for the drug's effect under the same injection-signalling condition that prevailed during the pretest phase of the experiment.

Since subjects participated in the experiment in squads of 4, the design of the experiment necessitated that 16 squads be run; thus about 1 yr was required for data collection. For simplicity and efficiency, all rats in a squad received the same number of sessions (either three or nine), and all were injected with the same substance (morphine or physiological saline) during the tolerance-development phase of the experiment. Within any squad, then, subjects differed only with respect to whether the tolerance-development injections were paired or unpaired with the complex environmental stimulus. Each squad was assigned to a session frequency and substance-injected condition in an irregular sequence.

All injections were subcutaneous in the dorsal surface of the neck. The morphine dose used throughout the experiment was 5 mg/kg of a 5 mg/ml solution of morphine sulfate (obtained from Allen and Hanburys, Toronto, Ontario, Canada). The volume of the physiological saline injection was 1 ml/kg.

Tolerance-Test Phase. The tolerance-test phase of the experiment followed the tolerance-development phase. Following either three or nine tolerance-development sessions (depending on the squad's treatment), subjects received three tolerance-test sessions, with a 48-hr interval separating each test session. These test sessions, which were conducted in the identical manner for all rats, consisted of the evaluation of the analgesic effect of morphine administrations in conjunction with the visual/auditory stimulus. For each test session, the vent fans were turned off and the drawer was opened (with the room being illuminated) and, 15 min later, the rat was injected with 5 mg/kg morphine. Thirty min after the opiate administration (corresponding to the termination of the signal during the tolerance-development phase of the experiment), each subject's analgesia level was assessed, and the drawer was then closed.

Responsivity to nociceptive stimulation was determined with the hot plate technique, in which pain sensitivity is assessed by observing the rat's latency to lick a paw when placed on a warm surface (longer paw-lick latencies are indicative of a greater analgesic effect; see Fennessy & Lee, 1975). Briefly, a copper plate $(30 \times 16 \times .6$ cm) was completely submerged in a constant temperature water bath (Narco Model 210) maintained at 54.2°C. A 12.5-cm inner diameter, upright, clear Plexiglas cylinder was affixed with a watertight seal in the center of the copper plate, isolating a dry circular surface on the plate on which to confine the rat and assess its sensitivity to heat. Thermistors in the water bath and imbedded in the plate were used to constantly monitor the temperature of the bath and copper plate. The hot plate apparatus was located about 2.5 m from the filing cabinet. When a rat was tested, it was removed from its cage in the cabinet and placed on the testing surface for 60 sec. The number of sec that elapsed before the rat licked one of its paws (paw-lick latency) was determined, with a stopwatch, by an experimenter who was unaware of the group assignment of the subject being tested. Each rat remained on the testing surface for the full 60 sec, regardless of its paw-lick latency. If a subject did not respond to the heat stimulation prior to the end of the test interval, the test was nevertheless terminated (to avoid tissue damage) and that subject was assigned a response latency of 60 sec for that session.

Results

Figure 1 presents the mean $(\pm 1 \ SE_M)$ paw-lick latencies on the hot plate for each of the three tolerance-test sessions for groups that received three (left panel) and nine (right panel) tolerance-development sessions. As can be seen in both panels of Fig. 1, for the very first tolerance-test session, rats with pretest experience with morphine in an unpaired manner responded more slowly on the hot plate (i.e., were less tolerant to the analgesic effect of the drug) than rats with the same amount of experience with morphine in a paired manner. Indeed, for this first test session,

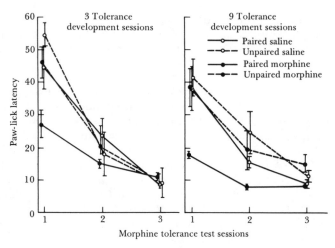

FIG. 1.   *Mean paw-lick latencies on the hot plate (± 1 SE_M) for each of the three tolerance-test sessions for groups which received three (left panel) and nine (right panel) tolerance-development sessions.*

both unpaired morphine groups responded about as slowly to the thermal stimulation as control groups, which received morphine for the very first time during tolerance testing.

Nonparametric Kruskal–Wallis analyses of variance indicated that following both three and nine tolerance-development sessions, the differences between the four groups on this first morphine test session were statistically significant: For groups tested following three tolerance-development sessions, $H(3) = 11.2$, $p < .02$; for groups tested following nine tolerance-development sessions, $H(3) = 13.9$, $p < .01$. Subsequent pairwise comparisons of the first test-session latencies (Mann–Whitney U tests) indicated that unpaired morphine subjects were less sensitive to the thermal stimulation than paired morphine subjects, both in groups tested following three tolerance-development sessions ($U = 7$, $p < .005$) and nine tolerance-development sessions ($U = .5$, $p < .001$). Unpaired morphine groups did not differ significantly from either signalled or unsignalled saline groups (for groups tested following three tolerance-development sessions, all $Us \geq 20$; for groups tested following nine tolerance-development sessions, all $Us \geq 31$).

The dramatic effect of morphine predictability on analgesic tolerance may clearly be seen by comparing the first-test-session response latencies of subjects with a history of three pretest paired morphine administrations with that of subjects with nine unpaired pretest morphine administrations. The group with the lesser experience with the opiate, but in a paired manner, was significantly more tolerant to the analgesic effect of the drug than the group with the greater experience with the opiate, but in an unpaired manner ($U = 15.5$, $p < .05$).

As indicated in Fig. 1, all groups displayed increasingly more rapid paw-lick latencies over the three tolerance-test sessions. As might be expected, the cue–injection relationship during the tolerance-development phase of the experiment did not affect the acquisition of morphine tolerance during tolerance testing when all pretest injections consisted of physiological saline; paired and unpaired saline groups did not differ significantly on any of the three tolerance-test sessions, this being the case when tolerance testing was conducted following either three or nine tolerance development sessions (all $Us \geq 25$). As also may be seen in Fig. 1, there was no evidence that pretest experience with unpaired morphine facilitated the acquisition of tolerance to cued drug administration over the three tolerance-test sessions. That is, following both three and nine tolerance-development sessions, the response latencies of unpaired morphine subjects not only did not differ significantly from that of either paired or unpaired saline subjects in the very first tolerance-test session, but they also did not differ significantly in any of the subsequent tolerance-test sessions (all $Us \geq 26$). Thus, pretest administrations of unpaired morphine not only led to less analgesic tolerance than equal experience with paired morphine, but also the previous unpaired morphine administrations did not facilitate the acquisition of tolerance to signalled morphine administration.

Discussion

Prior to the first morphine test session, following both three and nine tolerance-development sessions, paired morphine rats and unpaired morphine rats suffered the systemic effects of the same dose of morphine, administered at the same intervals, equally as often. According to any of the entirely systemic theories of tolerance, which assign no role to predrug cues in tolerance, there should be no difference in the level of tolerance displayed by paired and unpaired morphine groups, given the same number of tolerance-development sessions. However, according to the conditioning theory of tolerance, tolerance should be more pronounced in paired morphine groups than in unpaired morphine groups. This is because paired subjects, but not unpaired subjects, were tested for tolerance following morphine administration in conjunction with a cue that would be expected to have been associated with the opiate.

In agreement with the conditioning theory of tolerance, groups given paired pretest morphine administrations were much more tolerant to the analgesic effect of the drug than groups given the same number of unpaired morphine administrations.

The conclusion that morphine tolerance does not depend merely on the frequency of pharmacological stimulation, but rather on the number of pairings of a drug-predictive cue with the systemic effects of the drug, is clearly supported by the finding that subjects given a lesser number of pretest paired morphine administrations (three) were significantly more tolerant to the drug than subjects given a greater number of pretest unpaired morphine administration (nine).

The present demonstration that environmental signals of morphine play a critical role in analgesic tolerance acquisition is similar to earlier demonstrations by Mitchell and his colleagues that the display of morphine analgesic tolerance is specific to the environment in which the drug has previously been administered (e.g., Adams et al., 1969; Kayan et al., 1969). However, these investigators did not attribute their finding to the development of an association between the drug-administration environment and the drug. Rather, they suggested that subjects tested in the same environment in which they previously received morphine displayed a high level of tolerance, because only these subjects had pretest practice in making the analgesia-indicant response (Kayan et al., 1969), or because only these subjects suffered stress in conjunction with each morphine administration (Adams et al., 1969; see also Carder, 1978). Such interpretations are plausible in these prior demonstrations of the importance of contextual cues in tolerance, because tolerant subjects had more exposure than nontolerant subjects to the analgesia-assessment situation. In contrast, the results of the present experiment are *not* subject to such interpretations; prior to the first morphine test session, all groups given the same number of tolerance-development sessions had equal exposure to the complex visual/auditory stimulus, and no subject had any experience with the analgesia-assessment situation. Tolerance was displayed only when the effect of the drug was assessed following a stimulus which, in the past, reliably signalled the pharmacological stimulation. Thus, the present results lend credence to Siegel's (1975b, 1976) conditioning analysis of prior demonstrations (Adams et al., 1969; Kayan et al., 1969) of the situation specificity of tolerance.

In the present experiment, subjects with a history of unpaired morphine administrations showed *no* evidence of tolerance to the drug's analgesic properties; on the first test session, unpaired morphine rats were as sensitive to the analgesic effect of the opiate as rats receiving the drug for the very first time (i.e., paired and unpaired saline rats). Moreover, the unpaired morphine administration procedure did not lead to a "savings" in the acquisition of tolerance during the final phase of the experiment. That is, during tolerance testing, when all subjects received cued drug administrations, tolerance developed no faster for the unpaired morphine groups than for the saline groups, despite the fact that the unpaired morphine groups had pretest experience with morphine, whereas the saline groups had no such prior experience with the drug.

Although pretest unpaired morphine administrations did not facilitate the acquisition of tolerance during the test phase of the experiment, the unpaired procedure did not hinder the acquisition of tolerance either. If analgesic tolerance is an associative phenomenon, it might be expected, on the basis of contingency formulations of conditioning (e.g., Rescorla, 1967), that the unpaired drug administration procedure might actually impede the acquisition of tolerance. This is because there was a negative correlation between the visual/auditory CS and the pharmacological UCS for unpaired subjects, since they were not injected with morphine less than 2 hr after a drawer-opening-stimulus presentation. It has been suggested that such an "explicitly unpaired" schedule of CS and UCS presentations constitutes an inhibitory training procedure, which would be expected to retard subsequent excitatory training when the CS is paired with the UCS (see Rescorla, 1969). Although no evidence of retardation of tolerance was found in this investigation, the following factors should be considered when applying a contingency formulation of learning to this drug conditioning situation: (a) the contingency model, based primarily on studies using shock as the UCS (as indicated by Rescorla, 1969) may simply not be applicable with drug UCSs; (b) even if the contingency model was applicable to drug conditioning, the unusual parametric features of the situation (a very small ratio of CS-on time to CS-off time) may function to make the explicitly unpaired procedure indistinguishable from the presumably associatively neutral, truly random procedure (see Kremer, 1971; Quinsey, 1971); (c) even if the explicitly unpaired procedure in this experiment was inhibitory, it is possible that the number of tolerance-development trials (three or nine) may have been too small for detectable inhibitory properties to have accrued to the visual/auditory CS (see Rescorla & Wagner, 1972).

Although these results provided no evidence for inhibitory processes in tolerance acquisition, the techniques used here to manipulate the contingency between an arbitrary environmental cue and the drug permit further evaluation of such processes. Thus, the type of drug-administration preparation used in this experiment may be useful for assessing the similarities between pharmacological conditioning and more traditional conditioning preparations.

The results of the present experiment should be added to those of other experiments from this laboratory, which support the Pavlovian conditioning theory of morphine tolerance (see review by Siegel, 1978). According to this theory, drug-preparatory CRs, elicited in anticipation of the actual pharmacological assault, attenuate the pharmacological insult. Most models of tolerance stress only the effects of repeated pharmacological stimulation and do not assign any role to associative processes (see Hug, 1972; Kuschinsky, 1977). The present results, then, although expected on the basis of the conditioning analysis of tolerance, are inconsistent with most alternative formulations. However, it should be noted that some other investigators, while not committing themselves to this or any other specific associative model of tolerance, have also presented evidence implicating memory or learning processes in the development of morphine tolerance. For example, Cochin (1972) suggested that "a reaction analogous to memory" (p. 265) may be important in tolerance development because the phenomenon occurs with very long intervals—even 1 yr—between drug administrations.[2] Other investigators have provided evidence that a variety of manipulations, known to be effective in retarding many types of learning, similarly retard the development of morphine analgesic tolerance, and have suggested that such findings indicate a parallel between learning and tolerance; these manipulations include electroconvulsive shock (Kesner, Priano, & De Witt, 1976; Stolerman, Bunker, Johnson, Jarvik, Krivoy, & Zimmermann, 1976), electrical stimulation of the frontal cortex (Kesner et al., 1976), and administration of a variety of metabolic inhibitors (e.g., Cohen, Keats, Krivoy, & Ungar, 1965). Furthermore, administration of pituitary vasopressin facilitates both the acquisition of some learned responses and the acquisition of morphine tolerance (see Krivoy, Zimmermann, & Lande, 1974). All these findings generally support the view that learning plays a role in tolerance and are fully consistent with the Pavlovian conditioning theory of tolerance.

Notes
 [1] This research was supported by Research Grant DA-01200 from the National Institute on Drug Abuse. We thank Doreen Mitchell for assistance in data collection and Michael Leon for his comments on the manuscript.

[2] In fact, it has been reported that former opiate addicts retain their tolerance to the analgesic effect of morphine as long as eight years since their last experience with the drug (Andrews, 1943).

Reference Note
1. Siegel, S. *More evidence that morphine tolerance is an associative process: Learning and hyperthermic tolerance in the rat.* Manuscript submitted for publication, 1978.

References
Adams, W. H., Yeh, S. Y., Woods, L.A., & Mitchell, C. L. Drug-test interaction as a factor in the development of tolerance to the analgesic effect of morphine. *Journal of Pharmacology and Experimental Therapeutics,* 1969, *168,* 251–257.

Andrews, H. L. The effect of opiates on the pain threshold in post-addicts. *Journal of Clinical Investigation,* 1943, *22,* 511–516.

Carder, B. Environmental influences on marihuana tolerance. In N. A. Krasnegor (Ed.), *Behavioral tolerance: Research and treatment implications* (National Institute on Drug Abuse Research Monograph No. 18; U.S. Department of Health, Education, and Welfare Publication No. [ADM] 78–551). Washington, D.C.: U.S. Government Printing Office, 1978.

Cochin, J. Some aspects of tolerance to the narcotic analgesics. In J. M. Singh, L. Miller, & H. Lal (Eds.), *Drug addiction 1. Experimental pharmacology.* New York: Futura, 1972.

Cohen, M., Keats, A. S., Krivoy, W., & Ungar, G. Effect of actinomycin D on morphine tolerance. *Proceedings of the Society for Experimental Biology and Medicine,* 1965, *119,* 381–384.

Fennessy, M. R., & Lee, J. R. The assessment of and the problems involved in the experimental evaluation of narcotic analgesics. In S. Ehrenpreis & A. Neidle (Eds.), *Methods in narcotics research.* New York: Marcel Dekker, 1975.

Ferguson, R. K., & Mitchell, C. L. Pain as a factor in the development of tolerance to morphine analgesia in man. *Clinical Pharmacology and Therapeutics,* 1969, *10,* 372–383.

Guha, D., Dutta, S. N., & Pradhan, S. N. Conditioning of gastric secretion by epinephrine in rats. *Proceedings of the Society for Experimental Biology and Medicine,* 1974, *147,* 817–819.

Hug, C. C. Characteristics and theories related to acute and chronic tolerance development. In S. J. Mulé & H. Brill (Eds.), *Chemical and biological aspects of drug dependence.* Cleveland: CRC Press, 1972.

Kayan, S., Woods, L. A., & Mitchell, C. L. Experience as a factor in the development of tolerance to the analgesic effect of morphine. *European Journal of Pharmacology,* 1969, *6,* 333–339.

Kesner, R. P., Priano, D. J., & De Witt, J. R. Time-dependent disruption of morphine tolerance by electroconvulsive shock and frontal cortical stimulation. *Science,* 1976, *194,* 1079–1081.

Kremer, E. F. Truly random and traditional control procedures in CER conditioning in the rat. *Journal of Comparative and Physiological Psychology,* 1971, *76,* 441–448.

Krivoy, W. A., Zimmerman, E., & Lande, S. Facilitation of development of resistance to morphine analgesia by desglycinamide[9]-lysine vasopressin. *Proceedings of the National Academy of Science,* 1974, *71,* 1852–1856.

Kuschinsky, K. Opiate dependence. *Progress in Pharmacology,* 1977, *1* (Whole No. 2).

Pavlov, I. P. *The work of the digestive glands* (W. H. Thompson, trans.). London: Griffin, 1910.

Pavlov, I. P. *Conditioned reflexes:* (G. V. Anrep, trans.). London: Oxford University Press, 1927.

Quinsey, V. L. Conditioned suppression with no CS–US contingency in the rat. *Canadian Journal of Psychology,* 1971, *25,* 69–81.

Rescorla, R. A. Pavlovian conditioning and its proper control procedures. *Psychological Review,* 1967, *74,* 74–81.

Rescorla, R. A. Pavlovian conditioned inhibition. *Psychological Bulletin,* 1969, *72,* 77–94.

Rescorla, R. A., & Wagner, A. R. A theory of Pavlovian conditioning: Variations in the effectiveness of reinforcement and nonreinforcement. In A. H. Black & W. F. Prokasy (Eds.), *Classical conditioning II: Current research and theory.* New York: Appleton-Century-Crofts, 1972.

Russek, M., & Piña, S. Conditioning of adrenalin anorexia, *Nature,* 1962, *193,* 1296–1297.

Siegel, S. Conditioning of insulin-induced glycemia. *Journal of Comparative and Physiological Psychology*, 1972, *78*, 233–241.

Siegel, S. Conditioning insulin effects. *Journal of Comparative and Physiological Psychology*, 1975, *89*, 189–199. (a)

Siegel, S. Evidence from rats that morphine tolerance is a learned response. *Journal of Comparative and Physiological Psychology*, 1975, *89*, 498–506. (b)

Siegel, S. Morphine analgesic tolerance: Its situation specificity supports a Pavlovian conditioning model. *Science*, 1976, *193*, 323–325.

Siegel, S. Learning and psychopharmacology. In. M. E. Jarvik (Ed.), *Psychopharmacology in the practice of medicine*. New York: Appleton-Century-Crofts, 1977. (a)

Siegel, S. Morphine tolerance acquisition as an associative process. *Journal of Experimental Psychology: Animal Behavior Processes*, 1977, *3*, 1–13. (b)

Siegel, S. A Pavlovian conditioning analysis of morphine tolerance. In N. A. Krasnegor (Ed.), *Behavioral tolerance: Research and treatment implications* (National Institute on Drug Abuse Research Monograph No. 18; U.S. Department of Health Education, and Welfare Publication No. [ADM] 78–551). Washington, D.C.: U.S. Government Printing Office, 1978.

Stolerman, I. P., Bunker, P., Johnson, C. A., Jarvik, M. E., Krivoy, W., & Zimmermann, E. Attenuation of morphine tolerance development by electroconvulsive shock in mice. *Neuropharmacology*, 1976, *15*, 309–313.

Subkov, A. A., & Zilov, G. N. The role of conditioned reflex adaptation in the origin of hyperergic reactions. *Bulletin de Biologie et de Médécine Expérimentale*, 1937, *4*, 294–296.

Wikler, A. Conditioning of successive adaptive responses to the initial effects of drugs. *Conditional Reflex*, 1973, *8*, 193–210.

Woods, S. C., & Shogren, R. E., Jr. Glycemic responses following conditioning with different doses of insulin in rats. *Journal of Comparative and Physiological Psychology*, 1972, *81*, 220–225.

D. CONTINGENCY AND CONDITIONING

For many years, it was assumed that the critical determinant of Pavlovian conditioning was the pairing of CS and US, the occurrence of CS and US in close temporal contiguity. When CS and US are paired, the CS provides the organism with important information that the US is coming; this is information that the organism would not otherwise have. But it is possible to arrange things so that even though the CS and US are paired, the CS does not provide information. Consider an experimental session involving 10 presentations of the CS followed by the US. The CS is obviously informative. Now suppose we add 20 or 30 additional CSs that are not followed by USs. Is the CS still informative? Yes, it is, because the US never comes unless it has been preceded by a CS. But now suppose we also add 20 or 30 additional USs, without CSs. Now the CS provides little or no information, since the US may be just as likely to come without a CS as with one. Notice that we have eliminated the informativeness of the CS though the 10 CS–US pairings remain. Will such a procedure produce conditioning? Rescorla (1967) argued that it would not, because conditioning depends not just on pairings of CS and US, but on the informativeness, or predictiveness, of the CS. The following two articles by Rescorla and by Gamzu and Williams provide evidence for the importance of predictiveness from two quite different conditioning situations. Pavlovian conditioning seems to require contingency between CS and US and not just contiguity.

But does this mean that when a CS does not predict a US, there is no effect? The article by Seligman shows that sometimes unpredictable USs can have very dramatic effects. When rats that had been trained to respond for food received CSs and shocks arranged so that the CSs did not predict shocks, they stopped responding for food all together; in addition, they developed ulcers. Seligman used this finding to point out that one very important consequence of having a reliable signal for danger (shock) is that its absence is a reliable signal for safety (no shock). Without such a safety signal, one is afraid all the time.

4 Predictability and Number of Pairings in Pavlovian Fear Conditioning

ROBERT A. RESCORLA

Three groups of dogs were Sidman avoidance trained. They then received different kinds of Pavlovian fear conditioning. For one group CSs and USs occurred randomly and independently; for a second group, CSs predicted the occurrence of USs; for a third group, CSs predicted the absence of the USs. The CSs were subsequently presented while S performed the avoidance response. CSs which had predicted the occurrence or the absence of USs produced, respectively, increases and decreases in avoidance rate. For the group with random CSs and USs in conditioning, the CS had no effect upon avoidance.[1]

Traditional conceptions of Pavlovian conditioning have emphasized the pairing of CS and US as the essential condition for the development of a CR. As long as the CS and US occur in temporal contiguity, the conditions for Pavlovian conditioning are assumed to be met. In contrast, another view of Pavlovian conditioning argues that conditioning depends upon the degree to which the CS allows S to *predict* the occurrence of the US. If the CS is followed by a change in the probability of the US, Pavlovian conditioning will occur. If the CS forecasts an *increased* likelihood of the US, excitatory conditioning will occur; if the CS forecasts a *decreased* likelihood of the US, the CS will take on inhibitory properties. According to this view, the number of CS–US pairings may be irrelevant to the development of a CR if the CS does not predict a change in the probability of occurrence of the US.

The experiment reported here explores the fruitfulness of this second approach to Pavlovian fear conditioning. Three groups of dogs received different kinds of Pavlovian conditioning. For one group, CSs and USs occurred randomly and independently in such a way that CS occurrences provided no information about US occurrences. In a second group, CS occurrences were followed by an increase in the probability of US occurrences; however, Ss in this group received the same number of CS–US pairings as did Ss in the first group. For a third group, CS occurrences predicted the *absence* of USs. These CSs were then presented while S performed a previously trained avoidance response. Increases in the rate of avoidance responding produced by CSs were taken as evidence for excitatory fear conditioning and decreases were taken as indicating inhibition of fear. Such changes in rate of avoidance responding have been shown by Rescorla & LoLordo (1965) to be a sensitive index of the level of conditioned fear.

"Predictability and Number of Pairings in Pavlovian Fear Conditioning" by Robert A. Rescorla. *Psychonomic Science*, 1966, *4*, 383–384. Reprinted by permission of the Psychonomic Society and the author.

Method

Ss were 18 mongrel dogs, individually housed and maintained on ad lib food and water throughout the experiment. The apparatus was a two-compartment dog shuttlebox described in detail by Solomon & Wynne (1953). The two compartments were separated by a barrier of adjustable height and by a drop gate which, when lowered, prevented S from crossing from one compartment into the other. The floor was composed of stainless steel grids which could be electrified through a scrambler. Speakers, mounted above the hardware-cloth ceiling, provided a continuous white noise background and permitted the presentation of tonal stimuli.

The training procedure was similar to that described by Rescorla & LoLordo (1965). Each S was trained to jump the barrier separating the two sides of the shuttlebox to avoid electric shock. Brief shocks, 0.25 sec., were programmed on a Sidman avoidance schedule; the shock–shock interval was 10 sec. and the response–shock interval was 30 sec. The Ss received three initial days of avoidance training. On the first day the barrier height was 9 in. and the shock level 6 ma; on all subsequent days, the barrier height was 15 in. and the shock set at 8 ma.

Beginning with the fourth experimental day, S was confined to one-half of the shuttlebox and given Pavlovian fear conditioning. For the six dogs in Group R (random), 24 5-sec., 3 ma shocks were programmed on a variable interval schedule with a mean of 2.5 min. Twenty-four 5-sec., 400 cps tones were independently programmed randomly throughout the session in such a way that a tone onset was equiprobable at any time in the session. This was accomplished by a VI timer and a series of tapes. The six dogs in Group P (positive prediction) received a treatment identical to that of Group R except that they received only those shocks which were programmed to occur during the 30 sec. following each tone onset. The six dogs in Group N (negative prediction) received a treatment identical to that of Group R except that they received only those shocks which were *not* programmed to occur within 30 sec. after a tone onset. The treatments for Groups P and N were accomplished by having each CS onset reset a 30-sec. timer through which the pre-programmed shocks were gated. Thus, for Group P, CS occurrences predicted US occurrences; and for Group N, CS occurrences predicted absence of USs.

Pavlovian conditioning and Sidman avoidance training days were then alternated until S had received a total of seven avoidance and five conditioning sessions. On day 13 a single test session was given. During this session, S performed the avoidance response with the Sidman schedule remaining in effect. In addition, 24 5-sec., 400 cps tones were superimposed upon the avoidance behavior with a mean intertrial interval of 2.5 min. Changes in the rate of avoidance induced by these CSs were used as an index of the conditioned excitatory and inhibitory effects of the tones.

Results

The Sidman avoidance response was rapidly acquired by most animals and after several sessions all Ss were reliable responders. Figure 1 shows the results of the test session. Plotted in this figure are the mean number of responses per 5-sec. period of time over successive 5-sec. periods. Prior

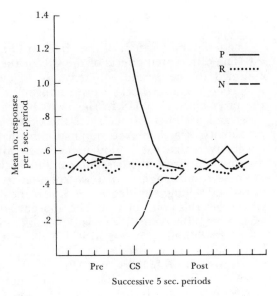

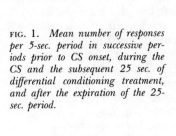

FIG. 1. *Mean number of responses per 5-sec. period in successive periods prior to CS onset, during the CS and the subsequent 25 sec. of differential conditioning treatment, and after the expiration of the 25-sec. period.*

to the occurrence of a CS, all groups responded at approximately the same rate. However, the occurrence of a CS led to markedly different results in the three groups. For Group P, CS onset produced an abrupt increase in response rate followed by a return to base rate. The rate increase was confined to the first few 5-sec. periods following CS onset. In contrast, the CS produced a sharp decrease in rate in Group N. Again the rate change was maximal immediately following CS onset. For Group R, the occurrence of a CS produced very little effect.

Comparisons among the groups were made with the help of suppression ratios. These ratios are of the form $A/(A + B)$ where B is the mean rate in the 30 sec. prior to CS onset and A is the rate for the period on which the two groups are to be compared. Using this measure, the rate increase during the CS was reliably greater for Group P than for Group R ($U = 0$; $p < .01$). Group R, in turn, responded more frequently during CS than did Group N ($U = 0$; $p < .01$). Similar conclusions result if the groups are compared on the rate during the entire 30 sec. following CS onset.

Discussion

The results of this experiment indicate that the degree to which a CS allows S to predict US occurrences is an important variable in Pavlovian fear conditioning. Stimuli which signalled increased probability of the US became elicitors of fear, resulting in an increased jumping rate, and stimuli which signalled decreased probability of the US became inhibitors of fear, resulting in a decreased jumping rate. The results, therefore substantiate the findings of Rescorla & LoLordo (1965), that active inhibition and excitation of fear can be induced by Pavlovian methods. However, these effects seem to be independent of the more traditionally emphasized effects of number of CS–US pairings. Despite the fact that Ss in Group R received at least as many pairings of the CS and US as Ss in

Group P, only the Ss in Group P showed evidence of Pavlovian fear conditioning.

The temporal location of the effect produced by the CS is also of interest. The differential effects of the CS for the three groups were primarily confined to the periods immediately following CS onset. Perhaps this happened because shocks were uniformly distributed, and for Group P the probability of a US in the next 30 sec. was maximal just after CS onset and declined as time since the CS increased; but for Group N, the probability of a shock was minimal immediately after CS onset. Another possibility is that the period immediately after CS onset is simply more discriminable from the baseline conditions than are subsequent periods.

These results suggest that we consider as a basic dimension of Pavlovian conditioning the degree to which the US is contingent upon prior CSs. From this point of view, the appropriate control procedure for nonassociative effects of Pavlovian conditioning, such as sensitization or pseudoconditioning, is one in which there is *no* contingency between CS and US. The two extremes in which CS predicts either the increased or the decreased probability of a US are seen in the present experiment to produce, respectively, excitation and inhibition. A procedure such as that of Group R in which there is *no contingency* between CS and US provides an appropriate control procedure against which to evaluate both of these effects.

Notes

[1] This research was supported by United States Public Health Service Grant MH-04202 to Richard L. Solomon. The author thanks Dr. Solomon for his advice and criticism.

References

Rescorla, R. A., & LoLordo, V. M. Inhibition of avoidance behavior. *J. Comp. Physiol. Psychol.*, 1965, 59, 406–412.

Solomon, R. L., & Wynne, L. C. Traumatic avoidance learning: Acquisition in normal dogs. *Psychol. Monogr.*, 1953, 67, No.4 (Whole No. 354).

5 Classical Conditioning of a Complex Skeletal Response

ELKAN GAMZU AND DAVID R. WILLIAMS

The pigeon's so-called "arbitrary" response of pecking an illuminated disk can be established and maintained by procedures resembling those of classical conditioning. This phenomenon was shown to be independent of the specific signaling relationships between illumination of the pecking disk and presentation of food; it will appear as long as the key is differentially associated with food. When a nondifferential condition is introduced, pecking "extinguishes" even if it has previously been established and even when the new condition involves as much reinforcement as the old one. Reinstating differential conditions reestablished pecking. The initial conditions determine the speed and apparently the asymptote of pecking rates in the differential condition; initial exposure to a nondifferential procedure retards subsequent acquisition, possibly quite permanently. These findings are discussed in the context of mechanisms of adaptive learning, not involving reward and punishment, which lead to selection of effective behaviors on a nonarbitrary basis.[1]

Brown and Jenkins (1) recently reported that hungry pigeons would spontaneously begin pecking a disk mounted on the wall of an experimental chamber if illumination of the disk signaled the forthcoming presentation of grain. The procedure closely resembled Pavlovian delay conditioning, and its effectiveness with pecking—a complex skeletal act directed outward at the environment—potentially represents a significant extension of the domain of classical conditioning. The delay conditioning procedure exerts such powerful control that birds frequently peck the disk even when conditions are changed so that pecking the disk prevents the opportunity to eat (2). Under these artificial laboratory conditions, such behavior appears maladaptive and is difficult to encompass in a biological approach to learning based on the reward value of external events.

In the experiments reported here, we explored the limits of applicability of the classical conditioning paradigm by using a procedure that avoids the specific "pairing" relationship between response key and food, which was characteristic of the earlier procedures. Pairing the response key with food according to the Pavlovian delay paradigm involves the precise signaling of the time of presentation of the unconditioned stimulus (for example, food). By circumventing this intimate signaling relationship, we hoped to determine whether the remarkable stimulus control over the act of pecking was attributable to a peculiarity of the Pavlovian procedures used earlier or whether it represents a more general manifestation of associative learning through classical conditioning.

The new procedure that we used was a variant of one introduced by Rescorla (3). Throughout the course of these experiments, a pecking disk was illuminated for 8.6-second periods, which were distributed randomly throughout each experimental session with a mean interstimulus interval of 30 seconds. In the presence of the illuminated disk, 4-second periods of access to a grain hopper were provided on a random basis; the probability of initiating such a period of access was .03 at the start of each second of key illumination. We compared pecking to the key under two conditions: a "differential condition," where the probability of access to grain when the disk was not illuminated was zero; and a "nondifferential" procedure, where the probability of grain presentation was the same in the presence and the absence of illumination of the disk. At no point in the experiment did the disk signal the actual time of presentation of reinforcement; it merely accompanied a condition where 4-second access to grain was provided on the average of once every 33 seconds.

Naive adult male Silver King pigeons maintained at 80 percent of their free feeding weight were tested in a standard pigeon chamber measuring 28 by 28 by 26 cm. One wall of the chamber housed a standard pecking disk, which could be transilluminated with white light. The disk was 19 cm above the floor of the compartment, and the grain hopper was centered 11 cm below the pecking disk. At the beginning of the first session, birds were trained to approach rapidly and to eat from the hopper whenever it was presented; they were then immediately exposed to the experimental procedure. A daily session comprised 50 trials of disk illumination, distributed geometrically with a range of 10 to 120 seconds between trials. In the presence of the key, an average of 13 reinforcements were typically presented during 50 daily trials. Grain presentation was always independent of the pigeons' behavior and could be initiated immediately at the onset of a trial or at the start of any other 1-second interval during the trial. Pecking had absolutely no effect on the experimental procedure.

Figure 1 traces the course of development of pecking for each of four birds studied under the differential procedure. Despite marked differences in rate of acquisition, all birds learned to peck the disk at rates substantially above one per second. Because illumination of the disk accompanied a change in the frequency of reinforcement but did not signal particular occurrences of reinforcement, it is clear that disk illumination need have no precise relationship to specific instances of food presentation. This property of the Pavlovian delay procedure, as such, is not necessary for the development of pecking.

To explore whether the pecking engendered by this procedure was dependent primarily on occasions of feeding in the presence of the disk or whether the differential association was a necessary aspect of the procedure, we began presenting grain in the absence of the illuminated disk at the same frequency as we had previously been presenting it in the presence of the illuminated disk, in sessions that immediately followed those illustrated in Fig. 1. Thus, we changed conditions only during the "intertrial interval" and not during the "trial interval" itself. Results from this nondifferential condition are shown in Fig 2. Levels of responding to the disk during its periods of illumination fell rapidly to zero. Although a modest "recovery" of rate was observed in one bird over a 4-day period, and in another for a single day, these elevated levels of performance were

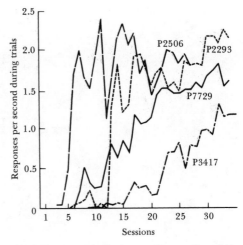

Fig. 1. *Individual acquisition curves indicate rate of responding within each session from the outset of the experiment.*

not sustained. Two other birds showed no tendency to resume respond-ing during the 14-day period. In addition, no bird developed sustained pecking during the interval between trials, when grain was presented but the disk was dark. It is apparent, then, that the presentation of grain in the presence of the illuminated disk is not a sufficient condition to engen-der pecking: the disc must at least accompany a change in the frequency of grain presentations. Figure 2 also shows that, when the differential condition was reinstated, pecking quickly regained its previous levels. These findings are similar to those of Rescorla, who used a classically conditioned fear response in dogs and rats (4).

The failure of the nondifferential condition to sustain pecking indicates that adventitious reward of pecking probably does not play a major role in this phenomenon. The rapid decline of pecking during periods of key illumination took place even though there was no change in response–reinforcer correlations (spurious or otherwise) in the presence of the illu-minated disk. If adventitious reward were effective during the differential condition, surely it would continue to be effective in sustaining a high rate of pecking in the nondifferential condition as well.

As a further check on the importance of the differential association of disk illumination with feeding, we studied five new birds on the nondif-ferential condition. After 14 days of nondifferential exposure to grain presentation, a total of ten pecks had been recorded for all five birds to-gether. All of these occurred during the intertrial interval when the key was not illuminated. Apparently, the decline in responding seen in the first experiment was not an artifact of changing the procedures, nor was it related to prior exposure to a difference in reinforcement density. Ac-quisition, as well as maintenance of pecking, is dependent on a differen-tial association of key and reinforcer.

When these new birds were shifted to the original differential proce-dure, all eventually began pecking the disk. Even after 35 days of expo-sure, however, the mean rate of response was only 20 per minute, and

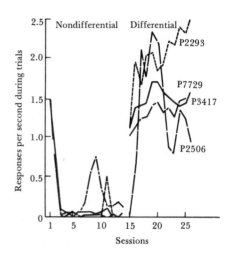

FIG. 2.   *Individual rates per session in sessions that immediately followed the sessions of Fig. 1. The rate declined under the nondifferential condition and recovered after reinstatement of the original procedure.*

there was no overlap between the rates of pecking of these birds and those of the first group, whose mean terminal rate was 101 responses per minute. Thus, there was a residual effect of nondifferential reinforcement, even after successful acquisition had taken place.

These results demonstrate three important aspects of the autoshaping phenomenon, all of which are consistent with the assumption that classical conditioning is a fundamental factor in the phenomenon. First, we have shown that a specific signaling relationship is not important for acquisition or sustained maintenance of behavior. Second, the necessity for differential pairing in maintenance, as well as acquisition, indicates that informational properties of the stimulus, rather than its mere association with feeding, are responsible for the phenonenon. Third, the phenomenon, although obviously susceptible to analysis by principles of classical conditioning, offers little basis for an account in terms of adventitious reinforcement.

The pecking engendered by autoshaping is directed to a significant part of the environment—that is, a part correlated with the opportunity to eat. The strong and direct control over behavior exerted by this part of the environment indicates the operation of a mechanism in pigeons by which skeletal acts are controlled without the involvement of reward and punishment. The findings of the Brelands (5) in a number of nonavian species suggest that such mechanisms are not peculiar to pigeons. Although study of the way in which complex activities are developed and learned has largely excluded effects other than those of reward and punishment, it now seems necessary to include some other factors as well, if the principles of adaptive learning are to provide an adequate account of the development and maintenance of effective but often nonarbitrary behavior. It is apparent that animals do not select behaviors randomly from their repertoire in new situations. The manifestation of associative learning that we have explored in this report may reflect a process by which organisms tailor their behavior nonrandomly to new environments, prior to any "shaping" effect by rewards and punishments.

Notes

This work was supported by grant G14055 from the National Science Foundation. T. Allaway, B. Schwartz, A. Silberberg, H. Williams, and K. Zonana contributed substantially to our development of this approach.

References

1. P. L. Brown and H. M. Jenkins, *J. Exp. Anal. Behav.* **11,** 1 (1968).
2. D. R. Williams and H. Williams, *ibid.* **12,** 511 (1969).
3. R. A. Rescorla, *Psychol. Rev.* **74,** 71 (1967).
4. _____, *J. Comp. Physiol. Psychol.* **66,** 1 (1968); *Psychonom, Sci.* **4,** 383 (1966).
5. K. Breland and M. Breland, *Amer. Psychol.* **16,** 681 (1961).

6 Chronic Fear Produced by Unpredictable Electric Shock

MARTIN E. P. SELIGMAN

Rats which had learned to bar press for food received CSs paired with electric shocks. For 1 group CSs and shocks were randomly interspersed, then new CSs predicted shocks; these Ss stopped bar pressing completely and formed extensive stomach ulcers. The group for which all shocks were predicted by CSs showed only transitory disruption of bar pressing and formed no ulcers. Experience with randomly interspersed CS and shock retarded acquisition of a CER when a new CS predicted shock. Implications for (a) a safety-signal explanation of the disruptive effects of unpredictable shock, (b) the learned helplessness hypothesis, and (c) the appropriateness of the random control group in conditioning are discussed.[1]

When a stimulus reliably predicts the occurrence of electric shock for an organism, safety, the absence of shock, is reliably predicted by the absence of the signal for shock. In Pavlovian language, the existence of a reliable CS+ for shock (an excitor of fear) logically implies the existence of a reliable CS− (a differential inhibitor of fear): The absense of the CS+ is a reliable CS− because it is never followed by shock. This prediction of safety may be at least as important for an organism as the prediction of danger.

In the standard conditioned emotional response (CER) experiment, the safety-signal view assumes that when S is placed in a bar-pressing situation and shocked, at first, all stimuli come to elicit fear. Then S learns which stimuli predict the absence of shock (the chamber in the absence of the CS+), as well as learning which stimuli reliably predict shock (the CS+). At asymptote of acquisition, the CS+ elicits fear (which is presumed throughout to be incompatible with bar pressing for food), and S does not bar press during the CS+. In the absence of the CS+ (the CS−) fear is actively inhibited, and S bar presses at a normal rate. Until that discrimination is made, however, S has no safety signal and so remains in fear. Hence, the common observation of little bar pressing in the early sessions of CER, followed in later sessions by a recovery of bar pressing when the CS+, is absent. The safety-signal hypothesis holds that what controls behavior in a situation in which shock occurs is the presence of a reliable predictor of the absence of shock, as well as the presence of a predictor of shock. In an aversive situation, an organism remains in chronic fear as long as no safety signal is present. It has been well established recently that animals can learn that a discrete stimulus predicts safety (the absence of shock) as well as learn that a stimulus predicts shock (e.g., Rescorla & LoLordo, 1965; Soltysik & Zielinski, 1962).

The experiment reported below tested the safety-signal hypothesis in the following way: Two groups of rats learned to press for food, and then received the same CSs and shocks. One group received CSs predicting the shocks (PR). For the other group, shocks were unpredictable (UN), as CSs and shocks were randomly interspersed. Since there was no CS predicting shock, this group also had no safety signal. Following this, both groups received two more cycles of new CSs predicting shocks (Cycles 2 and 3). Table 1 summarizes the procedure. The safety-signal hypothesis makes the following predictions concerning the bar pressing of the two groups. (*a*) Because the group which receives unpredictable shock has no safety signal, Ss should stop bar pressing altogether and show no recovery; they should not press either during the CS or in its absence, since neither predicts the absence of shock. (*b*) In Cycle 1, the group receiving predicted shock should show reduced bar pressing in the early sessions and then recover bar pressing in the absence of the CS, and fail to bar press only during the CS. (*c*) In subsequent cycles (following recovery of bar pressing by both groups with shock omitted) during which new CSs predict shock for both groups, the group with previous experience with predicted shock (PR) should show little disruption of pressing in the absence of the new CS, because the safety signal (the chamber with CS+ absent) is the same in all cycles. The group which had first experienced unpredictable shock (UN), however, should again show much overall disruption of bar pressing, and little or no recovery, because the new CS− (the chamber in absence of the CS+) was a danger signal in Cycle 1 and not only must a discrimination between CS+ and CS− now develop, but extinction of fear to the new CS− must also occur. (*d*) Finally, since stomach ulceration is frequently taken as a positive index of stress, and the UN group experiences chronic fear because shock is unpredictable, while the PR group is in fear only during the CS+, differences in ulceration might result (Sawrey, 1961).

Method

Subjects

Sixteen male albino rats of the Sprague-Dawley strain, obtained from the Holtzman Company, Madison, Wisconsin, were 90–120 days old at the beginning of the experiment. They were reduced to 75% of their ad-lib weight and maintained at this weight throughout the experiment.

TABLE 1. Stimuli for Successive Cycles for Various Groups

Group	Cycle 1	Cycle 2	Cycle 3	Cycle 4
UN-L	White light on	Tone on	Green light dimmed	—
UN-T	Tone on	White light on	Noise dropped	—
PR-L	White light on	Tone on	Green light dimmed	—
PR-T	Tone on	White light on	Noise dropped	Green light dimmed

Experimental sessions were conducted every day at the same time for each S for approximately 2½ mo.

Apparatus

The apparatus was four identical food reinforcement lever-press boxes described by Seligman (1966).

Four different CSs were used in the course of the experiment: L—a white light located over the lever was turned on for 1 min.; DL—a green light to the right of the lever was dimmed to half its wattage once per second (.5-sec. full, .5-sec. dim) for 1 min.; T—a tone which was audible above the masking white noise was turned on for 1 min.; ND—the white noise (normally on) was dropped from 80 db. (re .0002 dyne/cm²) to approximately 55 db. for 1 min. Thus two stimuli were visual and two auditory; one of each modality was normally on and was turned off as a CS, while one of each was normally off and was turned on as a CS.

Shocks were delivered through a multiple relay scrambler with a rate of 20 per sec. The circuit consisted of 600-v. ac source, with a 10 K and a 700 K resistor in series with S. Measured across the 10 K resistor, with sample rats completing the circuit, the current was approximately .88 ma. All shocks were 1 sec. long.

Stimuli and shock were programmed automatically by a Western Union tape reader (Model 1A). The controlling tapes were generated in the following way for predictable shock: Three different intervals were selected for each day of conditioning in a cycle; the CS began in these three randomly chosen intervals, followed by the US at the appropriate interval. No CS began less than 3 min. following the onset of a prior CS, and no CS began during the first minute of a session.

For unpredictable shock, the onset of the CS occurred at the same time as for the predictable shock tapes on the corresponding day. The shock was programmed to occur randomly with respect to the CS. A US could occur at any time (each with equal probability) and independently of the occurrence of a CS. Thus, occasionally, pairings of CS and US could and did occur. The basic findings on the UN group were later replicated using tapes in which the US occurred at the same time as for predictable shock tapes. For all groups, a different tape was used on each day of a given cycle, but the same tape was used on corresponding days of different cycles.

Presentations of stimuli and shock were independent of Ss' bar pressing and food reinforcement.

Procedure

Following magazine and CRF training, four Ss were randomly assigned to each of the four subgroups shown in Table 1. All groups then received 9 days on a variable interval 1-min. schedule (VI-1). On the tenth day of VI training, three CSs without shock were presented to assess unconditioned effects of the stimuli on bar pressing; this day is designated DA–1 (D stands for Day, A refers to the pretest of stimuli, and 1 refers to the cycle number).

Shock was introduced on the next day for all groups. This day is designated D1–1 (the first 1 refers to the day number within the cycle, the second 1 refers to the cycle number). The UN groups received three stimuli and two shocks randomly interspersed; one presentation of the stimulus occurred before the first shock was introduced to allow for further observation of the unconditioned effect of the stimulus.

On D1–1, the PR group received three CSs, the last two of which predicted shock. The second and third CS occurrences were both followed by a 1-sec. trace interval, followed by a 1-sec. shock. On each of 14 further daily sessions (D2–1 to D15–1), each group received three CSs and three shocks with the VI food schedule in effect, i.e., conditioning occurred on the base line.

All Ss then received 14 days of VI retraining, with no shock or CSs presented to allow the overall bar pressing of the groups to become equal again; DA–2 followed, i.e., three presentations of stimuli without shock.

During Cycle 2, the stimuli were counterbalanced so as to be new stimuli for each subgroup, e.g., the UN-L subgroup received T in Cycle 2. Then all groups received 10 days of predicted shock; the procedure for all groups was identical to the procedure for PR groups in Cycle 1. Following the 10 days of predicted shock in Cycle 2, all groups received 9 further days of VI retraining without CSs and shocks followed by DA-3 which was like DA-2, except that new stimuli (see Table 1) were presented.

This was followed by D1-3 through D10-3 of predicted shock with the new CSs. Following D10-3, the UN groups and the PR-L subgroup were sacrificed and examined for stomach ulcers.

Subgroup PR-T received 4 more days of VI retraining with no CSs or shock, and then a fourth cycle in which DL was the CS predicting shock. The procedure was identical with the past cycles. This group was then sacrificed and examined for ulcers.

Ulcers were observed and counted in the following way: The stomach was cut out by severing the cardiac and pyloric sphincters, and cut along the midline. It was then spread and ulcers were counted. The criterion for an ulcer was any fixed blood clot on the inner surface which could be seen by the naked eye. The size and location of each ulcer was recorded. Each ulcer count was performed by two different Os; no disagreements occurred. The stomachs were then preserved in formalin; sample stomachs were sectioned later and examined microscopically.

Response Measures

Base-Line[2] Drop. The amount of suppression of lever pressing for food occurring throughout a session was the major dependent variable of this study. The index for measuring the amount of base-line suppression was the ratio of the number of bar presses for the session to the number of bar presses on the most recent Day A, the last shock-free day. Statistical analyses revealed that the same results were found with either this ratio or the absolute number of bar presses.

Suppression to the CS. Suppression to the 1-min. CS was indexed by $B/(A + B)$, where B is the number of presses during the 1-min. CS and A is the number of presses for the 1 min. preceding the onset of the CS.

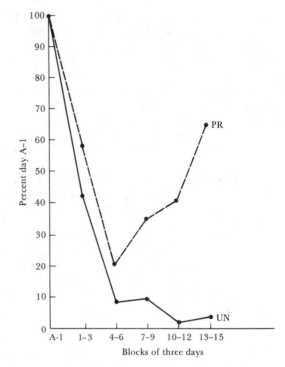

FIG. 1. *Mean percentage of Day A-1 bar pressing for blocks of 3 days in Cycle 1.*

Overall suppression to the CS for an entire day is given by the total presses during the three 1-min. CSs divided by the sum of itself and the total presses for the three 1-min. periods preceding CS onset: $\Sigma B/(\Sigma A + \Sigma B)$.

Results[3]

Cycle 1

As predicted by the safety-signal hypothesis, the base line of both UN and PR groups dropped initially. The base line then recovered for every S in the PR group, but it had not returned to its original rate at the end of 15 days. The base line did not recover at all for any S receiving unpredictable shock.

The individual records of each S looked like the means presented in Fig. 1. The PR group dropped to about 20% of its preshock base line in the first 6 days and then recovered sharply to about 65% of its preshock base line. The UN groups dropped monotonically to almost no bar pressing at all. On some of the latter days, the lowest presser in the PR group emitted some 20 times as many responses as the highest presser in the UN group. Analysis of variance revealed significant effects of Groups and Days, and a significant Groups × Days interaction ($ps < .001$).

During VI retraining, the UN group, which began at less than 10% of its preshock rate on the first VI retraining day, climbed rapidly, and merged with the PR group by about Day 8. The PR group began at about 60% of its preshock rate and climbed slowly to about 100% of its preshock rate. By the beginning of Cycle 2, both groups were bar press-

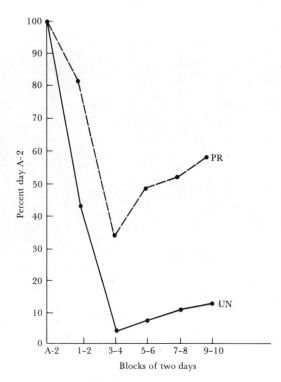

FIG. 2. *Mean percentage of Day A-2 bar pressing for blocks of 2 days in Cycle 2.*

ing at about the same rate. A significant Days effect ($p < .001$) and a significant Groups $\times$ Days interaction ($p < .01$) were revealed by analysis of variance.

Cycle 2

In Cycle 2 the predictions of the safety-signal hypothesis were confirmed as shown in Fig. 2. The UN group dropped to nearly zero pressing by Days 3 and 4, and showed only a very slight hint of recovery (7% on Days 5 and 6 to 12% on Days 9 and 10). The PR group dropped to about 35% of its DA-2 rate on Days 3 and 4 and then recovered to almost 60% of its DA-2 rate by Day 10. As in Cycle 1, little or no overlap occurred between Ss of the two groups on any given day. Analysis of variance revealed significant groups and blocks of days effects ($p < .001$). Newman–Keuls comparisons indicated significant recovery of pressing across days in the PR group ($p < .01$), but not in the UN group.

Did the two groups differ in the nature of the base-line drop changes from Cycle 1 to Cycle 2? The safety-signal hypothesis suggests that in the UN group little, if any, change should occur in the base-line drop in spite of the fact that shock was now predicted; this was because fear must extinguish to the chamber alone before recovery can be seen and was confirmed by comparison of Days 1–10 of Cycle 1 and Cycle 2. The UN group dropped to near zero on both cycles and did not recover. Newman—Keuls tests showed no significant differences from Cycle 1 to Cycle 2, except on Days 1 and 2, where more suppression occurred in Cycle 2 ($p < .05$).

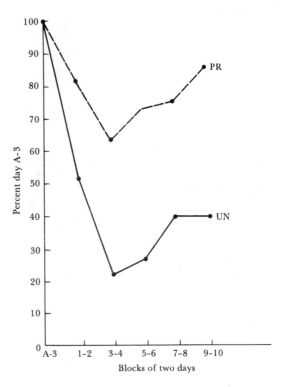

FIG. 3 *Mean percentage of Day A-3 bar pressing for blocks of 2 days in Cycle 3.*

In contrast, as suggested by the hypothesis, the PR group recovered faster in Cycle 2 than it did in Cycle 1. Analysis of variance on the PR group between Cycles 1 and 2 showed a significant Cycles effect ($p < .001$) and Cycles × Days interaction ($p < .01$).

During VI retraining, the UN group, which began at about 35% of its DA-2 rate, climbed to about 95% of its DA-2 rate by Day 7. The PR group began at almost 95% and stayed somewhat above 100% throughout. The groups did not differ significantly by the end of VI retraining.

Cycle 3

The safety-signal hypothesis predicts that during Cycle 3 the PR group should show little base-line drop and recover very rapidly to its normal pressing rate. The UN group should again lose its base line and show only gradual recovery. These predictions were confirmed as shown in Fig. 3. The PR group showed relatively little base-line drop (to 64% on Days 3–4) and then returned to about 85% of its DA–3 rate. In constrast, the UN group dropped to 22% of its DA-3 rate on Days 3–4 and recovered to only 40% of its DA-3 rate. As in Cycles 1 and 2, little or no overlap occurred among Ss of the two groups on a given day.

Analysis of variance showed significant Groups and Days effects and Stimuli × Days interaction ($ps < .001$). In Cycle 3, Newman–Keuls tests revealed the first signs of significant base-line recovery for the UN group during shock: More bar pressing occurred on Days 7–10 than on Days

3–4 ($ps<$ .05). Significant base-line drop followed by recovery was also observed in the PR group ($ps<$ .05).

Base-Line Drop across All Three Cycles

The safety-signal hypothesis predicts that the UN group should press less across all cycles than the PR group; this, of course, was confirmed ($p<$ .001). It predicts that overall bar pressing should increase with cycles; this was confirmed ($p<$ .001). It predicts that the PR group should show less and less disruption with cycles than the UN group; this Groups × Cycles interaction was confirmed ($p<$ .025). It predicts overall increases in bar pressing across blocks of days; this was confirmed ($p<$ .001). It predicts that the PR group should improve more with days than the UN group; this Groups × Blocks interaction was confirmed ($p<$ .001). It predicts that across both groups, base-line drop should be less on a given day as cycles progress; this Blocks × Cycles interaction was significant ($p<$ .001). Finally, within the UN group, collapsed over days, more pressing occurred in Cycle 3 than in Cycle 1 or 2 ($ps<$ .01). The same was true of the PR group ($ps<$ .01).

In summary of the base-line drop results, the safety-signal hypothesis made many specific predictions, all of which were confirmed.

Stomach Ulcers

Following D10-3, the UN group and half of the PR group were sacrificed and examined for stomach ulcers. The remaining four PR *Ss* were examined for ulcers following D10-4. Since the safety-signal hypothesis predicted that the UN group would form more ulcers than the PR group, the extra experience that half the PR group had with additional shock (and fear) should only have biased the results against the hypothesis. In spite of this, none of the eight *Ss* in the PR group showed any ulcers; while six of the eight *Ss* in the UN group formed ulcers, with a median of 4.5 ulcers and a mean of 9.1 ulcers each. Table 2 presents the ulcer count, along with an index of suppression across the three cycles for each *S* in the two groups.

TABLE 2. Number of Stomach Ulcers and Mean Percentage of DA Base Line for Individual *Ss*

Group UN-L		Group UN-T		Group PR-L		Group PR-T	
Number of ulcers	M percentage[b]	Number of ulcers	M percentage	Number of ulcers	M percentage	Number of ulcers	M percentage
7	28.8	5	52.8	0	49.1	0	53.3
1	17.0	4	22.5	0	49.4	0	74.2
0	8.1	9	14.7	0	63.0	0	56.6
0	19.6	>47	21.9	0	48.7	0	52.1

[a] For UN groups, mean number of ulcers = 9.1, median = 4.5.
[b] Mean percentage of DA base line for UN groups = 23.2 and for PR groups = 55.8.

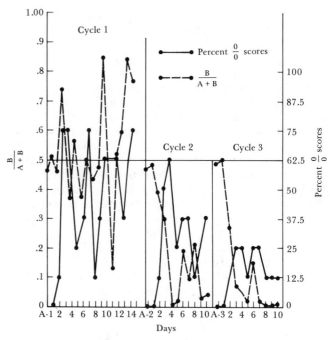

Fig. 4. *Mean daily* B(A + B) *scores and percentage of Ss with daily 0/0 scores in the UN group as a function of days across all three cycles.*

Conditioned Suppression to the CS

How can we compare what the two groups did during the CS? The conventional index of conditioned suppression is a ratio of the presses made during the CS to the presses made before the onset of the CS. This cannot be meaningful in this experiment, for the two groups differed sizably in their pre-CS rate. This point counts against the usefulness of the "truly random control" group (Rescorla, 1967) for on-the-base-line CER conditioning procedures. A typical S in the PR group showed a daily $B/(A + B)$ ratio of .02, $1/(49 + 1)$. In contrast, because bar pressing had dropped out almost completely in the UN group, a ratio of $0/(0 + 0)$ was not an uncommon finding. And what does a ratio of 0/0 mean either psychologically or mathematically? Moreover, when there are very many 0/0 scores, the overall suppression score to the CS for that group will be virtually determined by the choice of meaning for 0/0.

Figures 4 and 5 present concurrently both the mean daily $B/(A + B)$ score for each group, excluding the 0/0 scores, and the percentage of Ss in each group that had 0/0 scores for each day of the three cycles. Looking first at the percentage of 0/0 scores for each day (the number of scores omitted from the calculated suppression), it is obvious that the UN group had many more 0/0 scores than the PR group throughout. Meaningful comparison of calculated scores between the two groups were thus precluded.

Inspection of the non-0/0 scores in Fig. 4 reveals that the UN group

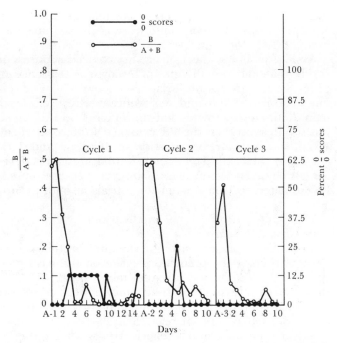

Fig. 5. *Mean daily* B/(A+B) *scores and percentage of Ss with daily*
0/0 scores in the PR group as a function of days across all three cycles.

did not show any systematic deviation from .50 in Cycle 1. This indicates
that fear of the CS did not differ from fear in the absence of the CS in
those Ss that showed measurable suppression. The PR group showed reliable acquisition of fear to the CS in Cycle 1. In Cycles 2 and 3, both
groups showed reliable (measurable) acquisition of suppression to the CS
(sign test, Day 1 vs. Day 10, $ps = .004$).

Associative Retardation

Seligman and Maier (1967) suggested that experience with one stimulus randomly interspersed with a US might retard the association between
that stimulus (or any other stimulus) and the US, once pairing was begun.
The appropriate comparison for looking at associative retardation in this
experiment is the acquisition of CER in the PR group in Cycle 1 vs. the
UN group in Cycle 2. This compares the acquisition of CER by naive Ss
(PR, Cycle 1) with acquisition by Ss that had first experienced shock and
a CS randomly interspersed (UN, Cycle 2). This comparison may be
meaningful in spite of the differential base-line drop in the two groups
because the effect of associative retardation is to be expected in the first
few trials of stimulus paired with shock, before differential base-line drop
was very great.

It should be noted that some 0/0 observations occurred in both groups
over the first five trials. Of the 40 scores in each group (eight Ss × five
trials), four 0/0 scores occurred in the PR group, and eight occurred in

the UN group. This difference was not significant ($\chi^2 = .88$, df = 1). For these 12 cases the score entered was the suppression ratio on the last non-0/0 trial for that S.

As Fig. 6 shows, the UN group acquired suppression to the CS more slowly than did the PR group. Analysis of variance on the suppression ratios of two groups on Trials 1–5 showed a significant Groups × Trials interaction ($p < .01$) and a significant effect of Trials ($p < .00$). New-man–Keuls tests showed that on Trials 4 and 5, the UN group showed less suppression than the PR group ($p < .05$, one-tailed). Further, the PR group showed more suppression on Trials 4 and 5 than on Trials 1–3 ($ps < .05$), while the UN group showed no such differences. This finding cannot be taken as conclusive, however, because suppression ratios had to be estimated for some Ss on some trials in both groups.

Discussion

Safety-Signal Hypothesis

The results present strong evidence for the safety-signal hypothesis. Each of the specific predictions made on the basis of the hypothesis was confirmed. (*a*) During unpredictable shock the UN group entirely stopped bar pressing for food and showed no recovery. The subjects showed a continual CER; throughout each session they avoided the bar and crouched in one place. When shock was removed, they gradually began bar pressing and after 15 days were pressing at about their pre-shock rate. When predictable shock was then introduced, they stopped pressing again and did not show signs of recovery until the end of the last cycle. Six of these eight Ss formed stomach ulcers. (*b*) In contrast, the PR group acquired a CER only to the signal predicting shock. When the sig-nal was on, they crouched in one place. In the absence of the signal, they pressed for food. With experience, they showed less initial extra-signal disruption of bar pressing when a new signal predicting shock was intro-duced. None of these eight Ss formed ulcers.

The safety-signal hypothesis is useful in understanding other results on the effects of predictable vs. unpredictable shock.

Choice of Predictable over Unpredictable Shock. The safety-signal hypothesis holds that Ss prefer signalled to unsignalled shock. This is well docu-mented (e.g., Lockard, 1963). Predictable shock is preferred not because the predicted shock is less aversive (via preparatory responses) but be-cause the situation in which predicted shock occurs is less aversive. On the predicted-shock side, S is in fear only when the CS + is on; when the CS + is not on, S is safe. On the unpredictable-shock side, S has no safety signal, and is in fear all the time. The shocks, then, are not differentially aversive, the entire situations are, and S chooses to stay on the predict-able side.

Choice of Immediate vs. Delayed Shock. The safety-signal hypothesis pre-dicts that Ss will choose immediate over delayed shock, as they do (e.g., Knapp, Kause, & Perkins, 1959). Since organisms cannot "time" per-fectly, the situation in which delayed shock occurs elicits fear for a longer period than the immediate-shock situation. In a chamber in which shock was delivered immediately and S released 45 sec. later (Knapp et al.,

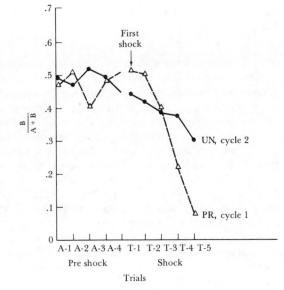

FIG. 6 *Mean trial-by-trial B/ (A + B) scores for the UN group in Cycle 2 and the PR group in Cycle 1. (On Trials A-1 through A-4 no shock was presented following the CS. The first shock occurred following the CS on Trial T-1.)*

1959), S received a shock, followed by 45 sec. of a CS $-$ (safety). In the chamber in which the shock was delayed for 45 sec., relatively less safety was present; Ss received 45 sec. of CS+ (fear) followed by the shock.

Differential Control over Shock. The safety-signal hypothesis predicts that a situation in which shock is uncontrollable (response-independent) should generate more fear than a situation in which shock is response-contingent. The feedback from a response can, of course, be a stimulus for an organism. When shock is response-contingent, withholding the response provides a safety signal. Making the response produces a CS+ for fear. As long as S withholds the response, it is in the presence of a fear-inhibiting stimulus. A yoked S (for which shock is response-independent) has no such safety signal, and remains in chronic fear. In an outstanding series of studies Weiss (1968) showed greater weight loss, more defecation, more stomach ulceration, and more suppression of drinking resulting from uncontrollable than controllable shock. Hearst (1965) and others have reported greater extra-S^d disruption of appetitive base lines for response-independent than for response-contingent shock.

One difficulty in completely specifying the safety-signal hypothesis concerns the intensity of fear. It is apparent that the UN group spent more time in fear than the PR group. One might expect that the intensity of fear per unit time might have been less for the UN group than during the CS for the PR group. After all, the probability of a shock was less during any given minute for the UN group than during the CS for the PR group. But the results suggest no difference in intensity of fear. The absence of bar pressing throughout the session for the UN group did not differ from the absence of pressing during the CS in the PR group. It is possible, however, that this negative result is merely a ceiling effect since both were near zero responding. Thus the present interpretation, strictly speaking, must rely on total time spent in fear and safety. The total amount of fear or the Time × Intensity function remains, for now, an unknown.

The Random Control Group in Pavlovian Conditioning

According to Rescorla (1967), the only appropriate control group for Pavlovian experiments is a group which receives the CS and US in a random relationship to each other. It is against this control that excitatory effects of pairing and inhibitory effects of nonpairing can be evaluated.

The present experiment raises an objection to the random control group for evaluation of on-the-base-line CER procedures. The UN group in Cycle 1 met the requirements of being a "truly" random control group" for the effects of the CS on the PR group. The CR of the "control" group, however, cannot be compared to the PR group, since the pre-CS pressing was much lower in the UN group. Since one cannot compute meaningful suppression ratios to the CS for the UN group, one cannot, of course, compare it to the PR group. Even if one could, the comparison would be of unknown validity, since the control group formed ulcers and the PR group did not. How do ulcers (and chronic fear) interact with the formation of a CR or lack thereof in the UN group? Since unpredictable (random) shock has strong effects of its own which might interact with CR formation, its uncritical use as a control procedure seems dubious.

Associative Retardation

Traditional learning theory has emphasized that only two relationships produce learning: explicit contiguity between events (acquisition) and explicit separation of two events (extinction). The central hypothesis of the theory proposed by Seligman and Maier (1967) and by Maier, Seligman, and Solomon (1968) to account for their learned helplessness results is that learning is also produced by a third relationship, independence between events. A testable consequence of this theory is that such learning will retard the association of two events when pairing begins. The learning of independence is conceived by Seligman and Maier to be an active form of learning, which can proactively interfere with associations.

This hypothesis was confirmed in the main experiment. Experience with CS1 and shock, randomly interspersed, somewhat retarded the acquisition of a subsequent CS-shock association: Over the first five trials in Cycle 2 for the UN group, no significant acquisition of CER was observed. Significant acquisition was observed over these trials for the PR group in Cycle 1 and Cycle 2.

For two reasons it seems unlikely that retardation resulted from disinhibition by the CS. There was no tendency for the UN groups to increase their rates during the CS, as observed by Brimer and Kamin (1963). Further, in their experiment, Pavlovian disinhibition occurred only with novel stimuli, but our UN group had seen the CS three times on the day before and twice on the same day that pairing of CS and shock began. More probably, the phenomenon is related to "latent inhibition" (Lubow & Moore, 1959). They observed that nonreinforced presentations of a CS made acquisition of a CR slower once that CS was paired with a US. It is not unlikely in their experiments that *S* came to ignore the CS when it was presented over and over without reinforcement (the orienting response habituated). It also seems possible that when a CS is rendered uninformative by being randomly interspersed with a US, similar inattention also occurs. Thus, the mechanism of both associative retardation and latent inhibition might be habituation of the orienting response to changes in the environment.

In conclusion, we have proposed a hypothesis which emphasizes the importance of the reliable prediction of the absence of shock in aversive situations. This hypothesis accounts for the disruptive effects of unpredictable shock, as well as the usual results of CER procedures. It predicts that removing a reliable predictor of safety from an aversive situation should result in chronic fear. We found this to be so: Experience with unpredictable shock eliminated instrumental responding for food and caused the formation of stomach ulcers.

Notes
[1] This report is based on a dissertation submitted by the author in partial fulfillment of the requirements for the PhD degree at the University of Pennsylvania. It was supported by a National Science Foundation predoctoral fellowship to the author, and by United States Public Health Service Grant MH-04202 and National Science Foundation Grant GB-2428 to R. L. Solomon. The author thanks R. L. Solomon, J. Geer, and P. Rozin, the members of the dissertation committee, and especially S. F. Maier, with whom many of the ideas herein had their beginnings.
[2] "Base line" refers throughout to the daily bar-press rate before shock was introduced (DA).
[3] All statistical statements are for two-tailed tests, unless otherwise indicated.

References
Brimer, C. J., & Kamin, L. J. Disinhibition, habituation, sensitization, and the conditioned emotional response, *J. Comp. Physiol. Psychol.*, 1963, **56**, 508–516.
Hearst, E. Stress induced breakdown of an appetitive discrimination. *J. Exp. Anal. Behav.*, 1965, **8**, 135–147.
Knapp, R., Kause, R., & Perkins, C. Immediate vs. delayed shock in T-maze performance. *J. Exp. Psychol.*, 1959, **58**, 357–362.
Lockard, J. S. Choice of a warning signal or no warning signal in an unavoidable shock situation. *J. Comp. Physiol. Psychol.*, 1963, **56**, 526–530.
Lubow, R. E., & Moore, A. V. Latent inhibition: The effect of nonreinforced pre-exposure to the conditioned stimulus. *J. Comp. Physiol. Psychol.*, 1959, **52**, 415–419.
Maier, S. F., Seligman, M. E. P., & Solomon, R. L. Pavlovian fear conditioning and learned helplessness. In B. A. Campbell & R. M. Church, (Eds.), *Punishment.* New York: Appleton-Century-Crofts, 1968.
Rescorla, R. A. Pavlovian conditioning and its proper control procedures. *Psychol. Rev.*, 1967, **74**, 71–79.
Rescorla, R. A. & LoLordo, V. M. Inhibition of avoidance behavior. *J. Comp. Physiol. Psychol.*, 1965, **59**, 406–410.
Sawrey, W. Conditioned responses of fear in the relationship to ulceration. *J. Comp. Physiol. Psychol.*, 1961, **54**, 347–348.
Seligman, M. E. P. CS redundancy and secondary punishment. *J. Exp. Psychol.*, 1966, **72**, 546–550.
Seligman, M. E. P., & Maier, S. F. Failure to escape traumatic shock. *J. Exp. Psychol.*, 1967, **73**, 1–9.
Soltysik, S., & Zielinski, K. Conditioned inhibition of the avoidance reflex. *Acta Biol. Experimentalis*, 1962, **22**, 157–167.
Weiss, J. M. Effects of coping responses on stress. *J. Comp. Physiol. Psychol.*, 1968, **65**, 251–260.

E. PREDICTABILITY AND ATTENTION

The demonstration that organisms are sensitive to the predictiveness of a CS changed the way in which researchers thought about Pavlovian conditioning, and opened up new areas of inquiry. Do organisms learn nothing about CSs that are not predictive of USs, or do they learn that these CSs are not predictive? And if they learn that a CS is not predictive, what is the consequence of that learning? And in situations in which there is more than one CS, do organisms selectively associate the most predictive CS with the US and not the others?

The article in this section illustrates the study of some of these issues. Suppose an animal is first exposed to pairings of a tone and shock until conditioning to the tone occurs; then a light is added so that trials now consist of a compound CS, tone and light, followed by shock. What does the animal learn about the light? On the one hand, we would expect the animal to become afraid of the light, because it is just as predictive of shock as the tone; but on the other hand, what information does the light provide that is not already provided by the tone? The answer is none. The light is redundant; and because it is redundant, it is blocked from conditioning. Kamin's article is a study of this blocking effect. *It appears that organisms will learn to ignore stimuli that are redundant. They will only pay attention to CSs if they are nonredundantly predictive of USs (see Mackintosh, 1975; Pearce and Hall, 1980).*

7 Predictability, Surprise, Attention, and Conditioning

LEON J. KAMIN

The experiments to be described here have no special relevance to the problem of punishment. The studies to be reported do employ the CER procedure (Estes & Skinner, 1941). This procedure, within which an aversive US follows a warning signal regardless of the animal's behavior, has been contrasted to the arrangements employed in response-contingent punishment (Hunt & Brady, 1955). This type of comparison, however, is not germane to the present research. The kinds of results considered in this chapter derive from rats in a CER procedure, with shock as the US; but very similar results have been obtained in the McMaster laboratory by H. M. Jenkins, using pigeons in a food-reinforced operant discrimination. What appears to be involved in these studies is a concern with phenomena often referred to as examples of "selective attention." To the degree that punishment contingencies may be brought under stimulus control, the present work might be related to other contributions in this volume.[1]

The present work arose from an interest in the possible role of attention in Pavlovian conditioning. The usual statement of the conditions sufficient for a Pavlovian CR asserts simply that a neutral, to-be-conditioned CS must be presented in contiguity with a US. What happens, however, when a compound CS consisting of elements known to be independently conditionable is presented in contiguity with a US? Are all elements of the CS effectively conditioned? Does the animal attend, and thus condition, more to some elements than to others? What kinds of experimental manipulations might direct the animal's attention to one or another element?

The first experimental approach to these questions was, in overview, as follows. First, condition an animal to respond to a simple CS, consisting of Element A. Then condition the animal to respond to a compound, consisting of Element A plus a superimposed Element B. Finally, test the animal with Element B alone. Will it respond to Element B? Put very naively, our primitive notion was that, because of the prior conditioning to Element A, that element might so "engage the animal's attention" during presentation of the compound that it would not "notice" the added Element B. The failure to notice the superimposed element might preclude any conditioning to it. To conclude that the prior conditioning to Element A was responsible for a failure to respond to Element B we must, of course, show that animals conditioned to the compound without prior conditioning to A do respond when tested with B. To control for amount of experience with the US, and variables correlated with it, we

Leon J. Kamin, "Predictability, Surprise, Attention, and Conditioning," in *Punishment and Aversive Behavior*, ed., by Campbell/Church, © 1969, pp. 279–296. Reprinted by permission of Prentice-Hall, Inc., Englewood Cliffs, N.J.

ought also to show that, if compound conditioning is followed by conditioning to A alone, the animal will respond when tested with B.

This relatively simple design has since expanded in a number of unexpected directions, and our original primitive notions about attention have been forcibly revised, if not refined. To date, we have utilized over 1200 rats as subjects in more than 110 experimental groups. There has been an earlier report of the first stages of this work (Kamin, 1968); in the present chapter, we shall review the basic preliminary findings, then focus on some of the more recent developments.

The basic CER procedure utilized in all these studies employs naive hooded rats as subjects, reduced to 75% of *ad libitum* body weight and maintained on a 24-hour feeding rhythm. The rats are first trained to press a bar for a food reward in a standard, automatically programmed operant conditioning chamber. The daily sessions are 2 hours in length, with food pellets being delivered according to a 2.5-minute variable-interval reinforcement schedule. The first five sessions (10 hrs.) produce stable bar-pressing rates in individual rats, and CER conditioning is then begun. During CER conditioning, the food-reinforcement schedule remains in effect throughout the daily 2-hour session, but four CS–US sequences are now programmed independently of the animal's behavior. The CS, typically, has a duration of 3 minutes and is followed immediately by a .5-second US, typically a 1-ma. shock. For each CER trial (four trials daily), a suppression ratio is calculated. The ratio is $B/A + B$, where B represents the number of bar presses during the 3-minute CS, and A the number of bar presses during the 3-minute period immediately preceding the CS. Thus, if the CS has no effect on the animal's bar pressing, the ratio is .50; but as the CS, with repeated trials, begins to suppress bar pressing, the ratio drops toward an asymptote very close to .00. We regard the learned suppression produced by the CS as an index of an association between CS and US, much as conditioned salivation to a metronome may be regarded as such as index.

The CS in the experiments to be described was either a white noise (typically 80 db), the turning on of an overhead house light (7.5-w. bulb diffused through milky plastic ceiling), or a compound of noise-plus-light presented simultaneously. The normal condition of the chamber is complete darkness. The various experimental groups received CER conditioning to various CS's, in different sequences. The precise sequences of CS's are detailed in the body of this report. Typically, following the CER conditioning, the animal was given a single test day, during which a nonreinforced CS was presented four times within the bar-pressing session. The data to be presented are suppression ratios for the first test trial. While no conclusions would be altered by including the data for all four test trials, the fact that the test CS is not reinforced means that test trials following the first contribute relatively little to differences between experimental groups.

The characteristic outcome of our basic conditioning procedure is depicted in Fig. 1, which presents median suppression ratios, as a function of acquisition trial, for three representative groups of subjects. The groups have been conditioned with either noise, light, or the compound as a CS. The major point to note at present is that after a very few trials

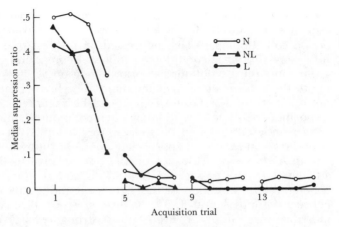

FIG. 1. *Acquisition of CER by trial, for three groups of rats, trained with either light, noise, or compound CS.*

all groups approach asymptotic suppression. It can also be observed that light has a slightly suppressing effect on the very first trial so that the light group tends to acquire slightly more rapidly than the noise group. Finally, the compound group acquires significantly more rapidly than either of the others.

The first experimental approach to attention is illustrated in the design outlined below. The code letter for an experimental group is indicated at the left of the paradigm. Then the CS employed with that group during consecutive phases of CER conditioning is noted; L, N, and LN refer, respectively, to a light, a noise, or a compound CS. The number of reinforced trials with each type of CS is indicated in parentheses immediately following the CS notation; four reinforced trials are given daily. Finally, the CS employed during the test trial is indicated, together with the median suppression ratio for the group on the test trial. The number of animals per experimental group varies, in the studies to be reported, between 8 and 20.

Group A:	LN (8)	N (16)	Test L	.25
Group B:	N (16)	LN (8)	Test L	.45
Group G:	—	LN (8)	Test L	.05
Group 2-B:	—	N (24)	Test L	.44

There are a number of relevant comparisons which can be made within the above set of four experimental treatments. The basic comparison is that between Groups G and B. The test result for Group G indicates, as a kind of base line, the amount of control normally acquired by the light as a result of eight reinforced compound conditioning trials. This is very significantly different from the result for Group B, within which the same compound conditioning trials have been preceded by prior conditioning to the noise element. Thus, our speculation that prior conditioning to an element might block conditioning to a new, superimposed element receives support. When we next compare Groups A and B, we again observe a significant difference. These two groups have each received the same number of each type of CER conditioning trial, but in a different sequence. Group B, for whom the noise conditioning preceded compound conditioning, is less suppressed on the test trial than is Group A, for whom the noise conditioning followed compound conditioning. This again supports the notion that prior conditioning to A blocks conditioning to the B member of the compound. The further fact that Group A is not as suppressed as Group G is not to be regarded as produced by interpolation of noise conditioning after compound conditioning. It must be remembered that four days elapse for Group A between the last compound trial and the test; appropriate control groups have established that Group A's poor performance on the test, relative to Group G's, can be attributed to the passage of time. This *recency effect*, of course, works counter to the direction of the significant difference we have observed between Groups A and B. The failure of Group B to suppress to light as much as does Group A, even with a strong recency effect working to Group B's advantage, suggests a fundamental failure of conditioning to the light in Group B. This is confirmed when we compare the test results of Groups B and 2-B. These groups each experience 24 times noise followed by shock, but for Group B light is superimposed during the final eight trials. The fact that the test trial to light yields equivalent results for B and 2-B indicates that the superimpositions have produced literally no conditioning to the light. The test ratios for both these groups are slightly below .50, indicating again that, independent of previous conditioning, an initial presentation of light has a mildly disruptive effect on ongoing bar-pressing behavior.

The blocking effect demonstrated by the experimental treatments described above is not specific to the particular sequence of stimuli employed. When four new groups of rats were trained, reversing the roles of the light and noise stimuli, a total block of conditioning to the noise member of a compound was produced by prior conditioning to the light element (Kamin, 1968). Further, it should be pointed out that we have tested many rats, after *de novo* conditioning to the light–noise compound, to each element separately. We have never observed a rat which did not display some suppression to each element. Thus, granted the present intensity levels of light and noise, the blocking effect depends upon prior conditioning to one of the elements; when conditioned from the outset to the compound, no animal ignores completely one of the elements.

We should also note that animals conditioned to noise alone after previous conditioning to light alone acquire at the same rate as do naive animals conditioned to noise alone. Prior conditioning to noise alone also does not affect subsequent conditioning to light alone. It seems very probable that this lack of transfer between the two stimuli, as well as some degree of equivalence between the independent efficacies of the stimuli, are necessary preconditions for the kind of symmetrical blocking effect which we have demonstrated.

The results so far presented indicate that, granted prior conditioning to an element, no conditioning occurs to a new element which is now superimposed on the old. This might mean, as we first loosely suggested, that the animal does not notice (or perceive) the superimposed element; the kind of peripheral gating mechanism popularized by Hernandez-Peon

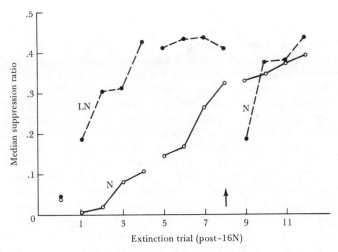

FIG. 2.   *Extinction of CER, by trial, following conditioning to noise. The groups were extinguished either to noise alone or to the compound. The arrow in the abscissa indicates the point at which the group extinguished to compound is switched to noise alone.*

(Hernandez-Peon et al., 1956) is an obvious candidate for theoretical service here. To speak loosely again, however, we might suppose that the animal does notice the superimposed stimulus but does not condition to it because the stimulus is redundant. The motivationally significant event, shock, is already perfectly predicted by the old element. The possible importance of redundancy and informativeness of stimuli in conditioning experiments has been provocatively indicated by Egger and Miller (1962). We thus decided to examine whether, in the case when the superimposed stimulus predicted something new (specifically, nonreinforcement), it could be demonstrated that the animal noticed the new stimulus. The following two groups were examined.

Group Y:	N (16)	LN, nonreinforced (8)	N, nonreinforced (4)
Group Z:	N (16)	N, nonreinforced (12)	

The results for both groups during nonreinforced trials are presented in Fig. 2.

Through the first 16 CER conditioning trials these groups are treated identically, and on the sixteenth trial the median ratio to noise was .02 for each group. When Group Y was presented with the compound on its next trial, its ratio increased to .18; on the equivalent trial, Group Z, presented with the familiar noise, had a ratio of .01. The difference between groups on this trial fell short of significance, but it is certainly suggestive. The animals in Group Y seem to notice the superimposed light, even before the compound is followed by nonreinforcement. It must be remembered that, until the moment of nonreinforcement on Trial 17, Group Y is treated identically to the blocked Group B in the original experiment. Thus, if this result can be replicated, we have evidence that animals do notice the superimposed element, at least on the first trial of its introduction. The evidence is in the form of an attenuation of the suppression which would have occurred had the new element not been superimposed.

To return to the comparison between Groups Y and Z, on the second nonreinforced trial Group Y's ratio was .31, Group Z's was .02. This difference was significant. Thus a single nonreinforced presentation of the compound was sufficient for Group Y to discriminate between noise (always reinforced) and the compound (nonreinforced). Clearly, the light element had been perceived by Group Y. The very rapid extinction in Group Y cannot be attributed to the mere failure to reinforce the noise element, as Group Z's performance makes perfectly clear. The nature of the discrimination formed by Group Y is further illustrated by comparing performance of the two groups throughout the extinction phase of the experiment. By the eighth nonreinforced trial, the ratios were .41 for Group Y and .33 for Group Z. Then, on the next trial, the stimulus for Group Y was changed to noise alone. The Group Y ratio on this trial was .17, the Group Z ratio was again .33. This was a significantly lower ratio for Group Y than had been observed on the preceding trial. Thus, to some degree, animals in Group Y had learned that it was the compound which was nonreinforced; the noise element per se had been protected from extinction.

We now see that, if the superimposed element provides new information, the animal not only notices the element but can utilize the information which it provides with truly impressive efficiency. Further, the attenuated suppression noted on the transitional trial, when the new element is first superimposed on the old, suggested that, even in the earlier experiments in which the new element was redundant, the animals may have noticed it. This suggestion was confirmed by examining all of our data. We had at last count conditioned 153 animals with 16 trials of noise alone, followed by at least one trial of the compound. The median ratio of these animals on the sixteenth noise trial was .02; on the transitional trial (before reinforcement or nonreinforcement of the compound can exert any differential effect) the median ratio was .15. (When the transitional trial was reinforced, the median ratio on the second compound trial was again .02). There were 106 subjects which displayed higher ratios on the transitional trial than on the sixteenth noise trial; 17 which displayed lower ratios on the transitional trial; and 30 which had equal ratios on the two trials. This is a highly significant effect. There is thus no doubt that, at least on the first transitional trial, an animal previously conditioned to a single element notices the superimposition of a new element.

This observation is clearly fatal to our original theoretical notions. There remains the possibility, however, that in the case when the transitional trial proves the superimposed stimulus to be redundant, some gating mechanism is activated at that point such that the new element is not perceived on subsequent compound trials. Thus, it is at least conceivable that perceptual gating (deficient attention) provides the mechanism through which redundant stimuli are made nonconditionable. This view can be contrasted to the notion that redundant stimuli, though perceived in an intact manner, are simply not conditioned. We shall return to this problem a little later, after reviewing briefly some of the parameters of the blocking effect.

The data gathered to date, much of which has been more fully described elsewhere (Kamin, 1968), indicates such facts as the following. The blocking effect, granted prior conditioning to Element A, remains total even if the number of compound conditioning trials is very substantially increased; on the other hand, if conditioning to Element A is terminated before suppression has become asymptotic, a partial block of conditioning to the B member of the compound occurs. The amount of blocking is very smoothly related to the amount of prior conditioning to Element A. The block can be eliminated by extinguishing suppression to A prior to beginning compound conditioning; if suppression to A is extinguished following compound conditioning (A having been conditioned prior to the compound), the block remains. When blocking experiments were conducted with new groups of animals, holding constant the intensity value of Element B, while varying for different groups the intensity of Element A, the amount of blocking was a clear function of the relative intensities of the two elements. That is, more blocking of conditioning to B occurs if A is physically intense than if A is physically weak. This, however, is confounded with the fact that the level of suppression achieved by conclusion of the conditioning trials to A varies with the intensity of A; and we have already indicated that blocking varies with the level of suppression conditioned to A.

We have, as well, examined the blocking effect under a large number of procedural variations which have had no effect whatever on the basic phenomenon. Thus, for example, if the standard experiment is repeated employing a 1-minute, rather than a 3-minute, CS, a complete block is obtained. The same outcome is observed if the experiment is performed employing a 3-ma., rather than a 1-ma., US throughout. And again, complete blocking is obtained if the first CS, on which light onset is superimposed as a new element, is the turning off of a background 80-db noise, rather than the turning on of an 80-db noise. To put matters simply, the blocking phenomenon is robust, and easily reproducible.

We turn now to consideration of a classical phenomenon to which the blocking effect seems clearly related; we shall later return to a more detailed analysis of blocking itself. The blocking effect demonstrated in these studies seems in many ways reminiscent of the overshadowing of a weak element by a strong element in a compound CS. The basic observation reported by Pavlov (1927, pp. 141 ff.) was that if a compound CS was formed of two stimulus elements differing greatly in intensity or strength, the weaker element, when presented on test trials, failed to elicit any CR, despite repeated prior reinforcement of the compound. This was true although the weaker element was known to be independently conditionable. The major distinctions between the Pavlovian finding and the present blocking effect are: first, that overshadowing was said to occur without prior conditioning of the stronger element; and second, that overshadowing was reported to depend fundamentally on a substantial difference between the relative intensities of the two elements. The available summaries of Russian protocols from Pavlov's laboratory, however, indicate that at least in some of the overshadowing studies the dog had in fact, at an earlier time in its lengthy experimental history, been conditioned to the stronger stimulus. Thus it seemed possible to us that overshadowing might not be obtained if naive animals were, from the outset of an experiment, conditioned to a compound consisting of strong and weak elements.

The data already reported make it clear that complete overshadowing is not obtained when naive rats are conditioned to a compound of 80-db noise plus light. Following sixteen such reinforced compound trials, animals tested either to noise or to light each display clear conditioning; the ratios are .05 to light and .25 to noise. We wished now to see whether overshadowing might be observed if the relative intensities of the light and noise elements were radically changed. To test this, new groups were conditioned (this time for eight trials) to a compound consisting of our standard light plus 50-db noise. The group then tested to light displayed a ratio of .03, while the group tested to noise had a ratio of .42. The weak noise was thus almost completely overshadowed by light. Further, animals conditioned to 50-db noise alone, following conditioning to the compound, did not acquire significantly more rapidly than did naive rats conditioned from the outset to 50-db noise. These results are entirely corroborative of the Pavlovian reports. There remains the problem of relating overshadowing, which is not dependent on prior conditioning to one of the elements, to blocking, which is so dependent.

There is at least one obvious way of incorporating both phenomena within the same framework. We could assume that, during the early trials of conditioning to a compound, independent and parallel associations are being formed between each element and the US. With the further assumption that the association to the stronger element is formed more rapidly than that to the weaker, the overshadowing experiment becomes a case in which, implicitly, precisely the same sequence of events takes place which is explicitly produced in the blocking experiment. That is, in the overshadowing case an association to one element (the stronger) is substantially formed before conditioning to a second element takes place. Thus, conditioning of the second element is blocked.

These assumptions might be made more plausible if we examined the rates at which independent groups of animals acquire the CER when conditioned to either light, noise, or the compound. The relevant acquisition curves for the first eight trials of conditioning are presented in Fig. 3. The upper left-hand panel of the figure presents curves for groups trained with light, 50-db noise, and the compound light plus 50 db, respectively. The group conditioned to light is asymptotically suppressed by Trial 5, before really substantial suppression is observed in the group conditioned to 50 db. The upper right-hand panel indicates that there is relatively little difference in the rates of conditioning to light and to 80-db noise. Thus, assuming the same rates of conditioning to each element within a compound as those observed when the elements are separately conditioned in independent groups, the overshadowing effect would be expected for the 50-db compound, but not for the 80-db compound.

There are further between-group comparisons possible within Fig. 3 which seem to support the argument. Within the upper right-hand panel,

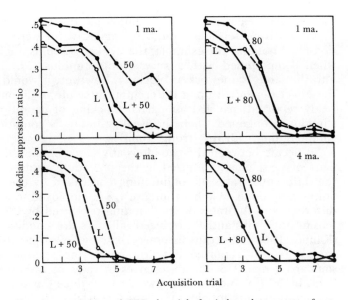

Fig. 3. *Acquisition of CER, by trial, for independent groups of rats trained with either 50-db noise, 80-db noise, light, or compound CS. The two upper panels are for groups trained with 1-ma. US, the two lower panels for groups trained with 4-ma. US.*

it can be observed that the compound group acquires significantly more rapidly than does either the light group or the 80-db group. That is, a clear summation of the two stimuli can be detected when conditioning to the compound. However, in the upper left-hand panel, there is clearly no summation; the compound group conditions at the same rate as the group trained to the stronger element, light. The 50-db element cannot be seen to affect in any way conditioning in the relevant compound group. Thus the presence or absence of overshadowing, measurable only after conditioning to a compound, is correlated with the presence or absence of a summation effect, detectable by comparing a compound group to other groups conditioned to single elements. This correlation of summation with overshadowing, it might be noted, seems relevant to Hull's (1943, Ch. 13) early interpretation of Pavlovian overshadowing. Basically, Hull regarded overshadowing as an extreme example of generalization decrement; the weaker member of the compound was assumed to be so dissimilar to the compound that it elicited no response. This view, which regards overshadowing as entirely dependent upon a postconditioning within-subject testing procedure, does not account for the association of overshadowing with the failure to observe summation in between-group comparisons made during conditioning. The very weak element in a compound CS really seems in some sense to be blotted out.

The weaker element in a compound, as has been noted, is one which, at least in independent groups, conditions less rapidly than the stronger element. The question thus arises whether overshadowing is a direct consequence of the relative intensities of the two elements, or whether the effect is mediated by the different rates of conditioning controlled by the separate elements. The finding that the effect depended directly upon relative intensities would be suggestive of perceptual and "attention-like" notions: for example, the weaker stimulus might not be noticed when compounded with a very strong stimulus. To fit overshadowing into the same framework as blocking, however, it would be convenient if the effect depended upon differential rates of conditioning. We have already reported that at least partial blocking of conditioning to a strong stimulus is obtained when the weak stimulus is conditioned prior to its compounding with the strong stimulus.

To decide between the two alternatives, we employed exactly the same pairs of CS elements utilized in the preceding studies, but manipulated the differential rates of conditioning controlled by the elements. This is quite easily done. When an intense US is employed in a CER procedure, differences in the rates of conditioning produced by CS's of different intensities are substantially reduced; all CS's are conditioned very rapidly (Kamin, 1965). We thus assumed that, by repeating the overshadowing studies already reported but now employing a 4-ma., rather than the standard 1-ma., US, the differences in rates of acquisition produced by light, by 50 db, and by 80 db would be reduced, with all groups tending to condition substantially in a very few trials. This in turn should mean that overshadowing, if it is dependent on the formation of a strong association to one element before substantial conditioning has occurred to the other, should be greatly reduced, if not eliminated.

The results were clear-cut. The groups conditioned with a 4-ma. US to the compound light plus 80 db, when tested with, respectively, light or 80 db, displayed virtually total suppression. The same result was obtained when groups conditioned with a 4-ma. US to the compound light plus 50 db were tested with either light or 50 db. These CS elements, of course, are identical to those employed in the preceding overshadowing studies. The fact that light does not overshadow 50 db when an intense US is employed makes it clear that overshadowing is not a simple, direct consequence of the relative intensities of conditioned stimulus elements and seems to eliminate a simple attentional interpretation of overshadowing. The alternative interpretation seems quite well supported by examination of the lower two panels of Fig. 3. These panels present CER acquisition curves for new independent groups, analogous to the curves in the upper panels, but with US intensity now set at 4 ma. The new groups acquire more rapidly than do corresponding groups conditioned to 1 ma. More important, all new groups acquire rapidly, and none of the single element groups appears to have conditioned substantially before conditioning in another such group was well under way. We do not have enough data to make any precise guess about how much conditioning must occur to one element, in how many trials, before how much conditioning to another element, in order for overshadowing to occur in animals for whom the two elements are compounded. The results do indicate clearly, however, that overshadowing is not the result of a simple interaction of sensory events. They suggest as well that the occurrence of overshadowing can be predicted from examination of the rates of acquisition of independent groups conditioned to the separate elements. We might note, finally, that in each of the lower two panels of Fig. 3 clear summation effects are detectable, once again associated with the failure to observe overshadowing.

We return now to some further experimental analyses of the basic blocking effect. Within the work previously reported, substantial prior conditioning to an element has invariably given rise to no evidence of conditioning to the superimposed element. Thus the block has appeared to be a dramatically all-or-none affair. We now ask whether the total block which we observed in our basic Group B was in part an artifact of the relatively blunt measure of conditioning which we employed. The test trial to light, following compound conditioning, measures transfer from the compound to the element. The savings method is known to be extremely sensitive in demonstrating transfer, much more so than is the recall method represented by our test. We now repeated the basic experiment, but the test was no longer a single test trial to light; instead, all animals were given four reinforced conditioning trials to light at the end of the experiment. The focus of interest is on rate of acquisition during this conditioning to light. The two basic groups are outlined below.

Group 2-A:	N (16)	LN (8)	L (4)
Group 2-B:	—	N (24)	L (4)

While Groups 2-A and 2-B have each experienced noise followed by shock 24 times before the conditioning to light alone, the difference is of course that Group 2-A has on the last eight trials experienced the light superimposed on the noise. Will Group 2-A therefore show any savings, relative to Group 2-B, when conditioned to the light alone? Or have the eight superimpositions of light literally left no effect on the animal?

There was, as our earlier results would have suggested, no significant suppression to the light by either group on the first conditioning trial to light. However, Group 2-A displayed significantly more suppression on each of trials 2, 3, and 4 than did Group 2-B. Thus, it is clear that the eight light superimpositions did indeed leave some trace, which was manifested in a significant savings effect. However, we are reminded that our earlier data already demonstrated that, in groups conditioned similarly to Group 2-A, the animals did notice the superimposed light at least on the first, transitional trial. Can it be the case that the significant savings exhibited by Group 2-A is entirely attributable to the first trial on which light is superimposed? Or, do the compound trials following the first also contribute to the savings effect?

To answer this question, Group 2-N was examined. The procedure is sketched below, and should be compared to those diagrammed in the immediately preceding paradigm.

Group 2-N:	N (16)	LN (1)	N (7)	L (4)

Group 2-N differs from Group 2-B only on the transitional trial; though the total number of reinforced experiences of noise is equated across Groups 2-A, 2-B, and 2-N, Group 2-N receives seven fewer light superimpositions than does Group 2-A. Nevertheless, the acquisition curves to light alone in the final phase of the experiment are virtually identical for Groups 2-N and 2-A; like Group 2-A, Group 2-N is significantly more suppressed than Group 2-B on each of Trials 2, 3, and 4. If we compute median suppression ratios over the four trials of light conditioning for each group, they are .28 for each of Groups 2-A and 2-N, but .38 for Group 2-B. Thus it is clear that the savings which we have demonstrated can be entirely attributed to the first, transitional trial. We had in any event independent evidence that the animal noticed the light on that trial, and it is now clear that the reinforcement at the termination of that trial does produce an increment in the associative connection between light and shock. There still, however, is nothing in the data which can allow us to conclude that the animal notices a redundant, superimposed element on any trial after the transitional trial; or at least, we have no indication that reinforced presentations of the superimposed element after the transitional trial in any way affect either the contemporaneous or the subsequent behavior of the animal. These results are obviously consistent with a perceptual gating concept, so long as the gating mechanism is not activated until after the transitional trial.

Where then do we stand now? The fact that the superimposed element proves to be redundant (that the US is already perfectly predicted by Element A) seems to be central to any interpretation of the blocking effect. Presumably, then, blocking would not occur if the superimposed element were made informative. We have earlier demonstrated that, if the compound is nonreinforced, the animal utilizes the information provided by Element B very efficiently. The strategy at this point was to perform a study within the blocking paradigm, reinforcing the compound trials, but at the same time making Element B informative. This was accomplished by radically increasing US intensity during the compound trials above the level employed during the prior conditioning to Element A, as with Group 2-M in the set of experimental treatments outlined below.

Group B:	N-1 ma. (16)	LN-1 ma. (8)	Test L	.45
Group 2-M:	N-1 ma. (16)	LN-4 ma. (8)	Test L	.14
Group 3-U:	N-4 ma. (8)	LN-4 ma. (8)	Test L	.36

The comparison between Groups B and 2-M is instructive. Here at last is a simple procedure which can virtually eliminate the blocking effect. Within Group 2-M, shock intensity is radically increased during the compound trials. The effect of this operation is to allow the formation of a clear association between the superimposed element and the US; Group 2-M, on the test trial, is significantly more suppressed than the standard Group B. This effect is not a simple consequence of employing an intense US during the compound trials. With Group 3-U, the same intense US is employed throughout the experiment, and a clear blocking effect is manifested: the test ratio of 3-U does not differ significantly from that of B, but does from that of 2-M. Thus, it is the change of shock intensity during the compound trials from that employed during prior conditioning which seems responsible for eliminating the block. These results provide clear support for the assumption that blocking occurs because of the redundancy of the superimposed element. The question remains, How does redundancy prevent the formation of an association between a CS element and a US with which it is continuously presented?

The most recent conception at which we have arrived seems capable of integrating all the data already presented. The notion is this: perhaps, for an increment in an associative connection to occur, it is necessary that the US instigate some mental work on the part of the animal. This mental work will occur only if the US is unpredicted, if it in some sense surprises the animal. Thus, in the early trials of a normal conditioning experiment, the US is an unpredicted, surprising event of motivational significance and the CS–US association is formed. Within the blocking experiment, the occurrence of the US on the first compound trial is to some degree surprising. This can be deduced, circularly, from the empirical observation that, on the transitional trial only, suppression is moderately attenuated; and some little learning about Element B can be demonstrated to have occurred on the transitional trial, but on no other compound trial. Finally, if in the blocking experiment US intensity is radically increased when compound training is begun, the new US is obviously surprising and no block is observed.

Precisely what mental work is instigated by a surprising US? The language in which these notions have been couched can be made more respectable, as well as more specific. Thus, as a first try, suppose that, for an increment in an associative connection to occur, it is necessary that the US provoke the animal into a backward scanning of its memory store of recent stimulus input; only as a result of such a scan can an association between CS and US be formed, and the scan is prompted only by an unpredicted US, the occurrence of which is surprising. This sort of speculation, it can be noted, leaves perception of the superimposed CS element intact. The CS element fails to become conditioned not because its input has been impeded, but because the US fails to function as a reinforcing stimulus. We have clearly moved some distance from the notion of attention to the CS, perhaps to enter the realm of retrospective contemplation of the CS.

These notions, whatever their vices, do suggest experimental manipulations. With the backward scan concept in mind, an experiment was performed which employed the blocking paradigm, but with an effort to surprise the animal very shortly after each presentation of the compound. Thus, animals were first conditioned, in the normal way, to suppress to the noise CS, with the usual 1-ma., .5-second US. Then, during the compound trials, the animal received reinforced presentations of the light-noise compound, again with a 1-ma., .5-second US. However, on each compound trial, 5 seconds following delivery of the US, an extra (surprising) shock (again 1 ma., .5 sec.) was delivered. When, after compound training, these subjects were tested with the light CS, they displayed a median ratio of .08. That is, the blocking effect was entirely eliminated by the delivery of an unpredicted shock shortly following reinforced presentation of the compound.

We have emphasized the close temporal relation between the unpredicted extra shock and the preceding compound CS. This emphasis is, of course, consistent with the backward scanning notion. There are, however, several alternative interpretations of the efficacy of the unpredicted shock in eliminating the blocking effect. There is the obvious possibility that the extra shock combines with the shortly preceding normal US to form, in effect, a US more intense than that employed during the prior conditioning to the noise element. We have already indicated that a radical increase of US intensity during the compound trials will eliminate the blocking effect. There is in the data, however, a strong indication that the extra shock functions in a manner quite different from that of an intense US. It is true that, if US intensity is increased from 1 ma. to 4 ma. during the compound trials, the blocking effect is eliminated; but it is also true that, if independent groups of naive rats are conditioned, with either a light, noise, or compound CS, paired with a 4-ma. US, they acquire the CER significantly more rapidly than do equivalent groups conditioned with a 1-ma. US. That is, acquisition of the CER is a clear positive function of US intensity. We have conditioned naive groups of animals, with either light or noise CS's, delivering the extra shock, 5 seconds after the normal US, from the outset of conditioning. In each case, the acquisition curve of rats conditioned with the extra shock was virtually superimposed on that of rats conditioned with the normal US. Thus, the extra shock does not appear to increase effective US intensity.

We have stressed the notion that the second, extra shock might cause the animal to scan the preceding sensory input, and that conditioning to the superimposed CS element occurs as a consequence of this scanning. There remains, however, the plausible alternative that the effect of the unpredicted, extra shock is to alert the animal in such a way that it is more attentive or sensitive to subsequent events, i.e., to the following compound trials. Thus, in this latest view, the extra shock does not increase the amount of conditioning taking place to the superimposed CS element on the first compound trial, but it does increase the amount of such conditioning taking place on all subsequent compound trials. Within the experiment already performed, there is unfortunately no way of deciding whether the extra shock facilitates conditioning to the CS which precedes it or to the CS which follows it. We do know, from appropriate control groups, that the extra shock does not cause the animal to suppress to extraneous exteroceptive stimuli which are subsequently presented.

There should be no great experimental difficulty in localizing the effect of the extra shock. We can, for example, deliver the extra shock to different groups at varying temporal intervals following the compound trials. Presumably, backward scanning should be less effective in forming an association when the extra shock is remote in time from the preceding trial. This approach, however, has the disadvantage that moving the extra shock away from the preceding trial moves it toward the subsequent trial. This problem in turn might be overcome by presenting only one compound trial a day. The sensitivity of the procedure seems to be such that employing a savings technique, we might demonstrate the facilitating effect of a single extra shock, delivered on a single compound trial, with no subsequent compound conditioning. This effect in turn might be related to the temporal interval between the compound trial and the extra shock. There is no dearth of potential experiments to be performed, and not much sense in attempting to anticipate their outcomes.

To sum up, the blocking experiment demonstrates very clearly that the mere contiguous presentation of a CS element and a US is not a sufficient condition for the establishment of a CR. The question, very simply is:

What has gone wrong in the blocking experiment? What is deficient? The experiment was conceived with a primitive hunch that attention to the to-be-conditioned stimulus element was a necessary precondition, and many of the results to date are consistent with the notion that the deficiency is perceptual, having to do with impeded input of the CS element. This blocked input was at first conceived as a consequence of a kind of competition for attention between the previously conditioned element and the new element. The results to date, however, make it clear that, if such an attentional deficit is involved, the redundancy of the new element is critical for producing it. The extra shock experiment, most recently, has suggested an alternative conception. The input of the new CS element can be regarded as intact, but the predictability of the US might strip the US of a function it normally subserves in conditioning experiments, that of instigating some processing of the memory store of recent stimulus input, which results in the formation of an association. There is also the possibility, of course, that the predictability of the US, by the time compound training is begun in the blocking experiment, strips the US of the function of alerting the animal to subsequent stimulus input.

There seems little doubt that, as experimentation continues, still other conceptions will be suggested. The experimental procedures are at least capable of discarding some conceptions and of reinforcing others. The progress to date might encourage the belief that ultimately these studies could make a real contribution toward answering the fundamental question toward which they are addressed: What are the necessary and sufficient conditions for the establishment of an association between CS and US within a Pavlovian paradigm?

Notes

[1] The research reported here was supported by a research grant from the Associate Committee on Experimental Psychology, National Research Council of Canada.

References

Egger, M. C., & Miller, N. E. Secondary reinforcement in rats as a function of information value and reliability of the stimulus. *Journal of Experimental Psychology*, 1962, **64**, 97–104.

Estes, W. K., & Skinner, B. F. Some quantitative properties of anxiety. *Journal of Experimental Psychology*, 1941, **29**, 390–400.

Hernandez-Peon, R., Scherrer, H., & Jouvet, M. Modification of electrical activity in cochlear nucleus during "attention" in unanesthetized cats. *Science*, 1956, **123**, 331–332.

Hull, C. L. *Principles of behavior*, New York: Appleton-Century, 1943.

Hunt, H. F., & Brady, J. V. Some effects of punishment and intercurrent "anxiety" on a single operant. *Journal of Comparative and Physiological Psychology*, 1955, **48**, 305–310.

Kamin, L. J. Temporal and intensity characteristics of the conditioned stimulus. In W. F. Prokasy (Ed.), *Classical conditioning*. New York: Appleton-Century-Crofts, 1965. Pp. 118–147.

Kamin, L. J. "Attention-like" processes in classical conditioning. In M. R. Jones (Ed.), *Miami symposium on the prediction of behavior, 1967: Aversive stimulation*. Coral Gables, Fla.: University of Miami Press, 1968. Pp. 9–31.

Pavlov, I. P. *Conditioned reflexes*. (Tr., G. V. Anrep.) London: Oxford University Press, 1927. (Reprinted, New York: Dover, 1960.)

F. SELECTIVE ASSOCIATION

For most of its history, the study of Pavlovian conditioning essentially ignored relations between CS and US aside from temporal contiguity and predictiveness. For example, what kind of stimulus one chose as a CS, in combination with what kind of US, was never a great concern. Researchers knew that not all CSs were equally effective. Some were more noticeable or salient than others and more salient CSs produced more rapid conditioning. Similarly, there were important differences in USs. They produced different kinds of responses, and some produced more powerful conditioning than others. However, there was no notion that the effectiveness of a CS might depend on what type of US it was combined with.

An important article by Garcia and Koelling changed this state of affairs. They studied a phenomenon known as taste aversion learning, along with more standard conditioning of fear with shock. Taste aversion learning involves presenting an animal with a food of distinctive taste and then making the animal sick to its stomach. The animal rapidly learns to avoid the taste, apparently associating it with illness. There are many striking characteristics of taste aversion learning that have made it the subject of a great deal of research activity (see Barker et al., 1977), but the one identified by Garcia and Koelling is of quite general significance. What they showed was that animals readily associate taste with stomach illness, but not with shock. Similarly, they readily associate lights and tones with shock, but not with stomach illness. There is a selectivity of association based upon qualitative relations between the stimuli being associated. While initially researchers thought this selectivity might be a peculiar feature of taste aversion, subsequent research has made it clear that such selectivity of association is quite general (see for example, LoLordo, 1979; Rescorla and Furrow, 1977).

8 Relation of Cue to Consequence in Avoidance Learning

JOHN GARCIA AND ROBERT A. KOELLING

An audiovisual stimulus was made contingent upon the rat's licking at the water spout, thus making it analogous with a gustatory stimulus. When the audiovisual stimulus and the gustatory stimulus were paired with electric shock the avoidance reactions transferred to the audiovisual stimulus, but not the gustatory stimulus. Conversely, when both stimuli were paired with toxin or x-ray the avoidance reactions transferred to the gustatory stimulus, but not the audiovisual stimulus. Apparently stimuli are selected as cues dependent upon the nature of the subsequent reinforcer.[1]

A great deal of evidence stemming from diverse sources suggests an inadequacy in the usual formulations concerning reinforcements. Barnet (1963) has described the "bait-shy" behavior of wild rats which have survived a poisoning attempt. These animals, utilizing olfactory and gustatory cues, avoid the poison bait which previously made them ill. However, there is no evidence that they avoid the "place" of the poisoning.

In a recent volume (Haley & Snyder, 1964) several authors have discussed studies in which ionizing radiations were employed as a noxious stimulus to produce avoidance reactions in animals. Ionizing radiation like many poisons produces gastrointestinal disturbances and nausea. Strong aversions are readily established in animals when distinctively flavored fluids are conditionally paired with x-rays. Subsequently, the gustatory stimulus will depress fluid intake without radiation. In contrast, a distinctive environmental complex of auditory, visual, and tactual stimuli does not inhibit drinking even when the compound stimulus is associated with the identical radiation schedule. This differential effect has also been observed following ingestion of a toxin and the injection of a drug (Garcia & Koelling, 1965).

Apparently this differential effectiveness of cues is due either to the nature of the reinforcer, i.e., radiation or toxic effects, or to the peculiar relation which a gustatory stimulus has to the drinking response, i.e., gustatory stimulation occurs if and only if the animal licks the fluid. The environmental cues associated with a distinctive place are not as dependent upon a single response of the organism. Therefore, we made an auditory and visual stimulus dependent upon the animal's licking the water spout. Thus, in four experiments reported here "bright–noisy" water as well as "tasty" water was conditionally paired with radiation, a toxin, immediate shock, and delayed shock, respectively, as reinforcers. Later the capacity of these response-controlled stimuli to inhibit drinking in the absence of reinforcement was tested.

"Relation of Cue to Consequence in Avoidance Learning" by John Garcia and Robert A. Koelling. *Psychonomic Science*, 1966, *4*, 123–124. Reprinted by permission of the Psychonomic Society.

Method

The apparatus was a light and sound shielded box (7 in. × 7 in. × 7 in.) with a drinking spout connected to an electronic drinkometer which counted each touch of the rat's tongue to the spout. "Bright–noisy" water was provided by connecting an incandescent lamp (5 watts) and a clicking relay into this circuit. "Tasty" water was provided by adding flavors to the drinking supply.

Each experimental group consisted of 10 rats (90 day old Sprague-Dawley males) maintained in individual cages without water, but with Purina Laboratory chow *ad libidum.*

The procedure was: A. One week of habituation to drinking in the apparatus without stimulation. B. Pretests to measure intake of bright–noisy water and tasty water prior to training. C. Acquisition training with: (1) reinforced trials where these stimuli were paired with reinforcement during drinking, (2) nonreinforced trials where rats drank water without stimuli or reinforcement. Training terminated when there was a reliable difference between water intake scores on reinforced and nonreinforced trials. D. Post-tests to measure intake of bright–noisy water and tasty water after training.

In the x-ray study an audiovisual group and a gustatory group were exposed to an identical radiation schedule. In the other studies reinforcement was contingent upon the rat's response. To insure that both the audiovisual and the gustatory stimuli received equivalent reinforcement, they were combined and simultaneously paired with the reinforcer during acquisition training. Therefore, one group serving as its own control and divided into equal subgroups was tested in balanced order with an audiovisual and a gustatory test before and after training with these stimuli combined.

One 20-min. reinforced trial was administered every three days in the x-ray and lithium chloride studies. This prolonged intertrial interval was designed to allow sufficient time for the rats to recover from acute effects of treatment. On each interpolated day the animals received a 20-min. nonreinforced trial. They were post-tested two days after their last reinforced trial. The x-ray groups received a total of three reinforced trials, each with 54 r of filtered 250 kv x-rays delivered in 20 min. Sweet water (1 gm saccharin per liter) was the gustatory stimulus. The lithium chloride group had a total of five reinforced trials with toxic salty water (.12 M lithium chloride). Non-toxic salty water (.12 M sodium chloride) which rats cannot readily distinguish from the toxic solution was used in the gustatory tests (Nachman, 1963).

The immediate shock study was conducted on a more orthodox avoidance schedule. Tests and trials were 2 min. long. Each day for four consecutive acquisition days, animals were given two nonreinforced and two reinforced trials in an NRRN, RNNR pattern. A shock, the minimal current required to interrupt drinking (0.5 sec. at 0.08–0.20 ma), was delivered through a floor grid 2 sec. after the first lick at the spout.

The delayed shock study was conducted simultaneously with the lithium chloride on the same schedule. Non-toxic salty water was the gustatory stimulus. Shock reinforcement was delayed during first trials and gradually increased in intensity (.05 to .30 ma) in a schedule designed to

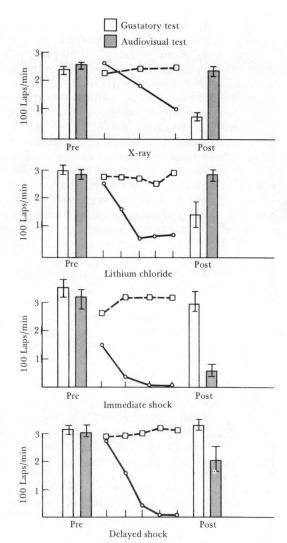

FIG. 1. *The bars indicate water intake (± St. Error) during a gustatory test (a distinctive taste) and an audiovisual test (light and sound contingent upon licking) before and after conditional pairing with the reinforcers indicated. The curves illustrate mean intake during acquisition.*

produce a drinking pattern during the 20-min. period which resembled that of the corresponding animal drinking toxic salty water.

Results and Discussion

The results indicate that all reinforcers were effective in producing discrimination learning during the acquisition phase (see Fig. 1), but obvious differences occurred in the post-tests. The avoidance reactions produced by x-rays and lithium chloride are readily transferred to the gustatory stimulus but not to the audiovisual stimulus. The effect is more pronounced in the x-ray study, perhaps due to differences in dose. The x-ray animals received a constant dose while the lithium chloride rats drank a decreasing amount of the toxic solution during training. Nevertheless, the difference between post-test scores is statistically significant in both experiments (p < 0.01 by ranks test).

Apparently when gustatory stimuli are paired with agents which produce nausea and gastric upset, they acquire secondary reinforcing properties which might be described as "conditioned nausea." Auditory and visual stimulation do not readily acquire similar properties even when they are contingent upon the licking response.

In contrast, the effect of both immediate and delayed shock to the paws is in the opposite direction. The avoidance reactions produced by electric shock to the paws transferred to the audiovisual stimulus but not to the gustatory stimulus. As one might expect the effect of delayed shocks was not as effective as shocks where the reinforcer immediately and consistently followed licking. Again, the difference between post-test intake scores is statistically significant in both studies (p < 0.01 by ranks test). Thus, when shock which produces peripheral pain is the reinforcer, "conditioned fear" properties are more readily acquired by auditory and visual stimuli than by gustatory stimuli.

It seems that given reinforcers are not equally effective for all classes of discriminable stimuli. The cues, which the animal selects from the welter of stimuli in the learning situation, appear to be related to the consequences of the subsequent reinforcer. Two speculations are offered: (1) Common elements in the time-intensity patterns of stimulation may facilitate a cross-modal generalization from reinforcer to cue in one case and not in another. (2) More likely, natural selection may have favored mechanisms which associate gustatory and olfactory cues with internal discomfort since the chemical receptors sample the materials soon to be incorporated into the internal environment. Krechevsky (1932) postulated such a genetically coded hypothesis to account for the predispositions of rats to respond systematically to specific cues in an insoluble maze. The hypothesis of the sick rat, as for many of us under similar circumstances, would be, "It must have been something I ate."

Notes
  [1] This research stems from doctoral research carried out at Long Beach V. A. Hospital and supported by NIH No. RH00068. Thanks are extended to Professors B. F. Ritchie, D. Krech, and E. R. Dempster, U. C. Berkeley, California.

References
  Barnett, S. A. *The rat: a study in behavior*. Chicago: Aldine Press, 1963.
  Garcia, J., & Koelling, R. A. A comparison of aversions induced by x-rays, toxins, and drugs in the rat. *Radiat. Res.*, in press, 1965.
  Haley, T. J., & Snyder, R. S. (Eds.) *The response of the nervous system to ionizing radiation*. Boston: Little, Brown & Co., 1964.
  Krechevsky, I. The hereditary nature of 'hypothesis.' *J. Comp. Psychol.*, 1932, 16, 99–116.
  Nachman, M. Learned aversion to the taste of lithium chloride and generalization to other salts. *J. Comp. Physiol. Psychol.*, 1963, 56, 343–349.

Part II
Operant Conditioning

Most of the behaviors that organisms engage in have consequences: When we write a term paper, we get a grade; when we invest in the stock market, our investment grows or shrinks; when we steal, we go to jail. Indeed, in the everyday language we use to talk about ourselves, we explain most actions precisely in terms of the consequences they are intended to produce. We think of ourselves as having purposes, intentions, or goals, and of our actions as designed to serve those intentions or realize those goals. Yet in research on Pavlovian conditioning no attention is paid to the consequences of conditioned responses; indeed, experiments are designed to that conditioned responses have no consequences.

The study of how behavior is influenced by its consequences is the province of another aspect of behavior theory. Pioneered by E. L. Thorndike (1874–1949), this aspect of behavior theory is known as *operant conditioning*. Thorndike (1898) argued that is was inappropriate to think of behavior as forward looking and purposive. Rather than acting to realize intentions, organisms simply act at random. Some actions would happen to be followed by positive consequences. Such positive consequences, called *rewards* or *reinforcers*, would work to make the behavior that preceded them more likely in the future. Other actions would happen to be followed by negative consequences. Such consequences, called *punishers*, would make the behavior that preceded them less likely in the future. Through the joint action of reinforcement and punishment, organisms would eventually develop behavior repertoires that seem intelligent and purposive in efficiently and effectively producing positive consequences.

That reinforcers increase and punishers decrease the future likelihood of behavior that precedes them, Thorndike called the *law of effect*. For behavior theorists, the study of how behavior is influenced by its consequences is the study of the law of effect. Some of the studies of Pavlovian conditioning in Section I of this book involved the operation of the law of effect. In the articles by Rescorla and LoLordo (p. 5) and Rescorla (p. 43), for example, Pavlovian conditioning was measured by the effects of CSs on jumping to avoid shock. Our understanding of Pavlovian conditioning may tell us why the CSs changed the rate at which the animals jumped. But why were they jumping in the first place? This is the province of the law of effect. The jumping response is an *operant*. The consequence of that response is positive—the prevention of shock. The positive consequence sustains the operant at high frequency. In the articles by Rizley and Rescorla (p. 16), Seligman (p. 52), and Kamin (p. 67) Pavlovian conditioning was measured by the effects of CSs on lever pressing for food. The lever press is an operant, maintained by its positive consequences. In this section we will focus on the law of effect, on how positive and negative consequences affect the future likelihood of operant behavior.

The most common experimental situations for studying operant conditioning involve either rats pressing levers or pigeons pecking lit, circular disks (keys). Unlike Pavlovian responses like salivation, these operants are not reflexes—they are not wired in. It is unlikely that a rat has ever pressed a lever or a pigeon ever pecked a key prior to experimental intervention. These operants must be established, or *shaped,* during the experiment. For just this reason, there is nothing special about a lever press or a key peck. They merely represent any of a host of different operants one might have established instead. It is assumed that by understanding how these operants are affected by their consequences, we will understand how all operant behavior—all behavior that is not reflex—is affected by its consequences.

The shaping process, the development of operants, is the subject of the article in Section A. In Section B, we turn to an examination of the conditions that are necessary for operant conditioning to occur. As we saw in the case of Pavlovian conditioning, the issue is this: Is temporal contiguity of operant and reinforcer enough to produce conditioning or is more required? Can organisms distinguish situations in which reinforcers merely happen to follow behavior from situations in which they are actually produced by behavior? In Section C, we present an article concerned with determining what makes an event a reinforcer. Is there some characteristic that all reinforcers have in common? Section D explores procedures by which events that are not reinforcers can become reinforcers, that is, can acquire the power to maintain operant behavior. Finally, in Section E we present a few examples of the failure of the law of effect, situations in which behavior is not controlled by its consequences. These examples highlight the importance of determining just how sweeping the domain of the law of effect actually is.

A. CREATING BEHAVIORAL UNITS

The law of effect tells us how an operant is increased or decreased in frequency by its consequences. But for an operant to have consequences, it must first occur. What gets operant behavior started?

There are a variety of answers to this question (see Staddon and Simmelhag, 1971). One of them is that new operants get created out of old ones. When a rat is being trained to press a lever for food, it moves about the chamber sniffing and exploring. While sniffing at the lever, it may inadvertently depress it. Food delivery follows. Now the rat spends more of its time around the lever, licking it, pawing it, sniffing it, and so on. Again the lever is inadvertently depressed, and again food comes. Gradually the rat learns that most of its activity around the lever is superfluous. Lever presses that are inadventent and variable in form give way to lever presses that seem purposive and which are highly efficient and stereotyped. A new operant has been created.

Usually this process happens very rapidly, because the required operant is so simple. But in the following article by Vogel and Annau the development of an efficient, stereotyped operant is more protracted. The operant is complex: pigeons must peck each of two keys three times. Order is irrelevant, so there is plenty of room for variability of response form. Nevertheless, each pigeon develops its own idiosyncratic, highly stereotyped sequential operant.

9 An Operant Discrimination Task Allowing Variability of Reinforced Response Patterning

RICHARD VOGEL AND ZOLTAN ANNAU

Five pigeons were trained to perform a discrimination task allowing variability of reinforced response patterning. The task consisted of moving a stimulus light within a 4×4 matrix of lights from the top left position to the bottom right position by pecking on two keys in succession in order to obtain a reinforcement. A peck on one key moved the light one position to the right and a peck on the other key moved it one position down. After preliminary training on 3 alternating fixed-ratio schedules of reinforcement, the birds could peck on either key in any order, but more than three responses on a key resulted in a blackout followed by the return of the stimulus light to the start position. Results indicate that initially the birds used a wide variety of response patterns to obtain reinforcement, but with continued practice, response patterns became more stereotyped.[1]

Continuous exposure to a particular schedule of reinforcement has been found to decrease the variability of response forms (Muenzinger, 1928; Skinner, 1938; Notterman, 1959; Antonitis, 1951). These studies were concerned with the topography of the individual instrumental motor "response." Muenzinger's study involved the part of the body used by guinea pigs in solving a puzzle box problem; Skinner's observations and Notterman's systematic description concern the force and duration of lever presses by rats; and Antonitis' study involved horizontal position of nose-thrusting responses of rats. In contrast with these results concerning variability of parameters of a single motor "response," the present study is concerned with variability of response patterning in a discriminative operant schedule in which many related but discrete patterns of responses are reinforced.

Method

Subjects

Five adult male Palmetto White Carneaux pigeons were maintained at approximately 80% of their free-feeding weight. All had previous experience with differential-reinforcement-of-low-rate (DRL) schedules of food reinforcement.

Apparatus

The experimental chamber was enclosed in an ice chest. A white noise generator and a ventilation fan provided masking noise. Two translucent plastic response keys were mounted 20 cm (8 in.) above the floor [behind

"An Operant Discrimination Task Allowing Variability of Reinforced Response Patterning" by Richard Vogel and Zoltan Annau. *Journal of the Experimental Analysis of Behavior*, 1973, *20*, 1–6. Copyright 1973 by the Society for the Experimental Analysis of Behavior, Inc. Reprinted by permission of the publisher.

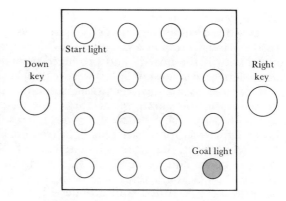

FIG. 1. *Diagram of the stimulus panel. A peck on the right key moved the lit position one column to the right and a peck on the down key moved the lit position one row down. Moving the lit position from the upper left position to the lower right (goal) position produced access to food. More than three responses on a key resulted in a blackout.*

2-cm (0.75-in.) diameter holes through one wall of the chamber], 10 cm (4 in.) apart on either side of a 6-cm (2.25-in.) square array of stimulus lights (see Fig. 1). When the keys were transilluminated by a white light, a force exceeding 0.015 N applied to the key broke an electrical contact that operated control and recording circuits. The keys were disconnected from the control circuitry when darkened. The square array of stimulus lights was made up of four rows of four 1-cm (0.5-in.) diameter translucent plastic capped lights. Fifteen of the caps were yellow, and the sixteenth cap in the lower right corner of the array was red. The control circuit allowed only one stimulus light to be illuminated at a time. The reinforcing event was a 2-sec presentation of mixed grain, which was accessible through a 5-cm (2-in.) square opening 7 cm (2.75 in.) below the stimulus lights. When grain was presented, the keys were darkened, the houselight went off, and the feeder opening was illuminated. The houselight, the stimulus light, the keylights, and the feeder light were the only sources of illumination in the chamber. A television camera permitted observation of the behavior.

Procedure

The birds did not require preliminary key training because of their previous conditioning history with DRL schedules. The shaping procedure consisted of three stages. In the first stage, none of the stimulus lights were lit. In succession, one, two, and finally three responses (fixed-ratio 3) on either of the illuminated keys were required to obtain reinforcement. Pecks on the preferred key were then not reinforced until the birds were reliably satisfying the FR 3 requirement on the nonpreferred key. In the last two stages, at the start of a trial, the top left yellow stimulus light was illuminated. During a trial period, a response on the key to the right of the stimulus array (the "right key") stepped the stimulus light to the right unless the lit stimulus light was one of the four lights in the right column. Similarly, responses on the key to the left of the stimulus light (the "down key") moved the lit position one row down unless the lit stimulus light was in the lowest row. The second stage required at least three responses on both keys in any sequence moving the lit position to the red "goal light" to produce food, but more than three responses on either key did not change the position of the lit stimulus light ("running off the board" was not possible). The final stage had the requirement of exactly three responses on each of the keys in any sequence to produce food—a fourth response on either key during a single trial "ran the stimulus light off the board" and produced a total blackout for 2 sec (as the houselight and stimulus lights were off) instead of reinforcement. This was defined as an incorrect trial; subsequently, the stimulus light was turned on in the start position for a new trial. Three responses on each key moved the cue light to the goal and resulted in the lighting of the lower-right red-capped stimulus light (the goal light) for 2 sec. While the goal light was lit, the pigeons had access to food with the hopper light on and the house and keylights off (key pecks during this period could not produce a blackout). This was defined as a correct trial. All response patterns were recorded with a Sodeco Printer.

Each session terminated automatically after 100 trials. Sessions were conducted daily with a few exceptions. Ten to 40 sessions were required for the individual subjects to attain stable baselines above 80% correct. For three of the pigeons, the baseline was maintained for 50 to 90 sessions after the 80% baseline was achieved to study changes in patterns of responding. Two of the pigeons served as controls with regard to the importance of the stimulus lights as cues. After maintaining a baseline accuracy better than 90% correct for 30 and 36 sessions, all stimulus lights were off while all other parameters of the schedule remained constant. Birds 25 and 26 were chosen for this "lights off" condition because in the early sessions they were consistently emitting a higher proportion of correct responses. After 39 sessions, the cue lights were reinstated for the final 24 sessions.

Results

Figure 2 represents the changes in percentage of reinforced trials per session for all five pigeons. The percentage of reinforced trials of the pigeons that were always provided with stimulus light cues (P21, P22, P24) is shown in Part A; Part B shows the performance of the two cue-light controls (P25, P26). Within 10 to 40 sessions, all five pigeons were emitting correct response sequences in more than 80% of the trials. The numbered sessions do not include the first two preliminary stages of shaping, which took between two to five sessions for the individual pigeons. Their pattern at the end of this period consisted of three to six responses on one key followed by three on the other. Within the first session of the final schedule (allowing "running off the board"), all pigeons adopted a variable mode of responding that tended to light the central, rather than the peripheral, cue lights. It might be noted that these patterns of responding with more than one key switch are less efficient in terms of motor output and that the one-switch pattern (i.e., three responses on one key followed by three on the other key) was the dominant pattern that the birds returned to with continuing training. The preferred (modal) patterns at the end of the experiment can be represented as sequences of r and d for right key and down key; they were rrrddd for two birds (P24 and P26) and dddrrr for three birds (P21, P22, and P25).

Figure 3 illustrates the changes in pattern frequency distribution dur-

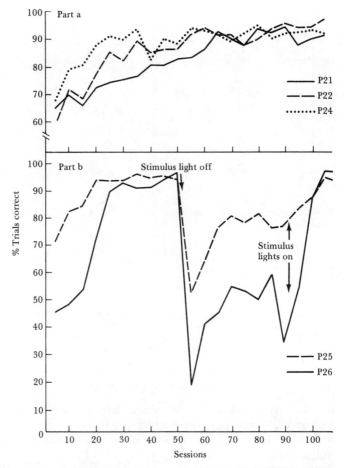

Fɪɢ. 2. *Mean percent correct trials as a function of training sessions. Each point represents the mean for five sessions. Part a: constant stimulus conditions (P21, P22, P24). Part b: cue light control (P25, P26).*

ing the experiment by showing a frequency histogram for the patterns used by P24 for a two-day period at the outset (Sessions 4 and 5, filled bars) compared to a final two-day period (Sessions 102 and 103, unfilled bars). The 50 possible patterns of responding for a single trial are arbitrarily numbered 1 to 50 on the nominal abscissa; the corresponding ordinate represents frequency of pattern occurrence as percentage of total trials during the sessions indicated. Patterns 1 through 20 represent the 20 possible correct response patterns; patterns 21 through 50 represent the 30 unreinforced possibilities. In the early sessions, more patterns were used while in later sessions one correct pattern dominated.

This decrease in variability of response patterns for all five subjects is presented graphically in Fig. 4. During the first two weeks of training, the mean number of correct patterns used per session was approximately 16 of a possible 20. After 100 sessions, the group of three pigeons not

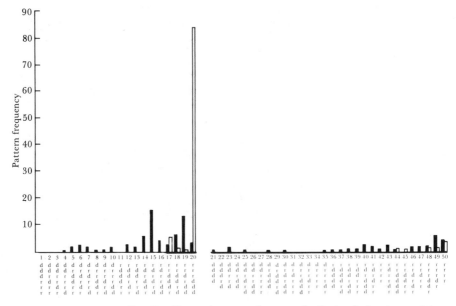

FIG. 3.   *Changes in pattern frequency distribution during the experiment. Frequency histogram for the patterns used by P24 for a two-day period at the beginning of training (Sessions 4 and 5; filled bars) compared to a final two-day period (Sessions 102 and 103; unfilled bars). Patterns 1 through 20 were reinforced, 21 through 50 were not reinforced. The columns of letters below each pattern number indicate the sequence of right (r) and down (d) responses in that pattern.*

exposed to a cueless control period had a mean use of three patterns per session of the 20 possible correct patterns.

Both control pigeons showed dramatic decreases in accuracy when cue lights were not illuminated (see Fig. 2b). P25 decreased 70 points in percentage accuracy from 97% with cue light to 27% without, while P26 made the maximum decrease of 100% between two days. The performance of both subjects partially recovered within 20 days to new baselines (80% for P25, 50% for P26). When the stimulus lights were returned, the improvement in performance was much less rapid than its previous disruption. Approximately 10 sessions were required by both pigeons before a 90 to 100% criterion was regained. Figure 4 shows that pattern variability increased significantly both with the removal of cue lights and their reinstatement, and that these control birds never regain the degree of stereotypy typical of the birds that had the cue light throughout the 110 sessions.

Discussion

The decrease in "response" variability with continued reinforcement supports previous findings by Muenzinger (1928), Skinner (1938), Notterman (1959), and Antonitis (1951), and extends the applicability of their conclusions concerning parameters of the single motor response to serial patterns of responding. In the previous studies on response variability, "trial" topography was relatively limited in that a single response was

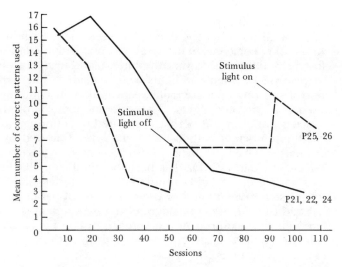

F_IG. 4. *Changes in mean number of correct patterns used per session during the course of the experiment. Each point represents a two-session mean for each of the two experimental groups: (1) the two pigeons subjected to a cueless control period (P25, P26) and (2) the three pigeons subjected to constant stimulus conditions (P21, P22, P24).*

required for reinforcement and the variability studied was in physical parameters of the single response. In the present study, the physical parameters (i.e., force, locus, duration) of the key pecks would be expected to become progressively stereotyped with continued training, but these were not measured. The concern here was with the additional variability of the patterns of sequences of two discrete responses.

From the initial training of the birds one could have expected a predominant pattern, the alternating FR 3, to be maintained, once the birds were allowed to "run off the board." The behavior of all four birds, however, changed dramatically during this phase of training in that a great variety of patterns were used. This variable response pattern may be understood better if one examines the consequences of running off the board. In this case, more than three responses made by the birds on any one key is followed by the blackout of the experimental chamber; therefore, one would expect the birds to reduce the number of consecutive responses emitted, i.e., to switch keys more frequently. Examination of the data reveals that this was indeed the case. A "centralizing" tendency in response patterns occurred with the simple alternation emerging as the modal pattern. As the birds eliminated errors, they slowly returned to the previous predominant and perhaps most efficient method of obtaining reinforcement, the alternating FR 3 pattern.

The "freedom of choice" in response patterning in the present paradigm is considerable and can be increased (or decreased) by changing the size of the matrix of stimulus lights. It is perhaps remarkable that the pigeons exercised this freedom to such a large extent, and that even after 10,000 trials the pattern of responding was far from completely stereotyped.

The initial disruption of performance in the removal of stimulus light control indicates that the cue lights were the discriminative stimuli maintaining the behavior. This is also supported by our observations over closed-circuit television that the birds made frequent observing responses between pecks when cue lights were available. The performance of both control pigeons only partially recovered with continued practice in the absence of the cue lights. The stimulus control of this cueless performance is not clear but perhaps is related to counting paradigms wherein a specific number of responses on one lever followed by a single response on another lever produces reinforcement (cf. Mechner, 1958; Mechner and Guevrekian, 1962). It is perhaps significant that in the final 24 sessions with the cue lights reinstated, these birds did not develop the degree of stereotypy typical of their pre-control period and that of the birds that had the cue lights throughout the experiment (see Fig. 4), suggesting that behavior acquired in the absence of cue lights may permanently reduce stereotypy. The control birds during these final sessions were at least as accurate as the others (see Fig. 2); thus, stereotypy is not necessary for success.

The results of previous workers (Muenzinger, 1928; Skinner, 1938; Notterman, 1959; Antonitis, 1951) have shown that variability of response topography decreases with continued training. The present results extend this conclusion to serial patterns of responding: continued practice decreases variability of trial topography. The success of the pigeons with this task also suggests that an extension of the paradigm might be useful as an interspecific comparative test of problem-solving ability.

Notes
[1] This research was supported by PHS Grants HL10342, HL05453, and ES00454. We wish to thank Dr. Allan Harris for his suggestions during the preparation of this paper, and Earl Winder, Sandra Murray, and Dennis Perman for their technical assistance.

References
Antonitis, J. J. Response variability in the white rat during conditioning, extinction, and reconditioning. *Journal of Experimental Psychology,* 1951, **42,** 273–281.

Mechner, F. Probability relations within response sequences under ratio reinforcement. *Journal of the Experimental Analysis of Behavior,* 1958, **1,** 109–121.

Mechner, F. and Guevrekian, L. Effects of deprivation upon counting and timing behavior in rats. *Journal of the Experimental Analysis of Behavior,* 1962, **5,** 463–466.

Muenzinger, K. F. Plasticity and mechanization of the problem box habit in guinea pigs. *Journal of Comparative Psychology,* 1928, **8,** 45–70.

Notterman, J. M. Force emission during bar pressing. *Journal of Experimental Psychology,* 1959, **58,** 341–347.

Skinner, B. F. *The behavior of organisms.* New York: Appleton-Century Crofts, 1938.

B. CONTIGUITY AND CONTINGENCY

Just as Pavlov thought that temporal contiguity of CS and US was all that was needed for Pavlovian conditioning, Thorndike thought contiguity between response and reinforcer was crucial to operant conditioning. For many years, this view was accepted, essentially unchallenged. The first article in this section, by B. F. Skinner, one of the leading figures in behavior theory, played an important role in sustaining this view. He simply presented food to pigeons periodically and observed that the pigeons developed stereotyped patterns of behavior that occurred with great regularity. He termed these behaviors "superstitions" and argued that they were a reflection of how accidental temporal contiguity between responses and reinforcers could strengthen those responses.

In recent years, however, this contiguity view of the conditioning process has been shown to be inadequate. Organisms can distinguish circumstances in which reinforcement happens to follow responses from circumstances in which it is produced by, or contingent upon responses. They distinguish situations in which they control reinforcement from situations in which they do not. Skinner's own observations have been called into question (Staddon and Simmelhag, 1971). In addition, as Hammond's article shows, when the degree of contingency between response and reinforcer is manipulated, the frequency of the response varies directly with the degree of contingency. Hammond's paper is the analogue, for operant conditioning, of Rescorla's demonstration for Pavlovian conditioning (p. 43).

Not only can organisms detect whether or not they have control, but also that not having control has substantial negative consequences. Seligman and Maier report a study in which dogs experience uncontrollable shocks and are then given the opportunity to escape and avoid shock by responding. Most of these dogs never learn to escape and avoid, though responding is acquired quite rapidly by dogs that have not experienced uncontrollable shocks. According to Seligman and Maier, when the dogs experience uncontrollable shocks, they learn that shock is uncontrollable. They learn that they are helpless. This learned helplessness *then generalizes to new situations in which the dogs can control shocks. Because they have learned to be helpless, they never discover that control is possible. Learned helplessness has now been studied extensively in a wide variety of different species, including humans. Seligman (1975) has implicated helplessness in clinical depression, the most common of all psychological disorders.*

10 "Superstition" in the Pigeon

B. F. SKINNER

To say that a reinforcement is contingent upon a response may mean nothing more than that it follows the response. It may follow because of some mechanical connection or because of the mediation of another organism; but conditioning takes place presumably because of the temporal relation only, expressed in terms of the order and proximity of response and reinforcement. Whenever we present a state of affairs which is known to be reinforcing at a given drive, we must suppose that conditioning takes place, even though we have paid no attention to the behavior of the organism in making the presentation. A simple experiment demonstrates this to be the case.

A pigeon is brought to a stable state of hunger by reducing it to 75 percent of its weight when well fed. It is put into an experimental cage for a few minutes each day. A food hopper attached to the cage may be swung into place so that the pigeon can eat from it. A solenoid and a timing relay hold the hopper in place for five sec. at each reinforcement.

If a clock is now arranged to present the food hopper at regular intervals *with no reference whatsoever to the bird's behavior,* operant conditioning usually takes place. In six out of eight cases the resulting responses were so clearly defined that two observers could agree perfectly in counting instances. One bird was conditioned to turn counter-clockwise about the cage, making two or three turns between reinforcements. Another repeatedly thrust its head into one of the upper corners of the cage. A third developed a "tossing" response, as if placing its head beneath an invisible bar and lifting it repeatedly. Two birds developed a pendulum motion of the head and body, in which the head was extended forward and swung from right to left with a sharp movement followed by a somewhat slower return. The body generally followed the movement and a few steps might be taken when it was extensive. Another bird was conditioned to make incomplete pecking or brushing movements directed toward but not touching the floor. None of these responses appeared in any noticeable strength during adaptation to the cage or until the food hopper was periodically presented. In the remaining two cases, conditioned responses were not clearly marked.

The conditioning process is usually obvious. The bird happens to be executing some response as the hopper appears; as a result it tends to repeat this response. If the interval before the next presentation is not so great that extinction takes place, a second "contingency" is probable. This strengthens the response still further and subsequent reinforcement becomes more probable. It is true that some responses go unreinforced and some reinforcements appear when the response has not just been made, but the net result is the development of a considerable state of strength.

" 'Superstition' in the Pigeon" by B. F. Skinner. *Journal of Experimental Psychology,* 1948, *38,* 168–172.

With the exception of the counter-clockwise turn, each response was almost always repeated in the same part of the cage, and it generally involved an orientation toward some feature of the cage. The effect of the reinforcement was to condition the bird to respond to some aspect of the environment rather than merely to execute a series of movements. All responses came to be repeated rapidly between reinforcements—typically five or six times in 15 sec.

The effect appears to depend upon the rate of reinforcement. In general, we should expect that the shorter the intervening interval, the speedier and more marked the conditioning. One reason is that the pigeon's behavior becomes more diverse as time passes after reinforcement. A hundred photographs, each taken two sec. after withdrawal of the hopper, would show fairly uniform behavior. The bird would be in the same part of the cage, near the hopper, and probably oriented toward the wall where the hopper has disappeared or turning to one side or the other. A hundred photographs taken after 10 sec., on the other hand, would find the bird in various parts of the cage responding to many different aspects of the environment. The sooner a second reinforcement appears, therefore, the more likely it is that the second reinforced response will be similar to the first, and also that they will both have one of a few standard forms. In the limiting case of a very brief interval the behavior to be expected would be holding the head toward the opening through which the magazine has disappeard.

Another reason for the greater effectiveness of short intervals is that the longer the interval, the greater the number of intervening responses emitted without reinforcement. The resulting extinction cancels the effect of an occasional reinforcement.

According to this interpretation the effective interval will depend upon the rate of conditioning and the rate of extinction, and will therefore vary with the drive and also presumably between species. Fifteen sec. is a very effective interval at the drive level indicated above. One min. is much less so. When a response has once been set up, however, the interval can be lengthened. In one case it was extended to two min., and a high rate of responding was maintained with no sign of weakening. In another case, many hours of responding were observed with an interval of one min. between reinforcements.

In the latter case, the response showed a noticeable drift in topography. It began as a sharp movement of the head from the middle position to the left. This movement became more energetic, and eventually the whole body of the bird turned in the same direction, and a step or two would be taken. After many hours, the stepping response became the predominant feature. The bird made a well defined hopping step from the right to the left foot, meanwhile turning its head and body to the left as before.

When the stepping response became strong, it was possible to obtain a mechanical record by putting the bird on a large tambour directly connected with a small tambour which made a delicate electric contact each time stepping took place. By watching the bird and listening to the sound of the recorder it was possible to confirm the fact that a fairly authentic record was being made. It was possible for the bird to hear the recorder at each step, but this was, of course, in no way correlated with feeding. The record obtained when the magazine was presented once every min. resembles in every respect the characteristic curve for the pigeon under periodic reinforcement of a standard selected response. A well marked temporal discrimination develops. The bird does not respond immediately after eating, but when 10 or 15 or even 20 sec. have elapsed it begins to respond rapidly and continues until the reinforcement is received.

In this case it was possible to record the "extinction" of the response when the clock was turned off and the magazine was no longer presented at any time. The bird continued to respond with its characteristic side to side hop. More than 10,000 responses were recorded before "extinction" had reached the point at which few if any responses were made during a 10 or 15 min. interval. When the clock was again started, the periodic presentation of the magazine (still without any connection whatsoever with the bird's behavior) brought out a typical curve for reconditioning after periodic reinforcement, shown in Fig. 1. The record had been essentially horizontal for 20 min. prior to the beginning of this curve. The first reinforcement had some slight effect and the second a greater effect. There is a smooth positive acceleration in rate as the bird returns to the rate of responding which prevailed when it was reinforced every min.

When the response was again extinguished and the periodic presentation of food then resumed, a different response was picked up. This consisted of a progressive walking response in which the bird moved about the cage. The response of hopping from side to side never reappeared and could not, of course, be obtained deliberately without making the reinforcement contingent upon the behavior.

The experiment might be said to demonstrate a sort of superstition. The bird behaves as if there were a casual relation between its behavior and the presentation of food, although such a relation is lacking. There are many analogies in human behavior. Rituals for changing one's luck at cards are good examples. A few accidental connections between a ritual and favorable consequences suffice to set up and maintain the behavior in spite of many unreinforced instances. The bowler who has released a ball down the alley but continues to behave as if he were controlling it by twisting and turning his arm and shoulder is another case in point. These behaviors have, of course, no real effect upon one's luck or upon a ball half way down an alley, just as in the present case the food would appear as often if the pigeon did nothing—or, more strictly speaking, did something else.

It is perhaps not quite correct to say that conditioned behavior has been set up without any previously determined contingency whatsoever. We have appealed to a uniform sequence of responses in the behavior of the pigeon to obtain an over-all net contingency. When we arrange a clock to present food every 15 sec., we are in effect basing our reinforcement upon a limited set of responses which frequently occur 15 sec. after reinforcement. When a response has been strengthened (and this may result from one reinforcement), the setting of the clock implies an even more restricted contingency. Something of the same sort is true of the bowler. It is not quite correct to say that there is no connection between his twisting and turning and the course taken by the ball at the far end of

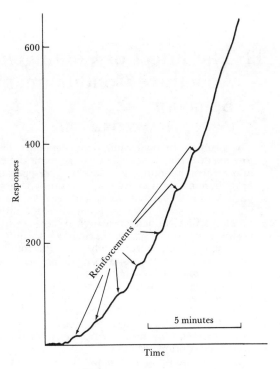

Fig. 1. *"Reconditioning" of a superstitious response after extinction. The response of hopping from right to left had been thoroughly extinguished just before the record was taken. The arrows indicate the automatic presentation of food at one-min. intervals without reference to the pigeon's behavior.*

the alley. The connection was established before the ball left the bowler's hand, but since both the path of the ball and the behavior of the bowler are determined, some relation survives. The subsequent behavior of the bowler may have no effect upon the ball, but the behavior of the ball has an effect upon the bowler. The contingency, though not perfect, is enough to maintain the behavior in strength. The particular form of the behavior adopted by the bowler is due to induction from responses in which there is actual contact with the ball. It is clearly a movement appropriate to changing the ball's direction. But this does not invalidate the comparison, since we are not concerned with what response is selected but with why it persists in strength. In rituals for changing luck the inductive strengthening of a particular form of behavior is generally absent. The behavior of the pigeon in this experiment is of the latter sort, as the variety of responses obtained from different pigeons indicates. Whether there is any unconditioned behavior in the pigeon appropriate to a given effect upon the environment is under investigation.

The results throws some light on incidental behavior observed in experiments in which a discriminative stimulus is frequently presented. Such a stimulus has reinforcing value and can set up superstitious behavior. A pigeon will often develop some response such as turning, twisting, pecking near the locus of the discriminative stimulus, flapping its wings, etc. In much of the work to date in this field the interval between presentations of the discriminative stimulus has been one min. and many of these superstitious responses are short-lived. Their appearance as the result of accidental correlations with the presentation of the stimulus is unmistakable.

11 The Effect of Contingency upon the Appetitive Conditioning of Free-Operant Behavior

LYNN J. HAMMOND

The problem of maintaining independence between response rates and reinforcement probabilities when determining the effect of varying the response reinforcement contingency upon free-operant behavior was solved by programming local reinforcement probabilities for response and no response on a second-by-second basis. Fifty-seven rats were trained to lever-press on schedules of water reinforcement involving different values of contingency. All rats were first trained on a high positive contingency and then shifted to less positive, zero, or negative contingencies. Under these conditions, rate of lever-pressing declined appropriately when the contingency between response and reinforcement decreased or was made negative. The decline in rate produced by a zero contingency cannot be attributed to extinction since the probability of reinforcement given the occurrence of a response was the same as for the positive contingency from which the shift to zero was made. That is, there was no change in the opportunity for response-reinforcement contiguity. It was concluded that the technique of programming local reinforcement probabilities offers promise for more critical examinations of the effects of contingency upon free-operant behavior.[1]

Key words: contingency, appetitive conditioning.

Contingency is often defined as the difference between the probability of reinforcement given a response and the probability of reinforcement given the absence of that response. When such a contingency definition is applied to free-operant paradigms, the experimenter faces a serious problem of how to program in advance the probabilities of the response and no response categories in a manner that is independent of response rate (see Gibbon, Berryman, & Thompson, 1974, p. 595). This technical problem, which has rarely been discussed, has effectively precluded examination of this type of contingency concept or any others which are also based on short-term reinforcement probabilities in the free-operant paradigm. The popularity of contingency explanations of operant behavior may stem from the well known rate-depressing effects of the shift from variable-interval (VI) reinforcement to free reinforcement on a variable-time (VT) schedule. However, such declines in response rate could be attributed to increases in the frequency of responses which are *not* followed by reinforcement on a VT as opposed to a VI schedule (e.g., Zeiler, 1968, p. 411).

Experiments which have been directly designed to evaluate the effect of contingency have all used a discrete-trial procedure (e.g., Neffinger & Gibbon, 1975), or one with many discrete-trial properties (e.g., Kop,

"The Effect of Contingency upon the Appetitive Conditioning of Free-Operant Behavior" by Lynn J. Hammond. *Journal of the Experimental Analysis of Behavior*, 1980, *34*, 297–304. Copyright 1980 by the Society for the Experimental Analysis of Behavior, Inc. Reprinted by permission of the publisher.

Kadden, & Schoenfeld, 1974). For some unknown reason all such studies have used shock as the reinforcing stimulus. Other experiments (such as Lattal, 1974; and Herrnstein & Hineline, 1966) were not designed to evaluate contingency effects and consequently are inadequate to do so. For example, in the Lattal study, the so-called free reinforcements are actually dependent upon the earlier occurrence of earned reinforcements.

The research described below illustrates the use of a technique that substantially, but not entirely, solves the problem of experimentally specifying reinforcement probabilities in the free-operant case. In addition, this research used an appetitive reinforcer paradigm. The advantages of this technique are: first, that the concept of contingency can now be investigated in a more precise fashion for free-operant paradigms; second, the technique can provide a critical comparison between response-reinforcement contiguity as the sole determiner of operant conditioning versus response-reinforcement contiguity as only one of several determinants of operant conditioning. For example, the lack of reinforcement for the absence of responding in the operant situation may play an important role in operant conditioning. Surprisingly enough, such a comparison has never been made, because, as noted above the lack of responding found on a VT schedule may be attributed just as readily to extinction as to lack of contingency.

The technique extends the discrete-trial paradigm to the free-operant paradigm by dividing the entire operant session into very brief unsignaled time periods each of which can be treated as a trial by the experimenter. Since these trials are unsignaled and there is no intertrial interval, the procedure is free-operant for the organism. In the present experiments the time base for a "trial" was one second. One momentary probability of water reinforcement could be assigned for each second in which at least one response occurred, while a second independent momentary probability could be assigned for each second in which no response occurred. In this way, it is possible to approximate the probability values for reinforcement given a response and for reinforcement given the absence of a response. In both experiments described below, rats were first trained on a high positive contingency and then shifted to a contingency of lower value or a negative contingency. The first experiment examined a shift from high positive to zero contingency, using an ABAB design. The second experiment examined shifts from high positive to lower positive contingencies, zero contingencies, or to a high negative contingency.

Experiment I

Method

Subjects Ten male albino rats with no previous experimental history served and were maintained on a 23-hr water deprivation schedule throughout the experiment.

Apparatus The experimental spaces consisted of ten Lehigh Valley Electronics (LVE) operant conditioning chambers, each equipped with one LVE retractable lever to the right of the LVE water dipper and a 28-V dc light with frosted-glass lens mounted just above the lever. Events in these chambers were scheduled by paper tape driven electromechanical equipment located in the next room. Responses were recorded on mechanical counters and monitored continuously on a 20 channel Esterline-Angus event recorder.

Procedure After one week of handling and deprivation, the rats were given a 1-hr session of magazine training in which they received 60, .03 cc water reinforcements on a variable-time (VT) 60-sec schedule, with the lever retracted from the chamber. After this single session of magazine training all rats were always exposed to one of the values of our particular procedure for programming contingency.

The programming equipment divided the session into a repeating 1-sec cycle. Reinforcements were delivered only at the end of a cycle and these reinforcements were conditional upon the occurrence of nonoccurrence of at least one response during that cycle and upon the predetermined holes in the paper tape. One channel of the paper tape was reserved for reinforcements when a rat did respond, and one for reinforcement when the rat did not respond in a given cycle. At the end of each 1-sec cycle the equipment detected whether the rat had, or had not, responded and then sampled the appropriate channel of the tape. If there was a hole in that channel, a reinforcement was delivered. Thus, when reinforcements occurred, they always came a constant fraction of a sec (programming time) after the end of the 1-sec cycle. When responses are reinforced some of the time, but no reinforcements occur following the absence of a response during a 1-sec cycle, this schedule is identical to what has been called a random-interval schedule with $T = 1$ sec (e.g., Millenson, 1963). Since rats are capable of responding more than once per sec, more than one response may have occurred in any given sec. Only one of the responses in any sec could actually produce reinforcement just as only the last response on an interval schedule has any influence upon reinforcement. The applicability of this technique to the study of contingency hinges upon these arbitrary assumptions about the temporal definition of a response and a nonresponse.

The actual sequence of experimental condition is shown in Table 1. The schedule for contingency will be labeled here as two reinforcement probabilities, the first for responding, the second for no responding. All ten rats received four sessions on the 1.0–0 schedule of reinforcement.

TABLE 1. Summary of Experimental Conditions in Experiment I

Condition	Number of sessions	$P_{RFT/R}$	$P_{RFT/R}$	Contingency
a	4	1.0	0	Very high positive
b	6	.2	0	High positive
c	14	.05	0	Moderately high positive
d	18	.05	.05	Zero
e	17	.05	0	Moderately high positive
f	18	.05	.05	Zero

The first two sessions were 60 min long, the second two sessions 50 min long. Thereafter they were shifted to a .2–0 schedule of reinforcement for six daily sessions of 40-min duration. Finally they were placed on a .05–0 schedule of reinforcement for 14 daily 1-hr sessions.

After this rather extensive history of reinforcement with a moderately high positive contingency between lever pressing and water delivery, all ten rats were shifted to a zero contingency produced by a .05–.05 schedule of reinforcement. Under these conditions the consequences of responding remained the same; only the consequences of not responding changed, from a probability of 0 to .05. Thus, a zero contingency was defined as a condition with equal likelihood of reinforcement for either a response or no response in any given sec.

The rats were maintained on the zero contingency of .05–.05 for 18 daily 1-hr sessions administered on a 5-day-a-week basis. At the end of this zero-contingency phase, these ten rats were returned to the moderately high positive contingency (.05–0) for 17 additional daily sessions and then shifted once again to the zero contingency (.05–.05) condition for 18 more sessions. In short, Experiment I involved an ABAB design.

Results

The mean response rate for all ten rats for each session throughout Experiment I is shown in the uppermost graph of Fig. 1. The response rates per session for two individual animals, R-8 and R-10, are shown in the middle and lower graphs of Fig. 1. R-8 and R-10 were selected for depiction because they represent the two extreme cases. The mean response rate for the last 5 trials (trials 10–14) of the .05–0 contingency was taken as the baseline rate. Performance on the zero contingency was assessed in terms of the percentage of the baseline rate. By this measure R-8 shows the greatest depression of response rate while R-10 shows the least.

As can be seen from the graph for R-10, all animals showed a substantial decline in responding upon introduction of the zero contingency. It is also the case that all rats showed a substantial decline the second time they were shifted to the zero contingency. In fact the decline was greater for the second than for the first shift. The mean percent baseline rate for the first shift was 22.7%, range 32.8% to 9.5%; while the average for the second shift was 12.1%, range 21.5% to 2.0%. These percent baseline rates were based in each case upon the mean of the last five sessions of the positive contingency and the mean for all sessions in each zero contingency. The difference in percent baseline rate between the first and second shift was significant (Wilcoxian, paired scores, signed ranks test, $T = 6$, $N = 10$, $p < .05$). Eight of the ten rats showed a greater rate-depressing effect the second time they were exposed to the zero contingency as compared with the first time.

Experiment II

The purpose of Experiment II was to examine the effects of a negative contingency and an intermediate positive contingency. In order to compare performance systematically on a wide range of contingencies, it was necessary to first develop a high rate of responding. For this reason all

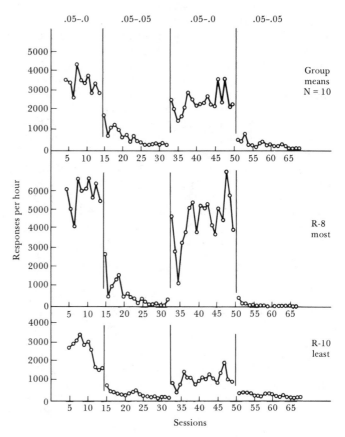

FIG. 1.   *Responses per hour for sessions of Experiment I. The top graph represents the mean response rate for all ten rats, the two lower graphs depict the two subjects which showed the most and the least effect of the shifted contingency.*

rats were always trained first on a high positive contingency and then shifted to a lower contingency as in Experiment I. Since Experiment I showed that exposure to an initial contingency shift changed performance on a second contingency shift identical to the first, it was necessary to make the comparisons in Experiment II between, rather than within, rats. A shift to zero contingency was included in each comparison.

Method

   Subjects Forty-seven male, experimentally naive albino rats served and were maintained as in Experiment I.

   Apparatus The apparatus was identical to that used in Experiment I.

   Procedure All rats were pretrained as before, including the magazine training for water reinforcement in their first experimental session. The sequence of experimental conditions following magazine training is shown in Table 2. First they were placed on a 1.0–0 schedule of reinforcement administered in the same manner as in Experiment I for one session. Rats

R-21 through R-29 constituted a zero contingency group which was compared to the negative contingency of Rats R-31 through R-38. These 17 rats were trained for 15 hourly sessions on a .05–0 schedule of reinforcement and then the zero group was shifted to a .05–.05 schedule and the negative group to a .0–.05 schedule for 22 hourly sessions.

The remaining 30 rats were divided into three equal groups to assess an intermediate contingency effect. These animals were trained and tested during 30 min sessions on higher reinforcement density schedules, because pilot work suggested that this might increase the discriminability of the intermediate contingency. They were trained initially on a .12–0 schedule for 25 half-hr sessions and then were shifted to either zero (.12–12), intermediate (.12–08), or were returned to the same positive (.12–0) contingency of reinforcement for an additional 25 sessions. Daily sessions were conducted on a five day per week schedule.

Results

The left side of Fig. 2 depicts the zero versus negative contingency comparison, while the right side depicts the comparisons for evaluating intermediate effects. As in Experiment I, the top graph (on each side) shows group means for each session, while the graphs below are for the rats with the most and least depressed performance following the particular contingency shift. The extreme cases were selected by the same criteria as before. There was no overlap in percent baseline between the eight rats of the negative group and the nine rats of the zero group (the mean for the zero group $= 20.6\%$; the mean for the negative group $= 2.9\%$; Mann–Whitney U score $= 0$, $p < .001$). As ancitipated, the negative contingency was much more effective than the zero contingency in suppressing behavior.

The intermediate contingency comparisons were less striking but were still in the expected direction. All 10 of the rats in the positive group, which was maintained on the same schedule (.12–0) throughout, actually

TABLE 2 Summary of Experimental Conditions in Experiment II

Rats	Condition	Number of Sessions	$P_{RFT/R}$	$P_{RFT/\cancel{R}}$	Contingency
R-21 through R-29	a	1	1.0	0	Very high positive
	b	15	.05	0	Moderately high positive
	c	22	.05	.05	Zero
R-31 through R-38	a	1	1.0	0	Very high positive
	b	15	.05	0	Moderately high positive
	c	22	0	.05	Strongly negative
R-51 to R-60	a	1	1.0	0	Very high positive
	b	25	.12	0	High positive
	c	25	.12	.12	Zero
R-31 to R-40	a	1	1.0	0	Very high positive
	b	25	.12	0	High positive
	c	25	.12	0	High positive
R-41 to R-50	a	1	1.0	0	Very high positive
	b	25	.12	0	High positive
	c	25	.12	.08	Intermediate positive

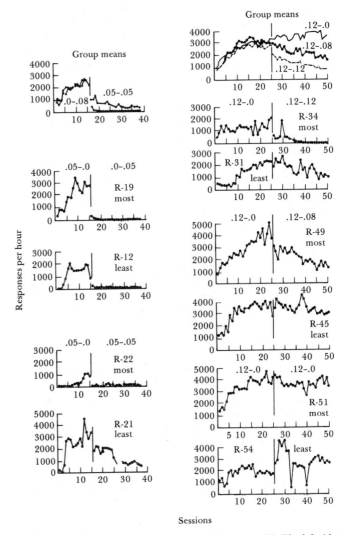

FIG. 2.   *Responses per hour for sessions of Experiment II. The left side represents a comparison between a shift to zero versus a shift to a negative contingency. The right side represents a comparison of an intermediate, positive contingency to a high positive and a zero contingency.*

increased their performance after the other groups were shifted; while both the degraded contingencies produced lower responding in 19 of 20 rats. Based on percent baseline rates, there was no overlap between the zero group (mean = 45.0%) and the positive group (mean = 121.9%; n_1, n_2 = 10, Mann–Whitney U = 0, p < .001); and there was only one instance of overlap between the intermediate (mean = 68.4%) and the positive group (U = 1, p < .001). But there was considerable overlap between the zero and intermediate groups (U = 21, p < .05) as can be seen by comparing the least depressed rat of the zero group, R-31, with the most depressed rat of the intermediate group, R-49. Although the intermediate contingency, generally speaking, produced intermediate rate depressing effects, individual differences in reactivity to these lowered contingencies were considerable.

Discussion

The major purpose of the present research was to examine a new technique for programming reinforcement probabilities following the occurrence of a response and the absence of that response in an appetitive free-operant paradigm in such a way that these probabilities would always be independent of the animal's overall rates of responding. Only when such independence is achieved can the components of a contingency (defined as the difference between the probability of reinforcement given a response and the probability of reinforcement given the absence of that response) be programmed in advance. Therefore only with such a technique can one begin to examine empirically the many predictions generated by contingency, as defined above, on free-operant behavior.

The present experiments demonstrate a relationship between behavioral change and changes in contingency. However, only widely separated contingency values were compared, and in this sense the demonstrated relationship is very crude. These findings then, do not incisively examine the effects of contingency, since the absolute difference between reinforcement given a response and reinforcement given no response is only one of a potentially large class of mathematical formulae specifying the relationship between the entries in the four cells of a contingency matrix (see Gibbon et al., 1974, p. 595).

What these results do clearly show is that the rate-depressing effects of response-independent reinforcement are not the result of simple extinction of responses previously strengthened by response-reinforcement contiguity. When rats were shifted to a zero contingency, the technique used here maintained the same opportunity for response-reinforcement contiguity as existed on the high positive contingency which established the behavior. One must look elsewhere for an explanation of the rate-depressing effects of response-independent reinforcement.

As noted before, the assessment of different contingency definitions (e.g., reinforcement probability difference versus statistical correlation between response and reinforcement) has not been possible in free-operant paradigms because methods were lacking for specifying the reinforcement probabilities following response and the absence of the response independently of overall response rate. The present technique appears to provide one approach to accomplishing the large scale effort required to make an assessment of contingency. However, one must accept certain assumptions upon which the technique is based. Most important, is it appropriate to define a response as an act in time (such as was done by Baum and Rachlin, 1969) rather than as a discrete act? With the particular values of the technique used here a response was defined as at least one lever press in any second, while a nonresponse was defined as the absence of any responses in a second. The question about the adequacy of this assumption arises because we have no idea whether or not the organism is best described on the basis of similar principles of response and no-response quantification. If the animal fails to press the lever for five seconds, should that be treated by the experimenter as five instances of the absence of a response (as was done here) or as one, or how should it be treated? Perhaps further research with different time cycles than once per second will help clarify this issue.

Notes

[1] The author would like to thank Walter E. Paynter, Jr. for extensive suggestions about the rationale of the experimentation, and Philip N. Hineline for his thorough suggestions and criticisms of the manuscript.

References

Baum, W. M. & Rachlin, H. C. Choice as time allocation. *Journal of the Experimental Analysis of Behavior,* 1969, **12,** 861–874.

Gibbon, J., Berryman, R., & Thompson, R. L. Contingency spaces and measures in classical and instrumental conditioning. *Journal of the Experimental Analysis of Behavior,* 1974, **21,** 585–605.

Herrnstein, R. J., & Hineline, P. N. Negative reinforcement as shock-frequency reduction. *Journal of the Experimental Analysis of Behavior,* 1966, **9,** 421–430.

Kop, P. F. M., Kadden, R. M., & Schoenfeld, W. N. Aversive schedules with independent probabilities of reinforcement for responding and not responding by rhesus monkeys: III. Recovery of avoidance baseline. *Journal of Comparative and Physiological Psychology, 1974,* **87,** 1198–1208.

Lattal, K. A. Combinations of response-reinforcer dependence and independence. *Journal of the Experimental Analysis of Behavior,* 1974, **22,** 357–362.

Millenson, J. R. Random interval schedules of reinforcement. *Journal of the Experimental Analysis of Behavior,* 1963, **6,** 437–443.

Neffinger, G. C., & Gibbon, J. Partial avoidance contingencies. *Journal of the Experimental Analysis of Behavior.* 1975, **23,** 437–450.

Zeiler, M. D. Fixed and variable schedules of the response-independent reinforcement. *Journal of the Experimental Analysis of Behavior,* 1968, **11,** 405–414.

12 Failure to Escape Traumatic Shock

MARTIN E. P. SELIGMAN AND STEVEN F. MAIER

Dogs which had first learned to panel press in a harness in order to escape
shock subsequently showed normal acquisition of escape/avoidance behavior in
a shuttle box. In contrast, yoked, inescapable shock in the harness produced
profound interference with subsequent escape responding in the shuttle box.
Initial experience with escape in the shuttle box led to enhanced panel pressing
during inescapable shock in the harness and prevented interference with later
responding in the shuttle box. Inescapable shock in the harness and failure to
escape in the shuttle box produced interference with escape responding after a
7-day rest. These results were interpreted as supporting a learned "helplessness" explanation of interference with escape responding: Ss failed to escape
shock in the shuttle box following inescapable shock in the harness because
they had learned that shock termination was independent of responding.[1]

Overmier and Seligman (1967) have shown that the prior exposure of
dogs to inescapable shock in a Pavlovian harness reliably results in interference with subsequent escape/avoidance learning in a shuttle box. Typically, these dogs do not even escape from shock in the shuttle box. They
initially show normal reactivity to shock, but after a few trials, they passively "accept" shock and fail to make escape movements. Moreover, if
an escape or avoidance response does occur, it does not reliably predict
future escapes or avoidances, as it does in normal dogs.

This pattern of effects is probably not the result of incompatible skeletal responses reinforced during the inescapable shocks, because it can be
shown even when the inescapable shocks are delivered while the dogs are
paralyzed by curare. This behavior is also probably not the result of adaptation to shock, because it occurs even when escape/avoidance shocks are
intensified. However, the fact that interference does not occur if 48 hr.
elapse between exposure to inescapable shock in the harness and escape/
avoidance training suggests that the phenomenon may be partially dependent upon some other temporary process.

Overmier and Seligman (1967) suggested that the degree of control
over shock allowed to the animal in the harness may be an important determinant of this interference effect. According to this hypothesis, if
shock is terminated independently of S's responses during its initial experience with shock, interference with subsequent escape/avoidance responding should occur. If, however, S's responses terminate shock during
its initial experience with shock, normal escape/avoidance responding
should subsequently occur. Experiment I investigates the effects of escapable as compared with inescapable shock on subsequent escape/avoid-
ance responding.

"Failure to Escape Traumatic Shock" by Martin E. P. Seligman and Steven F. Maier.
Journal of Experimental Psychology, 1967, 74, 1–9. Copyright 1967 by the American Psychological Association. Reprinted by permission of the publisher and author.

Experiment I

Method

Subjects. The Ss were 30 experimentally naive, mongrel dogs, 15–19 in. high at the shoulder, and weighing between 25 and 29 lb. They were maintained on ad lib food and water in individual cages. Three dogs were discarded from the Escape group, two because they failed to learn to escape shock in the harness (see procedure), and one because of a procedural error. Three dogs were discarded from the "Yoked" control group, two because they were too small at the neck to be adequately restrained in the harness; the third died during treatment. This left 24 Ss, eight in each group.

Apparatus. The apparatus was the same as that described in Overmier and Seligman (1967). It consisted of two distinctively different units, one for escapable/inescapable shock sessions and the other for escape/avoidance training. The unit in which Ss were exposed to escapable/inescapable shock consisted of a rubberized cloth hammock located inside a shielded, white sound-attenuating cubicle. The hammock was constructed so that S's legs hung down below its body through four holes. The S's legs were secured in this position, and S was strapped into the hammock. In addition, S's head was held in position by panels placed on either side and a yoke between the panels across S's neck. The S could press the panels with its head. For the Escape group pressing the panels terminated shock, while for the "Yoked" control group, panel presses did not effect the preprogrammed shock. The shock source for this unit consisted of a 500 v. ac transformer and a parallel voltage divider, with the current applied through a fixed resistance of 20,000 ohms. The shock was applied to S through brass plate electrodes coated with commercial electrode paste and taped to the footpads of S's hind feet. The shock intensity was 6.0 ma. Shock presentations were controlled by automatic relay circuitry located outside the cubicle.

Escape/avoidance training was conducted in a two-way shuttle box with two black compartments separated by an adjustable barrier (described in Solomon & Wynne, 1953). The barrier height was adjusted to S's shoulder height. Each shuttle-box compartment was illuminated by two 50-w. and one 7½-w. lamps. The CS consisted of turning off the four 50-w. lamps. The US, electric shock, was administered through the grid floor. A commutator shifted the polarity of the grid bars four times per second. The shock was 550 v. ac applied through a variable current limiting resistor in series with S. The shock was continually regulated by E at 4.5 ma. Whenever S crossed the barrier, photocell beams were interrupted, a response was automatically recorded, and the trial terminated. Latencies of barrier jumping were measured from CS onset to the nearest .01 sec. by an electric clock. Stimulus presentations and temporal contingencies were controlled by automatic relay circuitry in a nearby room.

White masking noise at approximately 70-db. SPL was presented in both units.

Procedure. The Escape group received escape training in the harness. Sixty-four unsignaled 6.0 ma. shocks were presented at a mean interval of

90 sec. (range, 60–120 sec.). If the dog pressed either panel with its head during shock, shock terminated. If the dog failed to press a panel during shock, shock terminated automatically after 30 sec. Two dogs were discarded for failing to escape 18 of the last 20 shocks.[2]

Twenty-four hours later dogs in the Escape group were given 10 trials of escape/avoidance training in the shuttle box; S was placed in the shuttle box and given 5 min. to adapt before any treatment was begun. Presentation of the CS began each trial. The CS–US interval was 10 sec. If S jumped the barrier during this interval, the CS terminated and no shock was presented. Failure to jump the barrier during the CS–US interval led to shock which remained on until S did jump the barrier. If no response occurred within 60 sec. after CS onset, the trial was automatically terminated and a 60-sec. latency recorded. The average intertrial interval was 90 sec. with a range of 60–120 sec. If S failed to cross the barrier on all of the first five trials, it was removed, placed on the other side of the shuttle box, and training then continued. At the end of the tenth trial, S was removed from the shuttle box and returned to its home cage.

The Normal control group received only 10 escape/avoidance trials in the shuttle box as described above.

The "Yoked" control group received the same exposure to shock in the harness as did the Escape group, except that panel pressing did not terminate shock. The duration of shock on any given trial was determined by the mean duration of the corresponding trial in the Escape group. Thus each S in the "Yoked" control group received a series of shocks of decreasing duration totaling to 226 sec.

Twenty-four hours later, Ss in the "Yoked" control group received 10 escape/avoidance trials in the shuttle box as described for the Escape group. Seven days later, those Ss in this group which showed the interference effect received 10 more trials in the shuttle box.

Results[3]

The Escape group learned to panel press to terminate shock in the harness. Each S in this group showed decreasing latencies of panel pressing over the course of the session ($p = .008$, sign test, Trials 1–8 vs. Trials 57–64). Individual records revealed that each S learned to escape shock by emitting a single, discrete panel press following shock onset. The Ss in the "Yoked" control group typically ceased panel pressing altogether after about 30 trials.

Table 1 presents the mean latency of shuttle box responding, the mean number of failures to escape shock, and the percentage of Ss which failed to escape nine or more of the 10 trials during escape/avoidance training in the shuttle box for each group. The "Yoked" control group showed marked interference with escape responding in the shuttle box. It differed significantly from the Escape group and from the Normal control group on mean latency and mean number of failures to escape (in both cases, $p < .05$, Duncan's multiple range test). The Escape group and the Normal control group did not differ on these indexes.

Six S's in the "Yoked" control group failed to escape shock on 9 or

more of the 10 trials in the shuttle box. Seven days after the first shuttle-box treatment, these six Ss received 10 further trials in the shuttle
box. Five of them continued to fail to escape shock on every trial.

Discussion

The degree of control over shock allowed a dog during its initial exposure to shock was a determinant of whether or not interference occurred with subsequent escape/avoidance learning. Dogs which learned
to escape shock by panel pressing in the harness did not differ from untreated dogs in subsequent escape/avoidance learning in the shuttle box.
Dogs for which shock termination was independent of responding in the
harness showed interference with subsequent escape learning.

Because the Escape group differed from the "Yoked" control group
during their initial exposure to shock only in their control over shock termination, we suggest that differential learning about their control over
shock occurred in these two groups. This learning may have acted in the
following way: (*a*) Shock initially elicited active responding in the harness
in both groups. (*b*) Ss in the "Yoked" control group learned that shock
termination was independent of their responding, i.e., that the conditional probability of shock termination in the presence of any given response did not differ from the conditional probability of shock
termination in the absence of that response. (*c*) The incentive for the initiation of active responding in the presence of electric shock is the expectation that responding will increase the probability of shock
termination. In the absence of such incentive, the probability that responding will be initiated decreases. (*d*) Shock in the shuttle box mediated
the generalization of *b* to the new situation for the "Yoked" control
group, thus decreasing the probability of escape response initiation in the
shuttle box.

Escapable shock in the harness (Escape group) did not produce interference, because Ss learned that their responding was correlated with shock
termination. The incentive for the maintenance of responding was thus
present, and escape response intiation occurred normally in the shuttle
box.

Learning that shock termination is independent of responding seems

TABLE 1. Indexes of Shuttle Box Escape Avoidance
Responding: Experiment I

Group	Mean latency (in sec.)	% Ss Failing to escape shock on 9 or more of the 10 trials	Mean No. failures to escape shock[a]
Escape	27.00	0	2.63
Normal control	25.93	12.5	2.25
"Yoked" control	48.22	75	7.25

[a] Out of 10 trials.

related to the concept of learned "helplessness" or "hopelessness" advanced by Richter (1957), Mowrer (1960, p. 197), Cofer and Appley (1964, p. 452), and to the concept of external control of reinforcement discussed by Lefcourt (1966).

In untreated Ss the occurrence of an escape or avoidance response is a reliable predictor of future escape and avoidance responding. Dogs in the "Yoked" control group and in the groups which showed the interference effect in Overmier and Seligman (1967) occasionally made an escape or avoidance response and then reverted to "passively" accepting shock. These dogs did not appear to benefit from the barrier-jumping–shock termination contingency. A possible interpretation of this finding is that the prior learning that shock termination was independent of responding inhibited the formation of the barrier-jumping–shock-termination association.

The Ss in the "Yoked" control group which showed the interference effect 24 hr. after inescapable shock in the harness again failed to escape from shock after a further 7-day interval. In contrast, Overmier and Seligman (1967) found that no interference occurred when 48 hr. elapsed between inescapable shock in the harness and shuttle-box training. This time course could result from a temporary state of emotional depletion (Brush, Myer, & Palmer, 1963), which was produced by experience with inescapable shock, and which could be prolonged by being conditioned to the cues of the shuttle box. Such a state might be related to the parasympathetic death which Richter's (1957) "hopeless" rats died. Further research is needed to clarify the relationship between the learning factor, which appears to cause the initial occurrence of the interference effect, and an emotional factor, which may be responsible for the time course of the effect.

The results of Exp. I provide a further disconfirmation of the adaptation explanation of the interference effect. If Ss in the "Yoked" control group had adapted to shock and, therefore, were not sufficiently motivated to respond in the shuttle box, Ss in the Escape group should also have adapted to shock. Further, the Escape and the "Yoked" control groups were equated for the possibility of adventitious punishment for active responding by shock onset in the harness. Thus it seems unlikely that the "Yoked" control group failed to escape in the shuttle box because it had been adventitiously punished for active responding in the harness.

Experiment II

Experiment I provided support for the hypothesis that S learned that shock termination was independent of its responding in the harness and that this learning inhibited subsequent escape responding in the shuttle box. Experiment II investigates whether prior experience with *escapable* shock in the shuttle box will mitigate the effects of inescapable shock in the harness on subsequent escape/avoidance behavior. Such prior experience might be expected (a) to inhibit S's learning in the harness that its responding is not correlated with shock termination and (b) to allow S to discriminate between the escapability of shock in the shuttle box and the inescapability of shock in the harness.

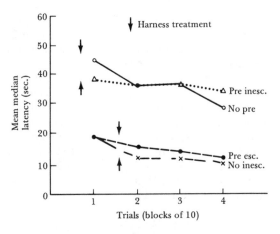

FIG. 1. *Mean median latency of escape/avoidance responding. (The position of the arrow denotes whether the harness treatment occurred 24 hr. before the first or second block of trials).*

Method

Subjects. The Ss were 30 experimentally naive, mongrel dogs, weight, height, and housing as above. Three dogs were discarded: two because of procedural errors and one because of illness. The remaining 27 dogs were randomly assigned to three groups of nine Ss each.

Apparatus. The two units described for Exp. I were used.

Procedure. The Preescape group received 3 days of treatment. On Day 1, each S received 10 escape/avoidance trials in the shuttle box as described in Exp. 1. On Day 2, approximately 24 hr. after the shuttle-box treatment, each S in this group received an inescapable shock session in the harness. All inescapable shocks were unsignaled. The inescapable shock session consisted of 64 5-sec. shocks, each of 6.0 ma. The average intershock interval was 90 sec. with a range of 60–120 sec. On Day 3, approximately 24 hr. after the inescapable shock, S was returned to the shuttle box and given 30 more escape/avoidance trials, as described for Day 1.

The No Pregroup received no experience in the shuttle box prior to receiving inescapable shock. On the first treatment day for this group, each S was placed in the harness and exposed to an inescapable shock session as described for the Preescape group, Day 2. Approximately 24 hr. later, S was placed in the shuttle box and given 40 trials of escape/avoidance training as described above. If S failed to respond on all of the first five trials, S was moved to the other side of the shuttle box. If S continued to fail to respond on all trials, it was put back on the original side after the twenty-fifth trial. Thus, if S failed to escape on every trial, it received a total of 2,000 sec. of shock.

The No Inescapable group was treated exactly as the Preescape group except that it received no shock in the harness. On Day 1, S received 10 escape/avoidance trials in the shuttle box. On Day 2, it was strapped in the harness for 90 min., but received no shock. On Day 3, it was returned to the shuttle box and given 30 more escape/avoidance trials.

Results

The No Pregroup showed significant interference with escape/avoidance responding in the shuttle box on Day 3. The Preescape and the No

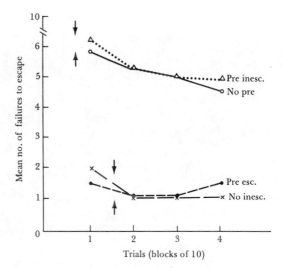

FIG. 2. *Mean number of failures to escape shock. (The position of the arrow denotes whether the harness treatment occurred 24 hr. before the first or second block of trials.)*

Inescapable groups did not show such interference. Figure 1 presents the mean median latency of jumping responses for the three groups (and a posterior control group, see below) over the four blocks of 10 trials. Analysis of variance on the three groups revealed that the effect of groups, $F(2, 24) = 3.55$, $p < .05$, and the effect of trial blocks, $F(3, 72) = 6.84$, $p < .01$, were significant. Duncan's multiple-range test indicated that the No Pregroup differed from the other two groups across all 40 trials, both $p < .05$. The Preescape and the No Inescapable groups did not differ from each other. Similar results held for the mean of mean latencies. A small, transitory disruption of improvement in shuttle-box performance following inescapable shock in the harness occurred in the Preescape group relative to the No Inescapable group. Difference scores for latencies between consecutive blocks of trials measure improvement in performance. A comparison of the Preescape group with the No Inescapable group on the difference between the mean latency on Trials 1–10 and the mean latency on Trials 11–20 revealed that the No Inescapable group showed significantly more improvement than the Preescape group, Mann–Whitney U test, $U = 15$, $p < .05$. No significant differences were found on difference scores for any subsequent blocks of trials.

Figure 2 presents the mean number of failures to escape shock for the three groups across the four blocks of trials. Analysis of variance revealed a significant overall effect of blocks, $F(3, 72) = 5.94$, $p < .01$, and a significant Groups × Blocks interaction, $F(6, 72) = 17.82$, $p < .01$. Duncan's tests indicated that the No Pregroup showed significantly more failures to escape than the other two groups across the 40 trials, both $p < .05$. The Preescape and the No Inescapable groups did not differ.

Figure 3 presents the total number of avoidance responses for the groups across the blocks of trials. Only the blocks effect was significant in the overall analysis of variance, $F(3, 72) = 27.90$, $p < .01$. No other effects were significant.

Panel presses made in the harness during the inescapable shock session were counted. On either side of S's head were panels which S could press;

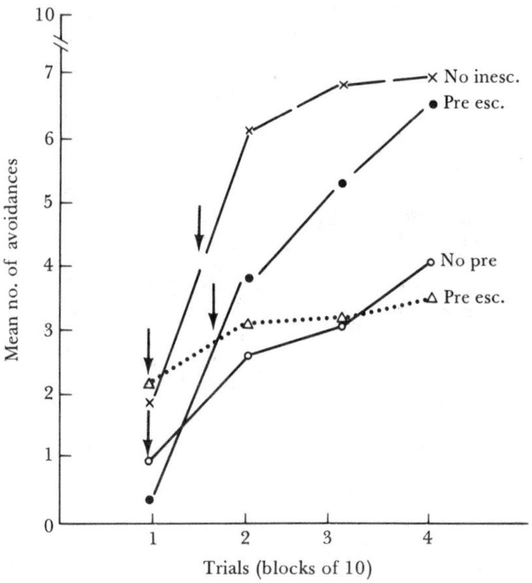

FIG. 3. *Mean number of avoidances. (The position of the arrow denotes whether the harness treatment occurred 24 hr. before the first or second block of trials.)*

panel pressing had no effect on the shock, but merely indicated attempts to respond and/or struggling in the harness. The Preescape group, having received 10 trials with *escapable* shock in the shuttle box the previous day, made more panel presses during the inescapable shock session than did the No Pregroup, the group for which the inescapable shock in the harness was the first experimental treatment, Mann–Whitney U test, $U = 9$, $p < .02$.

Posterior Control Group. Subsequent to this experiment, a control group was run to determine if the *escapability* of shock in the shuttle box on Day 1 for the Preescape group was responsible for its enhanced panel pressing in the harness and lack of interference with responding in the shuttle box. Or would the mere occurrence of inescapable shock for a free-moving animal in the shuttle box have produced these results? Nine naive dogs received the following treatment: On Day 1, Ss were placed in shuttle box and given 10 trials as for the Preescape and the No Inescapable groups. Unlike these groups, however, S's barrier jumping did not (except adventitiously) terminate the shock and CS, because trial durations were programmed independently of S's behavior. The duration of each of the 10 trials for this Preinescapable group corresponded to the mean trial duration for the Preescape and the No Inescapable groups on that trial. On Day 2, Ss received 64 trials of inescapable shock in the harness. On Day 3, Ss received 40 escape/avoidance trials in the shuttle box.

Figures 1, 2, and 3 present the escape/avoidance performance of the Preinescapable group on Day 3. In general this group performed like the No Pregroup. This impression was borne out by statistical tests. The Preinescapable group showed significantly slower median latency of barrier jumping than the Preescape and the No Inescapable groups across all 40 trials, both $p < .05$, Duncan's test. The Preinescapable group did not differ from the No Pregroup. Similar results held for the other indexes.

Analysis of the panel press data showed that the Preinescapable group made significantly fewer panel presses in the harness than the Preescape group, Mann–Whitney U test, $U = 14$, $p < .05$. The Preinescapable group did not differ significantly from the No Pregroup, $U = 26$.

Discussion

Three main findings emerged from Exp. II: (*a*) Ss (Preescape) which first received escapable shock in the shuttle box, then inescapable shock in the harness, did not react passively to subsequent shock in the shuttle box, as did Ss which either first received inescapable shock in the shuttle box (Preinescapable) or no treatment prior to shock in the harness (No Pre). (*b*) The Preescape group, having received experience with escapable shock in the shuttle box, showed enhanced panel pressing when exposed to inescapable shock in the harness, relative to naive Ss given inescapable shock in the harness. Such enhanced panel pressing was specifically the result of the *escapability* of shock in the shuttle box: The Preinescapable group did not show enhanced panel pressing. (*c*) The interference effect persisted for 40 trials.

The Ss which have had prior experience with *escapable* shock in the shuttle box showed more energetic behavior in response to inescapable shock in the harness. This contrasts with the interference effect produced by *inescapable* shock in Ss which have had no prior experience with shock or in Ss which have had prior experience with inescapable shock. Thus, if an animal first learns that its responding produces shock termination and then faces a situation in which reinforcement is independent of its responding, it is more persistent in its attempts to escape shock than is a naive animal.

General Discussion

We have proposed that S learned as a consequence of inescapable shock that its responding was independent of shock termination, and therefore the probability of response initiation during shock decreased. Alternative explanations might be offered: (*a*) Inactivity, somehow, reduces the aversiveness of shock. Thus S failed to escape shock in the shuttle box because it had been reinforced for inactivity in the harness. Since the interference effect occurred in Ss which had been curarized during inescapable shock, such an aversiveness-reducing mechanism would have to be located inward of the neuro-myal junction. (*b*) S failed to escape in the shuttle box because certain responses which facilitate barrier jumping were *extinguished* in the harness during inescapable shock. In conventional extinction procedures, some response is first explicitly reinforced by correlation with shock termination, and then that response is extinguished by removing shock altogether from the situation. Responding during extinction is conventionally not *un*correlated with shock termination; rather, responding is correlated with the total absence of shock. In our harness situation, no response was first explicitly reinforced, and shock was presented throughout the session. A broader concept of extinction, however, might be tenable. On this view, any procedure which decreases the probability of a response by eliminating the incentive to respond is an extinction procedure. If the independence of shock termination and responding eliminates the incentive to respond (as assumed), then our harness procedure could be thought of as an extinction procedure. Such an explanation seems only semantically different from the one we have advanced, since both entail that the probability of responding during shock has decreased because *S* learned that shock termination was independent of its responses.

Learning that one's own responding and reinforcement are independent might be expected to play a role in appetitive situations. If *S* received extensive pretraining with rewarding brain stimulation delivered independently of its operant responding, would the subsequent acquisition of a bar press to obtain this reward be retarded? Further, might learned "helplessness" transfer from aversive to appetitive situations or vice versa?

If dogs learn in one situation that their active responding is to no avail, and then transfer this training to another shock situation, the opposite type of transfer (avoidance learning sets) might be possible: If a dog first learned a barrier-hurdling response which avoided shock in the shuttle box, would that dog be facilitated in learning to panel press to avoid shock in the harness (to a different CS)? Our finding, that dogs which first successfully escape shock in the shuttle box later showed enhanced panel pressing in the harness, is consonant with this prediction.

Does learning about response–reinforcement contingencies have its analogs in classical conditioning? If *S* experienced two stimuli randomly interspersed with each other (adventitious pairings possible), would it be retarded in forming an association between the two stimuli once true pairing was begun? Conversely, pretraining in which one stimulus is correlated with a US might facilitate the acquisition of the CR to a new CS. Pavlov (1927, p. 75) remarked that the first establishment of a conditioned inhibitor took longer than any succeeding one.

In conclusion, learning theory has stressed that two operations, explicit contiguity between events (acquisition) and explicit noncontiguity (extinction), produce learning. A third operation that is proposed, independence between events, also produces learning, and such learning may have effects upon behavior that differ from the effects of explicit pairing and explicit nonpairing. Such learning may produce an *S* who does not attempt to escape electric shock; an *S* who, even if he does respond, may not benefit from instrumental contingencies.

Notes

[1] This research was supported by grants to R. L. Solomon from the National Science Foundation (GB-2428) and the National Institute of Mental Health (MH-04202). The authors are grateful to R. L. Solomon, J. Aronfreed, J. Geer, H. Gleitman, F. Irwin, D. Williams, and J. Wishner for their advice in the conduct and reporting of these experiments. The authors also thank J. Bruce Overmier, with whom Exp. I was begun.

[2] It might be argued that eliminating these two dogs would bias the data. Thus naive dogs which failed to learn the panel-press escape response in the harness might also be expected to be unable to learn shuttle box escape/avoidance. One of these dogs was run 48 hr. later in the shuttle box. It escaped and avoided normally. The other dog was too ill to be run in the shuttle box 48 hr. after it received shock in the harness.

[3] All *p* values are based upon two-tailed tests.

References

Brush, F. R., Myer, J. S., & Palmer, M. E. Effects of kind of prior training and intersession interval upon subsequent avoidance learning. *J. Comp. Physiol. Psychol.*, 1963, **56**, 539–545.

Cofer, C. N., & Appley, M. H. *Motivation: Theory and research.* New York: Wiley, 1964.

Lefcourt, H. M. Internal vs. external control of reinforcement: A review. *Psychol. Bull.*, 1966, **65**, 206–221.

Mowrer, O. H. *Learning theory and behavior.* New York: Wiley, 1960.

Overmier, J. B., & Seligman, M. E. P. Effects of inescapable shock on subsequent escape and avoidance learning. *J. Comp. Physiol. Psychol.*, 1967, **63**, 28–33.

Pavlov, I. P. *Conditioned reflexes.* New York: Dover, 1927.

Richter, C. On the phenomenon of sudden death in animals and man. *Psychosom. Med.*, 1957, **19**, 191–198.

Solomon, R. L., & Wynne, L. C. Traumatic avoidance learning: Acquisition in normal dogs. *Psychol. Monogr.*, 1953, **67**(4, Whole No. 354).

C. THE NATURE OF REINFORCEMENT

Almost from the beginning of research on operant conditioning, behavior theorists have attempted to develop an account of what makes certain events reinforcers. They have attempted to find some property that all reinforcers have in common. Most explanations of this issue focused on the idea that reinforcers reduce psychological drives that derive from biological needs; but the drive concept ultimately proved unsuccessful as a unifier of all reinforcers (see Bolles, 1967, for a discussion of the history of research on drive). Somewhat more successful was a theory developed by Premack (1965). Premack argued that reinforcement should be viewed as the opportunity to engage in certain highly preferred or probable activities. A given activity A could be reinforced by the opportunity to engage in any higher-probability activity, but the opportunity to engage in activity A could itself reinforce activities that were less probable than it. Thus reinforcers were relative. Engaging in the same activity could be a reinforcer for some activities and an operant for others. The following article by Premack demonstrates not only that reinforcement is relative, but also that the operant–reinforcer relation can be reversed. One can reinforce running in a wheel by providing opportunities to drink, but when running in the wheel has become highly probable, one can reinforce drinking by providing access to the wheel. While Premack's theory has been challenged and modified in recent years, it remains a powerful account of the nature of reinforcement (see Allison et al., *1979).*

13 Reversibility of the Reinforcement Relation

DAVID PREMACK

Parameters were identified for the rat which made both drinking more probable than running and running more probable than drinking. In the same subjects, depending upon which parameters were used, running reinforced drinking and drinking reinforced running. This relationship suggests that a "reward" is simply any response that is independently more probable than another response.

Food or water are used customarily to reinforce the bar press or running, but it is not asked, Can this relation be reversed? Will the bar press or running reinforce eating or drinking? The traditional account of reinforcement does not generate this question, for it assumes categorical reinforcers, food and water being prime examples (Hull, 1943, pp. 68–83; Skinner, 1938, pp. 61–115). Furthermore, the traditional account was not changed basically even by the finding that light and sound also reinforce (Barnes & Kish, 1961; Butler, 1953; Kish, 1955; Marx, Henderson, & Roberts, 1955). To incorporate these "new" reinforcers the reward category was simply enlarged, admitting unforeseen kinds of stimulation, and inferring additional drives and needs. The logic of the traditional account remains one that distinguishes between categories of positive and neutral events; only the events to which this logic is applied have changed.

We have proposed a model of positive reinforcement (Premack, 1959, 1961) whose major assumption is simply that, for any pair of responses, the independently more probable one will reinforce the less probable one. In this model the traditional vocabulary of drive, reward, and goal becomes either meaningless or misleading, for the model leads to the predictions that (i) the eating or drinking response is itself reinforcible[1] and, more important, (ii) the reinforcement relation is reversible.

Are there intervals of time in which eating or drinking are less probable than certain other responses, as well as other intervals in which the probabilities are reversed? Although the present model cannot make such predictions, but predicts only after the response probabilities are given, parameters were recently found in the rat that satisfy both conditions.

With free access to both food and an activity wheel, but access to water for only 1 hour per day, mean total drinking time for a group of six female rats was about 4 minutes, and mean total running time in the same period was only about 0.9 minute. With free access to both food and water, but access to the wheel for only 1 hour per day, mean total drinking time per hour was only about 28 seconds, and mean total running time in the same period was about 329 seconds. Thus it should be

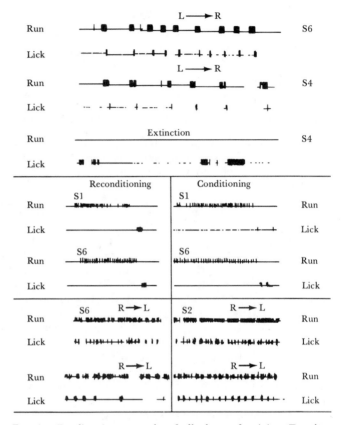

Fig. 1. *Esterline Angus samples of all phases of training. Top three records show the reinforcement of drinking by running* (L → R) *and subsequent extinction of drinking. Middle records compare the lick pattern for conditioning and reconditioning. Bottom records show the reinforcement of running by drinking* (R → L). R *designates running, where each 90 degrees of turn deflected the needle, and* L *represents drinking, where each lick deflected the needle. Records read from right to left.*

possible, according to the present model, not only to reinforce drinking with running but also to reverse the reinforcement relation in the same subject merely by changing from one set of parameters to the other.

Apparatus used to test these predictions was a modified Wahmann activity wheel equipped with a brake and a retractable drinkometer. Joint access to the wheel and water was provided by releasing the brake on the wheel and moving the drinkometer up to a hole on a stationary plate enclosing the open face of the wheel. Drinking contingent upon running was arranged by retracting the drinkometer, freeing the wheel, and making availability of the drinkometer contingent upon running. Conversely, running contingent upon drinking was arranged by locking the wheel, moving in the drinkometer, and making release of the wheel contingent upon drinking.

Because the outcome for the conventional experiment was not in doubt, the case of running contingent upon drinking was tested first.

Four female albino rats, about 200 days old, Sprague-Dawley strain, were given daily 1-hour conditioning sessions, followed by daily 1-hour extinction and reconditioning sessions. A fixed-ratio schedule was used in which each five licks freed the wheel for 10 seconds. Throughout this training, food and water were continuously available in the home cage; after the last reconditioning session water was removed from the home cage, and on the next day training was begun with the reverse contingency—drinking contingent upon running.

With running contingent upon drinking, total drinking time was increased in all subjects by a factor of from three to five. For operant-level drinking, with only the tube present, mean total drinking time was about 28 sec/hr; with both tube and wheel present, it was 23 sec/hr; and with running contingent upon drinking, 98 sec/hr. Moreover, the first extinction session further increased mean total drinking time to about 175 sec/hr.

Samples of all phases of training are shown in the Esterline Angus records of Fig. 1. The top records show the reinforcement of drinking by running in rats S-4 and S-6, characterized by alternating bursts of licking and running. A representative example of extinction—drinking no longer producing the opportunity to run—is provided by the record for rat S-4; both the atypical periodicity and brevity of the lick bursts have largely disappeared. Of interest in the middle records, which show fine-grain examples of conditioning and reconditioning, is the recovery of the noninstrumental lick pattern that followed extinction. Throughout the original conditioning, the five licks or more that were required for running tended to be dispersed, whereas during reconditioning, licking occurred in bursts typical of routine drinking. The picture is completed by the two bottom records; these provide examples of the evident increase in running subsequently produced by the conventional case, where 450 degrees of wheel turn were required for first 10 seconds and later 5 seconds of tube-time. Hence parameters were demonstrated which made running more probable than drinking, and vice versa, and subsequently, that it was possible not only to reinforce drinking with running, but also to reverse the reinforcement relation in the same subjects merely by changing from one set of parameters to the other.

Notes
    [1] Williams and Teitelbaum (1956) have reported the negative reinforcement of drinking—drinking turning off electric shock—but I can find no report of the positive reinforcement of eating and drinking reponses.

References
    Barnes, G. W., & Kish, G. W. *Exp. Psychol.*, 1961, **62**, 164.
    Butler, R. A. *J. Comp. Physiol. Psychol.*, 1953, **46**, 95.
    Hull, C. L. *Principles of Behavior*, New York: Appleton-Century, 1943, pp. 68–83.
    Kish, G. W. *J. Exp. Psychol.*, 1955, **48**, 261.
    Marx, M. X., Henderson, R. L., & Roberts, C. L. *J. Exp. Psychol.*, 1955, **48**, 73.
    Premack, D. *Psychol., Rev.*, 1959, **66**, 219.
    ———. *Exp. Psychol.*, 1961, **61**, 162.
    Skinner, B. F. *The Behavior of Organisms*, New York: Appleton-Century, 1938, pp. 61–115.
    Williams, D. R., & Teitelbaum, P. *Science*, 1956, **124**, 1294–1296.

D. CONDITIONED REINFORCEMENT

If organisms have the right kind of experience with neutral, nonreinforcing events, these events can become reinforcers. This phenomenon of conditioned reinforcement *(sometimes called* secondary reinforcement*) is of great significance for the extension of principles of behavior theory to the explanation of human behavior. Since so little of our behavior produces reinforcers like food, we must be able to explain how money, approval, good grades, and so on come to exert control over our activities.*

The question is, What is the right kind of experience? Early demonstrations of conditioned reinforcement made it seem that stimuli became conditioned reinforcers through Pavlovian pairing with unconditioned reinforcers. A rat might be trained to press a lever, with lever presses producing a click followed by food delivery. Later the rats would press the lever for the click alone. But we know now that pairing of a CS and a US is not enough to produce Pavlovian conditioning; the CS must also be informative. The article by Egger and Miller shows that the same is true of conditioned reinforcement: A neutral stimulus will become a conditioned reinforcer if it is a nonredundant predictor of the unconditioned reinforcer.

The other article in this section is an example of a type of conditioned reinforcement procedure that has become extremely important in applications of behavior theory (see p. 373). Kelleher trained chimpanzees to press a key. Every 125 presses produced a poker chip. When 50 poker chips had been collected, they could be exchanged for food. The chimpanzees responded reliably under these conditions. Thus, using poker chips, it was possible to get chimpanzees to perform 6250 responses between reinforcements. The poker chips are obviously analogous to money. This procedure is known as a token reinforcement *procedure. If tokens are associated with unconditioned reinforcers, organisms will work for the tokens themselves, as long as they are later given an opportunity to "cash them in" for unconditioned reinforcers.*

14 Secondary Reinforcement in Rats as a Function of Information Value and Reliability of the Stimulus

M. DAVID EGGER AND NEAL E. MILLER

Although secondary reinforcement has been of major importance to behavior theory, especially in explanations of complex learning phenomena (e.g., Hull, 1943; Miller, 1951; Skinner, 1938), little is known about the conditions for its occurrence in any but the simplest situations. The first hypothesis explored in the experiments reported here is that in a situation in which there is more than one stimulus predicting primary reinforcement, e.g., food, the more informative stimulus will be the more effective secondary reinforcer. Further it is asserted that a necessary condition for establishing any stimulus as a secondary reinforcer is that the stimulus provide information about the occurrence of primary reinforcement; a redundant predictor of primary reinforcement should not acquire secondary reinforcement strength. [1]

A possible situation in which to test this hypothesis is the following: a short stimulus always precedes the delivery of food. But it is made essentially redundant by being overlapped by a longer stimulus of slightly earlier onset which is also invariably followed by food. This situation is summarized in Fig. 1. The longer stimulus is labeled S_1 and the shorter, S_2. For an S trained with this series of stimulus events, S_2 is a reliable, but redundant, i.e., noninformative, predictor of food. Hence, according to our hypothesis, S_1 should be an effective secondary reinforcer; S_2 should acquire little or no secondary reinforcing strength, even though it is closer in time to the occurrence of food, and therefore in a more favorable position than is S_1 on the gradient of delay of reinforcement.

There is a way, however, to make S_2 informative. If S_1 occurs a number of times without S_2, unaccompanied by the food pellet, and randomly interspersed with occurrences of the stimulus sequence shown at the bottom of Fig. 1, then S_2, when it occurs, is no longer redundant; for now S_2 is the only reliable predictor of food. Thus, it is predicted that for a group of rats who receive the stimulus sequence depicted in Fig. 1 interspersed with occurrences of S_1 alone, S_2 will be a considerably more effective secondary reinforcer than for the group of rats who receive only the stimulus sequence depicted in Fig. 1.

It should be noted that both groups will receive exactly the same number of pairings of S_2 with food and in exactly the same immediate stimulus context, so that if a difference were found between the groups in the secondary reinforcing value of S_2, it could not be due to simple

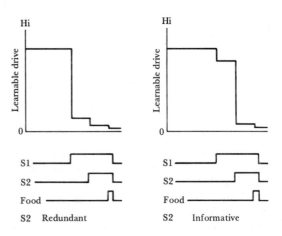

FIG. 1. *Schematic representation of the theoretical analysis of the two Main Experiment groups according to a strict interpretation of the drive-reduction hypothesis.*

patterning, stimulus-generalization decrement, or differences in association with food.

Our predicted results would be compatible with a strict interpretation of the drive-reduction hypothesis of reinforcement (Miller, 1959). Such a theoretical analysis is represented schematically in the upper portion of Fig. 1. According to the drive-reduction hypothesis, a stimulus acquires secondary reinforcing value by acquiring the ability to elicit a drive-reducing response. The left side of Fig. 1 illustrates that if most of the learnable drive already has been reduced by S_1, little drive-reduction remains to be conditioned to S_2. On the other hand, if S_1 sometimes fails to predict food, some of the conditioned drive-reduction to it should extinguish. Hence, as is depicted on the right side of Fig. 1, more of the drive-reduction should occur to, and be conditioned to, S_2.

From Fig. 1, one can also see that the drive-reduction analysis also demands that the secondary reinforcing value of S_1 should be greater when it is a reliable predictor (making S_2 redundant) than when it is an unreliable predictor (making S_2 informative). Thus we are led to our second hypothesis, namely, that in a situation in which a predictor of primary reinforcement exists which is both reliable and informative, this predictor should become a more effective secondary reinforcer than an unreliable predictor. Note that here we predict the opposite of a partial-reinforcement effect, which would be expected to increase the resistance to extinction of the unreliable predictor, that is, the stimulus which had been paired with food only part of the time. In any prolonged test for secondary reinforcement, this increased resistance to extinction should show up as a greater total secondary reinforcing effect.

Main Experiment

Method

Subjects. The Ss were 88 male rats of the Sprague-Dawley strain who were approximately 90 days old at the beginning of their experimental training. Owing to deaths and equipment failures, the data from 4 Ss were lost, and the data from another 4, selected at random, were discarded in order to have equal sized groups for an analysis of variance.

The Ss, fed once daily following the experimental session, were maintained at approximately 80% of their ad lib weight.

Apparatus. The apparatus consisted of two identical Skinner boxes, 19 in. long, 8 in. wide, and 6¾ in. high (inside dimensions). The floors of the boxes consisted of six ½ in.-diameter rods running parallel to the side containing the Plexiglas door. Each box was enclosed in a large, light-proof, sound-deadened crate into which a stream of air was piped for ventilation and masking noise. Inside each of the Skinner boxes were two lights, one located 2 in. above the food cup, another located in the middle of the long back wall, opposite the Plexiglas door. The food cup was in the center of the front, 8-in. wall; the bar, a bent steel strip 1½ in. wide, protruded ½ in. into the inner chamber of the box. The entire bar assembly was removable and, when withdrawn, its opening was sealed with a metal panel. The bar was located to the right of and slightly above the food cup. A downward force of at least 12 gm. on the bar activated a microswitch normally connected in the circuit of a Gerbrands feeder which delivered a standard .045-gm. Noyes pellet into the food cup. A loudspeaker was located 3 in. behind and slightly to the left of the front wall of the Skinner box. Both flashing lights (12 per sec.) and tones (750 cps) were used as stimuli.

Procedure. All training sessions lasted 25 min. per day. During the first three sessions, Ss were magazine-trained in the absence of the bar. Then the bar was inserted, and, for two sessions, each bar press was followed by a pellet of food. A few rats who did not spontaneously learn to press were given an extra remedial session during which bar pressing was "shaped." Over the next four sessions the required ratio of responses to reinforcements was gradually increased to 4:1.

Then, for the subsequent five sessions, the bar was removed, and Ss were randomly assigned to Group A (for whom S_2 was reliable but *redundant*) and Group B (for whom S_2 was reliable and *informative*). Group A received the following sequence of events during each of its five "stimulus-training" sessions: once every 56 sec. on the average, a pellet of food was delivered into the food cup. The pellet was inevitably preceded by 2 sec. of S_1 and 1½ sec. of S_2. Both stimuli overlapped the delivery of the food pellet by ¼ sec., and both terminated together.

Group B also received this stimulus sequence immediately preceding the delivery of the food pellet. But in addition, Group B Ss received aperiodically, interspersed with the stimulus–food sequence, 2 sec. of S_1 alone. The events for Group B occurred on the average of once every 30 sec.

For half the Ss in each group, S_1 was a flashing light and S_2 was a tone, and for the other half, the conditions were reversed: S_1 was a tone and S_2 was a flashing light.

During 5 days of such training, each group received 135 pairings of S_1 and S_2 with food, and Group B received in addition about 110 occurrences of S_1 alone. Thus for both groups S_2 was followed 100% of the time by food, while S_1 was followed by food 100% of the time for Group A, but only 55% of the time for Group B.

The above description of training applies to all but 16 Ss, 8 Group B and 8 Group A. For these Ss, training was exactly as described above except that the stimulus–food pairings occurred for both groups on the average of once every 75 sec. instead of 56 sec. and Group B received a stimulus event on the average of once every 15 sec. instead of 30 sec., so that S_1 was followed by food only 20% of the time for Group B. These 16 Ss were given seven 25-min. "stimulus-training" sessions. The data from these Ss were analyzed separately and not included in the overall analysis of variance.

Testing. On the day following the final stimulus-training session, Ss were tested as follows: the bar was reinserted and Test Session 1 began with each S pressing for food pellets on a fixed ratio of 3:1. The retraining presses continued until S had received 30 pellets. At this point the bar was disconnected and 10 min. of extinction ensued.

At the end of the 10 min., the bar was reconnected, not to the feeder, but to a timer which delivered on the same 3:1 schedule 1 sec. of whatever stimulus was being tested for secondary reinforcing strength. The test session continued until 25 min. had elapsed since the beginning of the extinction period, or until 10 min. after the first occurrence of a stimulus, whichever was longer.

In the foregoing procedure, relearning following experimental extinction was used as the measure of secondary reinforcing strength on the assumption that it would be more rapid and less variable than would de novo learning of the skill of pressing the bar. A preliminary study had validated this technique showing that in such a test more bar presses would occur when followed by a stimulus previously associated with food than when the stimulus had not been associated with food.

After an interval of 1 day, Test Session 2 was conducted, identical to the first, except that this time the stimulus delivered following the 10-min. extinction period was the opposite from that tested in Test Session 1: for half of the Ss, S_2 was tested in Test Session 1 and S_1 was tested in Session 2; for the other half of the Ss, trained and tested subsequent to the first half, the stimuli were tested in the opposite order.

For Ss tested first with S_2 and then with S_1, Test Session 3 followed another intervening day, this time with Ss pressing for S_2 again. Throughout the course of the 10-min. extinction and ensuing "pressing for stimuli" period, the cumulative total number of bar presses for each Ss was recorded each minute.

Response Measures. The total number of bar presses in a 10-min. period following the first occurrence of the stimulus was the measure of secondary reinforcing strength. Since there were significant between-S and within-S correlations ($r_b = .53$; $r_w = .34$) of this measure with the total number of bar presses in the 10-min. extinction periods, this total number of bar presses in extinction was used as a control variable in analyses of covariance. (It should be noted that most of the bar presses during extinction occurred within the first 2–4 min. of the 10-min. extinction period.)

Furthermore, since it was found that in no case would analyses based only on data from Test Session 1 have led to any substantially different conclusions from those reported below, the means and results of analyses reported (unless otherwise noted) are based on combined data from Test Sessions 1 and 2.

Since by Test Session 3, there no longer appeared to be any differences between the experimental groups, the data from this session were not included in the final analyses.

Results

Overall Analysis. Neither of the hypotheses being tested depended upon the significance of the main effects of the overall analysis, but instead upon comparisons between the means shown in specific subcells of Table 1. The marginal entries in Table 1 give the overall means for Groups A and B (rows), and for S_1 and S_2 (columns). The overall mean for each group is based on data from 32 Ss each tested with S_1 and with S_2; the overall mean for each stimulus position is based on data from all 64 Ss.

TABLE 1. Mean Responses during 10 min. of Extinction and 10 min. of "Pressing for Stimuli"

	S_1		S_2		
Group	Ext.	Pressing	Ext.	Pressing	$S_1 + S_2$
A	110.8	115.1	101.9	65.8	90.5
B	112.1	76.1	112.0	82.6	79.4
A + B		95.6		74.2	

Note. Test Sessions 1 and 2 combined.

TABLE 2. Summary of Analysis of Variance and Covariance: Test Sessions 1 and 2 Combined

	Analysis of variance			Analysis of covariance		
Source	df	MS	F	df	MS	F
Between Ss						
Experimental group (G)	1	3,916.12	2.36	1	6,062.17	4.98*
Modality of S_1 (M)	1	7,938.00	4.79*	1	4,792.37	3.93
Order of S_1,S_2 (O)	1	435.13		1	709.44	
G × M	1	2,907.03	1.75	1	573.36	
G × O	1	2,329.03	1.41	1	50.93	
M × O	1	9.03		1	37.41	
G × M × O	1	1,624.50		1	1,382.64	1.14
Error (b)	56	1,657.19		55	1,218.04	(r_b = .53)
Within Ss						
Stimulus position (P)	1	14,663.28	10.83**	1	12,168.39	9.97**
P × G	1	24,864.50	18.36***	1	21,613.81	17.71***
P × M = St	1	15,664.50	11.56**	1	10,316.32	8.45**
P × O = T	1	52,650.13	38.87***	1	1,594.90	1.31
P × G × M	1	87.78		1	546.78	
P × M × O	1	35.13		1	16.45	
P × G × O	1	5,330.28	3.94	1	3,168.95	2.60
P × G × M × O	1	5,781.27	4.27*	1	6,720.79	5.51*
Error (w)	56	1,354.57		55	1,220.64	(r_w = .34)

Note. St = modality of stimulus tested; T = test session (1 or 2).
*P < .05.
**P < .01.
***P < .001.

As seen from an inspection of Tables 1 and 2, Group A responded signif-icantly more than Group B and the position of S_1 was reliably more ef-fective than that of S_2.

It should be noted that although the groups were identically treated in all other respects, the 32 Ss tested with S_1 first and S_2 second were run subsequent to the 32 Ss tested with S_2 first and with S_1 second. No signifi-cant differences between these groups existed in the control variable, total presses in 10 min. of extinction. Nor did an analysis of covariance reveal any significant effects of order of testing (O), or of the interaction of order of testing with experimental group (G), or with stimulus position (P) (see Table 2).

Across all groups, the Ss responded more for the flashing lights than for the tones ($F = 8.45$; $df = 1/55$; $P < .01$, analysis of covariance).

Examination of the minute-by-minute response totals during the "pressing for stimuli" period revealed that the differences between groups tested at 10 min. had generally begun to appear after 3–5 min., and continued to increase out to 15 min., which was the longest period any S was permitted to bar press for stimuli during a given test session.

As expected from our hypotheses, the (P × G) interaction was highly significant ($F = 17.71$; $df = 1/55$; $P < .001$, anallysis of covariance). Hence, we were justified in making within experimental group and stimu-lus position comparisons.

S_2: *Group B vs. Group A*. On the basis of our first hypothesis, we ex-pected that Group B Ss, for whom S_2 was informative, should press more for S_2 than Group A Ss, for whom S_2 was redundant. The difference be-tween the group means on the secondary reinforcing measure was in the predicted direction and significant beyond the .05 level ($F = 4.03$; $df = 1/56$). (The means are given in Table 1). However, the effect was not statistically reliable in an analysis of covariance.

As mentioned above, 16 Ss, 8 each in Groups A and B, were trained with the number of occurrences of S_1 alone for Group B increased so that 80% of the stimulus events for Group B were unaccompanied occur-rences of S_1. For these Ss, tested with S_2 in Test Session 1, the means on the secondary reinforcing measure were in the predicted direction, 97.5 vs. 88.0, but the difference was short of statistical significance. However, when these data were analyzed in an analysis of covariance and combined by means of a critical ratio test with the data discussed above, the pre-dicted effect was significant beyond the .05 level. ($CR = 1.97$ if the data from these 16 Ss are combined with those from the 64 Ss tested with S_2 in Test Session 1 or Test Session 2; $CR = 2.02$ if the data are combined with those from the 32 Ss tested with S_2 in Test Session 1 only.)

S_1: *Group A vs. Group B* Our second hypothesis predicted that S_1 would be a more effective secondary reinforcer for Group A, for whom it was reliable and informative, than for Group B, for whom it was unreliable. This prediction was borne out by the data beyond the .001 level ($F = 15.71$; $df = 1/55$; analysis of covariance).

Group A: S_1 vs. S_2. As predicted from our first hypothesis, S_1 was a much more effective secondary reinforcer than S_2 for Group A. The dif-ference between the means for these two stimulus positions, 115.1 vs. 65.8, was significant beyond the .001 level ($F = 26.35$; $df = 1/27$; analysis of covariance).

Control Experiments

Pseudoconditioned and Unconditioned Control.

Fourteen *S*s, male albino rats, handled exactly as in the Main Experiment, were trained in groups of 7 *S*s each with stimulus sequences identical to those of Groups A and B, except that the stimuli were *never* paired with the occurrence of food, which was delivered at least 10 sec. after the occurrence of the stimuli. The two different patterns of stimuli used in training had no effect upon the pseudoconditioned rate of bar pressing. The mean for the 14 *S*s with both test sessions combined was 64.3. These 14 *S*s bar pressed for the stimuli significantly less in both Test Session 1 ($t = 3.41$; $df = 28$; $P < .005$) and Test Session 2 ($t = 2.72$; $df = 28$; $P < .02$) than did the 16 Group A *S*s bar pressing for the informative stimulus (S_1) in each of the Main Experiment test sessions. Hence, in a group predicted to show a large secondary reinforcing effect, we did indeed find such an effect produced by our training procedure.

Eight *S*s were exposed to the stimuli during training exactly as described above, except that the food pellets were eliminated entirely. The unconditioned rate of pressing for the stimuli was comparable to that of the pseudoconditioned group ($M = 73.4$).

The mean for the total group of pseudoconditioned and unconditioned *S*s with both test sessions combined was 67.6, indicating that the secondary reinforcing value of the redundant stimulus for Group A of the Main Experiment ($M = 65.8$), once the unconditioned rate of pressing for stimuli is taken into account, was small, if not zero, as we predicted from our first hypothesis. The estimates of the pseudoconditioned and unconditioned scores may be somewhat high, however, since these *S*s tended to have higher 10-min. extinction scores than did *S*s of the Main Experiment.

Activation Control.

To test whether the effects studied in the Main Experiment were related to secondary reinforcement or only to a possible activation effect of a stimulus formerly associated with food (Wyckoff, Sidowski, & Chambliss, 1958), 10 additional *S*s were trained exactly as in the Main Experiment, 5 as in Group A and 5 as in Group B. However, during the testing of these *S*s, the bar remained nonfunctional once it was disconnected from the feeder. Each *S* was tested at the same time as an identically trained *S* used in the Main Experiment. The yoked Activation Control *S* received only the stimuli earned by his Main Experiment partner. If the Main Experiment *S* pressed for a stimulus within $7\frac{1}{2}$ sec. of a yoked Activation Control *S*'s response, the stimulus for the Activation Control *S* was delayed so that it was not delivered until $7\frac{1}{2}$ sec. after his response. Hence spurious pairings of stimuli and pressing could not occur.

Thus, for these 10 *S*s, any pressing which occurred during the retraining test period could have been due only to the activation effects of the stimuli plus remaining operant level; the possibility of secondary reinforcement was eliminated.

In Test Session 1, all 10 of the Activation Control *S*s pressed less than did their secondary-reinforced partners ($P < .002$, binomial test, two-tailed). In Test Session 2, 9 out of 10 pressed less than did their yoked partners ($P < .02$, binomial test, two-tailed). Hence, we are quite certain that in the Main Experiment we were indeed studying secondary reinforcement.

Partial Reinforcement Effect Control.

In the Main Experiment we had found that in the presence of a reliable predictor (S_2), training with partial reinforcement of S_1 produced less total pressing for S_1 as a secondary reinforcer than did 100% reinforcement. This confirmed our hypothesis but was opposite to the effect of increased resistance to extinction usually found with partial reinforcement. In order to see whether the presence of the reliable predictor was indeed the crucial factor, we ran two special control groups of 8 Ss each, one with the usual partial reinforcement procedure and one with 100% reinforcement. These groups were identical in all respects to those of the Main Experiment, except that the reliable predictor, S_2, was omitted. When these groups were tested, the partial reinforcement group tended to press more for the stimuli than did the continuous reinforcement group (though the difference between the group means, 128.6 vs. 115.6, was not statistically significant). However, the difference between these two groups was in the opposite direction and significantly different ($F = 5.71$; $df = 1/35$; $P < .025$) from the difference found between Test Session 1 means of the 32 Ss of the Main Experiment tested with S_1 during Test Session 1. Thus it appears that the presence of S_2, the reliable predictor of food, did play the crucial role in determining the direction of the results obtained in our tests of the secondary reinforcing value of S_1.

Discussion

Our situation differed from those in which the effect of partial reinforcement on the establishment of secondary reinforcement has been studied (e.g., Klein, 1959; Zimmerman, 1957, 1959) in that during training all our Ss had a reliable predictor of food. The seemingly crucial importance of the presence or absence of a reliable predictor during training may help to explain the apparently conflicting results obtained from single-group vs. separate-group experimental designs in determining the effects of partial reinforcement on the strength of a secondary reinforcer (e.g., D'Amato, Lachman, & Kivy, 1958). It may be that partial reinforcement will increase resistance to extinction of a secondary reinforcer only if training occurs in the absence of a reliable predictor.

It should be noted that our formulation of the conditions necessary for the establishment of a secondary reinforcer is compatible with the well-known "discriminative stimulus hypothesis" of secondary reinforcement (Keller & Schoenfeld, 1950; Schoenfeld, Antonitis, & Bersh, 1950). Furthermore, our results with respect to S_2: Group B vs. Group A could perhaps be considered analogous to those reported by Notterman (1951) in studies using rats as Ss in both a Skinner box and a straight alley.

Summary

Albino rats ($N = 88$, male) were trained to press a bar for food, then divided randomly into two groups and trained as follows for 135 trials in the same Skinner boxes with the bars removed: two stimuli, when paired, ended together and always preceded food. For Group A, the second, shorter stimulus (S_2) was always redundant because the first stimulus (S_1) had already given reliable information that food was to come. But for Group, B, S_2 was informative, because for them S_1 also occurred sometimes alone without food.

After the training sessions, the bars were reinserted, bar pressing was retrained with food pellets, extinguished, and then retrained again, this time using 1 sec. of one of the training stimuli as a secondary reinforcer in place of the food. The total number of bar presses in 10 min. following the first occurrence of the secondary reinforcing stimulus was used as the measure of secondary reinforcing strength. The testing procedure was repeated after 48 hr. using the other training stimulus as secondary reinforcer, so that all Ss were tested with both stimuli in a balanced sequence.

Conrol experiments were run to provide baseline levels for pseudoconditioned and unconditioned rates of pressing, and for any activating effect of the stimuli.

As predicted, S_2 was a stronger secondary reinforcer when it was informative than when it was redundant; S_1 was a more effective secondary reinforcer than S_2 in that group for which S_2 was a redundant predictor of primary reinforcement. In addition, S_1 was a more effective secondary reinforcer when it had been a reliable predictor of food.

Notes

[1]This study was supported by funds from Grant MY647 from the National Institute of Mental Health, United States Public Health Service. We wish to thank Elizabeth Sherwood for her assistance in running the animals.

A portion of the data reported in this paper was presented by Neal Miller in his Presidential Address to the American Psychological Association.

References

D'Amato, M. R. Lachman, R., & Kivy, P. Secondary reinforcement as affected by reward schedule and the testing situation. *J. Comp. Physiol. Psychol.*, 1958, 51, 737–741.

Hull, C. L. *Principles of behavior.* New York: Appleton-Century, 1943.

Keller, F. S., & Schoenfeld, W. N. *Principles of psychology.* New York: Appleton-Century-Crofts, 1950.

Klein, R. M. Intermittent primary reinforcement as a parameter of secondary reinforcement. *J. Exp. Psychol.*, 1959, 58, 423–427.

Miller, N. E. Learnable drives and rewards. In S. S. Stevens (Ed.), *Handbook of experimental psychology.* New York: Wiley, 1951, Pp. 435–472.

Miller, N. E. Liberalization of basic S–R concepts: Extensions to conflict behavior, motivation, and social learning. In S. Koch (Ed.), *Psychology: A study of a science.* Vol. 2. New York: McGraw-Hill, 1959. Pp. 196–292.

Miller, N. E. Analytical studies of drive and reward. *Amer. Psychologist*, 1961, 16, 739–754.

Notterman, J. M. A study of some relations among aperiodic reinforcement, discrimination training, and secondary reinforcement. *J. Exp. Psychol.*, 1951, 41, 161–169.

Schoenfeld, W. N. Antonitis, J. J., & Bersh, P. J. A preliminary study of training conditions necessary for secondary reinforcement. *J. Exp. Psychol.*, 1950, 40, 40–45.

Skinner, B. F. *The behavior of organisms.* New York: Appleton-Century, 1938.

Wyckoff, L. B., Sidowski, J., & Chambliss, D. J. An experimental study of the relationship between secondary reinforcing and cue effects of a stimulus. *J. Comp. Physiol. Psychol.*, 1958, 51, 103–109.

Zimmerman, D. W. Durable secondary reinforcement: Method and theory. *Psychol. Rev.*, 1957, 64, 373–383.

Zimmerman, D. W. Sustained performance in rats based on secondary reinforcement. *J. Comp. Physiol. Psychol.*, 1959, 52, 353–358.

15 Fixed-Ratio Schedules of Conditioned Reinforcement with Chimpanzees

ROGER T. KELLEHER

In earlier studies of conditioned reinforcement, I investigated both fixed-interval and multiple schedules with fixed-interval and fixed-ratio components (2, 3, 4). These studies demonstrated several similarities between the characteristics of behavior maintained by conditioned reinforcers and behavior maintained by food reinforcers. However, one consistent difference was found in the general trend toward higher response rates as the time approached when the conditioned reinforcers could be exchanged for food. The purpose of this experiment was to extend the results of these earlier studies by elucidating the characteristics of performance maintained by fixed-ratio schedules of conditioned reinforcement.[1]

Subjects

The two Ss were 7-year old chimpanzees (Yerkes Laboratories, No. 117 and 119) maintained at about 80 per cent of normal body weight. The experimental histories of these animals, which included thousands of hours on schedules of conditioned reinforcement, have been presented previously (2, 3, 4).

Apparatus and Procedure

The animals had been trained to obtain poker chips (conditioned reinforcers) by pressing a telephone key in the presence of a white light. When 60 poker chips had been delivered or when 8 hours had elapsed, the white light went off and a red light appeared. When the white light was off, presses on the telephone key were ineffective. The animals had been trained to obtain food by inserting the poker chips through a slotted Plexiglas window in the presence of the red light. When the red light was off, poker-chip insertions were recorded but were otherwise ineffective. The animals were not physically restrained from inserting poker chips at any time. Further details concerning apparatus and procedure are presented elsewhere (2, 3, 4).

A 30-response, fixed-ratio schedule (FR 30) of conditioned reinforcement was in effect for 30 sessions. Under this schedule, one poker chip was delivered for every 30 presses on the telephone key. Over the next 10 sessions, the response requirement was gradually increased from FR 30 to FR 100. Each S had three sessions on FR 100. Following these three sessions, multiple schedules and variable-interval schedules were investigated for 3 months. The Ss were then returned to FR 60, and the

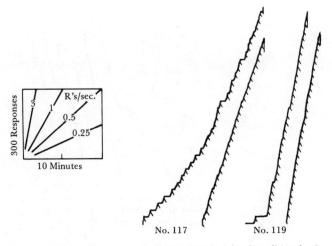

FIG. 1. *Final performances on the FR 30 schedule of conditioned reinforcement. The cumulative-response records have been telescoped along the abcissa as described by Ferster and Skinner (1, pg. 27). The short diagonal lines indicate the deliveries of poker chips which were exchanged for food at the end of each session. Coordinates and representative response rates are presented at the left of the figure.*

response requirement was gradually increased to FR 125 over 10 sessions. On FR 125 the Ss were required to obtain only 50 poker chips before the red light appeared to indicate that exchange for food was possible. After 20 sessions on FR 125, the poker-chip magazine was disconnected for a 6-hour extinction session. Each S was given 50 poker chips at the start of both the fortieth and fiftieth sessions on 125, but was still required to work for another 50 poker chips before exchange for food was possible. Each S had 60 sessions on FR 125.

Results

The individual rates of responding were bi-valued; that is, S was either not responding (pausing) or responding at a high, stable rate (the running rate). Figure 1 shows records on FR 30 for each S. Brief pauses usually occurred following poker-chip deliveries, but became less frequent in the later part of each session. The running rates were stable at 2 responses per second for No. 117 and 3 responses per second for No. 119.

Figure 2 shows the effects of increasing the response requirement to FR 100. The pauses in the early portions of each session became more prolonged, and the running rates were higher than at FR 30. Running rates were 3 responses per second for No. 117 and 4 responses per second for No. 119.

When the animals were returned from the variable-interval schedule to the FR 60 schedule of conditioned reinforcement, they rapidly recovered performances similar to those shown in Fig. 2. Once again as the response requirement was increased, the initial pauses became more prolonged and the running rates higher. Figure 3 shows a representative session on FR 125. One new characteristic of performance emerged

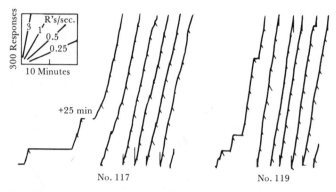

FIG. 2.   *Complete sessions on an FR 100 schedule of conditioned rein-forcement. A 25-minute pause was omitted from the record of No. 117 as indicated by the break in the record.*

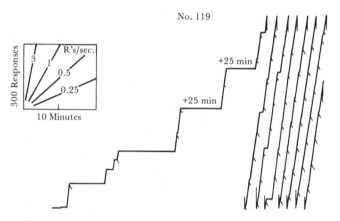

FIG. 3.   *Record of the tenth session for No. 119 on FR 125. Periods of pausing were omitted as indicated.*

clearly after experience on FR 125. The prolonged pauses which continued to occur in the early portions of each session were often initiated after responding had begun; that is, the running rates were interrupted by pauses. After several poker chips had been obtained, these running rates were sustained for the remainder of the session. When occasional brief pauses did occur, they usually followed poker-chip deliveries. The running rate of No. 117 was 3 responses per second, but in every other way the records of No. 117 at FR 125 were similar to those of No. 119. If the running rates which prevailed near the end of each session had been sustained throughout, each session would have ended within 35 minutes.

Segments from the first 2 hours of the extinction sessions are presented in Fig. 4. The pausing at the start of the session was followed by an abrupt shift to the running rates which had prevailed in the later portions of each session on FR 125. Number 117 sustained this running rate until about 1200 responses had been emitted, and No. 119 alternated bursts of

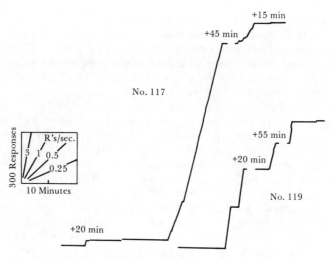

FIG. 4. *Records of the first 2 hours of extinction following FR 125. Periods of pausing were omitted as indicated, and the last 4 hours of the session were omitted.*

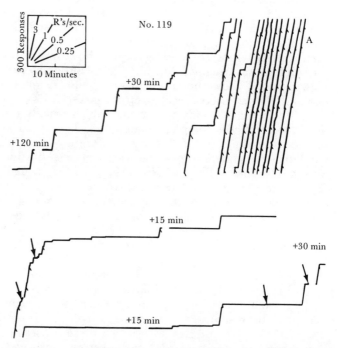

FIG. 5. *Cumulative-response records from a session in which poker chips could not be exchanged for food until 8 hours had elapsed. The two curves at the bottom of the figure are a continuation of the curves at the top. Periods of pausing were omitted as indicated, and the last part of this session was omitted.*

responding with increasing pauses until about 750 responses had been emitted. Both Ss responded only sporadically over the remainder of the extinction session. Except for the initial pauses, these extinction records are similar to those obtained after comparable schedules of food reinforcement; that is, most responding occurred at the running rates which had prevailed on FR 125.

Because of an apparatus failure in a subsequent session, the red light did not appear when 60 poker chips had been delivered. In fact, it appeared only after 8 hours had elapsed. The white light remained on for these 8 hours, and poker chips inserted during this time were wasted. The performances of both Ss were similar in this session, and only the records of No. 119 are presented in Fig. 5. The poker-chip magazine, which held approximately 103 poker chips, was emptied at about A. In the records just before A, No. 119 emitted 9000 responses at a rate of more than 3 responses per second. It is clear that S could sustain this high rate for at least 50 minutes. The two curves in the lower portion of Fig. 5 can be considered as another period of extinction, differing in at least two ways from the extinction curves of Fig. 4. During the session shown in Fig. 5, the poker-chip magazine continued to operate and S had in its possession the poker chips obtained in the first portion of the session. This extinction curve is, however, similar to those shown in Fig. 4. That No. 117 wasted only two and No. 119 only four poker chips indicates the extent to which the red light controlled poker-chip insertions.

The A records in Figs. 6 and 7 show representative performances on FR 125. Prolonged pauses prevailed for at least 2 hours at the start of each session. Once responding began, however, it was sustained except for brief pauses usually following poker-chip deliveries. The B records in Figs. 6 and 7 show the cumulative-response records from the following session in which each S was given 50 poker chips at the start of the session. The initial periods of pausing, which usually totalled more than 2 hours, were almost completely abolished. The 5-to 10-minute pauses that did occur at the start of this session were accompanied by hyperactivity, handling the poker chips, and vocalizations. In this session, No. 117 wasted one poker chip and No. 119, four. Occasionally, No. 119 wasted one or two poker chips late in control sessions, as shown in Fig. 7a; however, No. 117 never wasted poker chips in control sessions. In the sessions following those shown in the B records, both Ss again showed prolonged initial pausing. This procedure was repeated in a later session, and the same effects were observed with both animals.

Discussion

Performance on FR schedules of food reinforcement is characterized by high, stable rates of responding. Pauses may occur before responding begins if the response requirement is high (1, 6) or if sessions are prolonged (5). The frequency with which these pauses occur and their duration tend to increase as each session proceeds. These general characteristics were confirmed in the present investigation of FR schedules of conditioned reinforcement; however, the pauses in the first few FR segments of each session were extremely prolonged, and the animals often stopped responding before completing a ratio at FR 125. This gen-

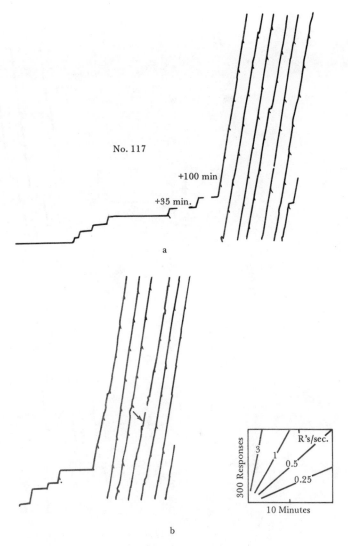

No. 117

+100 min

+35 min.

a

300 Responses

R's/sec.

3   1

0.5

0.25

10 Minutes

b

FIG. 6. *(a) FR 125; (b) the effect of delivering 50 poker chips at the start of a session. Arrows indicate poker-chip insertions.*

eral trend toward more sustained responding late in each session confirms the results found with other schedules of conditioned reinforcement.

The results demonstrate that the animals could sustain high response rates long enough to obtain more than 50 poker chips. (See Fig. 5). Indeed, they could have obtained 50 poker chips on FR 125 within 35 minutes if they had started responding at the start of each session. Thus, the prolonged initial pauses, which substantially delayed the receipt of food, are due to some aspect of conditioned reinforcement.

Informal observations indicated that the Ss were very inactive at the start of each session. They became extremely active when they had nu-

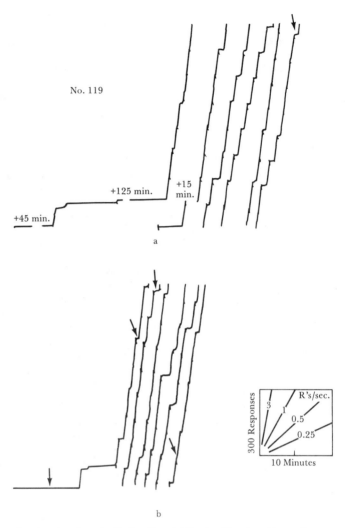

Fig. 7.   (a) FR 125; (b) the effect of delivering 50 poker chips at the start of a session. Arrows indicate poker-chip insertions.

merous poker chips, and continually manipulated several poker chips with one hand. Often, they held several poker chips in their mouths and rattled these against their teeth by vigorous head movements. All this activity was accompanied by high rates of responding as well as the screaming and barking which usually occurred during daily feedings in the home cages.

The formal as well as the informal observations suggested the feasibility of interpreting the FR schedule of conditioned reinforcement as a *chained FR schedule* (1). The delivery of each poker chip serves as a conditioned reinforcer for the preceding FR and increases the number of poker chips in the animal's possession. Since the number of poker chips in the animal's possession varies directly with the number of FR segments that have been completed, these poker chips could act as discriminative stimuli indicating the approach of the period of exchange for food. In the study of chained FR schedules with pigeons, for example, a different stimulus is associated with each component of the chain, and the response rates in each component vary directly with the proximity of food delivery. These differential response rates can be temporarily reversed by reversing the sequence of stimuli, If the chaining interpretation is applicable to the present procedure, high response rates might possibly be produced at the start of a session by when the stimuli are introduced which are usually present near the end of the session. This was accomplished by providing each animal with 50 poker chips at the start of a session. This change in procedure did generate high response rates and hyperactivity at the start of the session. Although this procedure was not repeated over several sessions in succession, the change in performance probably would last only until the animals formed a new discrimination. The stimulus control of the initial pausing, which could be characterized as a sort of psychological strain (6), is apparently quite powerful. Variables which would attenuate this control, especially those which might have more lasting effects, would certainly be of interest.

The development and maintenance of behavior by effective conditioned reinforcers is important for gaining an understanding of the behavioral processes involved in conditioned reinforcement *per se;* however, the technical advantages of having effective conditioned reinforcers should not be overlooked. Many reinforcers have immediate physiological effects which have a strong influence on subsequent behavior. For example, if food is the reinforcer, there may be progressive satiation as each session proceeds. The present method would enable one to investigate behavioral processes independently of the effects of food ingestion during a session. Such considerations could be crucial if one were attempting to use a drug as a reinforcer. For example, animals might work for ethyl alcohol, but progressive intoxication would influence results. With the use of poker chips which could be exchanged for alcohol, the reinforcing properties of the drug could be assessed in the absence of these side effects.

Summary

Ss pressed a telephone key to obtain conditioned reinforcers (poker chips) which could be exchanged for food at the end of each session. Fixed-ratio schedules of conditioned reinforcement ranging from FR 30 to FR 125 were investigated. The results were comparable to results obtained with FR schedules of food reinforcement except for prolonged pauses at the start of each session at the higher FR values. These prolonged pauses were eliminated when each S was given 50 poker chips at the start of a session. The results were discussed with respect to previous studies of conditioned reinforcement.

Notes
[1] This investigation was supported in part by Research Grant M-1005 from the Institute of Mental Health of the National Institutes of Health, U.S. Public Health Service, and in part by the National Science Foundation. This paper was presented at the annual meeting of the Eastern Psychological Association, Phila., Pa., April 1958.

References
1. Ferster, C. B., and Skinner, B. F. *Schedules of reinforcement.* New York: Appleton-Century-Crofts, 1957.
2. Kelleher, R. T. Intermittent conditioned reinforcement in chimpanzees. *Science,* 1956, **124,** 679–680.
3. Kelleher, R. T. Conditioned reinforcement in chimpanzees. *J. Comp. Physio. Psychol.,* 1957, **49,** 571–575.
4. Kelleher, R. T. A multiple schedule of conditioned reinforcement with chimpanzees. *Psychol. Rep.,* 1957, **3,** 485–491.
5. Sidman, M., and Stebbins, W. C. Satiation effects under fixed-ratio schedules of reinforcement. *J. Comp. Physiol. Psychol.,* 1954, **47,** 114–116.
6. Skinner, B. F. *Science and human behavior,* New York: Macmillan, 1953.

E. WHEN ORGANISMS MISBEHAVE

The law of effect clearly exerts powerful control over an organism's behavior, but there are circumstances in which other influences on behavior are even more powerful. This section presents a dramatic example by Breland and Breland. They describe some of their occasional failures in attempts to use the law of effect to induce animals to perform various entertaining stunts. What the Brelands report is a series of cases in which animals engage in activities that are counterproductive, that prevent reinforcement. In some cases, these activities emerge only after the animals have had prolonged experience responding under the control of reinforcement. According to the Brelands, these examples of "misbehavior" share a common feature, a feature they call "instructive drift." Under the right circumstances, biologically determined, species-typical behavior patterns will occur and persist at the cost of food. These instinctive behavior patterns are not themselves the product of the law of effect, and they override it. The lesson in these misbehaviors is that any complete account of behavior must involve an understanding of instinctive behavior along with an understanding of Pavlovian and operant conditioning.

16 The Misbehavior of Organisms

KELLER BRELAND AND MARIAN BRELAND

There seems to be a continuing realization by psychologists that perhaps the white rat cannot reveal everything there is to know about behavior. Among the voices raised on this topic, Beach (1950) has emphasized the necessity of widening the range of species subjected to experimental techniques and conditions. However, psychologists as a whole do not seem to be heeding these admonitions, as Whalen (1961) has pointed out.

Perhaps this reluctance is due in part to some dark precognition of what they might find in such investigations, for the ethologists Lorenz (1950, p. 233) and Tinbergen (1951, p. 6) have warned that if psychologists are to understand and predict the behavior of organisms, it is essential that they become thoroughly familiar with the instinctive behavior patterns of each new species they essay to study. Of course, the Watsonian or neobehavioristically oriented experimenter is apt to consider *instinct* an ugly word. He tends to class it with Hebb's (1960) other "seditious notions" which were discarded in the behavioristic revolution, and he may have some premonition that he will encounter this bête noir in extending the range of species and situations studied.

We can assure him that his apprehensions are well grounded. In our attempt to extend a behavioristically oriented approach to the engineering control of animal behavior by operant conditioning techniques, we have fought a running battle with the seditious notion of instinct.[1] It might be of some interest to the psychologist to know how the battle is going and to learn something about the nature of the adversary he is likely to meet if and when he tackles new species in new learning situations.

Our first report (Breland & Breland, 1951) in the *American Psychologist*, concerning our experiences in controlling animal behavior, was wholly affirmative and optimistic, saying in essence that the principles derived from the laboratory could be applied to the extensive control of behavior under nonlaboratory conditions throughout a considerable segment of the phylogenetic scale.

When we began this work, it was our aim to see if the science would work beyond the laboratory, to determine if animal psychology could stand on its own feet as an engineering discipline. These aims have been realized. We have controlled a wide range of animal behavior and have made use of the great popular appeal of animals to make it an economically feasible project. Conditioned behavior has been exhibited at various municipal zoos and museums of natural history and has been used for department store displays, for fair and trade convention exhibits, for entertainment at tourist attractions, on television shows, and in the production of television commercials. Thirty-eight species, totaling over 6,000 indi-

"The Misbehavior of Organisms" by Keller Breland and Marian Breland. *American Psychologist*, 1961, *16*, 681–684. Copyright 1961 by the American Psychological Association. Reprinted by permission of the publisher and author.

vidual animals, have been conditioned, and we have dared to tackle such unlikely subjects as reindeer, cockatoos, raccoons, porpoises, and whales.

Emboldened by this consistent reinforcement, we have ventured further from the security of the Skinner box. However, in this cavalier extrapolation, we have run afoul of a persistent pattern of discomforting failures. These failures, although disconcertingly frequent and seemingly diverse, fall into a very interesting pattern. They all represent breakdowns of conditioned operant behavior. From a great number of such experiences, we have selected, more or less at random, the following examples.

The first instance of our discomfiture might be entitled "What Makes Sammy Dance?" In the exhibit in which this occurred, the casual observer sees a grown bantam chicken emerge from a retaining compartment when the door automatically opens. The chicken walks over about 3 feet, pulls a rubber loop on a small box which starts a repeated auditory stimulus pattern (a four-note tune). The chicken then steps up onto an 18-inch, slightly raised disc, thereby closing a timer switch, and scratches vigorously, round and round, over the disc for 15 seconds, at the rate of about two scratches per second until the automatic feeder fires in the retaining compartment. The chicken goes into the compartment to eat, thereby automatically shutting the door. The popular interpretation of this behavior pattern is that the chicken has turned on the "juke box" and "dances."

The development of this behavioral exhibit was wholly unplanned. In the attempt to create quite another type of demonstration which required a chicken simply to stand on a platform for 12–15 seconds, we found that over 50% developed a very strong and pronounced scratch pattern, which tended to increase in persistence as the time interval was lengthened. (Another 25% or so developed other behaviors—pecking at spots, etc.) However, we were able to change our plans so as to make use of the scratch pattern, and the result was the "dancing chicken" exhibit described above.

In this exhibit the only real contingency for reinforcement is that the chicken must depress the platform for 15 seconds. In the course of a performing day (about 3 hours for each chicken) a chicken may turn out over 10,000 unnecessary, virtually identical responses. Operant behaviorists would probably have little hesitancy in labeling this an example of Skinnerian "superstition" (Skinner, 1948) or "mediating" behavior, and we list it first to whet their explanatory appetite.

However, a second instance involving a raccoon does not fit so neatly into this paradigm. The response concerned the manipulation of money by the raccoon (who has "hands" rather similar to those of the primates). The contingency for reinforcement was picking up the coins and depositing them in a 5-inch metal box.

Raccoons condition readily, have good appetites, and this one was quite tame and an eager subject. We anticipated no trouble. Conditioning him to pick up the first coin was simple. We started out by reinforcing him for picking up a single coin. Then the metal container was introduced, with the requirement that he drop the coin into the container. Here we ran into the first bit of difficulty: he seemed to have a great deal of trouble letting go of the coin. He would rub it up against the inside of the container, pull it back out, and clutch it firmly for several seconds. However, he would finally turn it loose and receive his food reinforcement. Then the final contingency: we put him on a ratio of 2, requiring that he pick up both coins and put them in the container.

Now the raccoon really had problems (and so did we). Not only could he not let go of the coins, but he spent seconds, even minutes, rubbing them together (in a most miserly fashion), and dipping them into the container. He carried on this behavior to such an extent that the practical application we had in mind—a display featuring a raccoon putting money in a piggy bank—simply was not feasible. The rubbing behavior became worse and worse as time went on, in spite of nonreinforcement.

For the third instance, we return to the galinaceous birds. The observer sees a hopper full of oval plastic capsules which contain small toys, charms, and the like. When the S_D (a light) is presented to the chicken, she pulls a rubber loop which releases one of these capsules onto a slide, about 16 inches long, inclined at about 30 degrees. The capsule rolls down the slide and comes to rest near the end. Here one or two sharp, straight pecks by the chicken will knock it forward off the slide and out to the observer, and the chicken is then reinforced by an automatic feeder. This is all very well—most chickens are able to master these contingencies in short order. The loop pulling presents no problems; she then has only to peck the capsule off the slide to get her reinforcement.

However, a good 20% of all chickens tried on this set of contingencies fail to make the grade. After they have pecked a few capsules off the slide, they begin to grab at the capsules and drag them backwards into the cage. Here they pound them up and down on the floor of the cage. Of course, this results in no reinforcement for the chicken, and yet some chickens will pull in over half of all the capsules presented to them.

Almost always this problem behavior does not appear until after the capsules begin to move down the slide. Conditioning is begun with stationary capsules placed by the experimenter. When the pecking behavior becomes strong enough, so that the chicken is knocking them off the slide and getting reinforced consistently, the loop pulling is conditioned to the light. The capsules then come rolling down the slide to the chicken. Here most chickens, who before did not have this tendency, will start grabbing and shaking.

The fourth incident also concerns a chicken. Here the observer sees a chicken in a cage about 4 feet long which is placed alongside a miniature baseball field. The reason for the cage is the interesting part. At one end of the cage is an automatic electric feed hopper. At the other is an opening through which the chicken can reach and pull a loop on a bat. If she pulls the loop hard enough the bat (solenoid operated) will swing, knocking a small baseball up the playing field. If it gets past the miniature toy players on the field and hits the back fence, the chicken is automatically reinforced with food at the other end of the cage. If it does not go far enough, or hits one of the players, she tries again. This results in behavior on an irregular ratio. When the feeder sounds she then runs down the length of the cage and eats.

Our problems began when we tried to remove the cage for photography. Chickens that had been well conditioned in this behavior became wildly excited when the ball started to move. They would jump up on the playing field, chase the ball all over the field, even knock it off on the floor and chase it around, pecking it in every direction, although they had never had access to the ball before. This behavior was so persistent and so disruptive, in spite of the fact that it was never reinforced, that we had to reinstate the cage.

The last instance we shall relate in detail is one of the most annoying and baffling for a good behaviorist. Here a pig was conditioned to pick up large wooden coins and deposit them in a large "piggy bank." The coins were placed several feet from the bank and the pig required to carry them to the bank and deposit them, usually four or five coins for one reinforcement. (Of course, we started out with one coin near the bank.)

Pigs condition very rapidly, they have no trouble taking ratios, they have ravenous appetites (naturally), and in many ways are among the most tractable animals we have worked with. However, this particular problem behavior developed in pig after pig, usually after a period of weeks or months, getting worse every day. At first the pig would eagerly pick up one dollar, carry it to the bank, run back, get another, carry it rapidly and neatly, and so on, until the ratio was complete. Thereafter, over a period of weeks the behavior would become slower and slower. He might run over eagerly for each dollar, but on the way back, instead of carrying the dollar and depositing it simply and cleanly, he would repeatedly drop it, root it, drop it again, root it along the way, pick it up, toss it up in the air, drop it, root it some more, and so on.

We thought this behavior might simply be the dilly-dallying of an animal on a low drive. However, the behavior persisted and gained in strength in spite of a severely increased drive—he finally went through the ratios so slowly that he did not get enough to eat in the course of a day. Finally it would take the pig about 10 minutes to transport four coins a distance of about 6 feet. This problem behavior developed repeatedly in successive pigs.

There have also been other instances: hamsters that stopped working in a glass case after four or five reinforcements, porpoises and whales that swallow their manipulanda (balls and inner tubes), cats that will not leave the area of the feeder, rabbits that will not go to the feeder, the great difficulty in many species of conditioning vocalization with food reinforcement, problems in conditioning a kick in a cow, the failure to get appreciably increased effort out of the ungulates with increased drive, and so on. These we shall not dwell on in detail, nor shall we discuss how they might be overcome.

These egregious failures came as a rather considerable shock to us, for there was nothing in our background in behaviorism to prepare us for such gross inabilities to predict and control the behavior of animals with which we had been working for years.

The examples listed we feel represent a clear and utter failure of conditioning theory. They are far from what one would normally expect on the basis of the theory alone. Furthermore, they are definite, observable;

the diagnosis of theory failure does not depend on subtle statistical interpretations or on semantic legerdemain—the animal simply does not do what he has been conditioned to do.

It seems perfectly clear that, with the possible exception of the dancing chicken, which could conceivably, as we have said, be explained in terms of Skinner's superstition paradigm, the other instances do not fit the behavioristic way of thinking. Here we have animals, after having been conditioned to a specific learned response, gradually drifting into behaviors that are entirely different from those which were conditioned. Moreover, it can easily be seen that these particular behaviors to which the animals drift are clear-cut examples of instinctive behaviors having to do with the natural food getting behaviors of the particular species.

The dancing chicken is exhibiting the gallinaceous birds' scratch pattern that in nature often precedes ingestion. The chicken that hammers capsules is obviously exhibiting instinctive behavior having to do with breaking open of seed pods or the killing of insects, grubs, etc. The raccoon is demonstrating so-called "washing behavior." The rubbing and washing response may result, for example, in the removal of the exoskeleton of a crayfish. The pig is rooting or shaking—behaviors which are strongly built into this species and are connected with the food getting repertoire.

These patterns to which the animals drift require greater physical output and therefore are a violation of the so-called "law of least effort." And most damaging of all, they stretch out the time required for reinforcement when nothing in the experimental setup requires them to do so. They have only to do the little tidbit of behavior to which they were conditioned—for example, pick up the coin and put it in the container —to get reinforced immediately. Instead, they drag the process out for a matter of minutes when there is nothing in the contingency which forces them to do this. Moreover, increasing the drive merely intensifies this effect.

It seems obvious that these animals are trapped by strong instinctive behaviors, and clearly we have here a demonstration of the prepotency of such behavior patterns over those which have been conditioned.

We have termed this phenomenon "instinctive drift." The general principle seems to be that wherever an animal has strong instinctive behaviors in the area of the conditioned response, after continued running the organism will drift toward the instinctive behavior to the detriment of the conditioned behavior and even to the delay or preclusion of the reinforcement. In a very boiled-down, simplified form, it might be stated as "learned behavior drifts toward instinctive behavior."

All this, of course, is not to disparage the use of conditioning techniques, but is intended as a demonstration that there are definite weaknesses in the philosophy underlying these techniques. The pointing out of such weaknesses should make possible a worthwhile revision in behavior theory.

The notion of instinct has now become one of our basic concepts in an effort to make sense of the welter of observations which confront us. When behaviorism tossed out instinct, it is our feeling that some of its power of prediction and control were lost with it. From the foregoing examples, it appears that although it was easy to banish the Instinctivists from the science during the Behavioristic Revolution, it was not possible to banish instinct so easily.

And if, as Hebb suggests, it is advisable to reconsider those things that behaviorism explicitly threw out, perhaps it might likewise be advisable to examine what they tacitly brought in—the hidden assumptions which led most disastrously to these breakdowns in the theory.

Three of the most important of these tacit assumptions seem to us to be: that the animal comes to the laboratory as a virtual *tabula rasa*, that species differences are insignificant, and that all responses are about equally conditionable to all stimuli.

It is obvious, we feel, from the foregoing account, that these assumptions are no longer tenable. After 14 years of continuous conditioning and observation of thousands of animals, it is our reluctant conclusion that the behavior of any species cannot be adequately understood, predicted, or controlled without knowledge of its instinctive patterns, evolutionary history, and ecological niche.

In spite of our early successes with the application of behavioristically oriented conditioning theory, we readily admit now that ethological facts and attitudes in recent years have done more to advance our practical control of animal behavior than recent reports from American "learning labs."

Moreover, as we have recently discovered, if one begins with evolution and instinct as the basic format for the science, a very illuminating viewpoint can be developed which leads naturally to a drastically revised and simplified conceptual framework of startling explanatory power (to be reported elsewhere).

It is hoped that this playback on the theory will be behavioral technology's partial repayment to the academic science whose impeccable empiricism we have used so extensively.

Notes

[1] In view of the fact that instinctive behaviors may be common to many zoological species, we consider *species specific* to be a sanitized misnomer, and prefer the possibly septic adjective *instinctive*.

References

Beach, F. A. The snark was a boojum. *Amer. Psychologist,* 1950, **5,** 115–124.

Breland, K., & Breland, M. A field of applied animal psychology. *Amer. Psychologist,* 1951, **6,** 202–204.

Hebb, D. O. The American revolution. *Amer. Psychologist,* 1960, **15,** 735–745.

Lorenz, K. Innate behavior patterns. In *Symposia of the Society for Experimental Biology.* No. 4. *Physiological mechanisms in animal behavior.* New York: Academic Press, 1950.

Skinner, B. F. Superstition in the pigeon. *J. Exp. Psychol.,* 1948, **38,** 168–172.

Tinbergen, N. *The study of instinct.* Oxford: Clarendon, 1951.

Whalen, R. E. Comparative psychology. *Amer. Psychologist,* 1961, **16,** 84.

Part III
Avoidance Learning

If a contingency is arranged so that a response eliminates a noxious or aversive stimulus, animals learn to perform the response. This kind of contingency between response and reinforcement is known as *escape.* Thus rats learn to press a lever, run down an alley, or jump across a hurdle to escape electric shock, and there is nothing mysterious in their ability to do this. But if a contingency is arranged so that a response prevents the occurrence of an aversive stimulus, animals also learn to perform the response. This kind of response–reinforcer contingency is known as *avoidance,* and from the perspective of the law of effect it is mysterious; for what is the reinforcer of avoidance responding? Can the absence of an event (like shock) be a reinforcer? It is difficult to think of the absence of an event as a reinforcer without also thinking that the animal expects that event if it does not respond; but the law of effect was intended to explain behavior without having to appeal to what organisms expect.

For this reason, the phenomenon of avoidance learning has generated a great deal of inquiry in behavior theory. In this section we present articles that illustrate four quite different explanations of avoidance: one that suggests that avoidance is not really avoidance at all, one that suggests explaining it is not really a problem, one that suggests we cannot explain avoidance without appealing to what animals expect, and one that appeals to biologically determined, species-typical behavior patterns.

A. TWO-FACTOR THEORY

A most ingenious and influential attempt to explain avoidance learning argued that avoidance was not really avoidance at all. Consider a rat being trained to jump across a barrier to avoid shock. A tone comes on for a few seconds, after which a shock is delivered. If the animal jumps during the shock, it escapes; but if it jumps during the tone, it avoids. Rats learn to jump during the tone. According to what has come to be known as two-factor theory, *the rat's avoidance response is actually an escape response. Through Pavlovian pairing, the tone comes to evoke fear just as the shock does. When the animal jumps to avoid shock, it is actually jumping to escape from the fear-provoking tone (Mowrer, 1947; Rescorla and Solomon, 1967). Thus the name "two-factor theory": One factor is the Pavlovian conditioning of fear; the other is the operant conditioning of escape. The following article, a classic demonstration by Miller, is designed to show that a stimulus paired with shock can motivate operant escape behavior. Rats learn to run in a wheel and press a lever when the consequence of these responses is to permit them to escape from a compartment that had been associated with shock. It is a small step from this demonstration to the argument that avoidance learning is also just escape from fear-provoking conditioned stimuli.*

17 Studies of Fear as an Acquirable Drive: I. Fear as Motivation and Fear-Reduction as Reinforcement in the Learning of New Responses

NEAL E. MILLER

An important role in human behavior is played by drives, such as fears, or desires for money, approval, or status, which appear to be learned during the socialization of the individual (1, 12, 16, 17, 18,). While some studies have indicated that drives can be learned (2, 8, 15), the systematic experimental investigation of acquired drives has been scarcely begun. A great deal more work has been done on the innate, or primary drives such as hunger, thirst, and sex.[1]

Fear is one of the most important of the acquirable drives because it can be acquired so readily and can become so strong. The great strength which fear can possess has been experimentally demonstrated in studies of conflict behavior. In one of these studies (3) it was found that albino rats, trained to run down an alley to secure food at a distinctive place and motivated by 46-hour hunger, would pull with a force of 50 gm. if they were restrained near the food. Other animals, that had learned to run away from the end of the same alley to escape electric shock, pulled with a force of 200 gm. when they were restrained near that place on trials during which they were not shocked and presumably were motivated only by fear. Furthermore, animals that were first trained to run to the end of the alley to secure food and then given a moderately strong electric shock there remained well away from the end of the alley, demonstrating that the habits motivated by fear were prepotent over those motivated by 46-hour hunger (9).[2] This experimental evidence is paralleled by many clinical observations which indicate that fear (or anxiety as it is called when its source is vague or obscured by repression) plays a leading role in the production of neurotic behavior (5, 6).

The purpose of the present experiment was to determine whether or not once fear is established as a new response to a given situation, it will exhibit the following functional properties characteristic of primary drives, such as hunger: (a) when present motivate so-called random behavior and (b) when suddenly reduced serve as a reinforcement to produce learning of the immediately preceding response.

Apparatus and Procedure

The apparatus used in this experiment is illustrated in Fig. 1. It consisted of two compartments: one white with a grid as a floor and the other black with a smooth solid floor. Both of these had a glass front to

"Studies of Fear as an Acquirable Drive: I. Fear as Motivation and Fear-Reduction as Reinforcement in the Learning of New Responses" by Neal E. Miller. *Journal of Experimental Psychology*, 1948, *38*, 89-101.

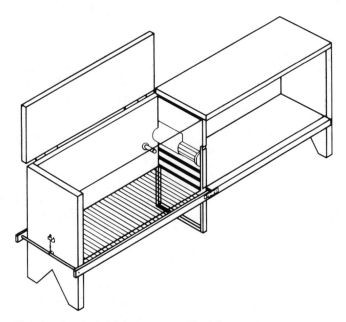

Fɪɢ. 1. *Acquired drive apparatus. The left compartment is painted white, the right one black. A shock may be administered through the grid which is the floor of the white compartment. When the animal is placed on the grid which is pivoted at the inside end, it moves down slightly making a contact that starts an electric timer. When the animal performs the correct response, turning the wheel or pressing the bar as the case may be, he stops the clock and actuates a solenoid which allows the door, painted with horizontal black and white stripes, to drop. The E can also cause the door to drop by pressing a button. The dimensions of each compartment are $18 \times 6 \times 8\frac{1}{2}$ in.*

enable the experimenter to observe the animal's behavior. The two compartments were separated by a door which was painted with horizontal black and white stripes. This door was held up by a catch operated by a solenoid and could be caused to drop in any one of three different ways: (a) by the E pushing a button, (b) by the rat moving a little cylindrical wheel made of horizontal rods stretched between bakelite disks and exposed above the right hand half of the door, (c) by a bar projecting $1\frac{1}{4}$ in. from the side of the apparatus in front of the upper left hand corner of the door.

The support of the grid was pivoted at the end near the door and held slightly above a contact by a little spring at the far end. Placing the rat into the apparatus caused the grid to move down a fraction of an inch and close the contact. This started an electric clock. When the animal caused the door to drop by rotating the wheel a fraction of a turn or pressing the bar (depending upon the way the apparatus was set), he stopped the clock which timed his response. The wheel was attached to a ratchet in such a way that the part of it facing the rat could only be moved downward. A brush riding on a segment of the wheel which projected through the back of the apparatus was arranged in such a way that each quarter of a revolution was recorded on an electric counter.

The animals used in this experiment were male albino rats approximately six months old. They had been tamed by handling but had not been used in any other experiment. They were allowed plenty of food and water in their home cages at all times.

The procedure involved the following five steps:

1. *Test for initial response to apparatus.* The animals were placed in the apparatus for approximately one min. with the door between the two compartments open and their behavior was observed.

2. *Trials with primary drive of pain produced by electric shock.* The procedure for administering shock was designed to attach the response of fear to as many as possible of the cues in the white compartment instead of merely to the relatively transient stimulus trace of just having been dropped in. This was done so that the animal would remain frightened when he was restrained in the compartment on subsequent non-shock trials. The strength of shock used was 500 volts of 60 cycle AC through a series resistance of 250,000 ohms. The animals were given 10 trials with shock. On the first trial they were allowed to remain in the white compartment for 60 sec. without shock and then given a momentary shock every five sec. for 60 sec. At the end of this period of time the *E* dropped the door and put a continuous shock on the grid.

As soon as the animal had run into the black compartment, the door was closed behind him and he was allowed to remain there for 30 sec. Then he was taken out and placed in a cage of wire mesh approximately nine in. in diameter and seven in. high for the time between trials. Since the animals were run in rotation in groups of three, the time between trials was that required to run the other two animals, but was never allowed to fall below 60 sec. This procedure was followed on all subsequent trials.

On the second trial the animal was placed into the center of the white compartment facing away from the door, was kept there for 30 sec. without shock, at the end of which time the shock was turned on and the door opened. On trials 3 through 10 the grid was electrified before the animal was dropped on it and the door was opened before he reached it. On odd numbered trials the animal was dropped at the end of the compartment away from the door facing it; on even numbered trials he was dropped in the center of the compartment facing away from the door.

3. *Non-shock trials with experimenter dropping door.* The purpose of these trials was to determine whether or not the animals would continue to perform the original habit in the absence of the primary drive of pain from electric shock, and to reduce their tendency to crouch in the white compartment and to draw back in response to the sound and movement of the door dropping in front of them.[3] Each animal was given five of these non-shock trials during which the *E* dropped the door before the animal reached it. As with the preceding trials the animals were dropped in facing the door on odd numbered trials and facing away from it on even numbered ones; they were allowed to remain in the black compartment for 30 sec. and were kept in the wire mesh cage for at least 60 sec. between trials.

4. *Non-shock trials with door opened by turning the wheel.* The purpose of these trials was to determine whether the continued running without

shock was the mere automatic persistence of a simple habit, or whether an acquired drive was involved which could be used to motivate the learning of a new habit. During these trials the *E* no longer dropped the door. The apparatus was set so that the only way the door could be dropped was by moving the wheel a small fraction of a turn. The bar was present but pressing it would not cause the door to drop. The animals that moved the wheel and caused the door to drop were allowed to remain 30 sec. in the black compartment. Those that did not move the wheel within 100 sec. were picked out of the white compartment at the end of that time. All animals remained at least 60 sec. between trials in the wire mesh cage. All animals were given 16 trials under these conditions. On each trial the time to move the wheel enough to drop the door was recorded on an electric clock and read to the nearest 10th of a sec.

5. *Non-shock trials with door opened by pressing the bar.* The purpose of these trials was to determine whether or not animals (a) would unlearn the first new habit of turning the wheel if this habit was no longer effective in dropping the door, and (b) would learn a second new habit, pressing the bar, if this would cause the door to drop and allow them to remove themselves from the cues arousing the fear. Animals that had adopted the habit of crouching in the white compartment till the end of the 100 sec. limit and so had not learned to rotate the wheel were excluded from this part of the experiment. These trials were given in exactly the same way as the preceding ones except that the apparatus was set so that turning the wheel would not cause the door to drop but pressing the bar would. During these trials there was no time limit; the animals were allowed to remain in the white compartment until they finally pressed the bar.[4] The time to press the bar was recorded on an electric clock to the nearest 10th of a sec. and the number of revolutions of the wheel was recorded on an electric counter in quarter revolutions.

Suggested Improvements in Procedure

In the light of further theoretical analysis and experimental results it is believed that the above procedure could be improved by the following changes: (a) Have the door drop down only part of the way so that it remains as a hurdle approximately two in. high over which the animals have to climb, thus introducing components of standing up and reaching into the initial response. This should favor the subsequent occurrence of wheel turning or bar pressing. (b) Connect the door to an electronic relay so that it will fall when touched and require the animals to touch it in order to make it fall during steps 2 and 3 of the experiment. This should tend to accomplish the same purpose as the preceding change and also insure that the animals have the response of running through the door attached to the stimulus produced by its dropping when they are very close to it. (c) Increase the number of non-shock trials in step 3 to approximately 12 in order to further counteract crouching. (d) At the end of the time limit in step 4, drop the door in front of the animal instead of lifting him out of the white compartment. This should tend to maintain the strength of the habit of going through the door and make it less likely that crouching or sitting will be learned.

Results

In the test before the training with electric shock, the animals showed no readily discernible avoidance or preference for either of the two chambers of the apparatus. They explored freely through both of them.

During the trials with primary drive of pain produced by electric shock, all of the animals learned to run rapidly from the white compartment through the door, which was dropped in front of them by the *E*, and into the black compartment. On the five trials without shock, and with the *E* still dropping the door, the animals continued to run. The behavior of the animals was markedly different from what it had been before the training with the primary drive of pain from electric shock.

When the procedure of the non-shock trials was changed so that the *E* no longer dropped the door and it could only be opened by moving the wheel, the animals displayed variable behavior which tended to be concentrated in the region of the door. They would stand up in front of it, place their paws upon it, sniff around the edges, bite the bars of the grid they were standing on, run back and forth, etc. They also tended to crouch, urinate, and defecate. In the course of this behavior some of the animals performed responses, such as poking their noses between the bars of the wheel or placing their paws upon it, which caused it to move a fraction of a turn and actuate a contact that caused the door to open. Most of them then ran through into the black compartment almost immediately. A few of them drew back with an exaggerated startle response and crouched. Some of these eventually learned to go through the door; a few seemed to learn to avoid it. Other animals abandoned their trial-and-error behavior before they happened to strike the wheel and persisted in crouching so that they had to be lifted out of the white compartment at the end of the 100 sec. period. In general, the animals that had to be lifted out seemed to crouch sooner and sooner on successive trials.

Thirteen of the 25 animals moved the wheel enough to drop the door on four or more out of their first eight trials. Since, according to theory, a response has to occur before it can be reinforced and learned, the results of these animals were analyzed separately and they were the only ones which were subsequently used in the bar-pressing phase of the experiment.[5] The average speed (reciprocal of time in seconds) with which these animals opened the door by moving the wheel on the 16 successive trials is presented in Fig. 2. It can be seen that there is a definite tendency for the animals to learn to turn the wheel more rapidly on successive trials. Eleven out of the 13 individual animals turned the wheel sooner on the 16th than on the first trial, and the two animals which did not show improvement were ones which happened to turn the wheel fairly soon on the first trial and continued this performance throughout. The difference between the average speed on the first and 16th trials is of a magnitude ($t = 3.5$) which would be expected to occur in the direction predicted by theory, less than two times in 1000 by chance. Therefore, it must be concluded that those animals that did turn the wheel and run out of the white compartment into the black one definitely learned to perform this new response more rapidly during the 16 trials *without* the primary drive of pain produced by electric shock.

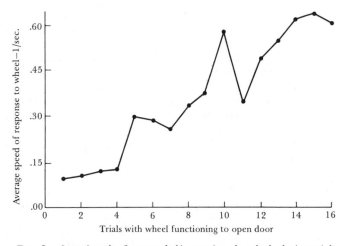

Fig. 2.   *Learning the first new habit, turning the wheel, during trials without primary drive. With mild pain produced by an electric shock as a primary drive, the animals have learned to run from the white compartment, through the open door, into the black compartment. Then they were given trials without any electric shock during which the door was closed but could be opened by turning a little wheel. Under these conditions the 13 out of the 25 animals which turned the wheel enough to drop the door on four or more of the first eight trials learned to turn it. This figure shows the progressive increase in the average speed with which these 13 animals ran up to the wheel and turned it enough to drop the door during the 16 non-shock trials.*

When the setting on the apparatus was changed so that the wheel would not open the door but the bar would, the animals continued to respond to the wheel vigorously for some time. It was obvious that they had learned a strong habit of responding to it. Eventually, however, they stopped reacting to the wheel and began to perform other responses. After longer or shorter periods of variable behavior they finally hit the bar, caused the door to drop, and ran through rapidly into the black compartment. On the first trial the number of complete rotations of the wheel ranged from zero to 530 with a median of 4.75. On successive trials during which turning the wheel did not cause the door to drop, the amount of activity on it progressively dropped till by the tenth trial the range was from 0 to 0.25 rotations with a median of zero. The progressive decrease in the amount of activity on the wheel is shown in Fig. 3. It is plotted in medians because of the skewed nature of the distribution. Twelve out of the 13 rats which were used in this part of the experiment gave fewer rotations of the wheel on the tenth than on the first trial. From the binomial expansion it may be calculated that for 12 out of 13 cases to come out in the direction predicted by the theory is an event which would be expected to occur by chance less than one time in 1000. Thus, it may be concluded that the dropping of the door, which is presumed to have produced a reduction in the strength of fear by allowing the animals to escape from the cues in the white compartment which elicited the fear, was essential to the maintenance of the habit of rotating the wheel.

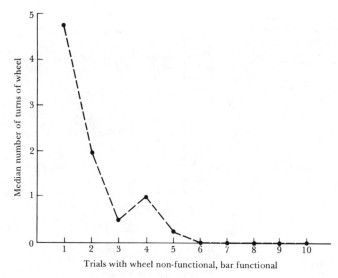

FIG. 3. *Unlearning of the habit of turning the wheel during trials on which it no longer serves to reduce the acquired drive. When conditions were changed so that turning the wheel was ineffective (and pressing the bar was effective) in causing the door to drop and allowing the animal to run from the white into the black compartment, the animals showed a progressive decrement in the response of rotating the wheel. Each point is based on the median scores of 13 animals.*

The results on bar pressing are presented in Fig. 4. It can be seen that the speed of bar pressing increased throughout the 10 non-shock trials during which that response caused the door to drop. Since the last trial was faster than the first for 12 out of the 13 animals, the difference was again one which would be expected by chance less than one time in 1000.

Discussion

On preliminary tests conducted before the training with electric shock was begun, the animals showed no noticeable tendency to avoid the white compartment. During training with the primary drive of pain produced by electric shock in the white compartment, the animals learned a strong habit of quickly running out of it, through the open door, and into the black compartment.

On non-shock trials the animals persisted in running from the white compartment through the open door into the black one. On additional non-shock trials during which the door was not automatically dropped in front of the animals, they exhibited so-called random behavior and learned a new response, turning the wheel, which caused the door to drop and allowed them to escape into the black compartment. This trial-and-error learning of a new response demonstrated that the cues in the white compartment had acquired the functional properties of a drive and that escape from the white into the black compartment had acquired the functional properties of a reward.

At this point the results of two later experiments which serve as controls should be briefly mentioned. One of these (13) demonstrated that

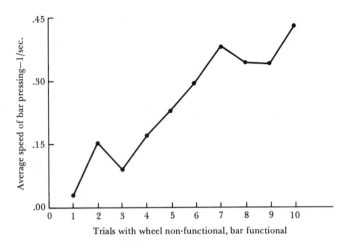

FIG. 4. *Learning a second new habit, bar pressing, under acquired drive. Conditions were changed so that only pressing the bar would cause the door to drop and allow the animals to run from the white compartment where they had been previously shocked, into the black one where they had escaped shock. During non-shock trials under these conditions, the animals learned a second new habit, pressing the bar. Each point is based on the average speed of 13 animals.*

the capacity of the cues in the two compartments to motivate and reinforce new learning was a function of the strength of the primary drive involved in the previous stage of the training. Animals put through the same procedure in every respect except that the primary drive was a weak one produced by a 90 volt electric shock showed no tendency to learn a new habit (which in this case was bar pressing) on subsequent non-shock trials. Animals, given their initial training with a stronger primary drive produced by a 540 volt shock, showed rapid learning of the new response on subsequent non-shock trials. For these two groups all other features of the experiment were exactly the same including possible initial preferences for the different features of the two compartments and trials of running in the apparatus with the last response to the cues in the white compartment being going through the door into the black one, etc. Therefore, the difference in learning during the non-shock trials must have been a function of the previous training, and more specifically a function of the strength of the primary drive involved in that training.

The second experiment which serves as a control demonstrated that if the non-shock trials were continued long enough, the new habit of pressing the bar and the older response of running through the door would both eventually extinguish (11). Thus, in this situation the primary drive of pain is essential not only to the establishment of the acquired drive, but also to its maintenance.

In the present experiment, when the animals were dropped into the white compartment on the non-shock trials following their training with shock, they exhibited urination, defecation, tenseness, and other forms of behavior which are ordinarily considered to be symptoms of fear. Furthermore, the procedure of having been given a number of moderately painful shocks in this compartment would be expected to produce fear. Therefore, it seems reasonable to conclude that the acquirable drive motivating the learning of the new response of turning the wheel was fear and that a reduction in the strength of this fear was the reinforcing agent. Thus, this experiment confirms Mowrer's (14) hypothesis that fear (or anxiety) can play a role in learning similar to that of a primary drive such as hunger.

In terms of the hypothesis put forward in Miller and Dollard (12) the cues in the white compartment acquire their drive value by acquiring the capacity to elicit an internal response which produces a strong stimulus. Whether this strong stimulus is produced by peripheral responses, such as those involved in the blanching of the stomach and the tendency for hair to stand on end, or by central impulses which travel from the thalamus to sensory areas of the cortex is a matter of anatomical rather than functional significance. Fear may be called a stimulus-producing response if it shows the functional characteristics of such responses, in brief, obeys the laws of learning and serves as a cue to elicit learned responses such as the verbal report of fear.

The general pattern of the fear response and its capacity to produce a strong stimulus is determined by the innate structure of the animal. The connection between the pain and the fear is also presumably innate. But the connection between the cues in the white compartment and the fear was learned. Therefore the fear of the white compartment may be called an acquired drive. Because fear can be learned, it may be called acquirable; because it can motivate new learning, it may be called a drive.

Running through the door and into the black compartment removed the animal from the cues in the white compartment which were eliciting the fear and thus produced a reduction in the strength of the fear response and the stimuli which it produced. This reduction in the strength of the intense fear stimuli is presumably what gave the black compartment its acquired reinforcing value.

If the reduction in fear produced by running from the white into the black was the reinforcement for learning the new habit of wheel turning, we would expect this habit to show experimental extinction when that reinforcement was removed. This is exactly what happened. During the first trial on which turning the wheel no longer dropped the door, the animals gradually stopped performing this response and began to exhibit other responses. As would be expected, the one of these responses, pressing the bar, which caused the door to drop and allowed the animal to remove himself from the fear-producing cues in the white compartment, was gradually learned in a series of trials during which the wheel turning was progressively crowded out. Thus, it can be seen that the escape from the white compartment, which presumably produced a reduction in the strength of the fear, played a crucial role, similar to that of a primary reward, in the learning and maintenance of the new habits.

Some of the implications of the principles which this experiment has demonstrated should be mentioned briefly. It can be seen that being able to learn a response (fear of the white compartment) which in turn is able to motivate the learning and performance of a whole category of new responses (turning the wheel, pressing the bar, and any other means of escape from the white compartment) greatly increases the flexibility of learned behavior as a means of adapting to a changing environment.

The present experiment has demonstrated the drive function of fear as a response which presumably produces a strong stimulus. But if fear is a strong response-produced stimulus, it will be expected to function, not only as a drive, but also as a cue mediating secondary generalization. Thus, when fear is learned as a new response to a given situation, all of the habits which have been learned elsewhere in response to fear, as well as the innate responses to fear, should tend to be transferred to that new situation. Evidence supporting this deduction has been secured in a recent experiment by May (7).

It seems possible that the potentialities of response-produced stimuli as mediators of secondary generalization and sources of acquirable drive may account in stimulus-response, law-of-effect terms for the type of behavior which has been described as "expectancy" and considered to be an exception to this type of explanation. If it should turn out that all of the phenomena of expectancy can be explained on the basis of the drive and cue functions of response-produced stimuli, expectancy will of course not vanish; it will be established as a secondary principle derivable from more primary ones.

The mechanism of acquired drives allows behavior to be more adaptive in complex variable situations. It also allows behavior to appear more baffling and apparently lawless to any investigator who has not had the opportunity to observe the conditions under which the acquired drive was established. In the present experiment the learning and performance of the responses of turning the wheel and pressing the bar are readily understandable. An *E* dealing with many rats, a few of which without his knowledge had been shocked in the white compartment, might be puzzled by the fact that these few rats became so preoccupied with turning the wheel or pressing the bar. In the present experiment, the white and black compartments are very obvious features of the animal's environment. If more obscure external cues or internal ones had been involved, the habits of turning the wheel and pressing the bar might seem to be completely bizarre and maladaptive. One hypothesis is that neurotic symptoms, such as compulsions, are habits which are motivated by fear (or anxiety as it is called when its source is vague or obscured by repression) and reinforced by a reduction in fear.[6]

Summary

Albino rats were placed in a simple apparatus consisting of two compartments separated by a door. One was white with a grid as a floor; the other was black without a grid. Before training, the animals showed no marked preference for either compartment. Then they were placed in the white compartment, received an electric shock from the grid, and escaped into the black compartment through the open door. After a number of such trials, the animals would run out of the white compartment even if no shock was on the grid.

To demonstrate that an acquired drive (fear or anxiety) had been established, the animals were taught a *new* habit *without further shocks*. The door (previously always open) was closed. The only way that the door could be opened was by rotating a little wheel, which was above the door, a fraction of a turn. Under these conditions, the animals exhibited trial-and-error behavior and gradually learned to escape from the white compartment by rotating the wheel.

If conditions were changed so that only pressing a bar would open the door, wheel turning extinguished, and a second new habit (bar pressing) was learned.

Control experiments demonstrated that the learning of the new habits was dependent upon having received moderately strong electric shocks during the first stages of training.

The following hypotheses were discussed: that responses which produce strong stimuli are the basis for acquired drives; that such responses may be the basis for certain of the phenomena of learning which have been labeled "expectancy," thus reducing this from the status of a primary to a secondary principle and that neurotic symptoms, such as compulsions, may be motivated by anxiety and reinforced by anxiety-reduction like the two new responses learned in this experiment.

Notes

[1] This study is part of the research program of the Institute of Human Relations, Yale University. It was first reported as part of a paper at the 1941 meetings of the A.P.A. The author is indebted to Fred D. Sheffield for assistance in the exploratory work involved in establishing the experimental procedure and for criticizing the manuscript.

[2] In both of these experiments the 46-hour food deprivation was made more effective by the fact that the animals had been habituated to a regular feeding schedule and maintained on a diet that was quantitatively restricted enough to keep them very thin but qualitatively enriched with brewer's yeast, cod liver oil, and greens to keep them healthy.

[3] During the training in the next step (learning to rotate the wheel), crouching would interfere with the type of responses necessary in order to hit the wheel and withdrawing would prevent the animals from going into the black compartment and having their fear reduced immediately after hitting the wheel. Apparently crouching occupies a dominant position in the innate hierarchy of responses to fear. Similarly withdrawing seems to be either an innate or a previously learned response to the pattern of fear plus a sudden stimulus in front of the animal. During the shock trials the response of fear is learned to the pattern of shock plus white compartment and the responses of running are learned to the pattern of shock plus stimuli produced by the fear response plus the cues in the white compartment. When the shock stimulus drops out of the pattern, the generalized fear and running responses elicited by the remainder of the pattern are weaker. The innate crouching response to fear is then in conflict with the generalized running responses to the pattern of fear plus cues in the alley. If the door is closed, the extinction of running and other related responses may reduce their strength to the point where crouching becomes dominant. If the door is dropped in front of the animal so that he can immediately run out of the white compartment, the reduction in the strength of fear will be expected to strengthen the relative dominance of running and related responses to the stimulus of fear plus the cues in the white compartment and the sight and sound of the door dropping.

[4] One animal which did not hit the bar within 30 min. was finally discarded.

[5] In a subsequent experiment (13) in which further steps suggested by the theoretical analysis (see footnote 3 and Suggested Improvements in Procedure) were taken to get rid of the crouching, none of the 24 animals in the group which had received the strong shock had to be eliminated for crouching; all of them learned to perform the new response during the non-shock trials.

[6] The author's views on this matter have been materially strengthened and sharpened by seeing the way in which Dollard (4), working with symptoms of war neuroses, had independently come to a similar hypothesis and been able to apply it convincingly to the concrete details of the case material.

References

1. Allport, G. W. *Personality.* New York: Henry Holt, 1937.

2. Anderson, E. E. The externalization of drive: III. Maze learning by non-rewarded and by satiated rats. *J. Genet. Psychol.,* 1941, **59**, 397–426.

3. Brown, J. S. Generalized approach and avoidance responses in relation to conflict behavior. New Haven: Dissertation, Yale Univ., 1940.

4. Dollard, J. Exploration of morale factors among combat air crewmen. *Memorandum to Experimental Section, Research Branch, Information and Education Division, War Department,* 9, March 1945.

5. Freud, S. *New introductory lectures on psychoanalysis.* New York: Norton, 1933.

6. Freud, S. *The problem of anxiety.* New York: Norton, 1936.

7. May, M. A. Experimentally acquired drives. *J. Exp. Psychol.,* 1948, **38**, 66–77.

8. Miller, N. E. An experimental investigation of acquired drives. *Psychol. Bull.,* 1941, **38**, 534–535.

9. Miller, N. E. Experimental studies of conflict behavior. In: *Personality and the behavior disorders* (Ed. J. McV. Hunt), New York: Ronald Press, 1944, 431–465.

10. Miller, N. E. Theory and experiment relating psychoanalytic displacement to stimulus–response generalization. *J. Abnorm. Soc. Psychol.* (In press)

11. Miller, N. E. Studies of fear as an acquirable drive: II. Resistance to extinction. (In preparation)

12. Miller, N. E., & Dollard, J. *Social learning and imitation.* New Haven: Yale Univ. Press, 1941.

13. Miller, N. E., & Lawrence, D. H. Studies of fear as an acquirable drive: III. Effect of strength of electric shock as a primary drive and of number of trials with the primary drive on the strength of fear. (In preparation)

14. Mowrer, O. H. A stimulus–response analysis of anxiety and its role as a reinforcing agent. *Psychol. Rev.,* 1939, **46**, 553–565.

15. Mowrer, O. H. & Lamoreaux, R. R. Fear as an intervening variable in avoidance conditioning. *J. Comp. Psychol.,* 1946, **39**, 29–50.

16. Shaffer, L. F. *The psychology of adjustment.* Boston: Houghton Mifflin, 1936.

17. Watson, J. B. *Psychology from the standpoint of a behaviorist.* Philadelphia: Lippincott, 1924.

18. Woodworth, R. S. *Dynamic psychology.* New York: Columbia Univ. Press, 1918.

B. REINFORCEMENT THEORY

Though two-factor theory has proven resilient over the years, there are aspects of avoidance learning that it has a very difficult time explaining. One of these is demonstrated in the following article by Sidman. Sidman developed a procedure for training avoidance responses in the absence of any signal paired with shock. The avoidance response has only the effect of avoiding shock. Animals reliably learn to avoid on such procedures. This fact prompted what we might call a reinforcement theory of avoidance. What reinforces avoidance is a reduction in the frequency of shock. Neither expectations nor conditioned fear need to be invoked (see Herrnstein, 1969).

18 Avoidance Conditioning with Brief Shock and No Exteroceptive Warning Signal

MURRAY SIDMAN

Experiments on avoidance behavior are usually divided, for the purpose of measurement, into trials.[1] A trial, by definition, begins with the presentation of a warning signal and ends with the occurrence of the noxious stimulus or of the response which avoids the noxious stimulus. The measure, occurrence or nonoccurrence of the avoidance response, is necessarily a gross one since there are no intermediate states between the extremes. Traditionally, two expedients have been resorted to for circumventing this difficulty. Either the number of responses emitted by a group of organisms is averaged for each trial, or the trials for a single animal are grouped into blocks of arbitrary length and the number of responses averaged for each block. In the first case, a continuous measure is obtained only by virtue of the fact that progress is not uniform among organisms. The behavior of no individual can be described. With the second procedure, the type of relation obtained, if any, depends upon the number of trials included in each block. With both procedures, the statistical techniques result in the loss of a considerable amount of descriptive information. The purpose of the present paper is to report a technique which eliminates the above difficulties in investigating avoidance behavior, and to present an example of a kind of descriptive data which previous investigators in this area have generally neglected. Use of the rate measure, which is a natural one once behavior is freed from arbitrary constriction into trials, permits continuous observation and measurement of avoidance responding while providing a sensative indicator of the effects of relevant variables (1).

White rats were the experimental organisms, with lever pressing selected as the avoidance reponse. Shocks of a fixed 0.2-sec duration were given to the animal through a grid floor at regular intervals unless the lever was depressed. Each lever depression reset the timer controlling the shock, thus delaying its appearance. If, for example, each lever press delayed the shock for 20 sec, a minimum interval of 20 sec was assured between avoidance behavior and shock. All other behavior was capable of being paired closely in time with the shock. Only the initial downward press on the lever reset the timer; holding the lever down had no effect upon the occurrence of the shock.

With no other contingencies between avoidance behavior and exteroceptive stimulation involved, approximately 50 animals have been successfully conditioned. Representative cumulated response curves for 4 of these animals are presented in Fig. 1. The letters refer to animals and the numbers to experimental sessions, each 3 hr in length. A striking characteristic of the initial curves is the abruptness with which the rate increases

"Avoidance Conditioning with Brief Shock and No Exteroceptive Warning Signal" by Murray Sidman. *Science*, 1953, *118*, 157–158. Reprinted by permission.

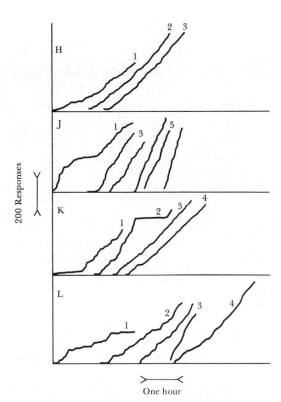

FIG. 1. *Cumulative records of avoidance responding by 4 albino rats.*

200 Responses

One hour

from its initial near-zero level. That these are not the unconditioned responses that hungry animals usually emit when the lever is first presented (2) was assured by making food and water continuously available to the animals in their home cages between experimental sessions, and by leaving the animals in the experimental cage, with the lever present, for 30 min before administering the first shock.

The initial curves are also characterized by their cyclic appearance and are composed of many small discontinuous segments. Responding of a more sustained nature is apparent as early as the final portion of the first session in some cases, but is most clearly demonstrated in later hours. With continued training the rate remains relatively stable not only within but also between sessions. Rates as high as 17 responses/min have been maintained by some animals during sessions totaling over 24 hr, with variations no greater than 0.1 responses/min appearing between the average rate for each session.

The behavior generated by this procedure can be explained by a model which holds that avoidance responding increases in rate at the expense of other behavior that is depressed by shock. An equivalent statement, in reinforcement terms, is that the avoidance response is strengthened when it terminates incompatible behavior that has been paired with shock (3, 4). Several lines of evidence indicate that the avoidance rate is not simply some form of temporal conditioning in which the responses are triggered off by the passage of a time interval. Once the response has developed, each occurrence automatically varies the interval between shocks. Furthermore, the relatively stable rates that finally emerge are considerably higher than are required by the shock schedule. If a temporal discrimination were to develop, it should, according to previous findings with the white rat in other situations, produce much more efficient responding than is displayed here (5, 6). Mitigating against a time discrimination, once the avoidance behavior appears, is the fact that the animal is provided with no indication that the end of an interval is approaching. While the shock can mark the start of a time interval of, i.e., 20 sec, once a response occurs this interval increases. It is, in fact, possible to vary the delay produced by each response, so that the amount of increase is completely unpredictable, even if the organism were to be provided with an internal resetting timer.

Notes

[1] This paper is a portion of a dissertation submitted in partial fulfillment of the requirements for the degree of Doctor of Philosophy in the Faculty of Pure Science, Columbia University. The writer is indebted to William N. Schoenfeld and Fred S. Keller for their constructive criticisms.

References
  1. Sidman, M. *J. Comp. Physiol. Psychol.* (in press).
  2. Schoenfeld, W. N., Antonitis, J. J., and Bersh, P. J. *Ibid.,* **43,** 41 (190).
  3. Hefferline, R. F. *Genet. Phychol. Monogr.,* **42,** 231 (1950).
  4. Schoenfeld, W. N. In P. H. Hoch and J. Zubin, Eds., *Anxiety,* New York: Grune and Stratton (1950).
  5. Bugelski, B. R., and Coyer, R. A. *Am. Psychol.,* **5,** 264 (abst.), (1950).
  6. Wilson, M. P., and Keller, F. S. *J. Comp. Physiol. Psychol.,* **46,** 190 (1953).

C. COGNITIVE THEORY

The reinforcement theory of avoidance is also not adequate; there are many aspects of avoidance behavior it can not explain. The failings of both two-factor theory and reinforcement theory prompted Seligman and Johnston to propose an alternative that explicitly acknowledges the importance of expectations to the phenomenon of avoidance. In the following article they present a detailed discussion of the shortcomings of other theories of avoidance. They then propose a theory in which avoidance responding depends upon the development of two expectancies, that responding leads to no shock and that not responding leads to shock. Any experience that strengthens these expectancies increases the likelihood of avoidance responding, while experiences that weaken these expectancies decrease the likelihood of avoidance responding. The author's account of avoidance is able to explain most of the findings that have been reported in studies of avoidance learning.

19 A Cognitive Theory of Avoidance Learning

MARTIN E. P. SELIGMAN AND JAMES C. JOHNSTON

In this chapter we review some of the problems that face existing theories of avoidance learning, and then propose a cognitive model which we believe successfully accounts for more of the relevant data. We discuss three different kinds of theories.[1]

1. *Two-process fear mediation theory* is treated at greatest length. We find that difficulties in verifying the mediation of fear have led to formulations that make fewer and fewer predictions. Even the more flexible versions, however, cannot be reconciled with the great resistance to extinction of avoidance and the concomitant absence of fear.

2. *Two-process aversion theory,* it will be argued, is silent about many important avoidance phenomena, particularly those involving fear, and is also incompatible with very high resistance to extinction.

3. *Discriminative stimulus theory* we find to be formulated in a manner that leaves it silent about so many phenomena that it risks becoming a vehicle only for a posteriori description, not prediction.

Our avoidance theory contains two components: one cognitive and one emotional. The cognitive component relies on the constructs of expectancies and preferences and is the primary mechanism supporting the avoidance response. We discuss a number of phenomena, particularly high resistance to extinction and the effects of response blocking, which are accounted for by this component of the theory alone. The emotional component consists simply of the classical conditioning of fear according to known Pavlovian laws. By adding this component, our theory can be made to account for many remaining avoidance phenomena, including the course of observed fear itself.

Difficulties with Previous Avoidance Theories

Miller (1948) viewed cognitive accounts of avoidance learning as unnecessary and even profligate. Why talk about cognition if a perfectly adequate account of avoidance can be given without it? Unfortunately, all alternative accounts of avoidance that we know of are seriously flawed. In the following sections, the difficulties facing three of the most favored contemporary avoidance theories will be reviewed. In many places we attempt to meet an alleged difficulty by constructing a rejoinder in the spirit of the theory under discussion. We hope to make it clear which difficulties can be overcome and which cannot.

Two-Process Fear Mediation Theory

The most popular theory of avoidance over the last 20 years has been a variant of general two-process theory in which classically conditioned fear

"A Cognitive Theory of Avoidance Learning" by Martin E. P. Seligman and James C. Johnston from *Contemporary Approaches to Conditioning and Learning* edited by F. J. McGuigan and D. Barry Lumsden. Abridged and reprinted by permission of Hemisphere Publishing Corporation.

mediates instrumental avoidance responding (Mowrer, 1947; Solomon & Brush, 1954; Soltysik, 1963; Rescorla & Solomon, 1967; Maier, Seligman, & Solomon, 1969). This theory has two key premises:

1. By classical conditioning, when a CS is paired with an aversive US (such as shock), the CS comes to elicit the conditioned response of fear.

2. Fear motivates the avoidance response. When the response is made, the CS terminates, fear is reduced, and the avoidance response is reinforced by this fear reduction.

This kind of theory eliminates the apparent forward-lookingness of avoidance. Rather than responding to ward off a shock in the future, an "avoider" is actually escaping from fear-evoking stimuli in the present.

Two-process fear mediation theory has recently come under heavy attack (Herrnstein, 1969; Bolles, 1970; D'Amato, 1970). Problems facing the theory are of three kinds: difficulties in specifying CSs; difficulties in verifying the existence of appropriate fear CRs; and difficulties in accounting for the very high resistance to extinction of most avoidance responding.

The Elusiveness of the CS

The crucial construct, fear, is asserted to be a Pavlovian CR, so its presence during avoidance must be produced by a Pavlovian CS. But identifying the effective CS has not been straightforward. In conventional avoidance training, of course, the onset and offset of the external CS present no trouble for fear theory. The CS is always on prior to the response and is therefore available for fear elicitation; it always terminates after the response, allowing fear reduction to occur. In the trace avoidance paradigm, however, the external CS terminates after a brief fixed time interval. CS termination occurs prior to responding and is independent of it. At first glance, this paradigm presents problems for fear theory. Avoidance should not be acquired because there is no CS around to evoke fear immediately prior to responding, and there is no CS termination after responding to provide reinforcement by fear reduction. Since dogs and rats *do* acquire trace avoidance conditioning (e.g., Kamin, 1954) albeit somewhat falteringly, the range of allowable CSs must be broadened. Fear theory might make the same move made by Pavlov (1927) to handle classical trace conditioning. If the memory trace of the external signal were the operative CS, the evocation of fear to motivate responding could be provided for. But how could reduction of fear by CS termination be handled? The memory trace of the external CS would not do, since there is no reason that the memory trace should terminate when the response is made.

A more promising move is to make the CS a compound of the memory trace *and* "internal stimuli" (Sidman, 1953; Dinsmoor, 1954; Anger, 1963) provided by proprioceptive, visual, and kinesthetic feedback from the avoidance response (hereafter designated "r") and from all other responses (hereafter designated "r̄"). Feedback from r̄ is paired with shock and should become a fear-evoking CS. Feedback from r is paired with no shock and should therefore elicit no fear. Thus engaging in r̄ after the external signal is turned off will elicit fear. Making r will reduce this fear, reinforcing r.

Similar problems arise, of course, for a fear theory account of Sidman avoidance. Making r postpones the shock for some number of seconds (the response–shock interval). If no response occurs, shocks are presented at some fixed interval (the shock–shock interval). By responding consistently with interresponse times smaller than the response–shock interval, the subject can avoid shock altogether. In spite of the fact that no external CS is presented, animals learn to avoid readily on this schedule (e.g., Sidman, 1953). A two-process fear theory can now postulate another compound CS: feedback from not having made the response (r̄) together with the length of time since the preceding response (see Anger, 1963). Increasing lengths of time in the presence of r̄ elicit increasing fear; making r terminates the compound CS and reduces fear. To account for Sidman avoidance, fear theory needs very little over and above what it needed for trace avoidance. It now gives the animal the ability to keep track of time since his last response. This assumption is not unreasonable since related assumptions are probably needed to explain scalloped responding on fixed-interval schedules.

Similar considerations account for Kamin's (1956) finding that rats could learn to avoid the US in spite of the fact that response-contingent CS termination was independent of responding. While this study makes it appear that CS termination is not necessary for avoidance, only *external* CSs were independent of responding. Feedback CSs, already needed to explain trace and Sidman avoidance, would explain Kamin's results equally well. Feedback CSs from r̄ are available to elicit the fear that motivates r; making r terminates these CSs and reduces fear. The fact that Kamin's rats did not learn to avoid as well as control rats which had both external CS termination and avoidance of the US contingent on the response need only lead a fear theorist to assert that terminating an entire compound of external and internal CSs is more fear-reducing than terminating only the feedback component.

Herrnstein (1969) discusses the elusiveness of the CS at length and adds some data of his own (Herrnstein & Hineline, 1966) which he argues are made more difficult for two-process theory to handle. While we are sympathetic with much that Herrnstein has to say, we think that the Herrnstein and Hineline data add no problems for two-process theory that were not there already. Herrnstein and Hineline's rats were exposed to two densities of shock—high and low. If they bar-pressed, they were shifted immediately from the high to the low shock density schedule. There were no external CSs correlated with the schedules. As Herrnstein (1969) noted, "The shock-free interval following a response is, on the average, greater than the shock-free interval measured from any other point in time. The average shock-free interval gradually shrinks back to its original value as time since a response increases [p. 59]." The rats eventually learned to respond although it took them thousands of trials. Herrnstein asserted that this kind of experiment puts two-process theory on the horns of a dilemma. Either two-process theory can formulate no plausible conditioned stimulus, or "the notion of a conditioned stimulus has retreated out of the range of empirical scrutiny [p. 57]." This is a serious overstatement: 1. two-process theory *can* plausibly postulate a CS to handle such experiments, *and* 2. the existence of such a CS is testable.

1. A plausible CS is the feedback from ř relied on earlier. Shocks are USs for the CR of fear. The feedback from ř regularly precedes shock. Hence, fear will be classically conditioned to ř. The fact that the interval between ř and shock fluctuates around some average interval need not handicap fear conditioning (e.g., Rescorla & LoLordo, 1965, experiment 1). The feedback from responding (r) also regularly precedes shock, but at a considerably longer interval. In accordance with the principle of inhibition of delay, this longer CS–US interval should lead to periods of lower fear *immediately* after the response. The longer interval may also lead to weaker fear conditioning *overall*. Thus conditioned fear elicited by feedback from r should be smaller than that elicited by feedback from ř; hence making r should reduce the fear level.

We can see no important additional assumptions that fear theory needs to make here. That feedback from ř and r could become conditioned fear stimuli is already necessary to account for trace and Sidman avoidance conditioning. That fear can be conditioned with a probabilistic US has been demonstrated (Rescorla, 1966). That a longer average CS–US interval would have produced greater inhibition of delay particularly after thousands of trials is likely (e.g., Kimmel, 1965; Seligman & Meyer, 1970), and the alternative assumption that weaker CRs would result from longer average intervals is at least plausible. That reduction of fear intensity from high to low is a reinforcer is highly likely.

Herrnstein (1969, p. 59) asserts that the reinforcer is the reduction in shock rate itself, not reduction of fear. This implies an ability of the animal to integrate over time to determine relative rates. While animals may well be able to make such a determination (e.g., Seligman, Maier, & Solomon, 1971), two-process fear theory does not even need this assumption to account for the results. A difference in shock rates is equivalent to a difference in average CS–US interval in the Herrnstein and Hineline (1966) study, and no new principles are needed to account for interval effects.

2. Herrnstein seems to feel quite strongly that a willingness to postulate such CSs takes the notion of conditioned stimulus out of the realm of testability. Elsewhere he claims that inferring the existence of such stimuli is an exercise in "sheer tautology [Herrnstein, 1969, p. 59]." We are puzzled by this claim. The hypothesis that these CSs are operative can be tested by traditional methods. A stimulus is a fear CS when it comes to evoke a fear CR. One could measure heart rate or any of the supposed fear indices following r and ř in the Herrnstein schedule. The two-process account under discussion suggests that heart rate will be higher following ř than following r, and that heart rate will lower consequent to r. Alternatively, if the animals were on a concurrent appetitive schedule, suppression should have been greater during ř periods than periods following r. The results of these tests are not logically implied by the data from which the CSs were inferred, and therefore their postulation is not a tautological exercise.

It is somewhat surprising that Herrnstein implies that postulation of such feedback CSs is tautological; for he ends this section of his paper by recounting evidence which he correctly considers to be an empirical "assault" on such CSs: Taub and Berman (1963, 1968) have found that monkeys could maintain trace avoidance responding even when locally or spinally deafferentated. These monkeys were deprived of (a) visual feedback from the response (the arm was hidden), (b) external CS feedback (the external CS was trace), and (c) proprioceptive and kinesthetic feedback. One yeoman monkey even persisted, albeit sleepily, without any of these and also without his cranial parasympathetic system and his vagal system. While the performance of the monkeys was *disrupted* considerably by deafferentiation, they came to avoid sufficiently well to make dubious the assumption that feedback CSs are necessary to mediate avoidance responding.

To account for these results, a fear theorist would need a new source of stimuli to serve as CSs. If feedback existed from commands to the motor system to make r and r̄ (Teuber, 1967) it might be able to serve as the CS. Except for the change in the type of feedback CSs relied on, the account could remain unchanged and very much alive. In this form, the theory would now be still more difficult to test. One can easily imagine, however, that physiologists might be able to deprive animals of even these CSs.

The foregoing arguments about the elusiveness of the CS were directed at the question of whether CS termination is *necessary* for avoidance learning. Fear theory has also been criticized on the grounds that CS termination is not *sufficient*. In Kamin's study (1956) referred to above, one group of rats could terminate the CS, but not prevent the US. They acquired the avoidance response considerably less strongly than rats which could both terminate the CS and prevent the US, and only slightly better than control rats which could do neither. This data need not bother a two-process fear theorist greatly. Kamin argued that when the CS is terminated, but shock still occurs, the animal is punished with some delay by shock onset. This should decrease the probability of the "avoidance" response. We prefer to conceive of the experiment as failing to meet fully the fear-reduction requirements deemed necessary for reinforcement by two-process theory. Since both the continuation of the external CS (when the animal fails to respond) and the noncontinuation of the external CS (when the animal responds) are paired with shock, both could elicit fear. Similarly, feedback from r and r̄ are both paired with shock and should elicit fear. So neither terminating the external CS nor responding will reduce fear. Therefore the two-process requirements for acquisition and maintenance of fear are simply not met.[2] In general, the paradigm of CS-escape with noncontingent delivery of USs *cannot* meet the reinforcement requirements of fear theory. By definition, if US presentation is noncontingent, the stimuli facing an animal after r and r̄ will lead to shock with equal probabilities and will be equally fear provoking. So fear reduction contingent on r will not occur. An alternative way of assessing the effectiveness of only the CS-termination contingency is to omit the US entirely and use a CS which acquired its fearfulness prior to the experiment. This was done long ago (Miller, 1951), and it was found that animals can learn to escape such a CS before fear extinguishes.

In summary, there is no reason to believe that the CS-escape mechanism proposed by two-process fear theory is not *sufficient* to produce avoidance responding. The considerations advanced earlier, however, leave the fear theorist with a somewhat elusive account of the *necessity* of the CS. The class of stimuli postulated as CSs has progressively expanded to include: *(a)* the internal feedback from not responding, *(b)* the passage of time since the last successful response, and *(c)* feedback from commands to the motor system. The animal's reliance on such CSs may be difficult to test, but mere difficulty of testing by no means justifies the claim that the theory has "passed over the line into irrefutable doctrine [Herrnstein, 1969, p. 67]." Gravity waves, whose existence is crucial to field theory, are also immensely hard to measure experimentally, but such difficulties do not take the question of *their* existence "over the line into irrefutable doctrine." In any case, two-process fear mediation theory makes predictions about other aspects of avoidance and indeed has been found wanting on other empirical grounds.

The Elusiveness of the Fear CR

Two-process theory holds that whatever the CS might be, a CR of fear motivates avoidance responding, and the termination of that fear reinforces responding. If this fear CR could be readily identified, the CS would become much less elusive: the CS would be the internal or external event whose onset reliably preceded the evocation of the fear CR and whose offset reliably preceded the reduction of the fear CR. Considerable data have been obtained about the extent to which various autonomic and behavioral measures of fear correlate with avoidance. After an extensive review of the literature, Rescorla and Solomon (1967) concluded that "in summary, we have not yet identified any peripheral CRs which are necessary to mediate avoidance behavior [p. 169]." We know of no development since 1967 which changes their conclusion. For example, claims that heart rate accelerates maximally during the CS up to the point of responding and then deccelerates immediately on the making of the response have not held up under empirical scrutiny (Black, 1959; Soltysik, 1960; Bersh, Notterman, & Schoenfeld, 1956; Wenzel, 1961). Space does not permit a review of the literature on peripheral concomitants of the fear CR.

The absence of peripheral CRs is especially striking in an animal which has learned to avoid asymptotically (i.e., is no longer receiving any shocks). Such animals may actually look nonchalant before and after the CS and make the avoidance response with aplomb (Solomon & Wynne, 1954; Maier, Seligman, & Solomon, 1969). There is often no autonomic arousal to the CS (Black, 1959), and imposing the CS onto appetitive behavior produces no suppression (Kamin, Brimer, & Black, 1963). There is simply no reason to believe that any peripheral fear CR mediates the avoidance response.

Rescorla and Solomon (1967) did not conclude from these considerations that two-process theory was in deep trouble. Rather, they suggested that fear might be a *central state*, with various observable peripheral events only occasionally associated with responding. They asserted that "what concomitance we do observe between instrumental behavior and peripheral CRs is due to mediation by a common central state [p. 170]." It seems from this statement that whenever concomitance is observed, this is supposed to constitute support for the fear mediation hypothesis.

Yet they clearly wish *failures*[3] to observe peripheral CRs concomitant with avoidance responding *not to disconfirm* the fear mediation hypothesis. We do not see how they can have it both ways without considering data on a basis of "heads we win, tails don't count." Rescorla and Solomon were apparently uncertain about how to cope with this problem. At one point they themselves suggest that looking for concomitance "becomes an irrelevant strategy." Yet they do not seem prepared to give up the connection between peripheral CRs and the central fear state; for in characterizing their theory in the concluding sentence of the paper, they again emphasize "that the concomitance we do observe between peripheral CRs and instrumental responding is mediated by a common central state [p. 178]."

If we are correct that Rescorla and Solomon's version of two-process theory can be neither confirmed nor disconfirmed on the basis of concomitance evidence, the appeal of such a theory diminishes considerably. When the fear CR was said to be peripheral, and concurrent measurement was a relevant strategy, the principle of fear mediation could be directly tested. Fear CRs themselves could be measured while avoidance responding was actually in progress. The mediation of Pavlovian fear could then be confirmed independently of avoidance responding. When we give up the measurement of mediating CRs, we are left with only one dependent measure—the avoidance response—from which to confirm both the Pavlovian and instrumental postulates of two-process theory. Where we once had two kinds of dependent variables to draw conclusions about two different processes, Rescorla and Solomon now leave us with only one.

If neither manipulation of external CSs nor observation of peripheral CRs will provide a critical test of two-process fear theory, what predictions from the theory remain to be tested? For Rescorla and Solomon the critical remaining claim is that whatever central state mediates avoidance must obey the laws of Pavlovian conditioning. One way they suggest of testing this assumption is to independently condition animals to respond to Pavlovian CSs and then impose these on avoidance responding. For example, Rescorla and LoLordo (1965) trained dogs to avoid on a Sidman schedule. They then imposed onto this schedule a CS+ and a CS− which had been paired with shock and no shock, respectively, in a separate Pavlovian procedure. The avoidance rate increased during CS+ and decreased during CS−. Rescorla and LoLordo assert that this finding confirms two-process theory on the following grounds: "If a CS+ is a Pavlovian excitor, then conditioned fear should be augmented by its presence and the instrumental responding rate should increase above the normal rate. In contrast, if CS− is a Pavlovian differential inhibitor, then it should actively suppress conditioned fear and the instrumental responding rate should decrease below the normal rate [p. 173]."

While Rescorla and LoLordo's results provide some comfort to two-process theory, their clear implications are quite limited. Such data do indicate that CSs established by Pavlovian procedures can modulate on-going avoidance responding. *What they do not show is that the state responsible for mediating avoidance in the first place obeys Pavlovian laws, much less that this state is central fear. They do not even show that the modulating effects of probe CSs are due to raising or lowering levels of whatever state was already*

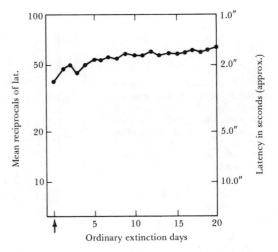

FIG. 1. *Mean response latency as a function of number of days of standard extinction, with 10 trials per day. (From Solomon & Wynne, 1954.)*

present. While Rescorla and LoLordo's data are certainly consistent with two-process theory, they also seem consistent with a number of alternative hypotheses including the cognitive one we will present later in this paper.

We are sympathetic with Rescorla and Solomon's review: The lack of concomitance between peripheral CRs and responding does suggest that avoidance is mediated by a central state. But we think there are several candidates for that state other than Pavlovian fear: (*a*) conditioned aversion, (*b*) the state underlying the ability to form a discriminative stimulus for avoidance, and (*c*) the expectations that responding leads to no shock and that not responding leads to shock.

Although modifications of two-process fear theory have tended to restrict its empirical implications, it is not untestable. We now turn to evidence which we believe shows that mediation of avoidance *cannot* be due to a Pavlovian CR, because the Pavlovian law of extinction is violated.

The Elusiveness of Extinction

Avoidance is, by and large, a remarkably persistent behavior. Animals will commonly respond for hundreds of trials without receiving a shock. Experimenters have often given up trying to extinguish the animal before the animal has given up responding. Just how difficult avoidance is to extinguish probably depends on a number of parameters.

Figure 1 presents the classic extinction curve for 13 dogs trained in a two-way shuttlebox to avoid intense shock by Solomon, Kamin, and Wynne (1953). The mean latency of responding was still getting shorter 200 trials after the last US was received. Solomon and Wynne (1954) also reported that "in return for a few intense shocks during acquisition of avoidance, dogs gave back as many as 650 avoidances without showing any sign of extinction [p. 359]." Similarly, Seligman and Campbell (1965), using a one-way shuttlebox, found that their rats were still avoiding with short latencies after 150 extinction trials. As Fig. 2 shows, the latencies seem to be lengthening slightly but are still considerably shorter than the CS–US interval. While very high resistance to extinction seems

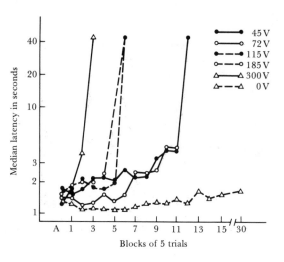

FIG. 2. *Median response latency for 0.15-sec.-duration punishment groups. Only the bottom curve (0 volt–unpunished group) is relevant to the effectiveness of standard extinction. (From Seligman & Campbell, 1965. Reprinted by permission of the author.)*

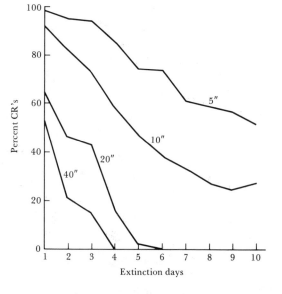

FIG. 3. *Percentage of avoidance responses by extinction days (10 trials per day) as a function of CS–US interval. (From Kamin, 1954.)*

to be the rule (e.g., F. R. Brush, 1957; Black, 1958; Miller, 1951; Baum, 1970), sometimes more rapid extinction is observed. For example, Fig. 3 shows extinction curves for Kamin's (1954) dogs run under trace avoidance procedures. With a 2-second CS followed by trace intervals of 20 or 40 seconds before shock, the dogs extinguished within about 50 trials. It should be noted that the more difficult the response was to learn, the more readily it extinguished. The groups with 5- or 10-second trace intervals were still showing some avoidance responding after 100 extinction trials. We cannot pinpoint the parameters that make extinction of avoidance more likely to occur, but we suspect the following to be relevant: preparedness or naturalness of the response (Bolles, 1970; Seligman, 1970), trace versus delay CS (Kamin, 1954), and reflexiveness of the re-

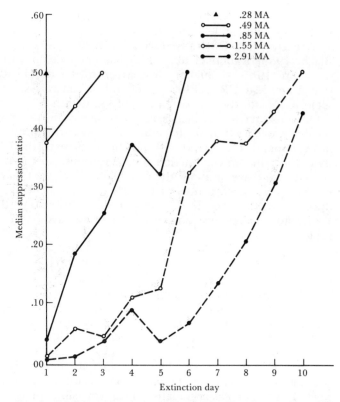

FIG. 4. *Median suppression ratio by extinction days (four trials per day) as a function of US intensity. (From Annau & Kamin, 1961. Reprinted by permission of the author.)*

sponse (Turner & Solomon, 1962). We can safely assert, however, that under a wide variety of conditions, avoidance responding is extremely resistant to extinction.

In contrast, classically conditioned responses extinguish very readily. Most Pavlovian CRs (e.g., salivation, GSR, eyelid) extinguish within several dozen nonreinforced trials. Figure 4 presents extinction data for CER established with different intensities of shock in rats (Annau & Kamin, 1961). Even with exceedingly intense shock for rats (2.91 milliamperes) extinction occurred within 40 trials. With less intense shock, extinction occurred even more rapidly. Church and Black (1958) found that classically conditioned heart-rate changes in the dog largely extinguished within 10 trials, with substantial extinction occurring after the very first shock omission. These results contrast strikingly with F. R. Brush's (1957) study of avoidance extinction in dogs. He varied intensity of shock from very mild to intense and found that all groups were still reliably avoiding after 200 extinction trials. We know of no form of classical conditioning, not excepting fear conditioning, which even approaches the usual resistance to extinction of avoidance.

The relative inextinguishability of avoidance responding was recognized as a serious problem for two-process theory by Ritchie (1951) and by Solomon and Wynne (1954). Since then it seems to have been swept under the rug, at least for theoretical purposes. The fact that animals apparently avoid fearlessly during extinction (Solomon & Wynne, 1954; Black, 1959; Kamin et al., 1963) has been dealt with by Rescorla and Solomon (1967) by making fear a central state. The deeper problem is that if any fear CR—either peripheral or central—*were* present, it would seem to violate the Pavlovian law of extinction.

On those trials in which a response occurs in the presence of the CS, no shock occurs. So, we have a Pavlovian extinction trial: the fear-evoking CS complex is paired with no shock. Fear to the CS should decrease monotonically, and extinction of the response in the presence of the CS should take place at about the rate of the Pavlovian fear extinction. After several dozen occurrences of the CS without the US, fear should be reduced to near zero. If the central state motivating the response were Pavlovian, as Rescorla and Solomon claim, avoidance would extinguish rapidly. . . .

The Cognitive Theory

Cognitive Precursors

Before presenting our theory, we would like to say a few words about its historical antecedents. Avoidance learning has long been recognized as a relatively favorable domain for cognitive theorizing. Hilgard and Marquis (1940), Osgood (1950), and Ritchie (1951) are among those who have taken a cognitive view of avoidance. Ritchie's views are of particular interest. He claimed two decades ago that high resistance to extinction presented a problem for prevalent S–R reinforcement theories. The purported problem was speculative, however, since he did not yet have data showing that classically conditioned fear extinguishes much more rapidly than avoidance. As an alternative to the S–R accounts, Ritchie suggested that extinction data could be readily handled by Tolmanian S–S expectancies. Ritchie contended that an animal in a traditional one-way shuttlebox avoidance situation expects to be shocked after some seconds in the start box, and expects not to be shocked in the goal box. During extinction, an asymptotically avoiding animal will leave the start box before he expects shock to arrive, so this expectancy will never be disconfirmed. One way to disconfirm it, Ritchie suggested, would be to block the response during extinction, and expose the animal to the start box through the time he expected shock to arrive. Ritchie noted Solomon and Wynne's (1950) preliminary report of a failure to extinguish dogs with response blocking and was willing to put his theory on the line as predicting that these early indications would not be upheld. Presumably, he would find modern data on response blocking much more congenial.

After a long dormant period, cognitive theory has recently emerged anew in an especially attractive form. In 1971, Francis W. Irwin published *Intentional Behavior and Motivation: A Cognitive Theory.* This book is, in our opinion, a signal achievement. Irwin has shown that a great deal of behavior can be handled in a single coherent framework relying on only two kinds of postulated states—*preferences* between outcomes, and *act–outcome expectancies*. Act–outcome expectancies are well-defined descendents of Tolman's (1932) "means–ends" relations. In a given situation, an animal is said to come to expect that a given act (a)—rather than some alternative act—will lead to a given outcome (o). A sufficient condition for making an act a_1 is having both (1) expectations that, in the situation at hand, a_1 leads to o_1, while a_2 leads to o_2, and (2) a preference of o_1 to o_2. Irwin presents rigorous empirical criteria for diagnosing the presence of such expectancies and preferences.

Our theory is stated within Irwin's situation–act–outcome (SAO) framework and uses a variant of Irwin's notation. We discuss in the appendix the relation of our theory to Irwin's approach.

Introduction to Our Theory

While we have called our account a cognitive theory, it actually has two components: one cognitive, the other emotional. The cognitive component makes use of pairs of act–outcome expectancies and a corresponding preference between outcomes.

In our theory, an expectancy is a hypothetical construct: a state of the organism which represents (stores information about) contingencies between responses and outcomes in a given situation. The general form of this three-term expectancy is S:rEo, which is read, "It is expected that in a given situation (S) a given response (r) leads to a given outcome (o)." A preference is also a hypothetical construct: a state of the organism which controls the choice of response on the basis of outcomes expected. The general form of the preference is o_1Po_2 which is read, "One outcome (o_1) is preferred to another outcome (o_2)."

The emotional component is based on classically conditioned fear as a response elicitor. Reinforcement by fear reduction plays no role in the theory.

Our exposition of the theory will be as follows. We will (I) present the cognitive component of the theory and (II) discuss empirical consequences that can be derived from it alone. We will then (III) present the theory's emotional component and (IV) discuss the additional empirical consequences that follow from a combination of the two components. We will next (V) discuss how our theory covers some further phenomena with the addition of subsidiary premises congenial to the theory. Lastly, (VI) we will mention some residual phenomena which our theory cannot easily explain.

I. The Cognitive Component

This part of the theory postulates that an animal has one preference and during avoidance learning acquires two related expectancies.

1. The animal prefers no shock (š) to shock (s); that is, šPs.

2. The animal expects that if he responds within a given time (r_t, where t is the length of the CS–US interval in signalized avoidance, or the R–S interval in unsignalized avoidance), no shock (š) rather than shock (s) will occur; that is, r_tEš.

3. The animal expects that if he does not respond within the appropriate time $(\bar{r}_t)$,[4] shock (s) rather than no shock (š) will occur; that is, $\bar{r}_t$Es.

4. Expectancies are strengthened when they are confirmed, and weakened when they are disconfirmed. Thus r_tEš is confirmed when r_t is followed by š, and disconfirmed when it is followed by s; $\bar{r}_t$Es is confirmed

when $\bar{r}_t$ is followed by s, and disconfirmed when it is followed by $\bar{s}$.[5]

5. Holding constant the preference for $\bar{s}$ rather than s, the *probability* of r_t is a monotonically increasing joint function of the strengths of both $r_t E\bar{s}$ and $\bar{r}_t Es$.[6]

II. Empirical Implications of the Cognitive Component Alone

Extinction. According to the rules of the cognitive component, r_t will decrease in probability when at least one of the following occurs: *(a)* $r_t E\bar{s}$ is disconfirmed, *(b)* $\bar{r}_t Es$ is disconfirmed, or *(c)* $\bar{s}Ps$ is weakened. The following phenomena can thus be accounted for:

1. Avoidance is extremely difficult to extinguish by the conventional procedure of omitting shock: $r_t E\bar{s}$ continues to be confirmed; $\bar{r}_t Es$ is not disconfirmed because $\bar{r}_t$ is never made and the contingency never sampled; $\bar{s}Ps$ is unchanged.

According to our theory, the high resistance to extinction of avoidance is not dependent on any special properties of aversive outcomes (as was the case with Solomon and Wynne's (1954) principle of partial irreversibility). It might be expected that if an animal on an appetitive schedule never sampled disconfirmation of the expectation that not responding leads to no reinforcement, high resistance to extinction would also be obtained. Schoenfeld (1973) found that this is indeed true. He put pigeons on an acquisition schedule in which they received grain at the end of a period of time if they had pecked a key during that interval. The birds were then shifted to an extinction schedule in which grain arrived at the end of the period whether or not key pecking occurred. Schoenfeld's pigeons failed to extinguish noticeably for as long as the schedule was continued. This experiment can be treated in a manner very similar to avoidance. The pigeon acquires the expectation that responding during the interval (r_t) leads to food (fd) $r_t Efd$—and that not responding during the interval $(\bar{r}_t)$ leads to no food $(\bar{fd})$—$\bar{r}_t E\bar{fd}$. The pigeon has a preference fdPfd. As in avoidance "extinction" the animal continues to respond during Schoenfeld's appetitive "extinction" schedule because the first expectancy continues to be confirmed, the second expectancy is not disconfirmed, and the relative preference for outcomes remains unchanged.

2. The efficacy of standard avoidance extinction procedures will, according to our theory, be a function of how likely the animal is to sample disconfirmation of $\bar{r}_t Es$. Anything that prevents an animal from producing r_t with total reliability should lead to more sampling and faster extinction. For instance, more sampling of disconfirmation and faster extinction should occur if the animal is required to make a "heavy-weight" response, e.g., one that is physically difficult to perform in the allotted time interval. We would also predict that an analysis of individual response records for a given experiment would show that less reliable responders at the start of extinction will reach a strong extinction criterion unusually fast.

At our present level of understanding we are largely ignorant of independent variables that produce greater or lesser sampling of $\bar{r}_t$. For the moment it is true that our theory can only assert that "weak responding leads to even weaker responding." (cf. Beecroft, 1971).

3. Omitting the avoidance contingency by allowing shock to occur (regardless of whether the animal responds) while continuing the CS-termination contingency, should produce extinction considerably faster than the standard procedure; $r_t E\bar{s}$ would be disconfirmed. So far as we know, this implication of our theory has not been tested yet.

4. Response blocking should facilitate extinction (e.g., Baum, 1970). In response blocking, r_t is prevented, and $\bar{r}_t Es$ is therefore directly disconfirmed. The more disconfirmation to which the animal is exposed, the more effective the procedure should be, as Baum (1969) has reported.

Unlike two-process theory, our theory asserts that *response extinction* occurs independently of Pavlovian *fear extinction*. It is therefore entirely possible according to our account that after response blocking some animals could still be afraid of the CS even though the avoidance response had entirely extinguished. Baum (1970) has reported observing this phenomenon.

5. Punishing the avoidance response by shock should facilitate extinction because $r_t E\bar{s}$ is disconfirmed and replaced by $r_t Es$. Evidence on this point is not yet decisive. F. R. Brush (1957) and Seligman and Campbell (1965), for example, have found punishment to be effective, but Brown (1969) has reviewed the contrary evidence.

6. The strength of sPs should be greater the longer the animal spends in the shock-free compartment. Reynierse and Rizley (1970) reported higher resistance to extinction (and superior acquisition) with longer shock-free reinforcement.

Acquisition. 1. If sPs (no shock is preferred to shock), acquisition will not occur. Very low shock intensities do not produce acquisition.

2. Circumstances which facilitate the occurrence of initial r_t's will facilitate avoidance acquisition. Once the avoidance response starts being made, the expectancy $r_t E\bar{s}$ will be confirmed, and the probability of r_t will increase. As before, this assertion is at present largely a statement that an animal must start making the avoidance response to learn to avoid—scarcely surprising. It does suggest looking at individual response records (see, e.g., Solomon & Wynne, 1953) to see if the acquisition curve is a sensible function of number of previous confirmations of $r_t E\bar{s}$.[7] Furthermore if we have independent means of predicting when r_t will be emitted, more impressive predictions become possible. The emotional component of our theory provides a start in this direction.

3. CS termination with no avoidance of shock should not produce much acquisition of r_t because $r_t E\bar{s}$ is disconfirmed.[8] Kamin (1956) obtained evidence for moderate acquisition under these circumstances, but Bolles, Stokes, and Younger (1966) have found virtually no acquisition when the contaminating effects of an escape contingency are removed. This is true even when the response is occurring with a relatively high base-line frequency.

4. A US avoidance contingency alone, without escape or CS-termination contingencies, should lead to acquisition if the response is emitted with enough probability to achieve reasonable confirmation of $r_t E\bar{s}$ (e.g., Bolles et al., 1966).

5. Avoidance learning need not be accompanied by fear at all. Only a preference for the nonaversive outcome is necessary. Ray (1972) and

Grant (1973) have reported that instrumental avoidance of air-puffs can be acquired by rats and men. There are no indications that subjects are actually afraid of the air-puff in these experiments. Unlike Rescorla and Solomon, we take the absence of peripheral fear signs as presumptive evidence that no fear is present.

6. Our theory accounts for Herrnstein and Hineline's (1966) finding that animals can learn to avoid an increase in shock density. The theory requires only that animals have the (quite plausible) preference for low shock density over high shock density. The theory then holds as before, with "low shock density" substituted for $\bar{s}$ and "high shock density" for s.

7. Our theory holds that punishment (passive) avoidance is produced in the same way as active avoidance. The only difference is that the animal acquires expectations rEs and $\bar{r}$E$\bar{s}$; his preference for $\bar{s}$ now causes $\bar{r}$ to be made. The roles of r and $\bar{r}$ are simply reversed from the active avoidance paradigm.

8. Under appropriate circumstances, animals can learn to respond to terminate a CS previously paired with shock but now shock-free (e.g., Miller, 1951). Pairings of the CS and shock should have established the expectation $\bar{r}$Es. When the shock is turned off and the animal is allowed to sample r, he will acquire the expectation that, during the CS, rE$\bar{s}$. This effect should depend on having a high enough initial probability so that rE$\bar{s}$ will become established, before the animal waits through enough CSs to lose the $\bar{r}$Es expectancy.

III. The Emotional Component

1. Fear is classically conditioned to a CS paired with shock.

2. Fear is classically extinguished to the CS when the CS is not followed by shock.

3. Fear can be indexed by autonomic responses and skeletal responses elicited by the CS. These skeletal responses may, with some probability, include the specified avoidance response or similar responses.

It should be noted that we are *not* offering a new analysis of the classical conditioning process. In particular, we are *not* asserting that it is mediated by expectancies of any kind.[9]

It should be noted that fear reduction plays no reinforcing role in our account. Fear serves only in the elicitation of responses.

It is not critical for our theory whether fear is considered to be peripheral or central. If it is the latter, however, it must at least be reliably indexed by peripheral skeletal and autonomic responses.

IV. Implications That Follow from the Cognitive and Emotional Components of the Theory Together

Extinction. 1. Fear, as indexed by autonomic responses, and CER will not be present during asymptotic acquisition or extinction (e.g., Black, 1959; Kamin et al., 1963). According to our theory, fear has classically extinguished to those *durations* of external and feedback CSs that have not been followed by shock. In fact, animals typically are *not* afraid of the CS that is controlling their asymptotic avoidance response (Maier et al., 1969; Solomon & Wynne, 1954).

2. Fear may be observed when long latency responses occur (Solomon & Wynne, 1954). This is because the animal now exposes himself to a duration of the CS which has not previously been classically extinguished by pairing with shock. Aside from eliciting fear, such a long latency trial is a classical extinction trial to this longer duration of the CS. Eventually no fear should be produced by even long-latency responses.

3. Fear should be observed during response blocking itself (e.g., Solomon et al., 1953; Baum, 1970). The animal is exposed to longer durations of the CS than had previously been classically extinguished during avoidance training.

4. As mentioned earlier, our theory permits the avoidance response to extinguish during response blocking without extinction of the fear CR (Baum, 1970). Extinction of the fear CR occurs when enough CS–no shock pairings have occurred for classical extinction. Disconfirmation of $\hat{r}_t$Es also requires CS–no shock pairings, but there is no reason why effective disconfirmation could not proceed at a faster rate than fear extinction.

5. We have already stated that factors which provide the animal with experience disconfirming $\hat{r}$Es will lead to faster avoidance extinction. One way for this to occur is if r_t is "unnatural"—that is, not similar to any part of the animal's species-specific defense repertoire (Bolles, 1970). In this case the animal will tend to emit other more natural responses which are incompatible with r_t and serve as effective instances of $\hat{r}_t$. If independent ethological observation is used to define the SSDR, there need be no circularity in a prediction that SSDR-incompatible responses will extinguish more readily.

Acquisition. 1. As noted earlier, circumstances which facilitate the occurrence of initial r_t's will facilitate the acquisition of avoidance. Initial r_t's should be facilitated if they are classically elicited by a fear-evoking CS or if they are part of an animal's SSDR. In either case the probability that r_t will be made, and r_tEs confirmed, increases.

2. If r_t is part of an animal's SSDR, avoidance conditioning will be retarded by any factor that retards classical conditioning of fear. Elicitation of early responses will be delayed. Evidence suggests that in fact techniques which can be presumed to suppress fear do retard avoidance acquisition. Sympathectomy, adrenalectomy, and administration of tranquilizers should lead to less effective avoidance learning because they retard the emission of the early avoidance responses elicited by fear (e.g., · Wynne & Solomon, 1955).

3. Concomitance of peripheral fear CRs and skeletal avoidance responses should be observed early in acquisition. Since fear elicits early r_t's, we would expect that the moment of onset of a peripheral CR would closely precede making the avoidance response. On the other hand our theory says nothing about the moment of onset of fear *reduction*, and we would not predict that making the avoidance response would reliably precede the decline of peripheral CRs. Black (1959), studying heart-rate acceleration in dogs, has reported just such a pattern of results in early acquisition: the *onset* of a peripheral fear CR reliably precedes making the

avoidance response, but this response is not closely followed by a reliable decline of the peripheral fear CR. We have not carried out a serious review of the huge literature that has accumulated on this topic, but we believe that a reevaluation of it with an eye toward only elicitation concomitance is in order.

4. CER to the CS will be seen early in avoidance because CER is also an index of fear (Kamin et al., 1963).

5. Autonomic fear CRs, and CER to the CS, will not be found late in acquisition (Black, 1959; Kamin et al., 1963). Fear has classically extinguished since the CS is never followed by shock if the animal responds reliably. . . .

Summary

We have reviewed several previous theories of avoidance learning. Two-process fear mediation theory was explored at greatest length and criticized for failing to account for the extraordinary persistence of responding under standard extinction procedures. Several variants of this theory were found to be incapable of handling this evidence while at the same time explaining why response blocking *does* produce a rapid decline in responding. Two-process aversion theory was also found to be unable to account for extinction data and, in addition, to be silent about fear-related phenomena in avoidance. Discriminative stimulus theory was found to be silent about an even wider range of phenomena.

We have proposed a cognitively oriented theory with two components. The cognitive component assumes that a subject has a preference for no shock over shock, and acquires two expectancies: that responding leads to no shock, and that not responding leads to shock. Behavioral criteria for diagnosing such expectancies and preferences were adapted from considerations advanced by Irwin (1971). According to the theory, the presence of the stated preference and pair of expectancies is a sufficient condition for responding to occur. The principles of the cognitive component were shown to account successfully for the troublesome data on the effects of extinction and response-blocking procedures, as well as some other extinction and acquisition data.

The theory also includes an emotional component based on the elicitation of responses by classically conditioned fear. The addition of the fear component extends our theory to cover most of the major facts of acquisition and extinction of avoidance. Several additional facts are handled with minor subsidiary principles such as stimulus generalization and pooling of separately established expectancies. Finally, we note several other phenomena which are not accounted for by this theory or by any of its competitors. . . .

Notes

[1] Supported by PHS grants MH 19604 to M. Seligman, MH 19989, and an NSF graduate fellowship to J. Johnston. We thank R. Bolles, H. Gleitman, R. Hendersen, R. Herrnstein, S. Mineka, and P. Rozin for many helpful comments on drafts of the chapter. We are also deeply grateful to two of our colleagues, F. W. Irwin and R. L. Solomon: Without the prodigious work of Solomon over the last two decades, there would be little data in the field of avoidance to theorize about. Without the conceptual framework provided by Irwin's cognitive theory, and without his patience and generosity at several stages in the writing of the chapter, there would be little theory we could offer.

[2] In Kamin's study, the group that can only terminate the CS shows some acquisition of "avoidance" responding. On escape trials, the CS terminates along with the shock; termination of both external and feedback CSs is paired with no shock. To the extent that the animal fails to discriminate between escape and avoidance conditions, these CSs in "avoidance" may provide some fear reduction. Bolles, Stokes, and Younger (1966) confirmed Kamin's results and also found that omitting the US-escape contingency reduced the number of "avoidance" responses markedly.

[3] Failure of concomitance between CER and avoidance (Kamin et al., 1963) also does not count against the central fear hypothesis. Rescorla and Solomon (1967) suggest that "the CER experiment is not an adequate index of the conditioned fear reaction. After all, there does not exist a closely reasoned account of the fact that the CER procedure produces *suppression* of the appetitively maintained operant. Why should we not instead find rate increases [p. 169]?"

[4] Technically we prefer to use $\bar{r}_t$ to refer to *making* another response that is a member of the set of responses consisting of all responses except r_t; $\bar{r}_t$ and r_t then refer to exclusive and exhaustive sets of responses.

[5] Clearly the theory will eventually have to be refined so that appropriate attention by the animal is a necessary condition for augmenting the strength of an expectancy. See item 3 in the section on unsolved problems below.

[6] It may be that $r_t E\bar{s}$ must have some minimal strength before increasing the strength of $\bar{r}_t E\bar{s}$ will have any effect on responding. Future analysis of failure to acquire avoidance may show this to be the case.

[7] Obviously if the animal responds too well, too early, it is in principle possible that $\bar{r}_t E\bar{s}$ will never become very strong. This seems rarely to be a relevant consideration in experiments so far conducted. When it is, the acquisition curve will be affected by individual differences in exposure to confirmations of this expectancy. In any case, a start at fitting acquisition data can be made in cases where $\bar{r}_t E\bar{s}$ can be sensibly considered asymptotic for all animals by the time of the first avoidance response.

[8] Some acquisition might occur if the animal prefers no fear to fear, and comes to expect that turning off the CS leads to less fear (see below). Since a US follows even when the CS has been turned off, however, fear will soon develop to the trace of a CS that has been recently escaped. Thus very little change in fear would be achieved, and the response would be acquired feebly if at all.

[9] Classical conditioning *might*, in fact, be mediated by expectancies of some kind, but our theory is neutral on this point.

References

Anderson, N. H., & Nakamura, C. Y. Avoidance decrement in avoidance conditioning. *Journal of Comparative and Physiological Psychology*, 1964, **57**, 196–204.

Anger, D. The role of temporal discrimination in the reinforcement of Sidman avoidance behavior. *Journal of the Experimental Analysis of Behavior*, 1963, **6**, 477–506.

Annau, Z., & Kamin, L. J. The conditioned emotional response as a function of intensity of the US. *Journal of Comparative and Physiological Psychology*, 1961, **54**, 428–432.

Baum, M. Rapid extinction of an avoidance response following a period of response prevention in the avoidance apparatus. *Psychological Reports*, 1966, **18**, 59–64.

Baum, M. Perseveration of fear measured by changes in rate of avoidance responding in dogs. Unpublished doctoral dissertation, University of Pennsylvania, 1967.

Baum, M. Extinction of an avoidance response following response prevention: Some parametric investigations, *Canadian Journal of Psychology*, 1969, **23**, 1–10.

Baum, M. Extinction of avoidance response through response prevention (flooding). *Psychological Bulletin*, 1970, **74**, 276–284.

Beecroft, R. S. Patterns in avoidance extinction. *Psychonomic Science*, 1971, **23**, 53–55.

Bersh, P. J., Notterman, J. M., & Schoenfeld, W. N. Extinction of a human cardiac-response during avoidance-conditioning. *American Journal of Psychology*, 1956, **59**, 244–251.

Black, A. H. The extinction of avoidance responses under curare. *Journal of Comparative and Physiological Psychology*, 1958, **51**, 519–524.

Black, A. H. Heart rate changes during avoidance learning in dogs. *Canadian Journal of Psychology*, 1959, **13**, 229–242.

Bolles, R. C. Species-specific defense reactions and avoidance learning. *Psychological Review*, 1970, **77**, 32–48.

Bolles, R. C., Stokes, L. W., & Younger, M. S. Does CS termination reinforce avoidance behavior? *Journal of Comparative and Physiological Psychology*, 1966, **62**, 201–207.

Brown, J. S. Factors effecting self-punitive behavior. In B. A. Campbell & R. M. Church (Eds.), *Punishment and aversive behavior*. New York: Appleton-Century-Crofts, 1969. Pp. 467–514.

Brown, J. S., & Jacobs, A. The role of fear in the motivation and acquisition of responses. *Journal of Experimental Psychology*, 1949, **39**, 747–759.

Brush, E. S. Traumatic avoidance learning: The effects of conditioned stimulus length in a free-responding situation. *Journal of Comparative and Physiological Psychology*, 1957, **50**, 541–546.

Brush, F. R. The effects of shock intensity on the acquisition and extinction of an avoidance response in dogs. *Journal of Comparative and Physiological Psychology*, 1957, **50**, 547–552.

Carlson, N. J., & Black, A. H. Traumatic avoidance learning: The effects of preventing escape responses. *Canadian Journal of Psychology*, 1960, **14**, 21–28.

Church, R. M., & Black, A. H. Latency of the conditioned heart rate as a function of the CS–US interval. *Journal of Comparative and Physiological Psychology*, 1958, **51**, 478–482.

Church, R. M., Brush, F. R., & Solomon, R. L. Traumatic avoidance learning: The effects of CS–US interval with a delayed-conditioning procedure in a free-responding situation. *Journal of Comparative and Physiological Psychology*, 1956, **49**, 301–308.

Coons, E. E., Anderson, N. H., & Myers, A. K. Disappearance of avoidance responding during continued training. *Journal of Comparative and Physiological Psychology*, 1960, **53**, 290–292.

D'Amato, M. R. *Experimental psychology: Methodology, psychophysics and learning.* New York: McGraw-Hill, 1970.

D'Amato, M. R., Fazzaro, J., & Etkin, M. Anticipatory responding and avoidance discrimination as factors in avoidance conditioning. *Journal of Experimental Psychology*, 1968, **77**, 41–47.

Denny, M. R., & Weisman, R. G. Avoidance behavior as a function of length of nonshock confinement. *Journal of Comparative and Physiological Psychology*, 1964, **58**, 252–257.

Dinsmoor, J. A. Punishment. I. The avoidance hypothesis. *Psychological Review*, 1954, **61**, 34–46.

Grant, D. A. Reification and reality in conditioning paradigms: Implications of results when modes of reinforcement are changed. In F. J. McGuigan and D. B. Lumsden (Eds.), *Contemporary approaches to conditioning and learning*. Washington, D.C.:V. H. Winston, 1973. Pp. 49–68.

Grossen, N. E. Effect of aversive discriminative stimuli on appetitive behavior. *Journal of Experimental Psychology*, 1971, **88**, 90–94.

Hammond, L. J. Increased responding to CS − in differential CER. *Psychonomic Science*, 1966, **5**, 337–338.

Herrnstein, R. J. Method and theory in the study of avoidance. *Psychological Review*, 1969, **76**, 49–69.

Herrnstein, R. J., & Hineline, P. N. Negative reinforcement as shock-frequency reduction. *Journal of the Experimental Analysis of Behavior*, 1966, **9**, 421–430.

Hilgard, E. R., & Marquis, D. G. *Conditioning and learning*. New York: Appleton-Century-Crofts, 1940.

Irwin, F. W. *Intentional behavior and motivation: A cognitive theory*. New York: Lippincott, 1971.

Kamin, L. J. Traumatic avoidance learning: The effects of CS–US interval with a trace-conditioning procedure. *Journal of Comparative and Physiological Psychology*, 1954, **47**, 65–72.

Kamin, L. J. The effects of termination of the CS and avoidance of the US on avoidance learning. *Journal of Comparative and Physiological Psychology*, 1956, **49**, 420–424.

Kamin, L. J., Brimer, C. J., & Black, A. H. Conditioned suppression as a monitor of fear of the CS in the course of avoidance training. *Journal of Comparative and Physiological Psychology*, 1963, **56**, 497–501.

Katzev, R. Extinguishing avoidance responses as a function of delayed warning signal termination. *Journal of Experimental Psychology*, 1967, **75**, 339–344.

Katzev, R., & Hendersen, R. W. Effects of exteroceptive feedback stimuli on extinguishing avoidance responses in Fischer rats. *Journal of Comparative and Physiological Psychology*, 1971, **74**, 66–74.

Kimble, G. A., & Perlmuter, L. C. The problem of volition. *Psychological Review*, 1970, **77**, 361–384.

Kimmel, H. D. Instrumental factors in classical conditioning. In W. Prokasy (Ed.), *Classical conditioning*. New York: Appleton-Century-Crofts, 1965.

Konorski, J. *Conditioned reflexes and neuron organization.* Cambridge: Cambridge University Press, 1948.

LoLordo, V. M. Similarity of conditioned fear responses based upon different events. *Journal of Comparative and Physiological Psychology,* 1967, **64,** 154–158.

LoLordo, V. M., & Rescorla, R. A. Protection of the fear-eliciting capacity of a stimulus from extinction. *Acta Biologiae Experimentalis,* 1966, **26,** 251–258.

MacCorquodale, K., & Meehl, P. E. On a distinction between hypothetical constructs and intervening variables. *Psychological Review,* 1948, **55,** 95–107.

MacCorquodale, K., & Meehl, P. E. Edward C. Tolman. In W. K. Estes (Ed.), *Modern learning theory.* New York: Appleton-Century-Crofts, 1954.

Maier, S. F., Seligman, M. E. P., & Solomon, R. L. Pavlovian fear conditioning and learned helplessness effects on escape and avoidance behavior of (a) the CS–US contingency and (b) the independence of the US and voluntary responding. In B. A. Campbell & R. M. Church (Eds.), *Punishment and aversive behavior.* New York: Appleton-Century-Crofts, 1969.

Miller, N. E. Studies of fear as an acquirable drive. I. Fear as motivation and fear reduction as reinforcement in the learning of new responses. *Journal of Experimental Psychology,* 1948, **38,** 89–101.

Miller, N. E. Learnable drives and rewards. In S. S. Stevens (Ed.), *Handbook of experimental psychology.* New York: Wiley, 1951.

Mowrer, O. H. On the dual nature of learning: A re-interpretation of "conditioning" and "problem-solving." *Harvard Educational Review,* 1947, **17,** 102–148.

Osgood, C. E. Can Tolman's theory of learning handle avoidance training? *Psychological Review,* 1950, **57,** 133–137.

Page, H. A. The facilitation of experimental extinction by response prevention as a function of the acquisition of a new response. *Journal of Comparative and Physiological Psychology,* 1955, **48,** 14–16.

Page, H. A., & Hall, J. F. Experimental extinction as a function of the prevention of a response. *Journal of Comparative and Physiological Psychology.* 1953, **46,** 253–255.

Pavlov, I. P. *Conditioned reflexes.* London: Oxford University Press, 1927.

Polin, A. T. The effect of flooding and physical suppression as extinction techniques on an anxiety-motivated avoidance locomotor response. *Journal of Psychology,* 1959, **47,** 253–255.

Ray, A. J., Jr. Shuttle avoidance learning and performance: Electric shock and air-stream aversive stimulation compared. Paper presented at the meeting of the Eastern Psychological Association, Boston, April 1972.

Rescorla, R. A. Predictability and number of pairings in Pavlovian fear conditioning. *Psychonomic Science,* 1966, **4,** 383–384.

Rescorla, R. A. Inhibition of delay in Pavlovian fear conditioning. *Journal of Comparative and Physiological Psychology,* 1967, **64,** 114–120.

Rescorla, R. A., & LoLordo, V. M. Inhibition of avoidance behavior. *Journal of Comparative and Physiological Psychology,* 1965, **59,** 406–412.

Rescorla, R. A., & Solomon, R. L. Two-process learning theory: Relationships between Pavlovian conditioning and instrumental learning. *Psychological Review,* 1967, **74,** 151–182.

Reynierse, J. H., & Rizley, R. C. Relaxation and fear as determinants of maintained avoidance in rats. *Journal of Comparative and Physiological Psychology,* 1970, **72,** 223–232.

Reynolds, G. S. *A primer of operant conditioning.* Glenview, Ill.: Scott Foresman, 1968.

Ritchie, B. F. Can reinforcement theory account for avoidance? *Psychological Review,* 1951, **58,** 382–386.

Schoenfeld, W. N. An experimental approach to anxiety, escape, and avoidance behavior. In P. J. Hoch & J. Zubin (Eds.), *Anxiety.* New York: Grune & Stratton, 1950. Pp. 70–99.

Schoenfeld, W. N., Cole, B. K., Lang, J., and Markoff, R., "Contingency" in behavior theory. In F. J. McGuigan and D. B. Lumsden (Eds.), *Contemporary approaches to conditioning and learning.* Washington, D.C.: V. H. Winston, 1973. Pp. 151–172.

Seligman, M. E. P. Chronic fear produced by unpredictable electric shock. *Journal of Comparative and Physiological Psychology,* 1968, **66,** 402–411.

Seligman, M. E. P. On generality of the laws of learning. *Psychological Review.* 1970, **77,** 406–418.

Seligman, M. E. P., & Campbell, B. A. Effects of intensity and duration of punishment on extinction of an avoidance response. *Journal of Comparative and Physiological Psychology,* 1965, **59,** 295–297.

Seligman, M. E. P., & Meyer, B. Chronic fear and ulcers in rats as a function of the unpredictability of safety. *Journal of Comparative and Physiological Psychology*, 1970, **73**, 202–207.

Seligman, M. E. P., Maier, S. F., & Solomon, R. L. Unpredictable and uncontrollable aversive events. In F. R. Brush (Ed.), *Aversive conditioning and learning*. New York: Academic Press, 1971. Pp. 347–400.

Shipley, R. H., Mack, L. A., & Levis, D. J. Effects of several response prevention procedures on activity, avoidance responding, and conditioned fear in rats. *Journal of Comparative and Physiological Psychology*, 1971, **77**, 256–270.

Sidman, M. Avoidance conditioning with brief shock and no exteroceptive warning signal. *Science*, 1953, **46**, 253–261.

Solomon, R. L., & Brush, E. S. Experimentally derived conceptions of anxiety and aversion. In M. R. Jones (Ed.), *Nebraska Symposium on Motivation*, 1954, **4**, 212–305.

Solomon, R. L., & Wynne, L. C. Avoidance conditioning in normal dogs and in dogs deprived of normal autonomic functioning. *American Psychologist*, 1950, **5**, 264.

Solomon, R. L., & Wynne, L. C. Traumatic avoidance learning acquisition in normal dogs. *Psychological Monographs*, 1953, **67** (4, Whole No. 354).

Solomon, R. L., & Wynne, L. C. Traumatic avoidance learning: The principles of anxiety conservation and partial irreversibility. *Psychological Review*, 1954, **61**, 353–385.

Solomon, R. L., Kamin, L. J., & Wynne, L. C. Traumatic avoidance learning: The outcomes of several extinction procedures with dogs. *Journal of Abnormal and Social Psychology*, 1953, **48**, 291–302.

Soltysik, S. Studies on the avoidance conditioning. II. Differentiation and extinction of avoidance reflexes. *Acta Biologiae Experimentalis*, 1960, **20**, 171–182.

Soltysik, S. Inhibitory feedback in avoidance conditioning. *Boletin del Instituto de Estudios Medicos y Biologicos*, Universidad Nacional de Mexico, 1963, **21**, 433.

Sutherland, N. S., & MacKintosh, N. J. *Mechanisms of animal discrimination learning*. New York: Academic Press, 1971.

Taub, E., & Berman, A. J. Avoidance conditioning in the absence of relevant proprioceptive and exteroceptive feedback. *Journal of Comparative and Physiological Psychology*, 1963, **56**, 1012–1016.

Taub, E., & Berman, A. J. The effect of massive somatic deafferentation on behavior and wakefulness in monkeys. In S. J. Freedman (Ed.), *The neuropsychology of spatially oriented behavior*. Homewood, Ill.: Dorsey Press, 1968.

Teuber, H. L. Lacunae and research approaches to them. In J. C. Eccles (Ed.), *Brain and conscious experience*. New York: Springer-Verlag, 1967. Pp. 182–216.

Tolman, E. C. *Purposive behavior in animals and men*. New York: Appleton-Century, 1932.

Tolman, E. C. There is more than one kind of learning. *Psychological Review*, 1949, **56**, 144–155.

Tolman, E. C., & Gleitman, H. Studies in learning and motivation. I. Equal reinforcements in both end-boxes, followed by shock in one end-box. *Journal of Experimental Psychology*, 1949, **39**, 810–819.

Turner, L. H., & Solomon, R. L. Human traumatic avoidance learning: Theory and experiments on the operant-respondent distinction and failure to learn. *Psychological Monographs*, 1962, **76** (40, Whole No. 559).

Weisman, R. G., & Litner, J. S. Positive conditioned reinforcement of Sidman avoidance behavior in rats. *Journal of Comparative and Physiological Psychology*, 1969, **68**, 597–603.

Wenzel, B. M. Changes in heart rate associated with responses based on positive and negative reinforcement. *Journal of Comparative and Physiological Psychology*, 1961, **54**, 638–644.

Wynne, L. C., & Solomon, R. L. Traumatic avoidance learning: Acquisition and extinction in dogs deprived of normal peripheral autonomic functioning. *Genetic and Psychological Monographs*, 1955, **52**, 241–284.

D. BIOLOGICAL THEORY

If we assume that the cognitive account of avoidance is correct, a question still remains. Before the appropriate expectancies can develop, organisms must begin making avoidance responses. What gets them to start responding in the first place? The article by Bolles suggests that organisms come to experiments equipped with a repertoire of different defensive responses, species-typical responses that occur, without learning, in danger situations. These are the responses they will make in an avoidance experiment. Thus, argued Bolles, the single most important determinant of whether, and how fast, an animal will learn to avoid is the relation between the avoidance response required of it and its repertoire of defensive responses. If the required avoidance response is part of its defensive repertoire, it will learn quickly; if not, it may not learn at all. Moreover, even if the animal makes the avoidance response, it may not associate it with successful avoidance unless the response is a part of its defensive repertoire. According to Bolles, conditioned fear and expectations take a back seat to biological predispositions as determinants of avoidance.

20 Species-Specific Defense Reactions and Avoidance Learning

ROBERT C. BOLLES

The prevailing theories of avoidance learning and the procedures that are usually used to study it seem to be totally out of touch with what is known about how animals defend themselves in nature. This paper suggests some alternative concepts, starting with the assumption that animals have innate species-specific defense reactions (SSDRs) such as fleeing, freezing, and fighting. It is proposed that if a particular avoidance response is rapidly acquired, then that response must necessarily be an SSDR. The learning mechanism in this case appears to be suppression of nonavoidance behavior by the avoidance contingency. The traditional approaches to avoidance learning appear to be slightly more valid in the case of responses that are slowly acquired, although in this case, too, the SSDR concept is relevant, and reinforcement appears to be based on the production of a safety signal rather than the termination of an aversive conditioned stimulus.[1]

Avoidance learning as we know it in the laboratory has frequently been used to "explain" how animals survive in the wild. The purpose of this paper is to turn this inferential process around and use the limited knowledge of natural defensive behavior to help account for some of the anomalies that have been found in laboratory studies of avoidance learning. Let us begin by recalling a little fable. It is a very familiar fable. It was already part of our lore when Hull gave his version of it in 1929, and the story has been told again many times since then. It goes something like this: Once upon a time there was a little animal who ran around in the forest. One day while he was running around, our hero was suddenly attacked by a predator. He was hurt and, of course, frightened, but he was lucky and managed to escape from the predator. He was able to get away and safely back to his home. The fable continues: Some time later our furry friend was again running around in the forest, which was his custom, when suddenly he perceived a conditioned stimulus. He heard or saw or smelled some stimulus which on the earlier occasion had preceded the attack by the predator. Now on this occasion our friend became frightened, he immediately took flight as he had on the previous occasion, and quickly got safely back home. So this time our hero had managed to avoid attack (and possibly worse) by responding appropriately to a cue which signaled danger; he did not have to weather another attack. And from that day hence the little animal who ran around in the forest continued to avoid the predator because the precariousness of his situation prevented, somehow, his becoming careless or forgetful.

The moral of this tale, we are told, is that little animals survive in nature because they learn to avoid big dangerous animals. The ability to learn to avoid has such obviously great survival value, we are told, that we should surely expect the higher animals to have evolved this ability.

We should also expect animals to be able to learn to avoid in the laboratory, and we should expand our theories of behavior to encompass such learning.

I propose that this familiar fable with its happy ending and plausible moral is utter nonsense. The parameters of the situation make it impossible for there to be any learning. Thus, no real-life predator is going to present cues just before it attacks. No owl hoots or whistles 5 seconds before pouncing on a mouse. And no owl terminates his hoots or whistles just as the mouse gets away so as to reinforce the avoidance response. Nor will the owl give the mouse enough trials for the necessary learning to occur. What keeps our little friends alive in the forest has nothing to do with avoidance learning as we ordinarily conceive of it or investigate it in the laboratory.

Species-Specific Defense Reactions

What keeps animals alive in the wild is that they have very effective *innate* defensive reactions which occur when they encounter any kind of new or sudden stimulus. These defensive reactions vary somewhat from species to species, but they generally take one of three forms: Animals generally run or fly away, freeze, or adopt some type of threat, that is, pseudo-aggressive behavior. These defensive reactions are elicited by the appearance of the predator and by the sudden appearance of innocuous objects. These responses are always near threshold so that the animal will take flight, freeze, or threaten whenever any novel stimulus event occurs. It is not necessary that the stimulus event be paired with shock, or pain, or some other unconditioned stimulus. The mouse does not scamper away from the owl because it has learned to escape the painful claws of the enemy; it scampers away from anything happening in its environment, and it does so merely because it is a mouse. The gazelle does not flee from an approaching lion because it has been bitten by lions; it runs away from any large object that approaches it, and it does so because this is one of its species-specific defense reactions. Neither the mouse nor the gazelle can afford to *learn* to avoid; survival is too urgent, the opportunity to learn is too limited, and the parameters of the situation make the necessary learning impossible. The animal which survives is one which comes into its environment with defensive reactions already a prominent part of its repertoire.

There is, of course, a considerable gulf between the wild animal of the field and forest and the domesticated animal of the laboratory. Our laboratory rats and dogs and monkeys are relatively approachable and are on relatively friendly terms with us. However, this good relationship changes as soon as the animal is placed in a box and given a few electric shocks. When shocked, the normally friendly, inquisitive laboratory animal shows a dramatic change in behavior. Exploration and grooming drop out; so does all of its previously acquired appetitive behavior—bar pressing, etc. Instead of its normal range of highly flexible, adaptive, and outgoing behavior, its behavior is severely restricted to those defensive reactions that characterize the wild animal. It is furtive, hostile, and will flee if given the opportunity to do so.

In short, I am suggesting that the immediate and inevitable effect of severe aversive stimulation on a domesticated animal is to convert it, at least temporarily, into a wild animal by restricting its response repertoire to a narrow class of species-specific defense reactions (SSDRs). I am suggesting further that this sudden, dramatic restriction of the subject's (S's) behavioral repertoire is of the utmost importance in the proper understanding of avoidance learning.

The concept of the SSDR repertoire enables one to make sense of what is one of the most challenging problems in avoidance learning, namely, that some responses either cannot be learned at all, or are learned only occasionally after extensive training. A particular S may be able to learn one avoidance response (R_a) with great facility and be quite unable to learn another R_a. In the latter case, the response may occur frequently, the presumed reinforcement contingencies may be regularly applied, and yet R_a fails to gain in strength. Such failures of learning indicate either that some responses are not acquirable, or that the reinforcement contingencies are not what they were thought to be.

These failures of Ss to learn in situations where the theories require them to, pose a serious challenge to contemporary behavior theory. Is it possible that some responses in S's repertoire actually are not acquirable as R_as? Such a conception defies one of the principal tenets of operant conditioning theory. The present paper argues for just this conclusion. I suggest that there is a restricted class of behaviors that can be readily acquired as R_as. Specifically, I am proposing that *an R_a can be rapidly acquired only if it is an SSDR.*

Is it possible, on the other hand, that the events which are ordinarily assumed to reinforce R_a actually are not effective in that capacity? I will argue that this is indeed the case, and that *an R_a is rapidly acquired only by the suppression of other SSDRs.* In other words, I propose that the primary effect of avoidance training is to get rid of competing behavior, and that this is accomplished mainly by the avoidance contingency.

The frequently reported failures of rats to learn certain R_as, such as wheel turning and bar pressing (e.g., D'Amato & Schiff, 1964; Meyer, Cho, & Wesemann, 1960; Smith, McFarland, & Taylor, 1961), should not be regarded as peculiar or as exceptions to the general applicability of operant conditioning principles, but rather as one end of a continuum of difficulty of learning. Learning the R_a in a shuttle box is likely to require about 100 trials, and a few rats apparently never acquire the response (Brush, 1966). Learning to run in a wheel proceeds considerably faster and more surely. All Ss learn the R_a within 40 trials (Bolles, Stokes, & Younger, 1966). But if we let the rat run down an alley to avoid shock, it may learn to do so in half a dozen trials (Theios, 1963). At the other extreme, if we place a rat in a box and shock it there, it may learn in one trial to jump out of the box (e.g., Maatsch, 1959). There is a continuum of difficulty here, and the parameter that is involved, what R_a the situation requires, is an enormously important one which accounts for more of the variance than any other so far discovered in avoidance learning. Indeed, the response requirement is the only really impressive parameter we know of, and it is a serious indictment of our major behavior theories that they pay no systematic attention to it.

By contrast, the SSDR hypothesis takes the fact that there are great differential rates of learning as its first principle. If we assume that the rat's SSDR repertoire consists of freezing, fleeing, or fighting (threat behavior), then it is clear why the jump-out box and the one-way apparatus should lead to such rapid acquisition. First, these situations provide abundant stimulus support for fleeing; more importantly, since freezing and aggressive behavior lead only to shock (because they fail to avoid it), these behaviors will be rapidly suppressed and the remaining SSDR, fleeing, will rapidly emerge as the most likely response in the situation. Running in the wheel and in the shuttle box are similar in that again freezing and fighting are punished by the nonavoidance of shock, but there is the difference that S cannot flee the situation. The S can make the right kind of response, but its effectiveness is compromised by the fact that in the wheel S does not actually change its environment, while in the shuttle box S must return to a place it has just left.

Bar pressing is certainly not an SSDR and, accordingly, we would have to predict that it cannot be learned as an R_a. The truth is that it frequently is not learned. It is also true, however, that it sometimes is learned, and this fact has to be dealt with. I suggest that when bar pressing is learned, the course of learning must necessarily be slow and uncertain because the processes involved are slow and uncertain. What is involved, apparently, is a stage of acquisition in which S freezes while holding onto the bar. Bolles and McGillis (1968) measured the latency of the bar-press escape response. (R_e) and found that within 40 trials it fell to values in the order of .05 second. Such short shocks appear to be the result of very fast, "reflexive" presses which occur, and which can only occur, if S is freezing on the bar. This behavior then has the effect of limiting the total amount of shock received to a value which does not disrupt S's ongoing behavior. Freezing anywhere else in the box or in any other posture will be disrupted by unavoided shocks, and punished by these shocks, and so too will any consistent efforts to get out of the box. In effect, the rat must end up freezing on the bar because that is the only response which on the one hand is an SSDR, and on the other hand can continuously survive the avoidance contingency. The observation of rats in this situation indicates that this is what happens. Even the attempts to "shape" the bar-press R_a in the manner that pressing for food is commonly shaped must start with S freezing on the bar (D'Amato, Fazzaro, & Etkin, 1968; Feldman & Bremner, 1963; Keehn & Webster, 1968). Thus, freezing on the bar appears to be a necessary stage in the acquisition of the bar-press R_a, just as the SSDR hypothesis suggests. How operant R_as can sometimes gradually emerge from this stage of respondent R_es is another story which will have to be considered later. The present discussion merely establishes that the SSDR hypothesis makes sense of the fact that some R_as are trivially easy to acquire while others evidently tax the limits of a particular species, and it provides, as far as I know, the first systematic account of these huge differences.

There is a trivial sense in which the SSDR hypothesis must be true, namely, that if the SSDR repertoire includes all of S's behavior in the aversive situation, then no other responses will occur there so no other responses can be reinforced there. The SSDR hypothesis is intended to mean something much more subtle and important than the obvious truth that a response must occur before it can be reinforced, however. When appetitive behavior is reinforced with food, it is profitable and convenient to define specific responses in terms of the movements involved, for example, when we "shape" the bar-press response. It is also convenient to define specific responses in terms of their effects on the environment, for example, whether or not it causes a bar to be depressed. These response-class definitions are serviceable because food reinforcement appears to have equivalent effects on all members of these classes. But we will shortly turn to data which indicate that neither of these kinds of response classes, equivalent movements or equivalent environmental effects, holds together in the case of avoidance learning, at least not with respect to the reinforcement operation. Consider the acquisition of a jumping R_a. It appears to be relatively difficult to establish a particular jump topography, and relatively difficult to train the rat to jump if jumping avoids shock and terminates the conditioned stimulus (discussed subsequently), but it is very easy to teach the rat to jump out of a box where it has been shocked (Maatsch, 1959). The critical feature of jumping as a flight response appears to be whether it is *functionally effective* in the sense that it actually makes flight possible. The possibility of flight appears to be much more important in establishing a flight response than either its topographical features or even whether it is effective in avoiding shock.

Consider running, which is also sometimes rapidly learned and sometimes is not. We must classify running as an SSDR because we observe that the rat runs in aversive situations (and out of them if it can). We can arrange aversive situations that provide different amounts of stimulus support for running, that is, we can change its operant rate and alter the whole SSDR repertoire by varying the situation. We can also arrange to make running effective in the sense that its occurrence prevents shock. But I contend that no matter how we arrange the situation, running will not be acquired as an R_a, at least not very readily, unless the running response is effective for flight, that is, effective in the functional sense that it takes the rat out of the situation. With other animals we should expect the case to be different if flight is functionally different. For example, whereas the rat and other small rodents flee from predators by getting completely away from them, an animal such as the dog needs to, and typically does, only stand off at some distance. From such observations the SSDR hypothesis suggests the inference that dogs might be much better than rats at learning to run in the shuttle box. Under some circumstances they are evidently quite good at it (e.g., Solomon & Wynne, 1953).

The argument so far can be summarized by giving an explicit statement of the SSDR hypothesis: For an R_a to be rapidly learned in a given situation, the response must be an effective SSDR in that situation, and when rapid learning does occur, it is primarily due to the suppression of ineffective SSDRs.

The Escape Contingency

One implication of the SSDR hypothesis is that the contingencies which have traditionally borne the theoretical burden of reinforcing avoidance behavior, namely, the escape contingency and the conditioned stimulus (CS) termination contingency, are relatively ineffectual. There is now considerable evidence suggesting that this is the case and indicating that neither of these familiar aspects of the normal avoidance training procedure is crucial for the establishment of avoidance behavior. Let us look briefly at some of this evidence.

At first, the phenomenon of defensive learning was viewed as an example of Pavlovian conditioning, and the earliest experimental procedures reflected this kind of theoretical orientation. Thus, there was no escape contingency; it was the unconditioned response (UCR) that was *elicited* by a brief inescapable shock that was supposed to become conditioned to the CS. Instrumental avoidance learning procedures arose from the discovery that Pavlovian techniques only seemed to work with autonomic responses and with reflexes. Other techniques had to be developed to train instrumental or operant defensive behavior. The Pavlovian heritage was still apparent, however. An avoidance response was first conditioned to the shock as an escape response (R_e), and it was called a UCR at this stage. Then, as it became conditioned to the CS, as it "gradually emerged," it was called a conditioned response (CR) (Solomon & Brush, 1956). In this view the escape contingency was a necessary part of the avoidance training procedure; it was essential for the maintenance of the UCR. This interpretation prevailed until Brogden, Lipman, and Culler (1938) and Mowrer (1939) began to demonstrate its inadequacy. Then, although a pure contiguity account of avoidance could no longer be defended, a semicontiguity or compromise position began to prevail. According to this view, which is still probably the predominant view today, R_a gains *some* of its strength by generalization, or through conditioning, from the strength of R_e. In practical terms, the escape contingency was supposed to help establish R_a, and accordingly, it became a regular part of the avoidance training procedure.

The simplest and methodologically most elegant way to assess the actual importance of the escape contingency is to permit shock escape to occur but to make its occurrence contingent on some response other than R_a. The first such study was conducted by Mowrer and Lamoreaux (1946), who demonstrated the possibility of training rats to make an R_a which was different from R_e. Some Ss were required to run to avoid shock and to jump in the air to escape shock following a failure to avoid. Other Ss were required to jump to avoid and to run to escape. Controls were required to learn identical escape and avoidance responses which were either jumping or running. The reported results indicated that the homogeneous groups, for which R_a and R_e were the same, showed a marked superiority over the heterogeneous groups, for which R_a and R_e were different. However, the important finding, according to Mowrer and Lamoreaux, was that the heterogeneous groups acquired R_a at all. The fact that the heterogeneous groups suffered a decrement relative to the homogeneous groups suggested to Mowrer and Lamoreaux that while the escape contingency was not essential, it did make a contribution to the strength of R_a.

This study and the few subsequent studies have left several basic theoretical questions unanswered, however. For example, it is not possible to say on the basis of the available evidence if independent R_as and R_es can be obtained as a general rule, or only under rather special circumstances. It is not known if independence of R_a and R_e can be shown for any se-

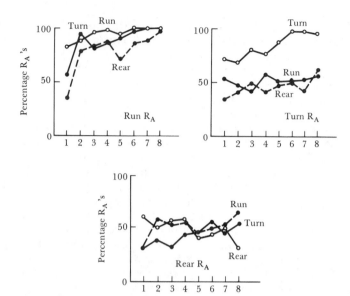

FIG. 1.   *Mean percentage of avoidances (R_as) on 10-trial blocks for rats required to run, turn, or rear to avoid shock and to run, turn, or rear to escape shock. (Labels on individual curves refer to the R_e requirement. Adapted from Bolles, 1969.)*

lected pair of responses, or whether this independence is restricted just to certain responses. In an attempt to answer this question, a larger study which involved three different responses was made. Rats were trained in a running-wheel situation and different groups were required either to run (resulting in a quarter turn of the wheel), to turn (an about-face without moving the wheel), or to rear (stand up on the hind legs). For different groups the nonoccurrence of shock was made contingent on one of these responses and, following a failure to avoid, the termination of shock was made contingent on either the same response or one of the other two responses. Thus there were three homogeneous groups and six heterogeneous groups.

The results of this experiment (Bolles, 1969) are summarized in Fig. 1. It is apparent, first, that some R_as are much more rapidly acquired than others, regardless of the R_e requirement. It is also apparent that whether there is a difference between homogeneous conditions, which permit generalization from R_e, and heterogeneous conditions, which preclude such generalization, depends entirely on what the R_a is. Thus, if R_a is chosen to be running, then it will be rapidly acquired more or less independently of other experimental conditions, including the escape contingency. Rearing, on the other hand, is not learned as an R_a, even with the escape contingency, at least not within 80 trials. Turning may be thought of as intermediate; it is not a flight response, but when other conditions are optimized it can be acquired through the joint action of the escape contingency and the avoidance contingency. It should be emphasized, however, that when the turning R_a is learned, the learning proceeds rather slowly.

These results indicate that the escape contingency does not play a consistent part in the acquisition of R_a, and that only in the case of one response, turning, did it make an appreciable contribution to avoidance learning. It is interesting to note that Mowrer and Lamoreaux's results also showed this type of specificity. They found that running in the shuttle box was as readily acquired as an R_a by homogeneous and heterogeneous groups, but that jumping in the shuttle box was not acquired as an R_a unless the R_e was also jumping. The usual conclusion drawn from their results, that is, that heterogeneous groups can learn to avoid but not as effectively as homogeneous groups, is obtained as a statistical artifact of lumping the different results for different R_as. Mowrer and Lamoreaux's data, as well as those shown in Fig. 1, also belie the frequently drawn conclusion that R_a can be any response drawn from S's repertoire. This simply is not true. In the case of rearing, the response occurred on about 40% of all trials. Its occurrence always avoided shock and terminated the CS, and for one group it also escaped shock on nonavoidance trials, but it never gained in strength. Rearing occurred, although it is not a flight response itself, in the context of flight, that is, in the attempt to climb the walls. But in this context it was ineffective because S was never able to climb out of the situation. This behavior persisted because all other behavior, that is, other attempts to escape, and freezing and aggressive reactions, were also punished. As noted in the previous section, for a flight response to be an effective SSDR for the rat, it must take S out of the situation (as in a one-way apparatus). It is not sufficient that the response has a high operant rate, or even that it might be effective in getting away in another situation.

It might be argued that running in the wheel also fails to get the animal away, so that this response should not have been learned either, according to the SSDR hypothesis. Perhaps this is the proper interpretation, and perhaps we have managed to discredit the SSDR hypothesis right at its inception. It cannot be argued that running in the wheel constitutes an effective SSDR while running in the shuttle box is marginally effective merely because the former is more rapidly acquired than the latter. From the viewpoint of the SSDR hypothesis, both situations are ambiguous in that they permit only limited or compromised flight. The running wheel has been recognized as a peculiar piece of apparatus by many investigators who have used it in general activity studies, however, and perhaps it does permit the rat to "get away" in some meaningful sense. Certainly it permits the rat to run continuously, to change cues in the immediate environment, including the ground underfoot, and to get away from the accumulation of its own odors. It may be immaterial that running in the wheel does not change extra-apparatus cues or the rat's location with respect to them. Further investigation is needed with various modifications of both the wheel and the shuttle box to pinpoint the critical factors and provide a real test of the SSDR hypothesis. The issue should be further illuminated by additional investigation in more naturalistic settings as well as with other kinds of animals to obtain a better idea of what constitutes effective flight in nature. The rat's facility with the running wheel may be relatively specific to the rat.

To return to the escape contingency, there have been a number of studies in which it has been eliminated in other ways. Bolles et al. (1966) trained Ss with shocks of .1-second duration, that is, too short to be response terminated, and found very little decrement relative to Ss that were required to terminate shock in the usual manner. Similar results have been reported by D'Amato, Keller, and DiCara (1964), Hurwitz (1964), and Sidman (1953) in the bar-press situation, although there is some question about whether there may still be some possibility of escape with the short shocks that were used. There are also a few instances in which negative transfer from R_e to R_a has been reported (Turner & Solomon, 1962; Warren & Bolles, 1967).

So much for the escape contingency. Knowledge about the escapability of shock does not permit us to predict how fast an animal will learn a particular R_a, or whether R_a will be learned at all. Other considerations are much more important, and one of the most important of these appears to be what the R_a is. The data suggest that R_a will be rapidly acquired if and only if it permits S to flee, freeze, or fight, and that whether there is an escape contingency is relatively inconsequential.

The CS-Termination Contingency

Another regular part of most avoidance experiments is the warning stimulus, or CS. Both its name and part of its assumed function derive from the Pavlovian tradition. The CS was assumed to be the stimulus to which the R_a (or CR) became conditioned. It has become fairly common in recent years to incorporate various control procedures for sensitization effects in order to determine if R_a is under the associative control of the CS. "Real" avoidance is attributed to performance beyond that displayed by sensitization control Ss. There is some irony in the fact that what counts in nature is not an animal's ability to learn this kind of discrimination but rather that it be subject to these sensitization effects! As observed in the introductory section, what keeps animals alive in nature is that they display SSDRs whenever there is any stimulus change in the environment. Some investigators have begun to suggest that perhaps in the laboratory, too, the stuff of which avoidance behavior is really made is rather indiscriminant defensive behavior (Bolles et al., 1966; D'Amato, 1967).

The major theoretical emphasis on the CS, of course, is not its discrim-

TABLE 1. Percentage of R_as in Two Different Situations as a Function of Whether S Could Avoid Shock (A), Escape Shock (E), or Terminate the CS (T)

Available contingencies	Apparatus	
	Shuttle box	Wheel
AET	70	85
AE	40	75
AT	37	79
ET	31	38
A	15	62
E	9	26
T	10	48
None	15	28

Note. Adapted from Bolles et al. (1966).

inative function but the reinforcement that is widely assumed to result from its termination. Some theorists introduce the additional element of fear; termination of the CS is assumed to lead to a reduction of fear which is reinforcing (e.g., Miller, 1951; Mowrer, 1939). Others contend that the fear construct is gratuitous here, and that it is sufficient to assume that because the CS is paired with shock it will become a conditioned negative reinforcer (e.g., Dinsmoor, 1954; Schoenfeld, 1950). According to either version of the story, however, termination of the CS is held to be an essential ingredient in avoidance learning. Hence, the termination of the CS is usually made contingent on the occurrence of R_a, and under these circumstances it is easy to point to CS termination as the source of reinforcement when learning occurs.

The argument gained considerable support from Mowrer and Lamoreaux's (1942) early demonstration that making CS termination coincident with the occurrence of R_a led to much faster acquisition than having it go off automatically before R_a occurred or having its termination delayed for some seconds after R_a occurred. There was a little room for concern that any learning was found under the latter conditions, but Kamin (1956) was able to account for it in terms of delay of reinforcement effects, and at this point the CS-termination hypothesis appeared to be quite secure.

There were still a few lines of evidence, however, that stubbornly resisted falling into line with the CS-termination hypothesis, and some of them suggested that the efficacy of CS termination might depend on what R_a was required of the animal (e.g., Mogenson, Mullin, & Clark, 1965). Bolles et al. (1966) attempted to extend the Mowrer and Lamoreaux and the Kamin design, first, by studying the effectiveness of the CS-termination contingency in two different situations, and, second, by experimentally separating all three of the potential reinforcement contingencies: CS termination, avoidance of shock, and escape from shock. This was a factorial study in which shock was either escapable or not (because it was too short), avoidable or not, and the CS either terminated with the R_a or was continued for some seconds after it. The Ss were trained either in a shuttle box or a running wheel. The results are summarized in Table 1.

An analysis of variance shows that in the shuttle-box avoidance, escape and CS termination accounted for, respectively, 39%, 22%, and 19% of the variance among groups. Thus the three contingencies contributed roughly equally to the performance in the shuttle box (also see Kamin, 1956). There was also a significant interaction which took the form that no one contingency by itself was able to produce learning. In the running wheel the pattern was quite different. Here, avoidance, escape, and CS termination accounted for, respectively, 85%, 0%, and 9% of the variance among groups. Thus, the avoidance contingency was vastly more important than the other two. Moreover, there was no interaction among the contingencies, and avoidance alone led to quite creditable acquisition. In short, the relative importance of the three contingencies depends on the situation, and, more specifically on what response is required of S. When R_a is running in the wheel, which I believe is an effective SSDR, the avoidance contingency itself is the big factor and CS termination is relatively unimportant. But in the shuttle box, where the effectiveness of R_a is more doubtful, the avoidance of shock and the termination of the CS assume more nearly equal importance.

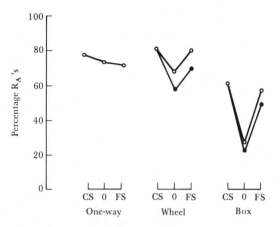

FIG. 2. *Mean percentage of* $R_a s$ *for rats trained with either CS termination (CS), FS presentation (FS), or neither (O). (Training comprised 20 trials in the one-way situation, 40 trials in the running wheel, and 80 trials in the shuttle box. Adapted from Bolles & Grossen, 1969).*

Bolles and Grossen (1969) have subsequently expanded this procedure by using situations in which the status of R_a is still more varied, namely, a one-way runway and a bar-press situation. These investigators also sought to analyze further the role of CS termination in those situations such as the bar press and the shuttle box where it does appear to be important. Is the crucial function of CS termination in these situations really reinforce- ment? It seems possible that when CS termination is made contingent on R_a, it is not reinforcing R_a in the usual sense but rather providing S with information, or feedback. CS termination may merely be a stimulus change which signals that the environment has been altered in some way. To test this possibility, groups of Ss were trained with no CS-termination contingency but with a feedback stimulus contingency. For these Ss a brief change in illumination conditions was made contingent on R_a. This feedback stimulus (FS) was presented only on avoidance trials, that is, it was never contiguous with shock. The important comparisons are among groups which had the normal CS-termination contingency, groups which had neither CS termination nor FS presentation, and groups which had no CS termination but did have the FS presentation. The results for rats trained under these conditions in three different avoidance situations are shown in Fig. 2. The black data points indicate the results for Ss run in a partial replication in which the CS-termination contingency was elimi- nated by using a trace conditioning procedure, that is, by using a short CS rather than one which continued for 5 seconds after the R_a. The gen- erally inferior performance of the trace Ss can presumably be attributed to the loss of the discriminative function of the CS.

In the one-way avoidance situation, learning proceeded very rapidly. There was no appreciable decrement in performance for Ss which lacked the CS-termination contingency, nor was there any improvement in per- formance for Ss which received the response-contingent FS. There were, in short, no differences among the three groups. In the running-wheel situation, acquisition was not as fast as in the one-way apparatus, but it was still quite fast. There was a small but statistically significant decre- mental effect of withholding the CS-termination contingency, and the in- troduction of the FS contingency returned performance nearly to the normal level. Then in the shuttle-box situation, where acquisition was considerably slower, the loss of the CS-termination contingency led to a serious decrement in acquisition, and the use of the FS again virtually eliminated this decrement. Sidman's (1953) procedure was used in the bar-press situation, which prevents a direct comparison of the results in terms of percentage of R_as, and these results are therefore not shown in the figure. But the bar-press results can easily be described. In the absence of a CS, and the CS-termination contingency, the median S failed to learn the response when there was no R_a-contingent feedback (a special bar was used which provided minimum auditory and kinesthetic feedback). By contrast, all Ss eventually learned the bar-press R_a when it produced a click and a brief change in illumination. Thus, in the bar-press situation, the FS made the difference between the group as a whole being able or not being able to learn the response. Bolles and Popp (1964) had earlier indicated the necessity of having some stimulus event contingent on the bar-press R_a.

There appears to be a striking parallel between the effectiveness of the CS-termination and the FS-presentation contingencies as the response requirement is varied. When learning is very rapid, that is, when R_a is an SSDR, neither contingency makes much difference. But when learning is slow and uncertain, that is, when R_a is not an SSDR, then learning depends on there being some response-contingent event, and it seems to make little difference whether it is CS termination or FS presentation. That these two procedures have such equivalent effects on performance strongly suggests that they may be functionally equivalent. Indeed, it is tempting to suppose that CS termination leads to avoidance learning, not because it causes a reduction in fear, nor because it reduces aversiveness, but merely because it provides response feedback. CS termination may merely tell the animal that it has responded; it has done something to affect the environment.

This interpretation is entirely consistent with the results of Bower, Starr, and Lazarovitz (1965), who found a direct relationship between the rate of acquisition of R_a and the amount of change in the CS which was made contingent on R_a. This kind of interpretation takes the problem of avoidance learning out of its traditional niche among reinforcement phenomena and puts it more into the realm of discrimination learning. D'Amato et al. (1968) have already urged such a move and these investigators, it should be noted, had previously obtained results in the bar-press situation very much like those of Bolles and Grossen (1969). The main difference was that D'Amato et al. used a discrete trial procedure, whereas Bolles and Grossen used Sidman's procedure. The fact that the introduction of an FS restores performance in both cases attests to the generality of the FS effect.

So much for the CS-termination contingency. It is clear that while the CS-termination contingency is of some importance in some situations, it is of little consequence in situations such as the one-way runway and the running wheel where R_a is very rapidly acquired. If we wish to predict whether R_a will be acquired or how fast it will be acquired, then knowledge about the CS-termination contingency will not give us nearly as much information as knowing what the R_a is. Moreover, even in those situations where CS termination is important, it turns out that it can be replaced by an entirely different kind of response contingency which produces learning just as effectively. It is becoming increasingly difficult to believe that avoidance learning occurs because the CS elicits fear or because it is aversive.[2] Let us look briefly at an alternative view of the role of the CS.

The Safety Signal Effect

The previous section suggested one interpretation of the CS-termination effect, namely, that termination of the CS serves as a source of feedback, or stimulus change. This is an attractive hypothesis and it is supported by some evidence (Bolles & Grossen, 1969; Bower et al., 1965; D'Amato et al., 1968). Bolles and Grossen have suggested that the reason some situations lead to such rapid avoidance learning may be that they furnish S with a great deal of *intrinsic* feedback. Accordingly, the addition of *extrinsic* feedback provided by the experimenter in the form of lights out or tone termination contributes relatively little to that already resulting from the occurrence of R_a. As we move on to situations which involve little intrinsic feedback, for example, the bar press, which requires little effort and which does not change S's environment, the acquisition of the response may depend on there being some extrinsic feedback. With the assumption that intrinsic feedback has greater weight (or a higher sampling probability) than extrinsic feedback, we would be in a good position to explain many of the findings that have been discussed above. The rate-of-learning effect, the CS-termination effect, and the FS-presentation effect would all fall neatly into line.

There are, however, some difficult problems with this interpretation, and some of the evidence does not fall into line so readily: (a) Why should intrinsic feedback be inherently more important than an arbitrarily selected external stimulus change, such as the termination of a tone? It is easy to argue that flight reactions necessarily produce a lot of stimulus change, but flight is not the only SSDR, and there is reason to believe that other SSDRs are also very rapidly acquired. For example, the author's observations, as well as those of Keehn (1967), indicate that freezing is acquired in very few trials, even though it is not a vigorous kind of behavior and does not change the situation. The rapid learning of the pseudo-flight response in the running wheel also indicates that the character of the response may be much more important than the simple quantity of stimulus change it produces. (b) Why does the rate of acquisition depend on the direction of stimulus change, that is, whether the stimulus goes on or off, and on its quality and modality (e.g., Myers, 1960, 1964)? Why is a change in geographical location such a particularly effective stimulus change? (c) Why does FS presentation or CS termination appear to be effective only with extended training? That is, if stimulus change is the critical factor, then why doesn't it seem to have an effect in a rapidly acquired R_a or in the early trials of a slowly acquired R_a?

This last point needs some illustration. The data shown at the far right in Fig. 2 represent the performance of rats with an FS in the shuttle box. Over the course of 80 trials, these Ss avoided nearly as well as those under the usual CS-termination condition. But the learning curves for the two groups were markedly different; the FS group showed a serious decrement during the first 40 trials, but then caught up with the CS group and eventually surpassed it. In short, the FS condition is not completely equivalent to the CS condition, it only produces the same mean performance over the course of the right number of trials. There seems to be a delay in the action of the FS contingency, such that it begins to be effective only after S has been in the situation for a number of trials, perhaps 40 or 50. D'Amato et al. (1968) found in their bar-press study that there was no FS effect during the first several hundred trials; it materialized only with continued training. One possibility is that the CS has functions beyond those it shares with the FS. It certainly has a discriminative function, and it may have others, including even an acquired aversiveness function.

A second possibility that is more interesting and more compelling is that the FS does more than provide information. Perhaps it actively reinforces R_a, and perhaps 40 or 50 trials (or more depending on the situation) are required for its reinforcing powers to be established. What I am suggesting is that the response-contingent FS acts as a *safety signal* of the sort that Rescorla and LoLordo (1965) have described.

Rescorla and LoLordo gave dogs a number of sessions in which one stimulus was repeatedly paired with unavoidable shock independently of the dogs' behavior, and a second, contrasting stimulus was explicitly paired with the absence of shock. The one stimulus thus became a danger signal (DS) while the second became a safety signal (SS). (It is difficult to know how to label these stimuli without begging the question of how they function; there is no intention to imply anything by the designation DS and SS beyond the procedural fact that the one stimulus is correlated with shock while the other is correlated with the absence of shock.) Several procedures were used in these sessions, and it seemed to make little difference precisely how the DS–SS contrast was made as long as the SS consistently predicted the absence of shock. Following this training, the stimuli were introduced momentarily while S was performing a previously well-established shuttle-box R_a. The DS was found to produce a short-term elevation in the rate of the R_a, whereas the SS was found to depress the rate of the R_a.

These dramatic results lend themselves to a variety of possible interpretations, but the one favored by Rescorla and LoLordo is that (a) the SS and DS acquire their behavioral effects through Pavlovian conditioning processes, and (b) the DS increases S's fear motivation, whereas the SS inhibits fear. They propose that fear is conditioned to the DS by a Pavlovian excitatory mechanism, and that in the test situation the momentary DS provides additional short-term motivation for the previously learned R_a. Similarly, the inhibition of fear by SS is assumed to be produced by a Pavlovian inhibitory mechanism so that brief presentation of the SS in the test situation provides a momentary reduction in S's prevailing fear motivation (also see Rescorla & Solomon, 1967).

Without necessarily denying the validity of this interpretation, I want to call attention to other potential properties of these DS and SS stimuli. I would emphasize that the presentation of a DS may be punishing and that the presentation of an SS may be positively reinforcing. Rescorla and LoLordo could not find such effects because their experimental situation was set up to demonstrate motivational (and de-motivational) effects. But Rescorla (1969) has subsequently found that an SS established in the same noncontingent manner can serve to reinforce an R_a when it is later introduced as a consequence of that R_a, that is, when it is made contingent on it. Similarly, Weisman and Litner (1968) have shown that an SS can be used as a reinforcer to produce either a high or a low rate of responding by making its occurrence differentially contingent on a high or low rate. Hendry (1967) has reported a related reinforcement effect in a conditioned suppression situation.

Let us make a logical extension: think of the R_a-produced feedback stimulus in the avoidance learning situation as gradually acquiring safety signal properties. Include among these properties the ability to reinforce R_a. A number of parallels may already be noted between the FS and the SS. For example, if there is an instrumental avoidance contingency, then the FS is surely correlated with the absence of shock, just as the SS is in Rescorla and LoLordo's noncontingent training sessions. The main difference is that the FS is by definition contingent on the occurrence of the response, while (at least so far) the SS is established independently of S's behavior. The noncontingent procedure provides a vivid demonstration that the DS and SS stimuli can acquire their behavioral powers independently of S's behavior. DiCara and Miller (1968) have reported an even more vivid demonstration of what appear to be SS and DS effects by using rats that were deeply curarized. But the possibility of establishing an SS independently of S's behavior does not mean that as SS cannot be established when it is response contingent. Indeed, a response-produced SS might be more discriminable and more readily established than if the stimulus was scheduled to appear intermittently without any antecedents. There have been no direct comparisons of SS and FS effects, but a comparison across studies using SS and FS techniques is suggestive. Thus, we have seen that establishing an effective FS seems to require 40 or 50 trials or perhaps more in some situations, while from the fact that the SS effect is typically reported in studies that involve 90 or so pairings of the SS with the absence of shock, we may presume that the effect requires approximately the same number. Hammond (1966) has claimed to have shown a more rapidly established SS effect in a conditioned suppression situation, but this interpretation seems doubtful in view of the transitory nature of the effect.

The author and his colleagues have recently conducted a series of studies with SS and DS procedures to determine if the SS and DS effects vary across situations with different R_a requirements in the same manner as we had previously found the FS and CS effects to vary. The results have been rather encouraging. Thus, in the one-way runway, where there was no CS-termination or FS-presentation effect, a total absence of SS and DS effects was found. In the running wheel, where the former effects had been found to be small (see Fig. 2), the latter were found to be small too, and unimpressive statistically. Then with the shuttle box, in the only one of these studies that has been published (Grossen & Bolles, 1968), large and highly reliable effects which mirrored the size of the CS and FS effects in that situation were found. In all of these studies, procedures like those of Rescorla (1966) were used, including 90 noncontingent pairings.

The chief difference in procedure was that we used rats, whereas Rescorla used dogs.

So far, then, the parallel between FS and SS effects suggests that they may be equivalent. The bar-press situation is critical, however, and our results there have unfortunately been largely negative. However, Weisman and Litner (1968) obtained impressive SS effects with a wheel-turn R_a, which is comparable to the bar-press R_a in a number of other respects. Perhaps there are unique features of the bar-press R_a that we have not sufficiently allowed for; perhaps its initial dependence on freezing is relevant; or perhaps there is a critical element of the SS–DS procedure that remains to be isolated. For example, it is not clear why SS effects have been reported thus far only in free-operant situations where the rate of responding is measured. We do not know if the effect is limited to rate measures of nondiscriminated avoidance or whether it can be obtained as well with other response measures in discriminated avoidance situations.

In spite of a number of such unanswered questions, it is tempting to hypothesize that the CS-termination effect, the FS-presentation effect, and the SS-reinforcing effect are all functionally equivalent. I propose that this is indeed the case, and further, that in those situations where CS termination is effective in strengthening an R_a, it is effective because it serves as response feedback, and that such feedback is positively reinforcing because it functions as a safety signal. CS termination tells the animal, in effect, that shock is not going to occur.

It should be emphasized that this SS mechanism appears to be limited to learning situations in which the R_a is acquired relatively slowly, for example, in 40 trials or more. The reason for this limitation is evidently that to become established, the SS mechanism requires a number of the pairings of the SS with the absence of shock. The implication of this limitation is that whenever an R_a is rapidly acquired, for example, in 40 trials or less, its acquisition must be based on mechanisms that have little to do with the SS, the response-contingent FS, or the CS-termination contingency.

Relation to Other Accounts of Avoidance Learning

The arguments that have been advanced here have been based in part on the finding that the escape contingency is not essential for the acquisition of avoidance learning. This finding is not new, of course; it has been known and widely accepted ever since Mowrer and Lamoreaux's (1946) classic study, and a purely Pavlovian or contiguity interpretation of avoidance has not been seriously advocated for some years. The prevailing accounts of avoidance learning appear to cast the escape contingency in the simple but not altogether bad role of increasing the operant rate of R_a. The question of choosing the right R_a involves much more than obtaining a suitably high operant rate, however. Thus, the data shown in Fig. 1 indicate what happened with three R_as with nearly equal operant rates. With one the escape contingency was apparently an essential ingredient in learning, with a second R_a it was unimportant because learning was so rapid without it, but with the third R_a the escape contingency was unimportant because neither it nor any other contingency produced learning. Meyer et al. (1960) suggested the appropriate conclusion some years ago: "However inconvenient the general implication, operants are *not* arbitrary; in avoidance learning, their selection is perhaps the most important of considerations [p. 227]."

The argument with regard to the CS-termination contingency is similar, but in the case of CS termination, it is nearly always cast in the leading role in avoidance learning. Fear-reduction theorists and operant theorists alike usually attribute the learning of R_a to response-contingent CS termination. The situation is only slightly complicated by the fact that some theorists attribute reinforcement to the reduction of the fear that is commonly assumed to become classically conditioned to the CS; CS termination is still assumed to be a critical agent in reinforcing R_a. The situation is complicated just a little more by the necessity to invent (or, more politely, to hypothesize the existence of) suitable CSs to explain the acquisition of avoidance when there is no observable CS. Sidman (1953) showed that rats could learn to avoid unsignaled shock, and it therefore became necessary to hypothesize that there were *implicit* CSs, the termination of which could be said to reinforce the R_a. This need was all the more urgent because, presumably, Sidman's situation provided S with no escape contingency.

The argument is now quite familiar: the proprioceptive and kinesthetic feedback from nonavoidance behavior serves as the needed CS. If S persists in some response, R_1, which fails to avoid shock, then the feedback from this behavior, S_1, will be paired with shock. After a number of such trials, S_1 will acquire conditioned, or secondary, aversiveness so that the subject will be reinforced for discontinuing R_1 and initiating some alternative response, R_2. If R_2 also fails to avoid shock the story will be repeated. Only R_a is exempt from the action of the avoidance contingency. The stimuli which earlier occasioned R_1, R_2, . . . ,must gradually gain discriminative control over R_a as the repeated transitions from the various R_i to R_a and the consequent terminations of the various S_i reinforce R_a. This theoretical mechanism, originally proposed by Schoenfeld (1950), Sidman (1953), and Dinsmoor (1954), has been subsequently elaborated by Anger (1963). Anger noted that while one stage of acquisition may depend on the aversiveness of S_1, S_2, . . . ,there must come a point at which the principal discriminative control and the principal source of reinforcement for R_a is the lapse of time since the last preceding R_a. Only in this way, Anger argued, can one explain the temporal distribution of R_as, or the continued improvement in performance as the subject becomes more proficient. So although there may be some question regarding just which implicit CSs are involved, there is rather widespread agreement that there are some implicit, response-produced stimuli, the termination of which reinforces avoidance learning.

I have no basic fault to find with the postulation of implicit CSs, but I think it important to point out that this conceptual scheme leads to some logical and empirical difficulties. One difficulty is that this account of avoidance involves a peculiar superfluity of explanatory mechanisms. The most common interpretation (e.g., Dinsmoor, 1954) involves what is basically an escape paradigm. While the avoidance contingency is clearly implicated as the principal contact of the situation with S's behavior, the S is not usually assumed to be avoiding in any real sense, but escaping. The assumed reinforcement mechanism is the termination of implicit CSs, the stimuli, $S_1, S_2, \ldots,$ that have been paired with shock.

Alternatively, we can think in terms of a punishment paradigm. We might suppose that the avoidance contingency is effective, not because it permits S to escape from the various S_i, but because it directly punishes, or suppresses, the various R_i, Dinsmoor (1954) has argued quite rightly that the punishment effect itself needs explication. He has attempted to reduce the phenomena of punishment to avoidance terms, and then to reduce the avoidance to escape from S_1. This tactic is certainly defensible, but is it superior to taking the phenomena of punishment as primary and using them to explain those of avoidance, and perhaps even escape? I have tried to show that in the special case of a very rapidly acquired R_a, that is, when R_a is an effective SSDR, the punishment paradigm is uniquely able to handle the facts. In the case of a rapidly acquired R_a, there hardly seems time to make all the necessary S_i aversive, especially if we cannot show that an environmental CS affects the behavior in the same amount of time! A much faster and more direct mechanism is needed in this case, and the punishment of competing SSDRs is such a mechanism.

The agreed upon importance of the avoidance contingency in unsignaled avoidance suggests another interpretation: an avoidance paradigm. We might suppose that S really is avoiding shock. Although recognizing that it is difficult to put such a concept into precise behavioral terms, some writers have argued that this is the best conception of the problem (e.g., D'Amato et al., 1968; Keehn, 1966). Other theorists (e.g., Herrnstein & Hineline, 1966; Sidman, 1966) have recently come to the similar conclusion that what really reinforces avoidance behavior is the overall reduction in shock density it produces. In the situations that are described, S is not able to avoid shock, or escape it, or to terminate CSs; S merely receives fewer shocks when R_a occurs. Under these conditions the rate of R_a increases. It should be emphasized, however, that the effects described by Herrnstein and Hineline and by Sidman are found after very extensive training. When Herrnstein and Hineline (1966) carefully eliminated all other sources of reinforcement besides reduction in shock density, the bar-press R_a only *began* to emerge after tens of thousands of shocks had been administered. Are we to believe then that this is the source of the reinforcement by which rats can learn other R_as in 100 trials, or 10 trials, or by which they learn to survive in nature? What Herrnstein and Hineline seem to have shown, quite to the contrary, is that avoidance itself, or response-contingent shock density reduction, *cannot* be the mechanism that produces the faster acquisition of R_a generally found under other conditions. We may marvel that such subtle control of the rat's behavior is possible, and we must admire the diligence of the experimenters who brought it about. But just because behavior can eventually be brought under the control of some stimulus and maintained by some contingency, it certainly does not follow that this stimulus controls the behavior under other circumstances or that the contingency is effective when others are available. Nor is there any reason to believe that the factors which can ultimately be used to govern some behavior are necessarily the same as those that were important in establishing it originally. We must look elsewhere for mechanisms to explain how the rat does most of its avoidance learning.

As a final alternative to the CS-termination hypothesis, we can consider an appetitive paradigm: The S learns to avoid shock, not because termination of S_i (or an explicit CS) is negatively reinforcing, but because R_a and the production of its feedback, S_a, is positively reinforcing. Denny and his students are among the few who have defended an appetitive paradigm (e.g., Denny & Weisman, 1964). Although Denny's relaxation theory emphasizes the response which becomes conditioned to the safety signal, whereas I am more concerned with the safety signal itself, there are many striking points of similarity between relaxation theory and the SSDR hypothesis, and both accounts generate similar predictions about avoidance behavior.

I have tried to show that the safety signal interpretation is especially able to handle the data in those cases where R_a is relatively slowly acquired, that is, when R_a is not an SSDR. In this case I assume that during the initial trials, S's behavior is restricted to a small set of SSDRs, and that learning will occur only if a number of rather delicate conditions are fulfilled. The first is that one of S's SSDRs (e.g., freezing) must be topographically compatible with the required R_a (e.g., bar pressing). Then shock must elicit enough reflexive bar presses so that S can either avoid some shocks (the postshock burst in Sidman's situation) or minimize their duration (when there is an escape contingency). With the minimization of shock, we may expect a gradual return of S's normal response repertoire, so that it is no longer restricted to SSDRs. This recovery process may be facilitated in the manner that Rescorla and LoLordo have suggested, that is, the R_a-contingent FS may become a safety signal and inhibit fear.[3] Finally, I assume that the safety signal actively reinforces R_a, and that eventually R_a may come under the control of still other, more subtle stimuli as their safety-signal properties gradually become discriminated. At this point we may be able to find S quite proficiently performing an R_a which is as unlikely and as unnatural as pressing a bar.

It is clear that an animal's defensive repertoire can be extended beyond the narrow limits set by its SSDRs. But it is unfortunate that our theoretical predilections have led us to be preoccupied with the ultimate limits to which this extension can be carried and with defending CS termination as the reinforcement mechanism. In retrospect, it hardly seems possible that the acquisition of the bar-press R_a could ever have been seriously attributed simply to the action of CS termination, but it was. These preoccupations have not really advanced our understanding of how such extensions occur, how other, more natural R_as are learned, or for that matter how animals survive in nature.

Notes

[1] The research reported here was supported by National Science Foundation Research Grant GB-5694.

[2] For example, Cole and Wahlsten (1968), Lockard (1963), and Sidman (1955) all show in different ways that the discriminative function of the CS can be much more important than its aversiveness.

[3] I have been careful to say nothing here about fear because I suspect we should let that tortured concept rest awhile and try to get along without it. However, if it is felt necessary to introduce the term, I would like to see it used as Rescorla and Solomon (1967) used it,

that is, to refer to some observed feature of instrumental behavior. The restriction of the animal's behavioral repertoire to a narrow set of SSDRs might just be an appropriate feature.

References

Anger, D. The role of temporal discrimination in the reinforcement of Sidman avoidance behavior. *Journal of the Experimental Analysis of Behavior,* 1963, **6,** 477–506.

Bolles, R. C. Avoidance and escape learning: simultaneous acquisition of different responses. *Journal of Comparative and Physiological Psychology,* 1969, **68,** 355–358.

Bolles, R. C. & Grossen, N. E. Effects of an informational stimulus on the acquisition of avoidance behavior in rats. *Journal of Comparative and Physiological Psychology,* 1969, **68,** 90–99.

Bolles, R. C., & McGillis, D. B. The non-operant nature of the bar-press escape response. *Psychonomic Science,* 1968, **11,** 261–262.

Bolles, R. C., & Popp, R. J., Jr. Parameters affecting the acquisition of Sidman avoidance. *Journal of the Experimental Analysis of Behavior,* 1964, **7,** 315–321.

Bolles, R. C., Stokes, L. W., & Younger, M. S. Does CS termination reinforce avoidance behavior? *Journal of Comparative and Physiological Psychology,* 1966, **62,** 201–207.

Bower, G., Starr, R., & Lazarovitz, L. Amount of response-produced change in the CS and avoidance learning. *Journal of Comparative and Physiological Psychology,* 1965, **59,** 13–17.

Brogden, W. J., Lipman, E. A., & Culler, E. The role of incentive in conditioning and learning. *American Journal of Psychology,* 1938, **51,** 109–117.

Brush, F. R. On the differences between animals that learn and do not learn to avoid electric shock. *Psychonomic Science,* 1966, **5,** 123–124.

Cole, M., & Wahlsten, D. Response-contingent CS termination as a factor in avoidance conditioning. *Psychonomic Science,* 1968, **12,** 15–16.

D'Amato, M. R. Role of anticipatory responses in avoidance conditioning: An important control. *Psychonomic Science,* 1967, **8,** 191–192.

D'Amato, M. R., & Schiff, D. Long-term discriminated avoidance performance in the rat. *Journal of Comparative and Physiological Psychology.* 1964, **57,** 123–126.

D'Amato, M. R., Keller, D., & DiCara, L. Facilitation of discriminated avoidance learning by discontinuous shock. *Journal of Comparative and Physiological Psychology,* 1964, **58,** 344–349.

D'Amato, M. R., Fazzaro, J., & Etkin, M. Anticipatory responding and avoidance discrimination as factors in avoidance conditioning. *Journal of Experimental Psychology,* 1968, **77,** 41–47.

Denny, M. R., & Weisman, R. G. Avoidance behavior as a function of length of nonshock confinement. *Journal of Comparative and Physiological Psychology,* 1964, **58,** 252–257.

DiCara, L. V., & Miller, N. E. Changes in heart rate instrumentally learned by curarized rats as avoidance responses. *Journal of Comparative and Physiological Psychology,* 1968, **65,** 8–12.

Dinsmoor, J. A. Punishment: I. The avoidance hypothesis. *Psychological Review,* 1954, **61,** 34–46.

Feldman, R. S., & Bremner, F. J. A method for rapid conditioning of stable avoidance bar pressing behavior. *Journal of the Experimental Analysis of Behavior,* 1963, **6,** 393–394.

Grossen, N. E., & Bolles, R. C. Effects of a classical conditioned "fear signal" and "safety signal" on nondiscriminated avoidance behavior. *Psychonomic Science,* 1968, **11,** 321–322.

Hammond, L. J. Increased responding to CS⁻ in differential CER. *Psychonomic Science,* 1966, **5,** 337–338.

Hendry, D. P. Conditioned inhibition of conditioned suppression. *Psychonomic Science,* 1967, **9,** 261–262.

Herrnstein, R. J., & Hineline, P. N. Negative reinforcement as shock-frequency reduction. *Journal of the Experimental Analysis of Behavior,* 1966, **9,** 421–430.

Hull, C. L. A functional interpretation of the conditioned reflex. *Psychological Review,* 1929, **36,** 498–511.

Hurwitz, H. M. B. Method for discriminative avoidance training. *Science,* 1964, **145,** 1070–1071.

Kamin, L. J. The effects of termination of the CS and avoidance of the US on avoidance learning. *Journal of Comparative and Physiological Psychology,* 1956, **49,** 420–424.

Keehn, J. D. Avoidance responses as discriminated operants. *British Journal of Psychology,* 1966, **57,** 375–380.

Keehn, J. D. Running and bar pressing as avoidance responses. *Psychological Reports,* 1967, **20,** 591–602.

Keehn, J. D., & Webster, C. D. Rapid discriminated bar-press avoidance through avoidance shaping. *Psychonomic Science,* 1968, **10,** 21–22.

Lockard, J. S. Choice of a warning signal or no warning signal in an unavoidable shock situation. *Journal of Comparative and Physiological Psychology,* 1963, **56,** 526–530.

Maatsch, J. L. Learning and fixation after a single shock trial. *Journal of Comparative and Physiological Psychology,* 1959, **52,** 408–410.

Meyer, D. R., Cho, C., & Wesemann, A. F. On problems of conditioning discriminated lever-press avoidance responses. *Psychological Review,* 1960, **67,** 224–228.

Miller, N. E. Learnable drives and rewards. In S. S. Stevens (Ed.), *Handbook of experimental psychology.* New York: Wiley, 1951.

Mogenson, G. J., Mullin, A. D., & Clark, E. A. Effects of delayed secondary reinforcement and response requirements on avoidance learning. *Canadian Journal of Psychology,* 1965, **19,** 61–73.

Mowrer, O. H. A stimulus–response analysis of anxiety and its role as a reinforcing agent. *Psychological Review,* 1939, **46,** 553–565.

Mowrer, O. H., & Lamoreaux, R. R. Avoidance conditioning and signal duration—A study of secondary motivation and reward. *Psychological Monographs,* 1942, **54**(5, Whole No. 247).

Mowrer, O. H., & Lamoreaux, R. R. Fear as an intervening variable in avoidance conditioning. *Journal of Comparative Psychology,* 1946, **39,** 29–50.

Myers, A. K. Onset vs. termination of stimulus energy as the CS in avoidance conditioning and pseudoconditioning. *Journal of Comparative and Physiological Psychology,* 1960, **53,** 72–78.

Myers, A. K. Discriminated operant avoidance learning in Wistar and G-4 rats as a function of type of warning stimulus. *Journal of Comparative and Physiological Psychology,* 1964, **58,** 453–455.

Rescorla, R. A. Predictability and number of pairings in Pavlovian fear conditioning. *Psychonomic Science,* 1966, **4,** 383–384.

Rescorla, R. A. Establishment of a positive reinforcer through contrast with shock. *Journal of Comparative and Physiological Psychology,* 1969, **67,** 260–263.

Rescorla, R. A., & LoLordo, V. M. Inhibition of avoidance behavior. *Journal of Comparative and Physiological Psychology,* 1965, **59,** 406–412.

Rescorla, R. A., & Solomon, R. L. Two-process learning theory: Relationships between Pavlovian conditioning and instrumental learning. *Psychological Review,* 1967, **74,** 151–182.

Schoenfeld, W. N. An experimental approach to anxiety, escape and avoidance behavior. In P. H. Hock & J. Zubin (Eds.), *Anxiety.* New York: Grune & Stratton, 1950.

Sidman, M. Two temporal parameters of the maintenance of avoidance behavior by the white rat. *Journal of Comparative and Physiological Psychology,* 1953, **46,** 253–261.

Sidman, M. Some properties of the warning stimulus in avoidance behavior. *Journal of Comparative and Physiological Psychology,* 1955, **48,** 444–450.

Sidman, M. Avoidance behavior. In W. K. Honig (Ed.), *Operant behavior: Areas of research and application.* New York: Appleton-Century-Crofts, 1966.

Smith, O. A., Jr., McFarland, W. L., & Taylor, E. Performance in a shock-avoidance conditioning situation interpreted as pseudoconditioning. *Journal of Comparative and Physiological Psychology,* 1961, **54,** 154–157.

Solomon, R. L., & Brush, E. S. Experimentally derived conceptions of anxiety and aversion. In M. R. Jones (Ed.), *Nebraska Symposium on Motivation,* 1956, **4,** 212–305.

Solomon, R. L., & Wynne, L. C. Traumatic avoidance learning: Acquisition in normal dogs. *Psychological Monographs,* 1953 **67**(4, Whole No. 354).

Theios, J. Simple conditioning as two-stage all-or-none learning. *Psychological Review,* 1963, **70,** 403–417.

Turner, L. H., & Solomon, R. L. Human traumatic avoidance learning: Theory and experiments on the operant-respondent distinction and failures to learn. *Psychological Monographs,* 1962, **76**(40, Whole No. 559).

Warren, J. A., Jr., & Bolles, R. C. A reevaluation of a simple contiguity interpretation of avoidance learning. *Journal of Comparative and Physiological Psychology,* 1967, **64,** 179–182.

Weisman, R. G., & Litner, J. S. Positive conditioned reinforcement of Sidman avoidance behavior in rats. *Journal of Comparative and Physiological Psychology,* 1969, **68,** 597–603.

Part IV
Intermittent Reinforcement and Choice

Very little operant behavior is reinforced each time it occurs. What is much more typical is reinforcement that is intermittent; sometimes responses produce reinforcement and sometimes they do not. Even when reinforcement is intermittent, it can sustain responding, but how much responding, and in what pattern, depends on the nature of the intermittency. The study of the effects of different types of intermittency of reinforcement has had a prominent place in behavior theory; it is known as the study of *schedules of reinforcement* (Ferster and Skinner, 1957). A schedule of reinforcement is simply a rule that describes a given type of intermittency. Thus, for example, a fixed-ratio 10 schedule specifies that every tenth response will be reinforced. A variable-ratio 10 schedule specifies that while on the average every tenth response will be reinforced, the number of responses to reinforcement will vary from ratio to ratio. A fixed-interval 1-minute schedule reinforces the first response that occurs 1 minute after the interval has begun, whereas a variable-interval 1-minute schedule reinforces responses once a minute on the average, though individual interreinforcement intervals will vary. Each of these schedules maintains responses in its own characteristic way.

We can make more than one schedule of reinforcement at a time available to an animal and examine its choices—how the nature of the schedules influences the animal's allocation of its behavior. Such procedures are known as *concurrent schedules of reinforcement* and they are the focus of this section. Are there any general principles that govern choice among a variety of sources of reinforcement? We will see in Section A that a principle known as the *matching law* can explain a great deal of what is known about choice behavior, and Section B will show how these principles of choice relate to strategies of behavior allocation that operate in the animal's natural environment.

A. CONCURRENT SCHEDULES OF REINFORCEMENT

A pigeon has two keys on which to peck. Pecks on each key are reinforced according to separately operating variable-interval schedules. How does the pigeon allocate its responses to the two keys? The article by Herrnstein tells us that the proportion of the animal's total responses that occur on one key is equal to the proportion of total reinforcements obtained for responses on that key. Thus if left key pecks are reinforced on a variable-interval 1-minute schedule and right key pecks are reinforced on a variable-interval 3-minute schedule, the pigeon pecks left three times as often as it pecks right. This relation between the relative response rate and the relative reinforcement rate is known as the matching law, *and it is a formulation of great power and generality (see Herrnstein, 1970; deVilliers, 1977).*

The second article, by Rachlin and Green, extends the matching law by showing that choice is sensitive not only to the relative rate of reinforcement, but also to the relative amount and relative delay of reinforcement. Animals tend to be impulsive; they prefer a small immediate reinforcer to a larger delayed one. However, Rachlin and Green show that if we force pigeons to make a choice between a small immediate reward and a large delayed reward far in advance of either, their preference shifts to the large delayed reward. The authors explain this effect of "early commitment" on "self-control" in terms of the matching law.

21 Relative and Absolute Strength of Response as a Function of Frequency of Reinforcement

R. J. HERRNSTEIN

A previous paper (Herrnstein, 1958) reported how pigeons behave on a concurrent schedule under which they peck at either of two response-keys. The significant finding of this investigation was that the relative frequency of responding to each of the keys may be controlled within narrow limits by adjustments in an independent variable. In brief, the requirement for reinforcement in this procedure is the emission of a minimum number of pecks to each of the keys. The pigeon receives food when it completes the requirement on both keys. The frequency of responding to each key was a close approximation to the minimum requirement.[1]

The present experiment explores the relative frequency of responding further. In the earlier study it was shown that the output of behavior to each of two keys may be controlled by specific requirements of outputs. Now we are investigating output as a function of frequency of reinforcement. The earlier experiment may be considered a study of differential reinforcement; the present one, a study of strength of response. Both experiments are attempts to elucidate the properties of relative frequency of responding as a dependent variable.

Method

Subjects

Three adult, male, White Carneaux pigeons, maintained at 80% of free-feeding weights, and experimentally naive at the start of the study, were used.

Apparatus

A conventional experimental chamber for pigeons (Ferster & Skinner, 1957) was modified to contain two response-keys. Each key was a hinged, translucent Plexiglas plate mounted behind a hole in the center partition of the chamber. The pigeons pecked at a circular area (diameter = 0.75 inch) of the plate, and a force of at least 15 grams was necessary to activate the controlling circuitry. Any effective response operated an audible relay behind the center partition; it has been found that the resulting auditory feedback stabilizes the topography of pecking. Behind each key was a group of Christmas-tree lamps of various colors, each group mounted in such a way that it cast significant amounts of light through only one key. The two keys were 4.5 inches apart (center-to-center) ar-

217

ound the vertical midline of the center partition and on a horizontal line about 9 inches from the floor of the chamber. Through a 2-inch-square hole in the center partition, 2 inches from the floor, the pigeon occasionally received the reinforcer—4 seconds' access to grain.

A masking noise and a low level of general illumination were provided.

Procedure

Preliminary training lasted for two sessions of 60 reinforcements each. During these sessions, a peck to either key was reinforced only when the just-previous reinforcement was for a peck to the other key. This alternating pattern of reinforcement led rapidly to a pattern of responding that consisted of almost perfect alternation between the two keys. The left key was always red; the right, always white.

During the experiment proper, responding to either key was reinforced on a variable-interval schedule. The schedule for one key was independent of the schedule for the other. Thus, at any given moment, reinforcement could be made available on neither key, on one key or the other, or on both keys. A reinforced response to one key had no effect on the programmer that scheduled reinforcements on the other.

The primary independent variable was the mean time interval between reinforcements on each key. These intervals were chosen so that the mean interval of reinforcement for the two keys taken together was held constant at 1.5 minutes.[2] The overall average value of 1.5 minutes was produced by a number of pairs of values for the two keys. The combined frequency of reinforcement from independent variable-interval schedules will be a constant if the values for each of the two keys are chosen according to the hyperbolic relationship:

$$\frac{1}{x} + \frac{1}{y} = \frac{1}{c};$$

in which x is the mean interval on one key, y is the mean interval on the other, and c is the combined mean interval for the two keys taken together. The pairs of values used were VI(3) VI(3); VI(2.25) VI(4.5); VI(1.8) VI(9); and VI(1.5) VI(∞)—*i.e.*, extinction on one of the keys.

During most of the experiment, the pigeons were penalized for switching from one key to the other. Each time a peck to one key followed a peck to the other key, no reinforcement was possible for 1.5 seconds. Thus, the pigeon never got fed immediately after changing keys. When the pigeon switched keys before the 1.5-second period was completed, the period simply started anew. At least two consecutive pecks on a given key were necessary before reinforcement was possible: the first peck to start the period, and the second after it was completed. This penalty for alternation will be referred to as the "change-over delay of 1.5 seconds," or COD (1.5″).

The sequence of pairs of values of the variable-interval schedules and the number of sessions at each pair of values are shown in Table 1. Key A is the left, red key; Key B is the right, white key. Sessions lasted for 60 reinforcements, which required approximately 90 minutes since the over-all mean interval of reinforcement was always 1.5 minutes. Whether the COD was present or absent is also shown.

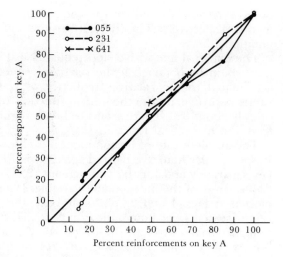

FIG. 1. *Relative frequency of responding to Key A as a function of relative frequency of reinforcement on Key A, for three pigeons; COD (1.5″) is present throughout.*

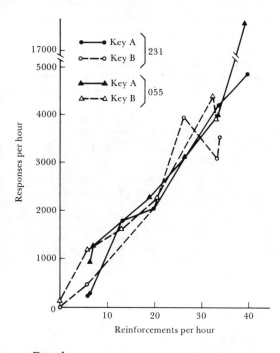

FIG. 2. *Rate of responding on each key as a function of rate of reinforcement on that key, for two pigeons; COD (1.5″) is present throughout.*

Results

Figure 1 shows the relative frequency with which the pigeon pecked on Key A as a function of the relative frequency with which it was reinforced on that key. Each point on the graph is a mean of the last five sessions under a given pair of values of the variable-interval schedule. The COD operated on all these sessions; the results without the COD will be given later. The ordinate and abscissa values were calculated by comparable methods. The number of responses (ordinate) or reinforcements (abscissa) on Key A was divided by the total number of responses or reinforcements, respectively. The five last sessions were pooled to make this computation.

The diagonal line with a slope equal to 1.0 in Fig. 1 shows the function that would be obtained if the relative frequency of responding were exactly equal to the relative frequency of reinforcement. The empirical values approximate the theoretical function with a maximum discrepancy of only about 8%. There seems to be no regular pattern to the deviations from the theoretical function.

The absolute rate of responding on each of the keys is shown in Fig. 2. Responses per hour are plotted against reinforcements per hour, for each key separately and for the two pigeons (231 and 055) that had an appreciable range of the independent variable. Data from the same sessions are plotted in Figs. 1 and 2. With one exception (Pigeon 055, Key A, at 40 reinforcements per hour), the points in Fig. 2 approximate a linear function that passes through the origin. It will be shown later that this relation between absolute rate of responding and absolute rate of reinforcement is the simplest one that is compatible with the relative-frequency function presented in Fig. 1.

The number of times a pigeon changed keys depended on the difference in frequency of reinforcement on the two keys. Figure 3 shows this relation for the three pigeons. The abscissa gives the difference, without regard to sign, between per cent of total reinforcement on one key and that on the other. Thus, when the two keys are characterized by equal

TABLE 1. Sequence of Procedures

Subject	VI on Key A (min)	VI on Key B (min)	No. of sessions	COD
055	3	3	20	no
	2.25	4.5	18	no
	2.25	4.5	43	yes
	3	3	44	yes
	3	3	25	no
	9	1.8	35	yes
	1.5	ext*	37	yes
	9	1.8	20	yes
	1.8	9	39	yes
231	3	3	35	yes
	3	3	17	no
	9	1.8	35	yes
	1.5	ext*	37	yes
	9	1.8	17	yes
	1.8	9	40	yes
	4.5	2.25	38	yes
641	3	3	17	no
	2.25	4.5	16	no
	2.25	4.5	45	yes
	3	3	34	yes
	3	3	16	no

* EXTINCTION.

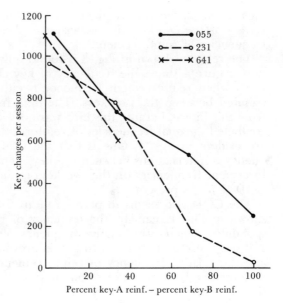

FIG. 3. *Number of alternations between the two keys as a function of the absolute difference between the per cent of reinforcements on each key, for three pigeons; COD (1.5") is present throughout.*

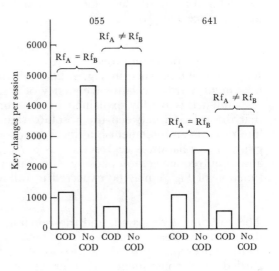

FIG. 4. *Number of alternations between the two keys when the COD was present or absent and when reinforcements were equally or unequally distributed between the two keys, for two pigeons.*

relative frequencies of reinforcement, the value on the abscissa is 0; when the responding to one key is extinguished, the value is 100, and so on. The ordinate gives simply the average number of times the pigeon switched from Key A to Key B, or vice versa. Once again, the data are from the same sessions that supplied those in Fig. 1. It should be noted, however, that in Fig. 3 there are only four values for Pigeons 055 and 231 whereas there were six in Figs. 1 and 2. This is the result of combining the three pairs of variable-interval schedules involving mean intervals of 9 minutes and 1.8 minutes (See Table 1). The data at abscissa values of about 70 per cent are, therefore, based on means of 15, instead of 5, sessions. The functions in Fig. 3 are less consistent than those in

Figs. 1 and 2, but the frequency of alternations between keys clearly decreases as the two keys are associated with increasingly different relative frequencies of reinforcement.

The relation shown in Fig. 3 is found only when the COD is in operation. Figure 4 shows the frequency of key changes with and without the COD when reinforcement frequency is either equally or unequally distributed between the two keys. The data from Pigeon 231 are omitted from this figure, because this bird was not exposed to any procedure that combined unequal frequencies of reinforcement with no COD. Two facts are evident in Fig. 4. One is that the COD markedly reduces the frequency of alternations between the keys. The other is that unequal reinforcement frequencies on the two keys reduce alternation only when the COD (1.5") is present.

The COD also seems to play a role in the production of the relation shown in Fig. 1, namely, the tendency of the relative frequency of responding to match the relative frequency of reinforcement. Pigeons 055 and 641 were both exposed to procedures in which the COD was absent and the relative frequency of reinforcement on Key A was about 66%. The relative frequencies of responding on Key A were 50% and 56% for the two pigeons, respectively. In both these cases the departures from matching are outside the range of departures obtained when the COD is present. (See Fig. 1.)

Discussion

The major problem posed by the present experiment is to explain the simple correspondence in Fig. 1 between the relative frequency of reinforcement and the relative frequency of responding. In a sense, this correspondence is readily explained by the curves in Fig. 2, which suggest that the relation between the absolute rate of responding and the absolute rate of reinforcement is a linear function that passes through the origin. If this relation is represented as $p = ke$, in which p and e denote the absolute frequencies of pecking and eating, then the simple matching function of Fig. 1 may be expected to follow the form

$$\frac{p_1}{p_1 + p_2} = \frac{ke_1}{k(e_1 + e_2)}$$

The constant, k drops out and the remaining expressions on each side of the equation denote relative frequencies of responding and reinforcement. The equality of these two relative frequencies may thus be regarded as a consequence of a linear relation, of any slope and zero intercept, between the absolute frequencies. Moreover, this relation between the absolute rates of responding and reinforcement is one that is consonant with a plausible view of response strength: Rate of responding is a linear measure of response strength, which is itself a linear function of frequency of reinforcement. The correspondence in Fig. 1 would thereby result from the fact that the behavior on each of the two keys obeys a simple linear rule governing strength of response. According to this point of view, the animals match relative frequency of responding to relative frequency of reinforcement not because they take into account what is happening on the two keys, but because they respond to the two keys independently.

The critical relation, $p = ke$, has been asserted before. Skinner (1938, p. 130) has discussed a quantity called the extinction ratio, which is the total number of responses divided by the number of reinforced responses in a fixed-interval schedule of reinforcement.[3] He presented a small amount of data that indicated that this quantity remained constant as the size of the fixed interval was varied. The constancy of the extinction ratio is merely another form, $p/e = k$, of the function we find.

Perhaps the greatest vulnerability of the foregoing account lies in its simplicity. If it were true that the rate of responding is so simply related to the frequency of reinforcement, the fact ought to have been well established by now. We should expect that behavior in a single-key situation would reveal the same linear relation shown in Fig. 2, and that with all the work done with the single-key problem, the nature of the relation between rate of responding and frequency of reinforcement would be known. Unfortunately, this information is not available. In few studies has the frequency of reinforcement been varied over an adequately wide range. Those which have done so have usually also involved manipulations in other, and possibly contaminating, variables.

A small amount of relevant material is shown in Fig. 5. These curves are adapted from earlier studies by Clark (1958), Wilson (1954), and Herrnstein (1955). These three experimenters observed the convention of plotting the independent variable as inter-reinforcement time, rather than frequency of reinforcement. Clark and Wilson used rats (Wilson used fixed-interval, instead of variable-interval, schedules); Herrnstein used pigeons. Rate of responding clearly increases with frequency of reinforcement. In these one-response situations, however, we do not obtain the linear function with zero intercept that was shown in Fig. 2. The relation suggested by Fig. 5 has downward concavity. Even if this concavity is taken to represent nothing more than a natural ceiling on the rate of responding, the function is still inappropriate, because the intercept is greater than zero.

Perhaps a more relevant comparison can be made with some data of Findley (1958), who devised a modification of concurrent scheduling not unlike the present procedure. A pigeon responds to a key and is reinforced on a variable-interval schedule. By pecking a second key, the pigeon alters the color of the first key. Each color on the first key signifies a particular value of the variable-interval schedule. The two variable-interval schedules are independent, just as in the present study. The difference between Findley's procedure and ours is in the character of the switching response. Switching required a peck on a second key in Findley's experiment, whereas in ours the pigeon had only to move over. In the present experiment, the discriminative stimuli for both schedules were concurrently visible; in Findley's, only one was present at a time, but the other was always available via a switching response. Figure 6 shows the relation between absolute rate of responding and absolute frequency of reinforcement obtained by Findley. Findley did not keep the total frequency of reinforcement constant as he varied the average inter-reinforcement interval associated with the two colors. Pigeons 5 and 6 had a constant value of 6 minutes in one color, and values ranging from 2 to 20 minutes in the other. The graphs are for the varying component.

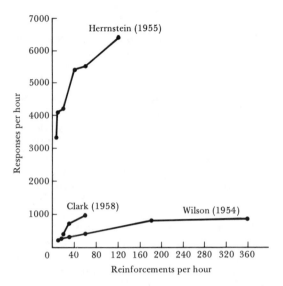

FIG. 5. *Data from previous experiments replotted to show rate of responding as a function of frequency of reinforcement.*

Responding in the other component was not, however, constant. Reynolds (1961) has demonstrated a similar kind of interaction in an ordinary multiple schedule. For Pigeons 2 and 4, the schedules were varied in both components. Only for Pigeon 5 does the function appear linear with an intercept of zero. For the three other pigeons, the pattern was the same as in Fig. 5: The relation is either concave downwards or linear with an intercept greater than zero.

Our results suggest that a relative-frequency function with a slope of less than 1.0 over part of the range would have been obtained if it were not for the COD. The precise correspondence between relative frequency of responding and relative frequency of reinforcement broke down when the COD was omitted. When the relative-frequency relationship has a slope of less than 1.0, then the absolute-frequency relationship must either be concave downwards or linear with a positive intercept. Thus, the present experiment shows excellent matching, on the one hand, and atypical absolute rate functions, on the other, probably because of the COD.

It remains to be explained why the COD has the effect of bringing the empirical points closer to the perfect-matching function. The data in Fig. 4 show that the COD greatly reduces the frequency of alternation between the two keys. Without the COD, switching is reinforced by the occasions when the first peck to a key produces food; with the COD, these occasions never occur. In a sense, then, switching is a third operant in the situation and is extinguished by the COD. The abundance of switching with no COD would tend to make the frequency of responding to the two keys more nearly equal than they would be if switching were not being reinforced. The reduction of switching by the COD probably does not, however, explain why the absolute rate of responding in the present experiment follows the simple linear function. At best, one would expect the absolute rate to behave the way it does in single-key experiments. Single-key experiments, including Findley's version of the concurrent schedule, yield functions between absolute rate of responding and abso-

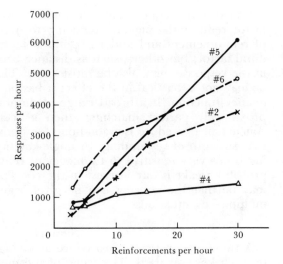

Fig. 6. *Data from Findley's experiment (1958) replotted to show rate of responding as a function of frequency of reinforcement. Numbers on curves refer to individual subjects (pigeons).*

lute frequency of reinforcement that predict nonmatching functions between relative frequency of responding and relative frequency of reinforcement. A way of characterizing this finding is to say that in the single-key situation, the animal responds too much at the low frequencies of reinforcement or too little at the high. Thus, the curves in Figs. 5 and 6 have intercepts greater than zero or are concave downwards. The same would apparently have been true in the present experiment had it not been for the COD. Why the COD has this effect is intuitively, if not scientifically, obvious. With a COD, two things are likely to happen; both follow from the fact that once the animal has switched to a key, it is likely to stay there for at least the duration of the COD. First of all, if the tendency to respond to a key is low, then the COD will probably push the tendency even lower because switching to the key calls for not one but a number of responses. Second, if the tendency is high, then the total number of pecks to the key will probably be increased because each switch to the key guarantees a number of responses. These presumed effects would change a function that is concave downwards or linear with a positive intercept toward a function that is linear with an intercept of zero. As an analogy, separating the two keys spatially may have effects similar to those of the COD. If the two keys were far apart, the animal would probably be less likely to go to the less lucrative key than if only a small distance were involved, and responding to the more lucrative key would be increased. A COD whose duration is longer than the 1.5 seconds used here might give a matching function with a slope greater than 1.0 and absolute-rate functions that are concave upwards or linear with intercepts less than zero.

The suggestion of the present discussion is that the surprisingly precise correspondence between relative frequency of responding and relative frequency of reinforcement arises from the function relating absolute frequency of responding and absolute frequency of reinforcement. When this function is linear with an intercept of zero, matching is found. In single-key situations, this linear relation is not obtained; and it is also not obtained under concurrent schedules unless some additional procedural factor reduces the pigeon's tendency to over-respond at low frequencies of reinforcement and under-respond at high. The COD is such a procedural factor; but others, such as distance between keys or effort involved in the response, may also be satisfactory. The duration of the COD may or may not be critical in the effect it has on the slope of the relative-frequency function. If a broad range of durations of the COD all give approximately perfect matching, then it seems correct to say that the concurrent procedure is a good one for studying absolute, as well as relative, strength of responding. In single-key situations, the rate of responding is not very sensitive to frequency of reinforcement. This insensitivity probably weakens our interest in the concept of strength of response. It may be that the concept can be given significant empirical support in multiple-key situations.

Summary

A two-key, concurrent procedure involving a variable-interval schedule on each key was used. The value of the mean interval on each key was varied over a range from 1.5 to 9 minutes, but the total frequency of reinforcement for the two keys taken together was held constant. The pigeon was penalized for alternating in response between the two keys by making reinforcement impossible for 1.5 seconds after every alternation. It was found that the relative frequency of responding on a given key closely approximated the relative frequency of reinforcement on that key.

Notes

[1] I wish to express my indebtedness to Dr. Douglas Anger of the Upjohn Company for his valuable comments concerning the interpretation of the data in this experiment. The work reported in this article was supported by Grant G-6435 from the National Science Foundation, Washington, D.C. to Harvard University.

[2] It should be noted that, by convention, the mean of a variable-interval schedule refers to the *minimum* average inter-reinforcement time and not to the *actual* inter-reinforcement time obtained under conditions of responding. Thus, if a particular animal responds very slowly, the actual mean interval of reinforcement may be larger than the value designated by the experimenter. The value designated is a minimum that is closely approached in practice because the animal's rate of responding is ordinarily high in comparison to the intervals in the reinforcement schedule.

[3] Skinner defined the extinction ratio as the number of unreinforced responses divided by the number of reinforced responses, but in actual computation he used the total number of responses divided by the number of reinforced responses. The difference is of no significance for the present discussion since both definitions imply a linear relation with zero intercept between absolute rate of responding and absolute rate of reinforcement.

References

Clark, F. C. The effect of deprivation and frequency of reinforcement on variable-interval responding. *J. Exp. Anal. Behav.*, 1958, 1, 221–228.

Ferster, C. B., and Skinner, B. F. *Schedules of reinforcement.* New York: Appleton-Century-Crofts, 1957.

Findley, J. D. Preference and switching under concurrent scheduling. *J. Exp. Anal. Behav.*, 1958, 1, 123–144.

Herrnstein, R. J. Behavioral consequences of the removal of a discriminative stimulus associated with variable-interval reinforcement. Unpublished doctoral dissertation, Harvard Univer., 1955.

Herrnstein, R. J. Some factors influencing behavior in a two-response situation. *Trans. N. Y. Acad. Sci.*, 1958, 21, 35–45.

Reynolds, G. S. Relativity of response rate and reinforcement frequency in a multiple schedule. *J. Exp. Anal. Behav.*, 1961, **2**, 179–184.

Skinner, B. F. *The behavior of organisms.* New York: D. Appleton Century Co., 1938.

Wilson, M. P. Periodic reinforcement interval and number of periodic reinforcements as parameters of response strength. *J. Comp. Physiol. Psychol.*, 1954, **47**, 51–56.

22 Commitment, Choice, and Self-Control
HOWARD RACHLIN AND LEONARD GREEN

When offered a choice (Choice Y) between a small immediate reward (2-sec exposure to grain) and a large reward (4-sec exposure to grain) delayed by 4 sec, pigeons invariably preferred the small, immediate reward. However, when offered a choice (Choice X) between a delay of T seconds followed by Choice Y and a delay of T seconds followed by restriction to the large delayed reward only, the pigeon's choice depended on T. When T was small, the pigeons chose the alternative leading to Choice Y (and then chose the small, immediate reward). When T was large, the pigeons chose the alternative leading to the large delayed reward only. The reversal of preference as T increases is predicted by several recent models for choice between various amounts and delays of reward. The preference for the large delayed alternative with long durations of T parallels everyday instances of advance commitment to a given course of action. Such commitment may be seen as a prototype for self-control.[1]

Commitment to a course of action is a form of self-control (Skinner, 1953) the utility of which depends on reversals of preference from time to time. Consider, for instance, a popular form of commitment, payroll savings. When a man signs a payroll savings agreement he prefers saving a certain portion of his paycheck to spending it. The utility of making this commitment rests on the fact that, when the man actually receives the money, he prefers to spend it rather than save it. Were it not for the reversal, there would be no reason to sign the payroll deduction agreement in the first place.

A similar reversal of preference underlies the effectiveness of a device invented by Azrin and Powell (1968) to limit chain smoking. The device consists of a cigarette case that locks for 2 hr when it is closed. When the user takes out one cigarette, the value of the next cigarette is minimal. It sinks below the value of limiting smoking and the case is cheerfully locked. Later, when the first cigarette is finished and the value of the next cigarette is greater than the value of limiting smoking, it is too late to have the cigarette. The availability of cigarettes from sources other than the locking case may limit the usefulness of the device, but if such a case were the only source of cigarettes and if the relative values of smoking and nonsmoking reversed, as hypothesized above, the method would be infallible.

Commitment, such as exhibited by the payroll saver or the user of the cigarette case, may be seen as an active process of self-control. A more parsimonious view, however, would see the commitment response as simple choice of a presently higher valued alternative. When the man signs the payroll savings agreement he is choosing to save his money. Not to sign the agreement would be to choose to spend his money. The apparent contingencies of the situation offer three alternatives:

"Commitment, Choice, and Self-Control" by Howard Rachlin and Leonard Green. *Journal of the Experimental Analysis of Behavior*, 1972, *17*, 15–22. Copyright 1972 by the Society for the Experimental Analysis of Behavior, Inc. Reprinted by permission of the publisher and author.

(a)   Make the commitment and save the money.
(b)   Do not make the commitment and spend the money.
(c)   Do not make the commitment but save the money anyway.
The third alternative, however, is not a real one. If it were, the commitment would not be necessary. In other words, the very fact that the commitment is made is evidence that the relative values of saving and spending reverse in time.

An account of choice that predicts reversals as a function of time is, thus, a prerequisite for the study of commitment. While it might seem that such reversals would be predicted only by complicated theories of human behavior, they are in fact predicted by several recent simple models, developed with animal subjects, for choice among various delays and amounts of reinforcement (Catania, 1963; Logan, 1965; Renner, 1967; Baum and Rachlin, 1969; Fantino, 1969; Herrnstein, 1970). Perhaps the simplest of these models is the one presented by Baum and Rachlin. They suggest a form of the matching law in which the ratio of the values of two reward alternatives differing in delay and amount is the product of the ratio of amounts and the inverse ratio of delays:

$$\frac{V_1}{V_2} = \frac{A_1}{A_2} \cdot \frac{D_2}{D_1}$$

Suppose A_1 was twice A_2, but was always delayed for 4 sec more than A_2. If D_1 was 4 sec and D_2 was 0 sec, the ratio, V_1/V_2, would be less than 1 ($A_1/A_2 = 2$; $D_2/D_1 = 0$). If, however, 10 sec are added to both delays, the ratio V_1/V_2 would be more than 1 ($A_1/A_2 = 2$; $D_2/D_1 = 10/14$). The change from a ratio less than one to a ratio more than one indicates a reversal of preferences as the two rewards are removed further from the choice point.

Figure 1a shows a set of contingencies by which such a reversal may produce commitment. Choice Y results in a preference for A_2 according to the matching formula ($A_1/A_2 = 2$; $D_2/D_1 = 0$). If A_2 is always chosen at Y, the choice at X is also between A_1 and A_2, but with longer delays involved than with the choice at Y. The upper branch alternative of A_1 is present, but not a factor at point X because it is never chosen. At point X, the matching formula predicts a choice of $A_1(A_1/A_2 = 2$; $D_2/D_1 = 10/14$). A_1 can be obtained only by choosing the lower branch. The only difference between the situation of Fig. 1a and a simple choice at X between A_1 with delay of 14 sec and A_2 with delay of 10 sec is the behavior at point Y of actually choosing A_2 instead of being forced to accept it. But there is ample evidence (Rachlin and Herrnstein, 1969) that choices such as at X are governed by the reward actually obtained and are independent of behavior *per se* between the choice and the reward. Therefore, there is good reason to believe that organisms at point Y will choose A_2 and at point X will choose A.

The choice of A_1 in Fig. 1a is predicted only on the basis of simple preference data. The only assumptions involved are that organisms will choose according to the matching formula, and that choice depends on the reward obtained and is independent of the behavior by which it is obtained. Both these assumptions are supported by evidence from previous experiments. As long as the choice responses are within the repertoire of the organism, commitment will be exhibited. The situation of

FIG. 1.(a) *A set of contingencies to study commitment. At choice point Y, the organism is expected to prefer the immediate, lesser reinforcement* (A_2) *over the delayed, greater reinforcement* (A_1). *At choice point X, however, the added delay between choice and reinforcement alternatives should lead the organism to reverse its preference. Reward A_1 will be obtained only when the lower branch is chosen. (b) Paradigm used in the free trials of the present experiment. The twenty-fifth peck on the right key in the initial link leads to the upper branch which presents a choice between delayed, greater reinforcement (green key) vs. immediate, lesser reinforcement (red key). The twenty-fifth peck on the left key in the initial link leads to the lower branch, which presents the green key only (greater, delayed reinforcement), the other key being darkened. T represents the delay between the end of the initial link (twenty-fifth peck) and the presentation of the red and green (Choice) or green only (No Choice) keylights.*

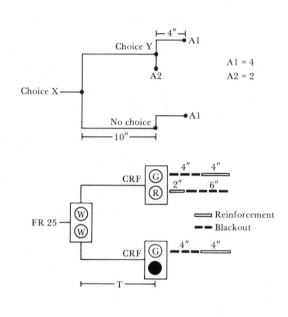

Fig. 1a parallels that of the payroll saver. The apparent alternatives at X are:

(a)   Choose the upper branch and A_2;
(b)   Choose the lower branch and A_1;
(c)   Choose the upper branch and A_1;

but, as with the payroll saver, alternative (c) is not a real one. While A_1 is preferred at X, A_2 will be preferred at Y. The only way to get A_1 is through commitment at X by choice of the lower branch.

The present experiment exposes pigeons to contingencies like those described by Fig. 1a and varies the time (T) between Choice X and Choice Y. With A_1 fixed at twice A_2 and T at 10 sec, pigeons at X should prefer the lower arm to the upper (should prefer No Choice to Choice Y). But, as T is decreased, the matching formula predicts that the preference should reverse. This experiment is similar to one by George Ainslie (described in Rachlin, 1970, 186–188) except that here, T is varied and choices are between one response and another; in Ainslie's experiment, the alternatives were response vs. non-response.

Method

Subjects

Five male adult, White Carneaux pigeons were maintained at about 80% of free-feeding weights. All five served as subjects in other experiments involving various delays and amounts of reward before the present experiment.

Apparatus

The experimental chamber contained two response keys, mounted 3.75 in. (8.9 cm) apart, which required a force of 0.15 N to be operated, and a food hopper that could provide variable access to mixed grain. The chamber was illuminated by two 7-w white bulbs on the ceiling and the response keys could be transilluminated by lights of various colors. White masking noise was continuously present. Scheduling and recording were automatic, with standard relay equipment located in an adjacent room.

Procedure

Each daily session consisted of 50 trials, 10 forced trials followed by 40 free trials. Figure 1b is a diagram of the free-trial procedure. Each trial was a chain of events, some produced automatically and some contingent on responding by the subject. At the beginning of a trial (the initial link), both keys were transilluminated with white light. Passage to the next link was governed by a fixed-ratio (FR) of 25 pecks, which could be distributed in any way on the two keys. If the twenty-fifth peck was on the right key (the upper key in Fig. 1b) both keys and the houselights darkened (blackout) for T seconds. After the blackout, the houselights and both keys were automatically reilluminated, one key with red light and the other key with green light. Which key was red and which green was determined randomly at each trial. A single peck on the red key (CRF) produced 2 sec of access to food, followed automatically by 6 sec of blackout. A single peck on the green key produced 4 sec of blackout, followed automatically by 4 sec of access to food. Thus, a peck on the red key produced a small immediate reinforcement while a peck on the green key produced a delayed but larger one. After the reinforcement or blackout, the keys were reilluminated with white light and a new trial began.

If, during the initial link, the twenty-fifth peck was on the left key (the lower key in Fig. 1b) there was a blackout for T seconds followed by reillumination of only one of the keys (randomly determined at each trial) with green light. The other key remained dark. A single peck on the green key produced a 4-sec blackout followed by 4 sec of access to food. Then, a new trial began immediately with both keys illuminated with white light. Pecks on dark keys throughout the experiment had no scheduled consequences.

A forced-choice trial differed from a free-choice trial in only one respect; the twenty-fifth peck during the initial link was effective on only one key (determined randomly at each trial), although both keys were lit. Responding on the inactive key advanced the fixed-ratio counter, but could not produce the blackout and subsequent reinforcement. Thus, during the forced trials, more than 25 pecks could be made in the initial link, while during free trials, the twenty-fifth peck was always effective in advancing to the next link.

Pigeons responding on concurrent fixed-ratio schedules such as those in the initial link tend to distribute all or almost all of their pecks on the preferred key (Herrnstein, 1958). This is desirable in the present experiment because large variations of T, according to the matching formula, produce relatively small preferences for one alternative over the other. The concurrent fixed-ratio schedules tend to amplify preferences and make it easier to determine at what value of T preferences switch from one alternative to the other. A disadvantage of concurrent fixed-ratio schedules for these purposes, however, is that once preferences are formed they are likely to persist through large changes of the independent variables. The forced-choice procedure was designed to force the pigeons to sample both alternatives during each session and to weaken strong key preferences.

For the first five sessions, T was set at 10 sec and only the right-hand key was available during the initial link (only the upper arm of the diagram of Fig. 1b was in effect). During these five sessions, each of the 50 trials was a form of forced trial, which differed from the forced trials described previously in that the inactive key was always the left key and its inactivity was signalled by darkening it.

After the first five sessions, both keys were lit and the 10 forced-trial and 40 free-trial sessions were instituted as described above. The value of T was constant during any single session but was varied between sessions for all pigeons. For 35 sessions, not counting the initial five training sessions, T was kept at 10 sec. Then, T was kept for 10 sessions at each of the following values in turn: 0.5, 1, 2, 4, 8, 16, 8, 4, 2, 1, and 0.5 sec.

Results

When exposed to the red and green keys together, all pigeons, within a single session, came to peck the red key on virtually all trials. This exclusive preference for the small immediate reinforcement over the large delayed one appeared for all pigeons during the initial forced-choice session and persisted through the five preliminary forced-choice sessions, during the 10 forced-choice trials at the beginning of subsequent sessions, and during the 40 free-choice trials of those subsequent sessions. Of course, this preference could be measured only when the right-hand key (upper branch of Fig. 1b) was chosen during the initial link. However, even during those sessions when the right key was chosen on only one or two of the 40 free-choice trials, the pigeons pecked the red key on those one or two trials. The percentage of responses on the red key during the CRF exposure to the red and green keys together was never less than 95% during a session for any pigeon after the first session. For most sessions, the red key was pecked whenever it appeared as an alternative.

With regard to behavior during the initial link, in the five preliminary forced-choice sessions with T = 10 sec, only the right key was available. At the sixth session, the left key was made available as well. Considering only behavior during the free-choice trials in the sixth session, two of the five pigeons pecked more on the left key and three pecked more on the right key. One of the pigeons that initially pecked more on the right key reversed its preference and came to peck more on the left key during the 35 sessions at T = 10. The other four pigeons showed no discernible changes in preference over the course of the 35 sessions.

Figure 2 shows, for each pigeon, median relative rate during the free-choice initial links (percentage of pecks on the left key) over the last five sessions at each value of T as T was increased from 0.5 sec to 16 sec and decreased again to 0.5 sec, the solid lines showing ascending, and the dotted lines, descending, values of T. Table 1 shows absolute rate of re-

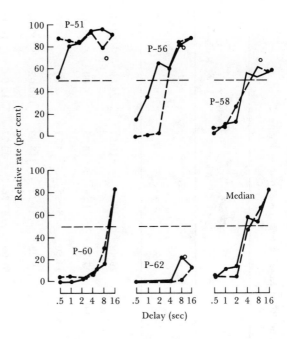

FIG. 2. *Relative rate (percentage of pecks on the left key) during the initial link for each pigeon. The rates are medians from the last five sessions at each value of T during the 40 free-choice trials. Solid lines are for ascending values and dotted lines for descending values of T. Circled points are for the last five sessions at T = 10 sec. The lower right function is the median of the five individual functions.*

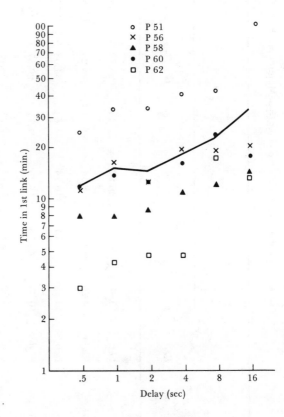

FIG. 3. *Total time spent in initial link at each value of T. The figures are the average times for each pigeon in the last five sessions at each ascending T value, averaged with the last five sessions at each descending T value, during the 40 free-choice trials. The line is the average of the five points at each value of T.*

TABLE 1. Absolute Rate of Responding (Per Minute) on the Left and Right Keys for Sessions Shown in Figure 2

Pigeon	Key	10	0.5	1	2	4	8	16	8	4	2	1	0.5
51	Left	10.08	20.80	36.22	26.43	23.79	27.68	8.20	29.49	18.45	19.97	24.69	57.08
	Right	4.26	18.55	8.34	4.71	1.25	0.85	0.65	7.79	1.28	3.98	4.00	8.04
56	Left	40.58	9.14	10.24	41.84	34.08	42.42	45.50	44.80	30.48	4.77	2.83	0.00
	Right	10.03	48.76	18.49	21.11	20.57	8.94	6.21	8.22	21.13	113.49	120.02	143.98
58	Left	48.72	4.39	13.87	18.28	55.72	51.93	43.11	51.09	47.36	30.77	12.69	10.08
	Right	22.27	129.16	109.08	110.81	41.67	42.14	31.57	30.15	54.17	80.71	122.94	119.12
60	Left	6.27	0.69	0.47	2.83	5.76	8.30	41.98	9.94	4.57	2.90	2.90	3.27
	Right	32.18	100.10	159.01	112.12	68.88	42.99	7.87	22.04	66.46	64.71	58.89	74.55
62	Left	10.39	0.00	0.23	0.00	0.68	16.77	8.78	0.92	0.58	0.00	0.23	0.00
	Right	35.67	287.19	239.44	226.86	233.41	52.77	58.51	92.03	199.03	217.16	231.60	254.46

sponding on left and right keys during those sessions shown in Fig. 2. The circled points in Fig. 2 are median relative rates for the last five of the initial 35 sessions at T = 10 sec. All of the curves increase as T increases, showing a tendency for pigeons to prefer the larger but longer delayed reinforcement over the smaller less-delayed one as the delay increases. The similarity between ascending and descending curves indicates that stability was reached during the sessions for which medians were taken. At T = 16 sec, four of the five pigeons pecked more on the left key, leading to the green key only (and the larger reinforcement). At T = 0.5 sec, four of the five pigeons pecked more on the right key, leading to a choice between the green key (larger reinforcement) and the red key (smaller reinforcement). Because the pigeons always pecked on the red key whenever both red and green keys appeared together, the only trials on which the larger reinforcement was obtained were those on which the left-hand key was pecked during the initial link.

The pigeons usually pecked on only one key during the initial link on the free-choice trials. However, when they switched, they switched more from the left to right keys than *vice-versa*. If relative entries from the left key to the next link were plotted in Fig. 2, instead of relative pecks on the left key, the curves would be parallel to those shown but slightly lower. This would be expected from the matching formula because it predicts that as the time to reinforcement grows shorter (while the 25 pecks are being made) the right key (leading to the smaller, less-delayed reinforcement) should be preferred.

Figure 3 shows the total time (cumulated over the last 40 trials of each session) spent in the initial link as a function of T. As T increased and the delay of both small and large reinforcements increased, the pigeons tended to spend more time in the initial link. The figure shows the average time in the initial link for the five pigeons. Some pigeons paused considerably less and some considerably more than the mean, but all pigeons spent more time in the initial link as T increased. Most of the increase in time during the initial link represents a pause at the beginning of a trial. However, on occasion, the pigeons would pause, then peck a few times on one key, then pause again and complete the ratio on the same key or on the other key.

The scheduled delay T and the additional 4-sec delay after pecking the green key do not comprise the entire time between the end of the initial link and reinforcement. In addition, there is the reaction time after T between presentation of the green or red and green keys and the peck on the green or red key. Figure 4 shows that reaction time increased with T. The time for choosing between red and green was not greater than the time for pecking the green key when it was presented alone. In fact, while there were no significant differences, the average curves show longer reaction times with the lone green key. This may have been due to the fact that delay of reinforcement was greater for the green key than the red key. The reaction times were a significant fraction of total delay time for low values of T. For values of T less than 2 sec, the reaction time was greater than T. Even at T = 16 sec, the reaction time comprised 17% of the delay between the initial link and the small reinforcement and 14% of the delay between the initial link and the large reinforcement.

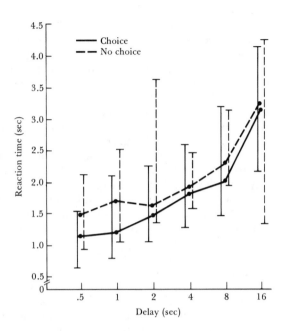

FIG. 4. *Reaction time (time from end of initial link to peck on red or green keys) at each value of T. Medians were determined for the last five sessions at each T value for each pigeon. Then, the ascending and descending medians at each T value were averaged. The solid line represents the reaction time for Choice trials (red and green keys) averaged across pigeons; the dotted line represents the reaction time for the No Choice trials (green key only) averaged across pigeons. The vertical solid and dotted lines indicate the range of median reaction times.*

Discussion

As T increases, the matching formula predicts a shift in preference from the more immediate (smaller) to the more delayed (larger) reinforcement. The fact that all the functions of Fig. 2 have upward slopes shows the tendency for preferences to shift in the predicted direction.

When the amounts and delays of the present experiment are substituted in the matching formula, an indifference point is predicted at $T = 4$ sec. But the nominal value of T is not the real value. In the case of the small reinforcement, for instance, the reaction time must be added to the nominal value of T to get the real delay between the twenty-fifth peck in the initial link and the reinforcement. A real delay of 4 sec would be experienced at about $T = 2.5$ sec since, in that region, the reaction time for both Choice (red and green keys) and No Choice (green key alone) is about 1.5 sec. The functions of Fig. 2 should cross the horizontal line at about $T = 2.5$ sec. Only one of the five functions can be said to cross near that point (P-56). The average curve crosses closer to $T = 4$ sec. Functions showing relative entries rather than relative rate of response in the initial link would cross at a still higher value of T ($T = 5.5$ sec for the average curve).

Because the individual functions varied so widely in slope, no simple equation could account for the data. The average function would cross near the predicted value only if reaction time were ignored. It may be that the reaction time is somehow not effective as delay. Evidently, there are some additional determinants of initial link behavior peculiar to individual pigeons which have not been accounted for. The FR schedules of the initial link generate strong key preferences that the forced-choice trials at the beginning of each session may not have counteracted. Furthermore, the amounts and delays as measured may not have equalled the amounts and delays actually in effect for each pigeon. For instance, a pigeon may start or stop eating at any time during the magazine presentation, even though the magazine is available for a fixed time. Chung (1965) found discontinuities in choice at short hopper times. In addition to the question of whether the obtained data could be accounted for by the proposed equation, there seems to be a more basic difficulty with the equation; it predicts that any immediate reinforcement $(D = 0)$ no matter how small would be preferred to any delayed reinforcement, no matter how large. When $D = 0$, the value of a reinforcement would be infinite. This is not, however, a real difficulty because D can never be zero. The equations purports to deal with choice behavior. If an alternative can be chosen it must also be capable of being rejected. Yet, an organism could not reject a reinforcement with no delay. To say $D = 0$ implies that the organism *has* the reinforcement. It is reasonable to consider preference to be infinite for a reinforcement already obtained. When the reinforcement is not yet obtained, when it still can be rejected, D can never be zero. Figure 3 implies a lower asymptote of about 1 sec for choice under the conditions of the present experiment.

It is worth noting that the proposed model for commitment is based on a reversal of preferences as the delay of alternatives changes. This reversal is a property of the particular matching equation of the introduction, but it is also a property of many other recently proposed quantitative accounts of choice (those cited in the introduction) as well as recent lexicographic models for choice (Coombs, 1964; Tversky, 1969). Thus, the model does not depend on a situation where the effective amounts and delays are expressible only in terms of hopper-time-up and hopper-time-down, as the proposed matching formula implies.

For the pigeons of the present experiment, commitment resulted in behavior often categorized as delay of gratification; the larger, more delayed reinforcement was obtained at the expense of the smaller, more immediate one. This raises the question of whether other instances of delay of gratification, and of self-control in general, rest on commitment.

In the illustrative examples of the introduction (the payroll saver and the user of the locking cigarette case) and for the pigeons of the present experiment, the commitment contingencies are overtly presented. That is, they are offered to the subject as strategies that he may take or leave. Payroll savings was invented by the bank, the cigarette case was invented by Azrin and Powell, and the electrical circuit that controlled the present experiment was built by the authors. For such situations, commitment would be predicted on the basis of reversal of preferences and presented contingencies. But commitment strategies may also be invented on the spot. When such commitment strategies are invented, rather than presented ready-made, we are more likely to regard the process as one of self-control. A recently cited classical example of self-control (Kanfer and Phillips, 1970) is Odysseus tying himself to the mast of a ship to avoid being tempted by the Sirens. Odysseus' behavior can be explained in terms of a reversal of values as the boat approached the Sirens. At a distance, the value of avoiding a crash on the rocks would be greater than whatever pleasure was to be gained by approaching the rocks. As Odysseus' boat approached closer to the rocks, these values would presumably reverse, with the value of approaching the Sirens rising above the value of avoiding a crash. The act of tying himself to the mast was a commitment similar in contingency to the choice of the lower arm of Fig. 1a by the pigeons. The difference between Odysseus and the pigeons is that he invented his own commitment strategy, whereas they were presented with theirs. Another example of a commitment strategy a person might invent is putting his alarm clock out of easy reach of his bed so that when it rings he is forced to get up to turn it off. This strategy would work (if it does work) because before going to sleep the value of getting up in the morning is greater than that of sleeping later, whereas next morning these values reverse. When we label these behaviors as self-control the part that should be attributed to the self is the invention of the commitment strategy. Once this is done, subsequent behavior would be predicted by the matching formula and the contingencies.

We might speculate that even in instances where no overt commitment strategies are apparent, they nevertheless operate covertly. Mischel and Ebbeson (1970) report that children when faced with a choice between an immediate small reward and a delayed large reward "spent their time psychologically doing something (almost anything) other than waiting." Some children tried to sleep during the delay period and one child actually succeeded. The child who slept may well have been overtly putting into effect mechanisms that other children, and adults, learn to activate covertly. These mechanisms may serve effectively to commit us to a previously chosen alternative so that an ostensible choice, when it is offered, is not a real one. We may not "see" the immediate small alternative because we have committed ourselves in advance to ignore it. One thinks of "perceptual defense" and "gating" of sensory input. Such strategies of commitment may be the only explanation for our apparent self-control.

Notes
[1] This research was supported by National Science Foundation Research Grant GB20802. The authors are grateful to Robert Liebert for his help and criticism. Reprints may be obtained from Howard Rachlin, Psychology Department, State University of New York, Stony Brook, New York, 11790.

References
Azrin, N. H., and Powell, J. Behavioral engineering: the reduction of smoking behavior by a conditioning apparatus and procedure. *Journal of Applied Behavior Analysis*, 1968, **1**, 193–200.

Baum, W. M., and Rachlin, H. Choice as time allocation. *Journal of the Experimental Analysis of Behavior*, 1969, **12**, 861–874.

Catania, A. C. Concurrent performances: A baseline for the study of reinforcement magnitude. *Journal of the Experimental Analysis of Behavior*, 1963, **6**, 253–263.

Chung, S. H. Effects of delayed reinforcement in a concurrent situation. *Journal of the Experimental Analysis of Behavior*, 1965, **8**, 439–444.

Coombs, C. H. *A theory of data.* New York: Wiley, 1964, P. 201.

Fantino, E. Choice and rate of reinforcement. *Journal of the Experimental Analysis of Behavior*, 1969, **12**, 723–730.

Herrnstein, R. J. Some factors influencing behavior in a two-response situation. *Transactions of the New York Academy of Sciences*, 1958, **21**, 35–45.

Herrnstein, R. J. On the law of effect. *Journal of the Experimental Analysis of Behavior*, 1970, **13**, 243–266.

Kanfer, F. H., and Phillips, J. S. *Learning foundations of behavior therapy.* New York: Wiley, 1970. Pp. 412–413.

Logan, F. A. Decision making by rats: Delay versus amount of reward. *Journal of Comparative and Physiological Psychology,* 1965, **59,** 246–251.

Mischel, W. Theory and research on the antecedents of self-imposed delay of reward. In B. A. Maher (Ed.), *Progress in experimental personality research.* Vol. 3. New York: Academic Press, 1966. Pp. 85–132.

Mischel, W., and Ebbesen, E. B. Attention in delay of gratification. *Journal of Personality and Social Psychology,* 1970, **16,** 329–337.

Rachlin, H. *Introduction to modern behaviorism.* San Francisco: W. H. Freeman and Co., 1970.

Rachlin, H., and Herrnstein, R. J. Hedonism revisited: On the negative law of effect. In B. Campbell and R. M. Church (Eds.), *Punishment and aversive behavior.* New York: Appleton-Century-Crofts, 1969. Pp. 83–109.

Renner, K. E. Temporal integration: An incentive approach to conflict resolution. In B. A. Maher (Ed.), *Progress in experimental personality research.* Vol. 4. New York: Academic Press, 1967. Pp. 127–177.

Skinner, B. F. *Science and human behavior.* New York: MacMillan, 1953.

Tversky, A. Intransitivity of preferences. *Psychological Review,* 1969, **76,** 31–48.

B. CHOICE UNDER NATURALISTIC CONDITIONS

How does an organism's choice behavior in the laboratory relate to its choice behavior in its natural environment? Concurrent schedules provide a highly constrained version of the problem of behavior allocation that animals face in nature, yet in recent years biologists have explained choice behavior in nature by appeal to principles that are similar to the ones used to explain choice among concurrent schedules (Charnov, 1976; Krebs, 1978). The article by Mellgren demonstrates this convergence of thinking among biologists and behavior theorists by studying how rats make choices in a laboratory situation designed to simulate the animals' natural environments.

23 Foraging in a Simulated Natural Environment: There's a Rat Loose in the Lab

ROGER L. MELLGREN

Rats were required to earn their food in a large room having nine boxes placed in it, each of which contained food buried in sand. In different phases of the experiment the amount of time allowed for foraging, the amount of food available in each food patch, and the location of the different available amounts were varied. The rats exhaustively sampled all patches each session but seemed to have fairly strong preferences for certain locations over others. If position preferences were for patches containing small amounts of food, the sensitivity to amount available was increased so that when location was compensated for, a pattern of optimal foraging was evident. The importance of environmental constraints in producing optimal behavior and the relation of the observed behavior to laboratory findings are discussed.[1]

Key words: foraging, amount of food, optimal behavior, seminatural environment, rats

In the past few years psychologists interested in animal behavior have become much less myopic in their outlook on what constitutes the appropriate procedure(s) and theoretical framework(s) for understanding behavior. On the theoretical side, economic models have been used to explain schedule effects (e.g., Allison, Miller, & Wozny, 1979; Hursh, 1980). Another related view is that learned behavior represents adaptation to environmental constraints on the basis of a homeostatic mechanism (e.g., Staddon, 1979). The influence of ecological and ethological theories of foraging behavior (e.g., Lea, 1979) has also served to broaden our theoretical perspective. On the procedural side, there has been a new appreciation for the "naturalness" of behavior and how the constraints of a learning situation affect naturally occurring activities (e.g., Shettleworth, 1975). To promote the idea of studying natural behavior, several researchers have also advocated the use of learning situations that require the animal to spend a significant amount of time (if not all the time) in the situation and work for all the daily food and/or water it will receive during this time (e.g., Collier, Hirsch, & Kanarek, 1977). These theoretical and procedural innovations are not independent but are mutually interdependent and compatible, promising a new look for animal psychology.

The present experiment represents an attempt to develop a procedure along the lines of a more natural or representative environment and procedure. It has the characteristics of a natural situation, but maintains some of the important controlled aspects of laboratory studies. This was done by allowing the rat to forage for its food in a large room containing nine food sources, or patches, and two water bottles. The patches consisted of boxes containing sand that had food buried in it. The room itself was in total disarray, with tables, chairs, and desks laid on their sides making it difficult for a human to move around in the room. With the contents of each patch being known and only one subject foraging at a time a quantitative test of optimal foraging theory (e.g., Krebs, 1978) is possible. In particular, this theory claims that a predator will capture prey in a patch so as to maximize the rate of return relative to the whole environment. In the present experiment the amount of food available in each patch was varied and the total amount was known. In the natural environment these parameters must often be guessed and are subject to fluctuation due to factors beyond the experimenter's control (e.g., weather, seasonal changes, other predators, etc.)

In the present experiment, the optimal foraging behavior is a function of the amount of food available in each patch. Consider the following situation where there are four food patches each containing a different number of prey: 10, 7, 4, and 1 prey, respectively. If we know the total number of prey captured by the forager is 12, then how should the optimal forager utilize the different patches? First it is assumed that average time between successive captures of prey items is inversely related to the number currently available. That is, a prey item will be found sooner if there are 10 available than if there are only 9. Second, it is assumed that the cost of searching for prey within a patch is relatively greater than the cost of traveling from one patch to another. If it was not costly to search and handle prey within a patch, as might be the case if soft pellets were available in a cup, then the predator should simply eat everything available before moving on to the next patch. Similarly, if the environment was very rich, meaning each patch had a very high density of prey available, the cost of traveling between patches would increase relative to the cost of staying in a patch since in a rich environment the cost of searching for prey is less than in a poor environment. Under these assumptions the optimal predator will act to minimize the time spent searching within a patch since such searching is the main cost in the situation. In the hypothetical example above the total number of prey obtained is known to be 12, and the predator therefore should have captured 7 from the 10 prey patch, 4 from the 7 prey patch, 1 from the 4 prey patch and 0 from the 1 prey patch. In this fashion the predator will have depleted each patch to 3 prey items available (except for the 1 prey patch, of course). A strategy that resulted in reducing a given patch below the 3 prey level is nonoptimal because it involves greater costs than the optimal.

The form of the optimal solution to predation in a patchy environment depends on the nature of the environment and constraints of the predator. For example, in the above prediction it was assumed that the cost (measured in some appropriate currency such as time or energy expended) of searching for prey within a patch was greater than the cost of traveling from one patch to another. Suppose that restrictions on travel were imposed. There might be either physical barricades between patches or the danger of becoming the prey of some other predator when traveling in the exposed areas between patches. In this case the optimal strategy would be to deplete each patch utilized to a greater degree than in the previous example since the cost of doing so is less than the cost of traveling to a new patch. Schoener (1971) discusses these and other cases and provides a mathematical formulation of the various possibilities.

In the present experiment 9 patches were made available, each containing differing numbers of prey items during the experimental phases. It was assumed that the cost of travel was less than the cost of searching within a patch (the first case discussed above). The optimal strategy would then be to reduce all patches to a given level, that level being determined by the total amount of food to be harvested and the distribution of food between patches. To simplify matters, the amount of food available was systematically varied in increments of 3 and 5 pellets per patch for the two subjects. This results in the optimal strategy being expressed as a linear relationship between amount available and amount eaten. This prediction is also consistent with the idea that the predator has a cutoff time for successive prey captures, and once this cutoff time is reached without finding a prey item the predator "gives up" and moves to a new patch (Charnov, 1976).

Method

Subjects

Two male hooded rats of the Long-Evans strain approximately 100 days old at the start of the experiment were obtained from Blue Spruce Farms, Altamont, N.Y.

Apparatus

A large windowless classroom and several smaller rooms, used for experimental psychology classes during the academic year, were used as the experimental apparatus. A floor plan and dimensions of the room are shown in Fig. 1. The patches were rubberized boxes 27.5 by 27.5 by 15 cm deep, filled with 3.71 liters (4.7 kg) of sand that was obtained from a local river bed. This volume of sand resulted in a depth of approximately 4 cm in each patch. During the time the subjects were in the apparatus no lights were on, although some illumination was caused by the gap under the two doors of the main classroom. Food pellets were Purina Hog Startina pellets with a mean weight of .119 g each. These pellets are very firm and will not crumble from the weight of a rat or by being handled. Two small water bottles were located in the apparatus as shown in Fig. 1, and each contained 100 ml of water when a subject was placed in the room.

Procedure

Both rats had extensive experience with foraging for food buried in sand prior to the start of this experiment, having served in one of M. W. Olson's dissertation experiments (Olson, 1980).

Phase 1 lasted for nine sessions, each 12 hours long for each subject. For the first five sessions 15 pellets were available in each patch and 20 pellets for the next session. There was a break of 10 days for extraexperimental reasons, followed by the last three sessions of this phase with 20 pellets in each patch. The rats were changed, food eaten was measured, patches were stocked, etc., at 9 a.m. and 9 p.m.

244   R. L. Mellgren

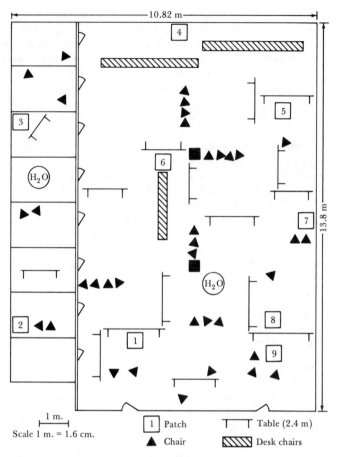

Fig. 1.   *A floor plan of the experimental rooms.*

Phase 2 lasted for six sessions with different numbers of pellets available in each patch, as shown in Table 1. An attempt was made to counterbalance small and large amounts by location between the two subjects, but any true counterbalancing would have required many more subjects. Foraging periods continued to last for 12 hours during this phase.

Phase 3 lasted for 15 sessions and was identical to Phase 2, except the rats were allowed only one hour of foraging time per session. Rat 9 foraged from 9 to 10 a.m. and Rat 10 foraged from 9 to 10 p.m.

Phase 4 lasted for 9 sessions of one hour duration. Number of pellets available in each patch was rotated so that each amount was represented once in each patch. This was accomplished by shifting the number of pellets for a particular patch to the next highest number patch and Patch 9 shifted to Patch 1. Thus, for Rat 9 on the first day of this phase, Patch 1 had 12 pellets in it, Patch 2 had 27 pellets, Patch 3 had 9 pellets, and so on. On the ninth session the amounts were as they were during Phases 2 and 3.

The sand from all patches was periodically mixed together and redistributed to prevent possible odor effects from differentially influencing the rat's behavior. No food was given to the rats in their homecages during the course of the experiment, except for the occasional feedings during Phases 3 and 4 at the time when the other rat was foraging. Such feedings occurred when a subject's weight dropped below 80% of its ad lib weight (during the 10-day break of Phase 1 food was available ad lib). Water was continually available in the home cage.

Data recorded were number of pellets eaten, number of feces, and evidence of urine for each patch. This was accomplished by sifting the sand after each session. Amount of urine was quantified by rating the amount of coagulated sand on a 1 to 10 scale. Amount of water drunk from each water bottle was measured and the weight of the rat at the start and finish of a session was also recorded. A note was made concerning the rat's location in the apparatus at the time the experimenter entered at the end of a session.

Results and Discussion

The data will be viewed in two different (but not exclusive) ways. First a theoretically neutral, descriptive account will be given, and then the relation of these data to optimality theory will be evaluated.

Descriptive Account

The subjects rapidly learned the location of the nine food patches. On the first foraging session, Rat 9 visited and ate from seven of the nine patches and ate from all of them on the second session. Rat 10 ate from six of the nine on the first session, and the others, except for Patch 9 which was closest to the front door, on the second session. It was not until the fifth session that Rat 10 ate from patch nine.

Although there were numerous occasions when food was not taken from a patch, it was almost always the case that every patch was visited and some indication was present of foraging having taken place, since the surface of each patch was smoothed over at the start of a foraging ses-

TABLE 1. Amount of Food (Number of Pellets)
Available in Each Patch for the Five Phases
of the Experiment

		Experimental phase		
	1	*2,3*		*4*
Patch number		*S9*	*S10*	
1	15,20	27	16	
2	15,20	9	41	
3	15,20	30	6	*Rotation*
4	15,20	21	1	
5	15,20	24	26	
6	15,20	15	11	
7	15,20	6	36	
8	15,20	18	21	
9	15,20	12	31	

sion, and disturbances due to digging in the sand were quite obvious. After the second session of Phase 1, Subject 9 visited 99.1% of available patches throughout the remaining phases, and Subject 10 visited 97.7% of the patches.

Phases 1 and 2 involved 12-hour foraging periods and that amount of time allowed the subjects to deplete almost completely all patches each session. Recorded occurrences of feces and urine were restricted to the patches, with only one exception. Both rats adopted a "home" in the rear corner of the large room. The home was in the area where books would be placed under a desk chair which was on its back on the floor. Rat 9 was first found in the home on the second session of Phase 1 and was subsequently found there frequently (five of six sessions during Phase 2). Rat 10 was found in the same location on the fifth and sixth sessions of Phase 2. Feces and urine were also found in this location, but unlike that found in the patches, it was not removed. Presumably, the odors left by Rat 9 induced Rat 10 to adopt the same home. During subsequent phases there was less consistency in where the rats were found, presumably because the foraging periods were restricted to one hour in these phases. It is interesting that during the phases with one-hour foraging sessions, when the session terminated with the rat in the open (i.e., not in a patch), it often ran to the home.

In order to evaluate the effect of having differing densities of food available in each patch, several correlation coefficients (Pearson's r) were computed. These correlations are used as a descriptive device to indicate the degree of relationship between patch densities and patch utilization. Scattergrams and regression lines for the correlations are shown in Fig. 2. A correlation between the proportion of total food available in a particular patch and the proportion of food actually eaten in that patch was computed for each rat on the average data of the first five days of Phase 3. For Subject 9 this correlation was $-.41$, indicating that this subject ate proportionately less from higher density patches than from lower density patches. However, for Subject 10 the same correlation was $+.66$. We interpret this to mean that the placement of patches for Subject 9 was contrary to its preferences for location at the start of this phase, but they were consistent for Subject 10. Evidence that Subject 9 changed its preferences for patches comes from the correlation computed between proportion available and proportion eaten over the average of the last five days of Phase 3. Now the correlation was $+.35$ for Rat 9 and $+.71$ for Rat 10. This suggests that Rat 9 adjusted its foraging pattern to reflect more closely the relative availability of food, but Rat 10, since it already had a preference for the more dense patches, showed little change.

Data from Phase 4 support the hypothesis that Rat 9 was forced to readjust its preference for patch location by being more sensitive to patch density, but Rat 10 was not. During Phase 4 the density of food available in each patch was systematically varied so that each density occurred once in each location. Correlations were again computed for amount available and amount eaten so that a subject sensitive to patch density should show a positive correlation, but one insensitive to density and concerned (primarily) with location should show a low correlation. The correlation was .85 for Rat 9 and .18 for Rat 10. These findings are consistent with the hypothesis that Rat 9 adjusted its foraging pattern because the density–

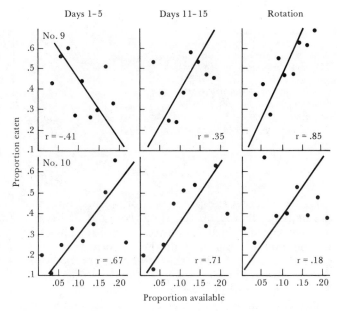

FIG. 2. *The proportion of food available in the environment plotted against the actual proportion of food eaten that came from that patch during the first and last five days of constant patch locations and all nine days with food availability rotated through all locations.*

location relationship originally experienced in Phase 3 was inefficient. The efficiency of foraging could be increased by Rat 9 through increased sensitivity to patch density. Rat 10 had preestablished preferences for patch locations that also happened to be some of the more dense patches, so it would be expected that little pressure was put on this subject to increase his foraging efficiency and responsivity to patch density differences.

Although there were two water sources available in the foraging environment, surprisingly little water was consumed. Generally no more than 10 ml was consumed from either bottle, with the average amount being between 6 and 7 ml per session during the 12-hour phases and less than 5 ml during the one hours phases.

Optimal Foraging Theory

According to this theory organisms will act in such a way as to optimize their patterns of foraging to provide the greatest return (energy gain, caloric intake, etc.) with the minimal expenditure (energy expended, exposure to predation, etc.). Most tests of optimality theory have involved unifactor manipulations in the sense that only one aspect of the test situation was varied to test predictions of the theory. Size of prey or other aspects of the prey have been the favorite standard for testing the theory (e.g., Krebs, 1978), although occasionally travel time between patches has been used. The method employed in the present experiment was designed to be similarly unifactor, with the density of prey in a patch being the variable of interest.

Days 11–15 constant location

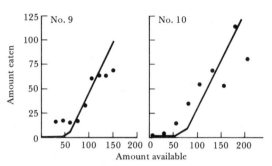

Fig. 3. *Predictions of Optimal Foraging Theory (solid lines) for amount eaten as a function of the amount available for the last five days of constant patch locations.*

Figure 3 shows the prediction of optimal foraging theory in relation to the density of prey on the final five days of Phase 3 (one hour foraging sessions, constant patch-density locations). The predictions were derived by the method outlined in the introductory part of this report. This method involves taking the total number of pellets consumed by each subject and determining the optimal pattern of patch utilization under the assumption of increasing costs of searching with decreasing prey availability and relatively greater costs for searching within a patch relative to travel between patches. The fit of data and theory is not overly impressive.

The deviations from predicted behavior are systematic and similar for each subject. Those patches containing low densities of prey are overutilized and those containing high densities are underutilized. This behavior indicates that the subjects are too conservative relative to optimality theory. The subjects do not exploit the high density patches to the degree that optimality theory predicts and instead, sample from lower density patches, overexploiting them. Changing the assumption concerning relative costs of searching within a patch and travel between patches will not help the fit. If travel between patches was actually more costly than originally assumed, the slope of the predicted line in Fig. 3 and 4 would be increased and the intercept would be shifted to the right, making the fit even worse. It is interesting that there is a parallel phenomenon in research on decision making by humans. Our species underutilizes the diagnostic value of information relative to the optimal (Bayes Theorem in this case), showing a more conservative pattern of behavior than is optimal (e.g., Edwards, Lindman, & Phillips, 1965).

Optimal foraging theory makes nearly identical predictions concerning patch utilization regardless of whether patch densities maintain constant locations from one foraging session to the next, or if the locations vary in nonsystematic fashion. The only difference between these two situations is the fact that when patch densities vary in location, it will take some time for the subject to discover the rate of return in a particular location, thereby increasing the probability that a low density patch will be overforaged relative to the condition where patch densities and their locations remain constant. Figure 4 shows the predictions of optimal foraging theory and the outcome of Phase 4 of the experiment (densities rotated among all patch locations). Although Rat 10 shows essentially the same pattern of deviation from what optimal foraging theory predicts—also ev-

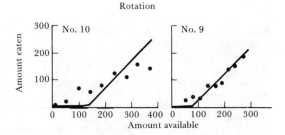

FIG. 4. *Predictions of Optimal Foraging Theory (solid lines) for amount eaten as a function of the amount available for the nine days of patch densites rotated among patch locations.*

ident in the previous phase of constant patch-density locations (overutilizes low density, underutilizes high density)—Rat 9 shows fairly impressive agreement with the predictions of the theory. Excluding the two lowest density patches, a chi-square goodness-of-fit procedure indicated that the predicted and observed number of prey eaten were not significantly different [$\chi^2(6) = 12.47$, $p > .05$].

The finding that Rat 9 was consistent with predictions from optimal foraging theory also supports the earlier argument that Rat 9 was forced to be more sensitive to patch densities than Rat 10 because of the mismatch between Rat 9's initial patch preferences and what was available in those patches. By being forced to be more sensitive to the contents of a patch, Subject 9 shows an optimal pattern of foraging, but Subject 10 does not. It appears then that optimal foraging is not a necessary result of biological programming, but depends on how such programming interacts with environmental constraints for its occurrence.

The main results of the experiment may be summarized as follows: (1) rats are exhaustive samplers of their potential food sources. Both rats showed evidence of visiting virtually every patch available on each session. (2) Rats tend toward conservatism in the sense of preferring a particular location for foraging over what is available in that location, except when preferred locations contain very small amounts of food. (3) When the environment is structured so that preferred locations do not contain rich food sources, there appears to be increased sensitivity to the richness of the food source. When location is subsequently not a factor, there is optimization of the utilization of differentially rich food sources. It is also interesting that at least one subject showed more efficient behavior in a changing environment than a constant one. This may reflect the fact that more than one kind of learning is called for in an environment as complex as the one used in this experiment. Learning about where food sources are and learning about the nature of the food sources and how to obtain the food they contain may be relatively independent processes. Such different components of foraging are more dramatically evident in other species such as birds which fly to a beach area and then walk on the beach probing the sand with their beaks for worms (e.g., Goss-Custard, 1977).

In conclusion, the procedure described in this experiment is an effective method for evaluating the operation of variables that have been shown to affect behavior in the lab and the interaction of such variables in a situation that is more complex than is normally studied in the lab but maintains sufficient control and precision to allow for meaningful conclusions about environmental constraints that govern behavior.

Notes

[1] The generous assistance of Jill and Scott Mellgren in data collection and Mark Olson for maintaining the subjects is gratefully acknowledged. Dr. P. Schwagmeyer provided helpful suggestions on the manuscript.

References

Allison, J., Miller, M., & Wozny, M. Conservation in behavior. *Journal of Experimental Psychology: General,* 1979, **108**, 4–34.

Charnov, E. L. Optimal foraging, the marginal value theorem. *Theoretical Population Biology,* 1976, **9**, 129–136.

Collier, G., Hirsch, E., & Kanarek, R. The operant revisited. In W. K. Honig & J. E. R. Staddon (Eds.), *Handbook of operant behavior.* Englewood Cliffs, N.J.: Prentice-Hall, Inc. 1977.

Edwards, W., Lindman, H., & Phillips, L. D. Emerging technologies for making decisions. In Barron et al. (Eds.), *New directions in psychology II.* New York: Holt, Rinehart, & Winston, 1965.

Goss-Custard, J. D. Optimal foraging and the size selection of worms by redshank, *Tringa totanus,* in the field. *Animal Behaviour,* 1977, **25**, 10–29.

Hursh, S. R. Economic concepts for the analysis of behavior. *Journal of the Experimental Analysis of Behavior,* 1980 **34**, 219–238.

Krebs, J. R. Optimal foraging: Decision rules for predators. In J. R. Krebs & N. B. Davies (Eds.), *Behavioral ecology.* Sunderland, Mass.: Sinauer Associates, Inc., 1978.

Lea, S. E. G. Foraging and reinforcement schedules in the pigeon: Optimal and non-optimal aspects of choice. *Animal Behavior,* 1979, **27**, 875–886.

Olson, M. W. *Reinforcement schedules and patterns of persistence in running and digging in rats.* Unpublished doctoral dissertation, University of Oklahoma, 1980.

Schoener, T. W. Theory of feeding strategies. In R. F. Johnston, P. W. Frank, & C. D. Michener (Eds.), *Annual review of ecology and systematics.* (Vol. 2). Palo Alto, Calif.: Annual Reviews, 1971.

Shettleworth, S. J. Reinforcement and the organization of behavior in golden hamsters: Hunger, environment, and food reinforcement. *Journal of Experimental Psychology: Animal Behavior Processes,* 1975, **104**, 56–87.

Staddon, J. E. R. Operant behavior as adaptation to constraint. *Journal of Experimental Psychology: General,* 1979, **108**, 48–67.

Part V
Stimulus Control: Discrimination and Generalization

Developing an effective repertoire of behavior requires learning not only what responses to perform, but also under what conditions to perform them. Operants are not generally reinforced under all circumstances. The young child must learn when to cross the street and when not to. Learning to cross only when the light is green does not involve learning an operant; the operant (crossing the street) has already been learned. What it does require is learning under what stimulus conditions (green light) crossing the street is appropriate. Learning of this type is called operant *discrimination learning*. It is the process by which operant behavior comes under the control of environmental stimuli. Thus it is sometimes referred to as *stimulus control*.

We encountered examples of discrimination learning earlier. The development of conditioned excitation to a Pavlovian CS^+ and inhibition to a Pavlovian CS^- is an example of discrimination learning, in this case Pavlovian (p. 5). Concurrent schedules depend upon discrimination learning (pp. 217 and 228). Animals could not respond differentially to the schedules if they had no means of telling which one was operative for which alternative response. But we should be clear about what discrimination learning involves. Suppose a pigeon is confronted with a procedure in which pecks when the key is green produce food and pecks when the key is red do not. The pigeon must learn to discriminate the consequences of pecking green (reinforcement) from the consequences of pecking red. If it does so, it will stop pecking red. But the pigeon's learning of this discrimination does not involve learning the difference between red and green any more than for the young child learning how to cross streets. The pigeon (and the child) already knows the difference between red and green. What learning the discrimination requires is learning that red and green make a difference in terms of the consequences of pecking a key (or crossing the street).

Discrimination learning is just one aspect of the stimulus control of operant behavior; the other aspect is the phenomenon of *stimulus generalization*. It turns out that if a pigeon, for example, is trained to peck a green key for food and is then presented with key colors other than green, it may generalize from its experience with green to these other colors and peck at them as well; and indeed, how much it pecks at these other colors may depend upon how similar they are to the green training stimulus.

In this part of the book we explore the phenomena of discrimination and generalization. Section A presents a demonstration of generalization of both excitation and inhibition. Section B explores the determinants of discrimination. What is required for a stimulus to exert discriminative control over behavior? Finally, in Section C we see that operant discrimination learning may involve selectivity of association, just as Pavlovian conditioning does (p. 83).

A. GENERALIZATION GRADIENTS

When an organism learns to respond in the presence of a particular stimulus, how will that training generalize to other stimuli? And when an organism learns not to respond in the presence of a particular stimulus, how will that training generalize to other stimuli? The following paper by Honig and co-workers addresses these issues. Two groups of pigeons learn a discrimination. For one group a vertical line on the key signals that food will be delivered for pecking. The absence of the vertical line signals no food. For the second group, the vertical line signals no food, and its absence signals food. After both groups have learned the discrimination and are responding almost exclusively in the presence of the stimulus signaling food, generalization tests are conducted. Lines differing in orientation from the vertical are presented and generalization gradients are obtained.

The question of interest is how much responding occurs during these generalization tests. Suppose that animals in each group respond at equal rates to all line orientations; that is, variations in line orientation make no difference. This result would suggest that the orientation of the line was not controlling responding. Perhaps some other feature of the line, like its brightness, was. On the other hand, suppose different line orientations produce different amounts of responding. For the first group, responding is maximal to the vertical line and decreases systematically as line orientations become increasingly horizontal. For the second group, responding is minimal to the vertical line and increases as line orientations become increasingly horizontal. This kind of result would indicate that line orientation was controlling responding. This was the result reported by Honig and co-workers and it shows that discriminative stimuli signaling reinforcement become excitatory, while discriminative stimuli signaling nonreinforcement become inhibitory. It also demonstrates the generalization of both excitation and inhibition (see Honig and Urcuioli, 1981).

24 Positive and Negative Generalization Gradients Obtained after Equivalent Training Conditions

WERNER K. HONIG, C. ALAN BONEAU,
K. R. BURSTEIN, AND H. S. PENNYPACKER

Positive and negative gradients were compared on the dimension of angular orientation (tilt) following discrimination training with the presence of a vertical line being positive and its absence being negative for one group of pigeons, and the opposite discrimination for another group. The gradients were initially very similar in form, although the negative gradient became flatter in the course of testing. Equivalent training conditions therefore produced similar positive and negative gradients; previously obtained differences between gradients of acquisition and extinction are presumably due to differences in pretest training procedures.[1]

Orderly generalization gradients for acquisition (Blough, 161; Guttman & Kalish, 1956) and extinction (Honig, 1961) have been obtained on the spectral continuum from pigeons. These are dissimilar; the acquisition gradients are peaked, and the decrement is negatively accelerated with increasing distance from the training stimulus. The extinction gradients are relatively flat, or "bowl shaped"; the decrement (represented by an increase in responding) is positively accelerated. These differences in form may be due to the training procedures prior to the generalization tests (Honig, 1961). Acquisition gradients were obtained after exposure to a single stimulus value, at which the Ss were reinforced on an intermittent schedule. For extinction gradients, positive training with 13 stimulus values was followed by extinction on the central value of the series, after which the gradients were obtained. The training procedure provided a baseline against which the extinction decrement could be assessed. But equal reinforcement presented over the range of stimulus values subsequently used in testing may have reduced any tendency for Ss to respond differentially to the different stimuli on the generalization test.

The present study was undertaken with the aim of minimizing differences in pretest training procedures, so that gradients of acquisition and extinction could more justifiably be compared. While it is possible to provide positive training against a baseline of no responding or a very low operant rate, one cannot assess the effects of extinction without producing responding first by positive training of some kind. This problem was attacked in the present study by training two groups to discriminate between the presence and the absence of a vertical black line on an illuminated response key; for one group the presence was positive, and for

"Positive and Negative Generalization Gradients Obtained after Equivalent Training Conditions" by Werner K. Honig, C. Alan Boneau, K. R. Burstein, and H. S. Pennypacker. *Journal of Comparative and Physiological Psychology*, 1963, *56*, 111–116. Copyright 1963 by the American Psychological Association. Reprinted by permission of the publisher and author.

another it was negative. Generalization was then tested for the dimension of angular orientation, or "tilt," of the black line in order to obtain positive and negative gradients around the vertical line.

Since this procedure employs discrimination training prior to testing, we will refer to positive and negative gradients rather than gradients of acquisition and extinction. But it should be noted that the discrimination is not formed between two values lying on a given continuum, such as two different orientations of the black line. Such a procedure would provide a postdiscrimination gradient which could be obtained from an interaction of positive and negative gradients generated at the respective stimulus values, as suggested by Spence (1933). The contributing positive and negative gradients could not be independently evaluated from such a procedure.

Method

Subjects

The experiment was carried out twice, each time with 12 White Carneau pigeons at 75% of ad lib weight. In Study 1, the pigeons had been used in a student laboratory course and had been exposed to a variety of procedures which did not involve any of the present stimuli. Study 2 was carried out to check the reliability of the results of Study 1 with naive birds. The procedures were made as similar as possible for the two studies. The only systematic difference between the experienced and the naive groups of birds appears to have been that the former attained higher response rates during training and testing.

Apparatus

Two identical operant behavior boxes were used. Half the Ss from the positive and the negative groups were trained in each box. All generalization tests were run in one box in order to provide identical testing conditions for all animals. A slide projector illuminated S's response key. Each slide projected a sharply defined disc of white light 1 in. in diameter, surrounded by a black background. The slide used for the "line absent" condition had nothing else on it. Six other slides were used for the "line present" conditions. On these, a black line ⅛-in. wide divided the white disc in half. Six different orientations of this line were presented; 0°, 30°, 60°, 90°, 120°, and 150°. The key light provided the only illumination in the box save for a magazine light that came on during reinforcements. White noise was used to mask extraneous sounds.

Procedure

After magazine and key-peck training, necessary in Study 2 but not for the experienced birds of Study 1, all birds were given daily sessions of 30 1-min. periods of stimulus presentation alternating with 10 sec. of blackout. For the first 2 days, only the stimulus that was later to be positive in the discrimination was presented, and responding to it was reinforced on a 1-min. variable interval schedule by 3-sec. presentations of grain. Discrimination training began with the third session. The positive stimulus (S+) was presented for 15 periods, with responding reinforced as before. The negative stimulus (S−) was presented for the other 15 periods in extinction, and during these presentations, the operation of the reinforcement programmer was interrupted. The order of conditions was haphazard, but neither condition was presented on more than two successive periods. For half the birds in each study, the presence of the vertical (90°) line was S+ while the line absent condition was S−. For the remaining birds, these reinforcement contingencies were reversed. The two groups will be called *line positive* and *line negative* respectively.

Discrimination training ended with the session at which *S* gave 90% or more of its total responses to S+, and responded during every presentation of S+. On the following day, a generalization test was administered. This commenced with a warm-up period of 10 min. of discrimination training. Reinforcement was then discontinued and the periods of stimulus presentation were shortened to 30 sec. Each of the seven stimulus conditions described above was then presented 12 times, once in each of 12 randomized blocks. The line absent and the 90° conditions were, of course, S+ or S− for each *S*. Tests were identical for all birds except for the specific random orders of the stimulus values.

Results

Generalization gradients in terms of mean total responses to each test stimulus are presented in Fig. 1. The points at 0° and 180° represent only a single set of measurements and are duplicated in the interest of symmetry. A comparison of values obtained with 90° and with the line absent shows clearly that each group maintained the trained discrimination during testing. Overall response levels are higher for Study 1 than for Study 2, and they are higher for the positive than the negative gradients if the line absent condition is ignored.

Standard errors associated with each mean value are given in Table 1. While each individual animal showed the expected positive or negative gradient, there were considerable differences, particularly in overall response level. Such differences tend to affect the gradient in multiplicative fashion, and the positive relationship between errors and means is to be expected. The line negative group from Study 1 shows greater variability than the others due to one deviant *S* with exceptionally high rates.

While the negative gradients are by inspection flatter than the positive ones (Fig. 1), the difference in shape is not nearly as great as it is for the acquisition and extinction gradients previously obtained for the spectral dimension. Furthermore, differences in overall response level must be taken into account, and the effects of systematic changes due to testing in

TABLE 1. Standard Errors Associated with Mean Total Responses Obtained for Each Test Stimulus.

	0°	30°	60°	90°	120°	150°	No Line
Study 1							
Line positive group	27.1	21.4	40.1	36.6	51.5	36.0	12.1
Line negative group	61.5	62.6	43.1	34.5	41.8	58.2	76.6
Study 2							
Line positive group	11.6	9.5	22.1	34.2	20.8	13.3	9.1
Line negative group	24.1	28.0	23.8	17.3	21.8	29.4	50.9

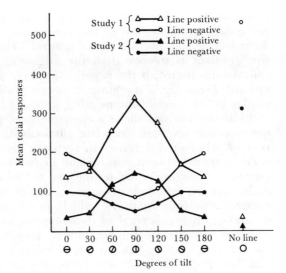

FIG. 1. *Generalization gradients obtained from the line positive and line negative groups.*

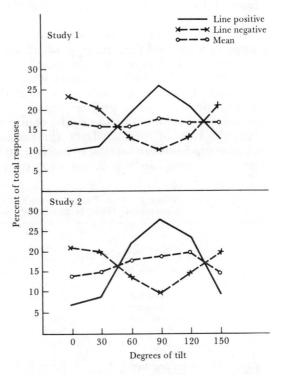

FIG. 2. *Positive, negative, and mean percentage gradients for Studies 1 and 2.*

extinction should be evaluated. Gradients obtained at different response levels can be compared by expressing the number of responses emitted to each stimulus as a percentage of the total responses on the gradient. This was carried out for the four gradients presented in Fig. 1 (omitting responses to the line absent condition); the outcome is presented in Fig. 2. To facilitate the comparison of the corresponding positive and negative gradients, they were averaged to yield a mean percentage gradient. If the percentage gradients are of the same form but inverted, the mean gradient will be flat and will hover around 17% (i.e., 100%/6). If the positive gradient is steeper than the negative, the mean gradient will be concave downward; if the negative gradient is steeper, it will be concave upward. From Fig. 2 it appears that the gradients from Study 1 are quite similar in form, while the negative gradient is flatter from Study 2.

While this analysis allows a comparison of gradients obtained at different response levels, it does not eliminate this difference. The question remains whether differences in response level are responsible for differences in form between positive and negative gradients. Furthermore, the effects of changes during testing are not examined when data from the entire test are included. In order to answer these questions, each test was divided into four quarters, which provided (for the two studies) 16 quarter-gradients. Several of these were selected to provide positive and negative gradients obtained at similar response levels. In order to examine the effects of testing, averaged quarter-gradients of high, medium, and low response levels are presented in Fig. 3. The total reponses obtained for each of the contributing quarter-gradients are shown in Table 2.

At a high response level, the positive and negative gradients are very similar in form, and their mean gradient is almost flat. With medium and low response levels, the mean gradient becomes concave downward, indicating that the line positive gradient is steeper. This difference is due to a flattening of the line negative gradient at the lower response levels, the form of the line positive gradient changing rather little. The flattening is presumably due to extinction in the course of testing.

On the basis of these analyses, the possibility remains that the flatter negative gradients are specific to Study 2 and not due to extinction in the course of testing. In Fig. 2, the negative gradients are flatter only for

TABLE 2. Mean Total Responses of Quarter-Gradients
Representing High, Medium, and Low Response Levels

	Source	Total responses
High response level		
Line positive	Study 1, 2nd Quarter	345
Line negative	Study 1, 1st Quarter	305
Medium response level		
Line positive	Study 1, 3rd Quarter	209
	Study 1, 4th Quarter	221
	Study 2, 1st Quarter	241
Line negative	Study 1, 2nd Quarter	212
	Study 2, 1st Quarter	208
Low response level		
Line positive	Study 2, 3rd Quarter	90
	Study 2, 4th Quarter	57
Line negative	Study 2, 3rd Quarter	68
	Study 2, 4th Quarter	88

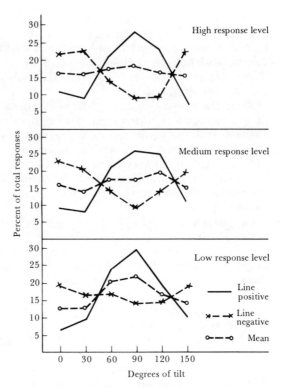

FIG. 3. *Positive, negative, and mean percentage gradients representing high, medium, and low response levels.*

Study 2; from Table 2 it is evident that the quarter-gradients chosen to represent high response levels in Fig. 2 are all from Study 1, while those chosen to represent low response levels are from Study 2. To check on this possibility, some further comparisons were made, although these are not shown separately. The first quarter-gradients from Study 2 are very similar to those representing high response levels (from Study 1), and the mean percentage gradient is quite flat. These were obtained before much extinction had taken place, and they show that the similarity of positive and negative gradients is not specific to Study 1. Furthermore, the last negative quarter-gradients from Study 1 are flatter than the last positive ones, as in the low response level panel of Fig. 3. This shows that flatter negative gradients are not specific to Study 2, though the flattening is not as marked as for Study 2, presumably because extinction was slower in Study 1. Actually, the gradients shown at medium response level in Fig. 3 represent a combination of these cases, being taken from early quarter-gradients from Study 2 and late ones from Study 1, and this results in a mean percentage gradient which is mildly concave downward.

Discussion

The present results leave little doubt that positive and negative generalization gradients, when generated with the present method, are at least initially very similar in form. The comparability of pretest training conditions appears to be crucial in the proper evaluation of positive and negative gradients. Recent findings by Thomas and Lanier (1962) with human Ss support his conclusion. Modifying a technique developed by Kalish (1958), they first presented a given stimulus value, then instructed half of their Ss to respond only to this value when presented in a series of values, and half of them to respond to all the values except this one. They obtained a negative gradient that was almost a perfect inversion of the positive gradient.

After the present research had been completed, a different comparison of gradients of reinforcement and extinction for the orientation of an isosceles triangle projected on a pigeon's key was published by Reynolds (1961). He trained a discrimination between two adjacent positive values "embedded" in a series of negative ones, or the reverse, and used data obtained in training. In spite of the differences in procedure, his results are similar to ours in that the two kinds of gradients are much alike in form.

One asymmetry which our analysis did not bring out, is that for the positive gradients the level of responding at the extreme value (0°) comes a good deal closer to the level of the no line stimulus than it does for the negative gradient. In this sense, the negative gradients are flatter, since there is never enough decrement in the inhibitory effect to allow the level of responding at any point along the gradient to approach that of S+. The converse is not true: the decrement on the positive gradient is great enough to produce a level of responding not too different from that obtained from S−. But this asymmetry reflects differential degrees of generalization between line present stimuli and the line absent condition; it is not an asymmetry along the dimension of interest on which the generalization gradients have been compared.

The question may be raised whether the present discrimination procedure produced gradients that can be considered equivalent to the "pure" gradients of acquisition and extinction, or whether it introduced a distortion. As noted above, the discrimination was formed between the absence and presence of a portion of the stimulus pattern; not between two values on the dimension under study. It is hard to conceive how generalization of the positive or negative response strength associated with the absence of the line could have contaminated gradients on the dimension of angular orientation. It might have influenced gradients of width or length, or total luminous flux from the key, but hardly orientation. The positive gradients are very similar to acquisition gradients obtained in other studies after simple acquisition (e.g., Blough, 1961; Guttman & Kalish, 1956). Furthermore, they show the same relationship to overall response level in that there is little change in the basic form during extinction.

A further consideration is important here: It is quite possible that *all* acquisition gradients and extinction gradients result from either explicit or implicit training procedures, so that ours are not different in kind from any others. In some cases (Sidman, 1961) there is discrimination training between stimuli on the dimension being studied; in others, there is differentiation between the presence and the absence of a relevant stimulus, as in our case, Jenkins and Harrison (1960), for example, obtained very flat gradients for auditory frequency until they introduced discrimination training between the presence and the absence of a tone, at which point the gradients became quite steep. In other studies where such training procedures are not explicit, the development of some kind of discrimination seems inevitable. In spectral generalization studies, *S* must learn *where* to respond, i.e., at an illuminated key; he may learn to discriminate unilluminated time-out periods; and so forth. With regard to the extinction gradient, Honig, Thomas, and Guttman (1959) found no specific effect of extinction on the generalization gradient until explicit discrimination training was introduced between a positive and a negative stimulus. In the case where extinction gradients were obtained without explicit discrimination training (Honig, 1961), the author himself suggested that this gradient was not a simple primary gradient of extinction, but that it resulted from the differential extinction of a number of summated acquisition gradients produced by positive training before extinction was introduced.

Notes

[1] This study was supported by Grant No. M-3917 to Norman Guttman and M-2414 to the first author, both from the National Institute of Mental Health, and by National Science Foundation Grant C-9592 to the second author. The contribution of the final author was supported by United States Public Health Service Predoctoral Fellowship MF-13,327. The authors are much indebted to Normal Guttman for advice and for the use of his research facilities, and to David R. Thomas for a critical reading of the manuscript.

References

Blough, D. S. The shape of some wave length generalization gradients. *J. Exp. Anal. Behav.*, 1961, **4**, 31–40.

Guttman, N., & Kalish, H. I. Discriminability and stimulus generalization. *J. Exp. Psychol.*, 1956, **51**, 79–88.

Honig, W. K. Generalization of extinction on the spectral continuum. *Psychol. Rec.*, 1961, **11**, 269–278.

Honig, W. K., Thomas, D. R., & Guttman, N. Differential effects of continuous extinction and discrimination training on the generalization gradient. *J. Exp. Psychol.*, 1959, **58**, 145–152.

Jenkins, H. M., & Harrison, R. H. Effect of discrimination training on auditory generalization. *J. Exp. Psychol.*, 1960, **59**, 246–253.

Kalish, H. I. The relationship between discriminability and generalization: A re-evaluation. *J. Exp. Psychol.*, 1958, **55**, 637–644.

Reynolds, G. S. Contrast, generalization, and the process of discrimination. *J. Exp. Anal. Behav.*, 1961, **4**, 289–294.

Sidman, M. Stimulus generalization in an avoidance situation. *J. Exp. Anal. Behav.*, 1961, **4**, 157–170.

Spence, K. W. The differential response in animals to stimuli varying within a single dimension. *Psychol. Rev.*, 1937, **44**, 430–444.

Thomas, D. R., & Lanier, W. G. A comparison of stimulus generalization of tendencies to respond and not to respond. *Psychol. Rec.*, 1962, **12**, 61–65.

B. ATTENTION AND PREDICTABILITY

In any operant conditioning situation there are multiple stimuli that might conceivably control responding. When a pigeon pecks a key for food, its pecking could be controlled by the color of the key, its brightness, its size, its shape, its location, or many of these properties in combination. What determines which of the many potential controlling stimuli will be the actual controlling stimuli?

We encountered this very same issue in Part I on Pavlovian conditioning, and we discovered there that the most predictive stimulus will be the controlling one. When multiple stimuli are equally predictive, they may all control behavior, and if some are more salient than others, the more salient stimuli may overshadow the less salient ones. We concluded that Pavlovian conditioning in part involved learning to pay attention to predictive stimuli and learning to ignore irrelevant ones (p. 67).

The articles in this section show that the same conclusion can be drawn about operant discrimination learning. In the article by Rudolph and Van Houten, pigeons were trained to peck a key in the presence of a 1000-Hz tone. Some of them were trained to peck with the lights on in the experimental chamber, and some with the lights off. Rudolph and Van Houten expected that in a lit chamber a variety of visual stimuli might compete with and overshadow the tone, whereas in a dark chamber the tone would be more likely to control responding. How did they test for control by the tone? They did so by conducting a generalization test, presenting tones differing in pitch by varying amounts from the 1000-Hz training tone. They reasoned that if the tone was not controlling responding, changes in its pitch would not matter. Thus the pigeons would respond equally to all pitches during the generalization test. On the other hand, if the tone was controlling responding, then pigeons would decrease their rate of pecking as test tones were increasingly different from the training tone. They found much less evidence of control by the tone for animals trained with lights on than for animals trained with lights off.

The second article in this section, by Mackintosh and Little, provides evidence that operant discrimination learning involves learning to pay attention to predictive stimuli. Pigeons were exposed to a two-phase experiment. In the first phase they learned a discrimination. The discriminative stimuli were combinations of key colors and line orientations, and for some pigeons color was predictive of reinforcement, whereas for others line orientation was predictive of reinforcement. In the second phase of the experiment the pigeons learned another discrimination, which also involved key colors and line orientations, but the colors and orientations were all different from those used in the first phase. For some pigeons, color was the predictive stimulus in both phases of the experiment; for others line orientation was predictive in both phases; and finally, for others color was predictive in one phase and line orientation was in the other. These pigeons learned the second discrimination much more slowly than the other two groups. What this indicates is that in learning the first discrimination, pigeons learned to pay attention to the predictive stimulus (color or line orientation), and they continued to pay attention to this stimulus in the second phase (see Mackintosh, 1975).

25 Auditory Stimulus Control in Pigeons: Jenkins and Harrison (1960) Revisited

ROBERT L. RUDOLPH AND RONALD VAN HOUTEN

Pigeons were trained to peck a key in the presence of a 1000-Hz tone on a variable-interval one-minute schedule of reinforcement. One group was trained with an illuminated key; the other was trained in a totally dark chamber. During a generalization test on tonal frequency, subjects trained and tested with the key illuminated produced rather shallow gradients around the training value; subjects trained and tested in the dark produced steeper generalization gradients. These data replicate Jenkins and Harrison's (1960) finding that tone acquires relatively little control over responding and demonstrate that this absence of control is a function of the presence of the keylight.[1]

Key words: auditory control, overshadowing, keylight, key peck, pigeons

The amount of stimulus control, as measured by the slope of a generalization gradient, may be markedly affected by apparently minor procedural changes. Key-peck training in the presence of a tone produces relatively little control by tonal frequency (Jenkins and Harrison, 1960), whereas similar training in the presence of a key illuminated with a spectral value produces considerable control by that spectral value (Guttman and Kalish, 1956). In discussing this discrepancy, Jenkins and Harrison (1960) stated: "Since the training procedures appear to be the same in all important respects it may be concluded that the difference lies in the use of a visual—as compared with an auditory stimulus." Furthermore, they noted that "the visual stimulus appeared directly on the response key, whereas the auditory stimulus was diffuse and probably unlocalized" (p. 252). Heineman and Rudolph (1963) tested this hypothesis that stimulus control is a function of the degree of localization. They trained pigeons to peck an illuminated disc, which varied in size for different groups, and found that the amount of stimulus control on the visual-intensity dimension was inversely related to the size of the stimulus. Thus, greater localization did produce more stimulus control.

Some evidence, however, indicates that localization of color on the key is not a necessary condition for obtaining stimulus control on the spectral dimension. Rudolph (1971) obtained spectral control with a localized monochromatic light off the key; Mackintosh *(personal communication)* also obtained spectral control with a diffusely illuminated overhead Plexiglas panel. Certainly the lights in these studies were not as diffuse as the tones in the Jenkins and Harrison (1960) experiment. Nevertheless, these results with rather diffuse stimuli cast doubt on an explanation based entirely on the degree of localization of the training stimulus.

Another possible interpretation of the discrepancy between Jenkins and

"Auditory Stimulus Control in Pigeons: Jenkins and Harrison (1960) Revisited" by Robert L. Rudolph and Ronald Van Houten. *Journal of the Experimental Analysis of Behavior,* 1977, 27, 327–330. Copyright 1977 by the Society for the Experimental Analysis of Behavior, Inc. Reprinted by permission of the publisher and author.

Harrison (1960) and Guttman and Kalish (1956) is based on the phenomenon of overshadowing. Overshadowing occurs when the presence of one stimulus reduces the amount of control obtained by another stimulus (Miles, 1965). Van Houten and Rudolph (1972) tested this notion indirectly. Pigeons were trained to peck a key in the presence of an airflow that emerged from the key. Different groups of subjects were trained with a back-illuminated key, a houselight, or with no light. Generalization gradients obtained on the dimension of airflow velocity were steep in the no-light condition but were relatively flat in both the houselight and illuminated-key conditions. These results indicated that the presence of a light during training and testing reduced control by airflow. Van Houten and Rudolph (1972) suggested that a similar overshadowing effect might have been present in the Jenkins and Harrison (1960) experiment, *i.e.*, that the keylight may have overshadowed control by tones.

The purpose of the present experiment was to test this overshadowing hypothesis by training pigeons to peck a key in the presence of a tone, with the key illuminated for some subjects but not for others. The amount of tonal stimulus control was assessed by giving the subjects a generalization test on the tonal-frequency dimension.

Method

Subjects
Ten six-month-old experimentally naive Silver King Pigeons were maintained at 80% of their free-feeding weights.

Apparatus
The apparatus is presented schematically in Fig. 1. The chamber was designed to facilitate responding in the dark, and thus differed from a standard pigeon chamber in three ways. (1) The response key was larger than the standard key, measuring 5.08 by 6.35 cm. (2) The response key was located in a small (8.89 by 6.35 by 8.89 cm) recessed "alcove," which could provide tactual cues to the key's location. (3) The magazine was also located in this small alcove directly below the key, so that when the magazine cycle terminated the subject was in position to respond again.

Tones were produced by a 10-cm speaker mounted on top of the chamber. Intensity of the 1000-Hz stimulus used in training varied from 65 to 95 dB depending on the area of the chamber in which the measurement was taken. The large range of tonal intensities was presumably a function of standing waves produced in the small aluminum chamber. Though a precise integration of intensity over area was not performed, a number of readings taken at various locations in the chamber indicated that the average tonal intensity was approximately 85 dB. The average intensities of the 300-, 670-, 1500-, and 3500-Hz test stimuli were approximately 95, 90, 75, and 85 dB, respectively.

Procedure
All subjects were trained to peck a lighted key in the absence of tone and were presented with 4 sec of access to mixed grain for each of 30 key pecks on the first day of training. Throughout the experiment, grain presentation was signalled by a magazine light for all subjects. On the second and third days of training, each of 30 key pecks was reinforced. During

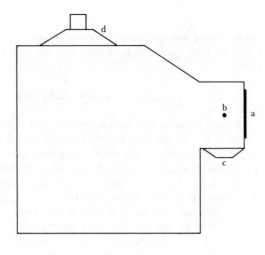

FIG. 1. *A side and top view of the apparatus, "a" is the key, "b" is the magazine light, "c" is the magazine aperture, and "d" is the speaker.*

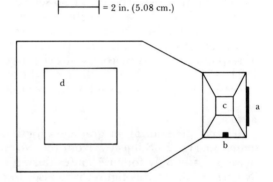

the first 15 reinforcements on the second day, the 1000-Hz tone was faded in. When this was accomplished, the keylight was faded out for five of the subjects (No-Keylight group). Fading was continued on the third day and was completed by the end of that day.

During the next 10 days of training, subjects were given 30 reinforcements per day. The reinforcements were delivered on a variable-interval 15-sec (VI 15-sec) schedule, in which the first response after an average interval of 15 sec was reinforced, for the first five days, and then on VI 30-sec. When the No-Keylight subjects were placed in the chamber it was dark. If they failed to start responding in the dark, the keylight was dimly illuminated until the subject started responding; then it was quickly faded out (generally within about five reinforcements). On the final 10 days of training, responding was reinforced on a VI 1-min schedule for 30 min each day. Throughout all phases of training the 1000-Hz tone was on when the subjects were put into the chamber and when they were taken out. The five Keylight subjects were treated just like the No-Keylight subjects, except that the key was always illuminated for these subjects.

After a 5-min warmup on the training conditions, a tonal-frequency generalization test was administered in extinction, with the key illuminated for the Keylight group and not illuminated for the No-Keylight group. The test stimuli were 300, 670, 1000, 1500, 3500 Hz, and No-tone. These six test conditions were presented in a counterbalanced order over 10 blocks of trials, with each stimulus occurring for 30 sec in each block.

Results and Discussion

Acquisition

Little difficulty was encountered in training the No-Keylight subjects to respond in the dark. These five subjects all responded in the dark during the third day of continuous reinforcement training. On the first day of VI 15-sec training, none of the subjects started responding when placed in the dark chamber, and thus the keylight was dimly illuminated for a few reinforcements. However, four of the five subjects began responding in the dark on the second day of VI 15-sec training and the fifth subject began responding in the dark on the fourth day of VI 15-sec training. Subjects in the No-Keylight group tended to emit fewer responses than subjects in the Keylight group, particularly early in training. For example, on the first two days of VI 30-sec training, the lowest number of responses emitted by a Keylight subject was greater than the highest number emitted by a No-Keylight subject. This difference decreased with continued training, and on the last day of VI 1-min training the number of responses emitted by the No-Keylight group (Subjects 1 to 5) was 599, 1321, 471, 836, and 1165; the Keylight group (Subjects 6 to 10) emitted 1514, 1138, 1418, 401, and 1067, respectively.

Testing

Relative generalization gradients for nine of the 10 subjects are presented in Fig. 2. (Subject 3 from the No-Keylight group was omitted because it made only four responses during the test, all to 1500 Hz on the first test trial.) In this figure, responses to each of the test stimuli are expressed as a percentage of total responses emitted during the test. Total responses for each subject during the test are presented in Fig. 2.

Each subject in the No-Keylight group exhibited a decremental gradient that peaked at 1000 Hz. Two subjects in the Keylight group also exhibited decremental gradients with a peak at 1000 Hz, but neither peak was as high as the peaks of any subject in the No-Keylight group. The other three subjects in the Keylight group exhibited rather flat gradients, with the percentage of responses in 1000 Hz being essentially equivalent to the percentage given in No-Tone. The difference in the gradients indicates that the presence of the keylight during training and testing reduced the amount of tonal control, *i.e.,* light overshadowed control by tone. Since the results of the Keylight group are similar to the results of Jenkins and Harrison's (1960) group that received similar training, it may also be concluded that light overshadowed control by tone in their group. Thus, the discrepancy between strong spectral control obtained by Guttman and Kalish (1956), and weak tonal control obtained by Jenkins and Harrison (1960), appears to be resolved by noting that considerable tonal control is obtained if a visual stimulus is not present to overshadow tonal control.

The question remains why control develops with either auditory or visual stimuli when subjects' responding is reinforced in the presence of a

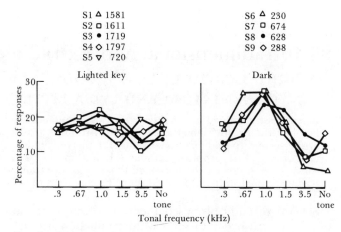

FIG. 2. *Percentage of total responses given to each of the tones during the generalization test. Total responses made on the test are presented in the subject legend.*

stimulus. We would suggest that in both instances, unscheduled sources of differential training produce the observed control. Possible sources of differential training are readily apparent when a visual stimulus is located on the response key, *e.g.*, responses to the stimulus on the key are reinforced, whereas responses to other stimuli off the key are not reinforced. Possible sources of differential training are not so apparent when an auditory stimulus is employed. However, one possible source concerns the fact that responses are reinforced in the chamber in the presence of the tone and are not reinforced outside of the chamber in the absence of the tone. Thus, the tone may inform the subject that the environment containing the possibility of reinforcement is present. Notice that this cue property of the tone might well be overshadowed by visual stimuli, given that a pigeon normally identifies its environment on the basis of visual stimuli.

Notes
 [1] This research was supported by Grants APA 297 and A 8352 from the National Research Council of Canada. We thank Sue Bell and Victor Day for their assistance in the experiment and W. K. Honig for his comments on a draft of this paper.

References
 Guttman, N., and Kalish, H. I. Discriminability and stimulus generalization. *Journal of Experimental Psychology*, 1956, **51**, 79–88.
 Heinemann, E. G., and Rudolph, R. L. The effect of discriminative training on the gradient of stimulus-generalization. *American Journal of Psychology*, 1963, **76**, 653–658.
 Jenkins, H. M., and Harrison, R. H. Effect of discrimination training on auditory generalization. *Journal of Experimental Psychology*, 1960, **59**, 246–253.
 Miles, C. G. *Acquisition of control by the features of a compound stimulus in discriminative operant conditioning.* Unpublished doctoral dissertation, McMaster University, 1965. P. 14.
 Rudolph, R. L. Effects of interdimensional discrimination training on stimulus control in monochromatically reared chicks. *The Psychological Record*, 1971, **21**, 257–264.
 Van Houten, R., and Rudolph, R. L. The development of stimulus control with and without a lighted key. *Journal of the Experimental Analysis of Behavior*, 1972, **1**, 217–222.

26 Intradimensional and Extradimensional Shift Learning by Pigeons

N. J. MACKINTOSH AND LYDIA LITTLE

Pigeons were trained consecutively on two simultaneous visual discriminations. For half the Ss, the dimension relevant in the first problem remained relevant in the second (intradimensional shift); for the remainder, the dimension irrelevant in the first problem became relevant in the second (extradimensional shift). As is predicted by two-stage theories of discrimination learning, the intradimensional shift was learned more rapidly than the extradimensional shift.[1]

Several recently proposed theories of discrimination learning have assumed that in order to solve a discrimination problem, Ss must not only learn which value of the relevant dimension is associated with reinforcement, but must also learn to identify, observe, or attend to the relevant dimension itself (Lovejoy, 1968; Sutherland, 1964; Zeaman & House, 1963). One prediction that follows from such a theory is that training on one problem with a given dimension relevant may selectively facilitate the learning of a new discrimination problem involving the same relevant dimension even though no direct transfer based on the response requirements of the two tasks could be expected. Lawrence's experiments on the acquired distinctiveness of cues, in which transfer between successive and simultaneous discriminations was assessed, provided the earliest support for this prediction (Lawrence, 1949); but the procedure has since been criticized by Siegel (1967) on the grounds that some direct transfer might have occurred.

A second appropriate experimental design, used in studies of human concept learning, involves comparing intradimensional shift (IDS) and extradimensional shift (EDS) learning. Ss are trained on a discrimination problem with Dimension A relevant and Dimension B irrelevant; in the second stage of the experiment new values of the two dimensions are chosen, and Ss learning the IDS problem are again trained with A relevant and B irrelevant, while Ss learning the EDS problem are trained with B relevant and A irrelevant. If Ss during Stage 1 learn to attend to A and ignore B, and if these attentional changes transfer to the new values of A and B used in Stage 2, then the IDS problem should be learned more rapidly than the EDS problem.

Although there is ample evidence that human Ss, from 4-year-old children (Trabasso, Deutsch, & Gelman, 1966) to college students (Isaacs & Duncan, 1962) learn IDS problems more rapidly than EDS problems, only one study with animals (rats) has shown such an effect (Shepp & Eimas, 1964). The present experiment was designed to see whether pigeons would show any difference in rate of learning the two kinds of problems.

"Intradimensional and Extradimensional Shift Learning by Pigeons" by N. J. Mackintosh and Lydia Little. *Psychonomic Science*, 1969, *14*, 5–6. Reprinted by permission of the Psychonomic Society.

Subjects

The Ss were 16 White Carneaux pigeons, six months old. They were maintained at 80% of their ad lib weights.

Apparatus

The apparatus was a three-key pigeon chamber, with the center key blacked out except during initial shaping. The stimuli were projected onto the rear of the two side keys by means of in-line projectors, and consisted of three colored lines on a white background. The colors were red, yellow, green, or blue; and the orientation of the lines was 0, 90, 45, or 135 deg.

Procedure

After being shaped to peck at a white center key, Ss were given 50 noncorrection trials each day for the remainder of the experiment. At the beginning of each trial, the house light was turned off and the two side keys were illuminated. A correct response led to 5-sec access to grain; an error led to 8-sec time-out in darkness. At the end of each trial, the house light was turned on and a 25-sec intertrial interval followed. All events were controlled by external programming equipment, and responses were recorded on counters.

Experimental Design

All Ss learned two simultaneous discriminations. In Stage 1, the stimuli were red and yellow, 0-deg and 90-deg lines. For eight Ss, color was the relevant dimension (half being trained with red positive, half with yellow positive), and orientation irrelevant. For the remaining Ss, orientation was relevant (0-deg positive for half, 90-deg positive for the other half) and color was irrelevant. The position of the positive and negative stimuli, and the values of the irrelevant dimension, were determined by selected Gellermann orders. All Ss received 250 trials.

In Stage 2, the stimuli were blue and green, 45-deg and 135-deg lines. Half of each of the above groups was trained on a color problem (blue positive) with orientation irrelevant, and half was trained on an orientation problem (45-deg positive) with color irrelevant. All Ss were trained to a criterion of 40 correct responses in a day.

There were, therefore, four main experimental groups distinguished by the dimensions relevant in Stages 1 and 2: Color–color, and orientation–orientation (these groups learned an IDS problem in Stage 2); color–orientation, and orientation–color (these groups learned an EDS problem in Stage 2). Within these four groups, equal numbers of Ss had been trained in opposite directions in Stage 1.

Results

Table 1 shows the average number of errors made during the 250 trials of Stage 1. The color discrimination was substantially easier than the orientation discrimination ($F = 42.71$, $df = 1/2$, $p < .001$), but Ss subsequently learning EDS and IDS problems were closely matched for Stage-1 scores ($F < 1$). All Ss achieved a criterion of 40 correct responses in a day.

Table 1 also shows the number of errors to criterion in Stage 2. Again, the color discrimination was easier than the orientation discrimination ($F = 49.67$, df $= 1/12$, p $< .001$). The IDS problem was learned faster than the EDS problem ($F = 5.67$, df $= 1/12$, p $< .05$); and there was no interaction between dimensions and type of shift ($F < 1$). Finally there was little sign of any direct (response-based) transfer between the two problems. Of the eight Ss that learned color in Stage 1, those trained with red positive selected blue on 64.5% of trials on the first day of Stage 2, while whose trained with yellow positive selected blue on 54% of trials. Similarly, of the Ss trained on orientation in Stage 1, those trained with 0 deg positive selected the 45-deg lines on 58.5% of trials, while those trained with 90 deg positive selected the 45-deg lines on 50% of trials. neither of these differences approached significance (in both cases, p $> .20$).

TABLE 1.

Groups	Stage 1 Errors in 250 trials	Stage 2 Errors to criterion
Color–color	25.25	13.50
Orientation–color	77.50	30.50
Orientation– orientation	74.75	54.00
Color–orientation	24.50	67.00

In conclusion, therefore, pigeons, like rats and humans, learn IDS problems faster than EDS problems. Although the effect was a relatively small one, the results suggest that transfer between problems may occur which cannot be explained simply in terms of differential response tendencies. It appears that learning to attend to the relevant dimension is part of what is involved in learning a discrimination problem.

Notes
[1] This research was supported by Grant APA-259 from the National Research Council of Canada.

References
Isaacs, I. D., & Duncan, C. P. Reversal and nonreversal shifts within and between dimensions in concept formation. *Journal of Experimental Psychology*, 1962, **64**, 580–585.

Lawrence, D. H. Acquired distinctiveness of cues: I. Transfer between discriminations on the basis of familiarity with the stimulus. *Journal of Experimental Psychology*, 1949, **39**, 770–784.

Lovejoy, E. *Attention in discrimination learning*. San Francisco: Holden-Day, 1968.

Shepp, B. E., & Eimas, P. D. Intradimensional and extradimensional shifts in the rat. *Journal of Comparative & Physiological Psychology*, 1964, **57**, 357–361.

Siegel, S. Overtraining and transfer processes. *Journal of Comparative & Physiological Psychology*, 1967, **64**, 471–477.

Sutherland, N. S. The learning of discriminations by animals. *Endeavour*, 1964, **23**, 148–152.

Trabasso, T., Deutsch, J. A., & Gelman, R. Attention in discrimination learning of young children. *Journal of Experimental Child Psychology*, 1966, **4**, 9–19.

Zeaman, D., & House, B. J. The role of attention in retardate discrimination learning. In N. R. Ellis (Ed.), *Handbook of mental deficiency; Psychological theory and research*. New York: McGraw-Hill, 1963. Pp. 159–223.

C. BIOLOGICAL SELECTIVITY OF STIMULUS CONTROL

The articles in the previous section suggest that the best predictor of reinforcement will control operant responding. When there is no best predictor, the most salient of equally good predictors will control responding. But what determines how salient a stimulus will be? For many years, it was assumed that salience was simply a property of an organism's sensory sensitivity to different stimuli; a loud tone would be more salient than a soft one. Tones might be more salient than lights for rats, while the reverse was true for pigeons. The article by Foree and LoLordo makes it clear that there is more to salience than this. They show, with pigeons, that the relative salience of auditory and visual discriminative stimuli depends upon the nature of the events the stimuli predict. Auditory stimuli overshadow visual ones when shock is signaled, and visual stimuli overshadow auditory ones when food is signaled. Thus there is selectivity of association in operant discrimination learning just as there is in Pavlovian conditioning (p. 83 and LoLordo, 1979).

27 Attention in the Pigeon: Differential Effects of Food-Getting versus Shock-Avoidance Procedures

DONALD D. FOREE AND VINCENT M. LOLORDO

Groups of pigeons were trained to depress a treadle in the presence of a compound stimulus consisting of a tone and a red house light (*a*) to avoid electric shock or (*b*) to obtain grain. Responding in the absence of the compound stimulus postponed its next occurrence. After performance had stabilized, the degree to which the compound and each element controlled treadle pressing was determined. In the appetitive test, many responses were made in the presence of the compound and the light alone, but very few were made to the tone alone. In the avoidance test, very few responses occurred in the presence of the light alone, an intermediate number to the tone alone, and most in the presence of the compound.[1]

When discriminative stimuli (S^Ds) on several dimensions are simultaneously correlated with the availability of reinforcement, and other values on these same dimensions are correlated with nonreinforcement, one dimension frequently exerts much more control over the reinforced response than do the others, i.e., it overshadows them. Reynolds (1961) trained 2 pigeons to peck a key in the presence of a white triangle on a red background and not to peck in the presence of a white circle on a green background. When the 4 stimulus elements were tested separately, one bird pecked only in the presence of the triangle, and the other pecked only in the presence of red. Reynolds concluded that each bird was paying attention to only one S^D, although in subsequent research (Farthing & Hearst, 1970) a more sensitive test procedure revealed that there was some control of responding by each dimension. In any case, these findings exemplify overshadowing, which has been observed in many studies of classical and operant conditioning (see Kamin, 1969; Miles, 1969; Pavlov, 1927). Baron (1965) proposed that when (*a*) overshadowing occurs in a particular redundant relevant cue experiment, (*b*) the same stimulus dimension exerts the "lion's share" of the control over responding for all subjects, and (*c*) the subjects are experimentally naive, we have reason to postulate the presence of a species-characteristic attending hierarchy, or ordering of the extent to which each stimulus dimension will come to control responding. This hierarchy, which was the proposed basis of stimulus selection, was assumed to be modifiable by differential reinforcement of values on the various stimulus dimensions treated separately.

In a recent model of Pavlovian conditioning. Rescorla and Wagner (1972) explained overshadowing without recourse to a selective attentional process. They argued that overshadowing may occur when the learning rate parameters (αs) characteristic of the 2 elements, which roughly represent their saliencies, are quite different. In such cases the associative strength of the more salient stimulus approaches the asymptote much more rapidly than the associative strength of the less salient. According to the model, the increment in the associative strength of any element as a result of reinforcement is directly, proportional to the difference between the asymptotic associative strength and the sum of the associative strengths of all elements present on that trial. Consequently, the rapid growth in the strength of the more salient stimulus will keep the less salient from ever catching up, and overshadowing will occur.

Shettleworth (1971) asserted that neither selective attention theory nor the associative model of Rescorla and Wagner (1972) predicts a *reversal* of the direction of overshadowing with changes in the reinforcer.

There have been no experiments testing the hypothesis that the relative degree of control exerted over an instrumental response by elements of a compound S^D will vary with the reinforcer. The present experiment compares the control of lever pressing by auditory and visual elements of a compound S^D when responding is reinforced by food vs. the avoidance of shock.

Method

Subjects

Subjects were 12 experimentally naive male White Carneaux pigeons. The birds were housed in individual home cages with free access to water in a colony room that was lighted at all times. On the day prior to its first experimental session, each bird was implanted around the pubis bones with stainless steel wire electrodes. The electrodes were connected to a double banana plug, which was attached to a leather harness worn by the birds at all times (Azrin, 1959; Coughlin, 1970). All birds were run under both an appetitive- and an avoidance-training condition. Birds 810, 811, 831, 833, 834, and 846 were in Group App–Av, which received the appetitive training first. Birds 790, 817, 826, 827, 848, and 849 were in Group Av–App. which received avoidance training first. All birds were maintained at 75%–80% free-feeding weight for the appetitive portion of the experiment. In addition, Birds 831, 833, 834, and 846 were maintained at 80% weight for the avoidance portion. A thirteenth bird, 770, was dropped from the experiment prior to the test because of a history of illness in conjunction with an abnormally low level of performance.

Apparatus

The experimental chamber was a $30 \times 30 \times 30$ cm. ventilated sound-attenuating box with 2 opposing white wooden walls and 2 removable, unpainted aluminum walls. A 15×20 cm. one-way mirror was centered in one wooden wall. Through a hole in the center of one aluminum wall extended a bakelite bar, to which a 9×7 cm. masonite treadle was attached. The treadle, which was similar to one used by Smith and Keller (1970), was tilted down from the wall at a 30° angle to the floor with the lower edge 3.5 cm. from the hardware cloth floor when held in its rest position by a spring. A downward force of 50 gm. (.49 N.) on the treadle activated a microswitch, defining a response. To the left of the treadle in the same wall was a 5×4.5 cm. opening through which grain could be presented. The ceiling consisted of a piece of translucent white Plexiglas, above which were mounted 2 7.5-w. white lights, a 7.5-w. and a 40-w. red light, and a Utah SP25A loudspeaker.

To provide the shock, a 60-Hz. 110-v. ac was first put through a variable transformer and then through a 10-kΩ resistor. Shock was transmitted via a cable connected at one end to a swivel in the ceiling of the chamber and at the other end to a banana plug which was attached to the plug on the bird's harness immediately prior to each session. Masking noise was provided by the ventilation fan, which was on at all times.

Procedure

All sessions in a given condition were run on consecutive days for 1 hr. each day. After being tested on the first condition, some birds were run under the new condition on the following day, but up to 58 days separated conditions for others.

Appetitive Training

The birds were trained to eat from the food hopper in the presence of a compound stimulus (C) consisting of a 440-Hz. tone, which increased the sound level from 81 to 83 db., and illumination of the 7.5-w. and 40-w. red house lights. After magazine training, which took less than one session for all birds in Group App–Av and 1–5 sessions for birds in Group Av–App. the birds were shaped to depress the treadle on a continuous reinforcement schedule for a 5-sec. access to grain. During shaping, an intertrial stimulus consisting of illumination of the 2 7.5-w. white house lights and the absence of tone followed each reinforcement for .5 sec. When treadle pressing was established, the duration of the intertrial stimulus was lengthened to 15 sec. and the duration of the C stimulus was reduced to 5 sec. over a period of 2–3 days. Each response in the intertrial period reset the intertrial interval and caused a brief (160 msec.) darkening of the chamber accompanied by a relay click.

The final training schedule thus consisted of an intertrial period of at least 15 sec. during which white house lights and no tone were on. Each response in the intertrial period extended the period for 15 sec. from the time of the response, at the end of which time a 5-sec. trial period began. During the trial the red house lights and tone were on, and the first response produced a 5-sec. access to grain. During the 5-sec. reinforcements the tone and all house lights were off and the grain magazine was illuminated (see Fig. 1).

The birds were run under these conditions until (*a*) they responded on at least 75% of the trials in a session or (*b*) they received 19 days of training. They were tested on the day following fulfillment of this criterion. The appetitive test was begun with a 15-min. warm-up period in which the training conditions were in effect. The next 60 trials consisted of 20 presentations each of the compound training stimulus (C) and its elements (red light alone [L] and tone alone [T] in a random order. Then a short retraining period of 10 C trials was presented, followed by 11 more presentations each of C, T, and L trials in a random order. Data

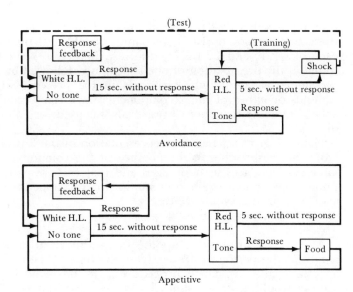

FIG. 1. *Diagrammatic representation of the avoidance (top) and appetitive training procedures. (Note the similar consequences of responding in the presence of "white house light–no tone" in the 2 procedures. Also note the different consequences of failing to respond in the presence of "red house light–tone" during test vs. training in the avoidance condition.)*

from the 10 retraining trials were not included in the analysis. Throughout the test, responses to the compound stimulus or either of its components were reinforced.

Avoidance Training

The avoidance training procedure was similar to the signaled avoidance procedure used by Foree and LoLordo (1970). Each response in the presence of the intertrial stimulus (white house lights and no tone, as in the appetitive procedure) reset the intertrial duration to 15 sec. Feedback for intertrial responses consisted of a brief darkening of the chamber (160 msec.) accompanied by a relay click. After 15 sec. without a response in the intertrial condition, the compound stimulus (again consisting of the red house lights and tone) came on. A response in the presence of this stimulus reinstated the intertrial conditions. Failure to respond within 5 sec. after onset of C resulted in a brief (120-msec.) shock. The C stimulus remained on with the shock presented every 5 sec. until a response was made. No hand shaping was employed.

The shock voltage was set at 30 on the first day of training and was increased 10 v. each day to a maximum of 60 v. for Birds 817, 827, 790, 848, 849, 846, and 833. For Birds 826, 810, 831, 834, and 811, voltage was increased subsequently to 65, 70, 70, 75, and 80 v., respectively.

As in the appetitive case, birds were trained until they either (*a*) responded on 75% or more of the trials in a session or (*b*) received 19 days of training.

The test was given on the day following attainment of the criterion and was similar to the appetitive test. After a 15-min. warm-up period on the training schedule, 20 trials each of C, T, and L were presented. Then there was a block of 10 C (retraining) trials, and finally 11 more trials each of C, T, and L. During the test, failure to respond on a trial resulted in the presentation of one shock only, followed by reinstatement of the intertrial conditions. Responses in the presence of the compound stimulus or either of the 2 components were reinforced by shock avoidance. The same sequence of test trials was used for all birds in both conditions.

Figure 1 gives a schematic representation of the 2 training procedures. Note that responding in the absence of the compound stimulus has the same consequences in both cases and that each response in C results in reinforcement i.e., grain presentation in the appetitive case and shock avoidance in the avoidance case.

Results

As Fig. 1 indicates, a response in the intertrial period extended the length of this period by 15 sec. from the time of the response in both the appetitive and avoidance procedures. In the avoidance case, such responses would postpone shock by 20 sec. and thus be reinforced, but in the appetitive case such responses would reduce reinforcement rate and presumably be punished. Despite this apparent asymmetry in the consequences of responding in the intertrial period, very similar patterns of responding developed under the 2 procedures. After the first 2 or 3 days of training very few responses occurred in the intertrial period. However, when the compound trial stimulus came on, the birds would make 1 or often a short burst of 2–4 responses. This pattern of responding has been noted under avoidance schedules similar to the one employed in the present study in rats (Ulrich, Holz, & Azrin, 1964) and pigeons (Foree & LoLordo, 1970). It should be noted that after the first 2 days of avoidance training, only very rarely did a bird receive more than one shock on a trial before responding. Typically a shock was followed after a very short latency by depression of the treadle. Thus the pattern of avoidance responding was such that there was virtually no change in the average length of the conditioned stimulus (CS) or the number of shocks per CS from training to test, despite the procedural change illustrated in the top panel of Fig. 1.

The number of training sessions required to reach criterion was comparable under the 2 training procedures, and the order in which the birds received the procedures affected this measure little. For Group App–Av the mean number of days to criterion for the appetitive task was 6.7 with a range of 3–19 days; for the avoidance task the mean was 12.3 days with a range of 4–19 days. For Group Av–App the mean for the appetitive task was 10.2 days with a range of 4–19 days; for the avoidance task the mean was 11.9 with a range of 3–19 days.

The similarities noted above ensured that the birds received approximately the same total amount of contact with the compound stimulus in the 2 training procedures.

The primary measure of interest was the number of responses to the 3 test stimuli during the test session. Figure 2 illustrates for each bird the total number of responses out of 31 opportunities to respond in the pres-

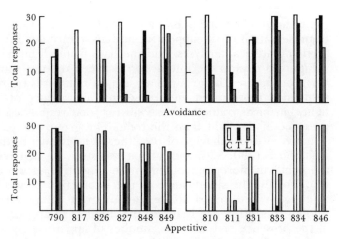

FIG. 2. *Total number of responses made to each of the 3 test stimuli in both the avoidance (top) and appetitive conditions for each of the 12 birds. (The open bar represents responses in compound; solid black, responses in tone alone; and gray, responses in light alone. The 6 birds in Group Av–App are to the left of the center line, and those in Group App–Av are to the right.)*

ence of each stimulus in both the avoidance and appetitive tests. Although the overall level of responding in the last training session and in the test session varied widely across birds, the relative amount of responding to the 3 stimuli remained generally the same for birds within either the avoidance or the appetitive procedures. In the appetitive test, the largest number of responses was made in the presence of the compound S^D; about the same number was made in the light alone; and few responses were made in the presence of the tone alone. Bird 790, which responded on almost every trial to all 3 stimuli, is the one exception to this generalization. In the avoidance test the compound stimulus again controlled responding to the greatest extent. The light alone controlled relatively little responding, but the tone alone controlled responding at an intermediate level. The 2 exceptions to this generalization are Birds 826 and 849.

The number of nonrunning days separating conditions had no obvious effect upon the outcome of the second test. Furthermore, the pattern of results obtained from Birds 831, 833, 834, and 846, all of which were maintained at 80% of free-feeding weight during avoidance training and testing, did not differ from the pattern obtained from the other birds. Birds 831, 833, 834, and 846 did respond more often to the tone during the avoidance test than did the other birds.

Figure 3 illustrates the mean number of responses made in the presence of each of the 3 test stimuli under the appetitive and avoidance procedures. Data from the 2 groups are presented separately. In order to compare the 2 groups, a multivariate analysis of variance was performed using each of the 6 points shown in a panel of Fig. 3 as a variable in the analysis. That is, for each bird the number of responses to each of the 3 stimuli in each test situation was one variable. The groups did not differ significantly from one another ($F = 2.21$, $p < .2$). Consequently the order of presentation of the appetitive and avoidance conditions was ignored in further statistical analyses, and the data from all birds were pooled.

Figure 3 depicts the interaction between the test stimuli and the training procedures. The group data suggest that birds trained to avoid shock responded more often in the test in the presence of the tone than the light, but birds trained to respond for food responded more often in the presence of the light than the tone. The group curves are strictly representative of the behavior of 9 of the 12 individual birds. For the remaining 3 birds (790, 826, and 849) it was still true that relative to the tone, the light was more controlling in the appetitive test than in the avoidance test. To test the significance of the interaction between test stimuli and training procedures, a single measure was computed for each bird by finding the difference between the number of appetitive responses made in the presence of L and the number of appetitive responses made in the presence of T, and subtracting from this quantity the difference between the number of avoidance responses made in the presence of L and the number of avoidance responses made in the presence of T, i.e., (App L − App T) − (Av L − Av T). This quantity, which was positive for all birds, was found to be significantly different from zero (Student's $t = 6.01$, $df = 11$, $p < .001$). Thus with the procedures and stimuli used here, auditory control increases and visual control decreases when the reinforcer for responding in the presence of an auditory–visual compound stimulus is avoidance of shock as opposed to the presentation of food.

Discussion

The nature of the reinforcer for the pigeon's treadle-pressing response determines whether the auditory or the visual element of a compound S^D will exert more control over that response. The auditory component is stronger in the avoidance procedure; the visual element is stronger when food is the reinforcer. This result was true both between and within subjects. In many cases a stimulus which exerted very strong control with one reinforcer lost this control in subsequent training with the other reinforcer. For example, the responding of Birds 834 and 846 (Fig. 2) was strongly controlled by the light in the appetitive test, which they received first, yet this control was markedly diminished during the subsequent avoidance test, though avoidance responses in the presence of the light were always reinforced. Birds 817 and 849 provide analogous examples of loss of control by the tone in the appetitive procedure.

The outcome obtained in the present experiment is not predicted by selective attention theory or the sort of associative model proposed by Rescorla and Wagner (1972). It requires that attending hierarchies or the α values assigned to CSs (S^Ds) be reinforcer specific, or at least that they be different for food vs. shock avoidance.

There are several outcomes reported in the psychological and ethological literature which are consonant with the present result. Baerends (1958) allowed herring gulls to choose between wooden egg models which differed in size, shape, color, and pattern. When the gull was returning eggs to incubate them, color and speckling were more important

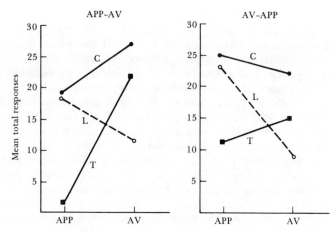

Fig. 3. *Mean total responses to the 3 test stimuli (C = compound, T = tone alone, L = light alone) under both the appetitive (App) and avoidance (Av) conditions for Group App–Av and Group Av–App.*

than shape, but when it was stealing eggs to eat, shape was more important than speckling or color. Turning to data from experimental psychology, Gilbert (1969) noted that auditory control was stronger than visual control in a number of studies in which rats pressed levers to avoid electric shock. Other studies, which required more complex response chains to produce either food or shock avoidance, suggested that visual stimuli were more effective than auditory stimuli for rats. Gilbert argued against species-characteristic attending hierarchies on the basis of these studies.

Shettleworth (1972b) allowed water-deprived chicks to drink in both the presence and absence of an auditory–visual compound S^D, but punished drinking with electric shock or quinine in only one of the conditions in a counterbalanced design. When the elements were presented separately, drinking was nearly completely controlled by the flashing light. On the other hand, when the compound was followed by electric shock in a classical conditioning experiment which did not involve positive reinforcement, the auditory stimulus exerted stronger control over increases in calling and general activity than did the visual stimulus. As Shettleworth (1972a) noted, in her experiments and those discussed by Gilbert more than the reinforcer was manipulated within each study. The nature of the responses and deprivation conditions were also varied. Consequently, it cannot be concluded from these studies that changes in control were due to changes in the reinforcer. The outcome of the present study does warrant that conclusion.

Several studies of food aversion are similar to the present work insofar as they varied the reinforcer in essentially parallel experiments in order to determine how the distribution of stimulus control changed with the reinforcer. Garcia and Koelling (1966) allowed 2 groups of rats to drink salty water, with each lick also producing a click and a flashing light. Half the rats then received a delayed electric shock, and the others suffered visceral upset caused by administration of lithium chloride. In the test the gustatory and audiovisual cues were presented separately. Only the salty taste was avoided by those rats which had been poisoned, but only the "bright, noisy water" was avoided by the rats which had been shocked. Domjan and Wilson (1972) replicated this effect in a study in which the tasty solution was infused through an oral cannula, thereby minimizing differences in the reception of gustatory and audiovisual stimulation.

The present study suggests that the dependence of the direction of overshadowing upon the reinforcer is a reasonably general phenomenon. It occurs in a situation which differs from the food aversion procedure in several potentially important respects: (a) The aforementioned food aversion studies used rats, but the present experiment used pigeons; (b) the food aversion studies compared gustatory with auditory–visual stimulation; we compared auditory with visual stimuli; (c) the food aversion studies compared 2 aversive reinforcers (unconditioned stimuli); we compared positive and negative reinforcement; (d) the food aversion studies used response-independent reinforcement; we used response-contingent reinforcement.

More work must be done to determine which of the specific aspects of our procedure are necessary for the observed outcome. One interesting question concerns the function of shock. Does the auditory S^D exert more control than the visual S^D in our shock avoidance procedure because (a) there is an avoidance contingency or (b) because shocks are delivered? The first possibility suggests the use of aversive stimuli other than shock in a procedure which maintains the avoidance contingency. The second possibility suggests the use of procedures which include shock but no avoidance contingency. Analysis of this phenomenon would also be extended by the use of a positive reinforcer which, like electric shock, is not localized in the external environment, e.g., positively reinforcing electrical stimulation of the brain.

The present outcome is consonant with our knowledge of the lives of wild pigeons. Pigeons are said to find their food by sight, but according to Goodwin (1967) they often rely upon auditory cues, e.g., the noise of wing flapping or the alarm calls of other pigeons, when predators approach. We are not arguing that the stimuli used in the present study are "natural" by any means, but we are suggesting that the birds bring into the experiment the neural mechanisms which facilitate certain associations but not others (see Garcia & Ervin, 1968; Rozin & Kalat, 1971; Seligman, 1970; Shettleworth, 1972a for general discussions of this issue).

Notes
    [1] This research was supported by National Institute of Mental Health Grant MH-15468-03 and National Science Foundation Grant GB-31065 to Vincent M. LoLordo. Donald D. Foree was supported by National Institute of Mental Health Training Grant T01-MH-12383 to the University of North Carolina. We would like to thank Kathleen Bloom, Robert Rescorla, Anthony Riley, and Sara Shettleworth for their helpful comments on an earlier version of this report.

References
    Azrin, N. H. A technique for delivering shock to pigeons. *Journal of the Experimental Analysis of Behavior*, 1959, **2**, 161–163.
    Baerends, G. P. The contribution of ethology to the study of the causation of behavior. *Acta Physiologica et Pharmacologica Néerlandica*, 1958, **7**, 466–499.

Baron, M. R. The stimulus, stimulus control, and stimulus generalization. In D. I. Mostofsky (Ed.), *Stimulus generalization.* Stanford: Stanford University Press, 1965.

Coughlin, R. C., Jr. Inexpensive pubis electrodes for delivering shock to pigeons. *Journal of the Experimental Analysis of Behavior,* 1970, **13,** 368–369.

Domjan, M., & Wilson, N. E. Specificity of cue to consequence in aversion learning in rats. *Psychonomic Science,* 1972, **26,** 143–145.

Farthing, G. W., & Hearst, E. Attention in the pigeon: Testing with compounds or elements. *Learning and Motivation,* 1970, **1,** 65–78.

Foree, D. D., & LoLordo, V. M. Signalled and unsignalled free-operant avoidance in the pigeon. *Journal of the Experimental Analysis of Behavior,* 1970, **13,** 283–290.

Garcia, J., & Ervin, F. R. Gustatory–visual and telereceptor–cutaneous conditioning—Adaptation in internal and external milieus. *Communications in Behavioral Biology,* 1968, **1** (Part A) 389–415.

Garcia, J., & Koelling, R. A. Relation of cue to consequence in avoidance learning. *Psychonomic Science,* 1966, **4,** 123–124.

Gilbert, R. M. Discrimination learning? In R. M. Gilbert & N. S. Sutherland (Eds.), *Animal discrimination learning.* New York: Academic Press, 1969.

Goodwin, D. *Pigeons and doves of the world.* Portsmouth: Grosvenor Press, 1967.

Kamin, L. J. Predictability, surprise, attention and conditioning. In B. A. Campbell & R. M. Church (Eds.), *Punishment and aversive behavior.* New York: Appleton-Century-Crofts, 1969.

Miles, C. G. A demonstration of overshadowing in operant conditioning. *Psychonomic Science,* 1969, **16,** 139–140.

Pavlov, I. P. *Conditioned reflexes* (Trans. by G. V. Anrep). New York: Oxford, 1927.

Rescorla, R. A., & Wagner, A. R. A theory of Pavlovian conditioning: Variations in the effectiveness of reinforcement and nonreinforcement. In A. H. Black & W. F. Prokasy (Eds.), *Classical conditioning II: Theory and research.* New York: Appleton-Century-Crofts, 1972.

Reynolds, G. S. Attention in the pigeon. *Journal of the Experimental Analysis of Behavior,* 1961, **4,** 203–208.

Rozin, P., & Kalat, J. W. Specific hungers and poison avoidance as adaptive specializations of learning. *Psychological Review,* 1971, **78,** 459–486.

Seligman, M. E. P. On the generality of the laws of learning. *Psychological Review,* 1970, **77,** 406–418.

Shettleworth, S. Constraints on learning. In D. S. Lehrman, R. A. Hinde, & E. Shaw (Eds.), *Advances in the study of behavior 4.* New York: Academic Press, 1972a.

Shettleworth, S. Stimulus relevance in the control of drinking and conditioned fear responses in domestic chicks *(Gallus gallus). Journal of Comparative and Physiological Psychology,* 1972b, **80,** 175–198.

Smith, R. F. & Keller, F. R. Free-operant avoidance in the pigeon using a treadle response. *Journal of the Experimental Analysis of Behavior,* 1970, **13,** 211–214.

Ulrich, R. E., Holz, W. G., & Azrin, N. H. Stimulus control of avoidance behavior. *Journal of the Experimental Analysis of Behavior,* 1964, **7,** 129–133.

Part VI
Cognitive Processes

The traditional aim of behavior theory has been to delineate the relations between environmental inputs and behavioral outputs. Little work has been devoted to exploring the internal processes that mediate between inputs and outputs. Such processes, which we may call *cognitive processes,* must surely occur. When an organism experiences an environmental event, it must first *perceive* the event; if it is to profit from its past experience, it must *remember* that past experience; and if it is to discern the relevance of past experience to the present, it must *categorize* its experiences in such a way as to make the similarities between past and present apparent. If an organism did none of these things, it could never learn anything. Each time it pressed a lever and received food would be like the first time; each time it experienced a pairing of tone and shock would be like the first time.

Attempting to understand relations between environmental inputs and behavioral outputs without appeal to mediating cognitive processes is like trying to understand the functioning of a computer by looking at inputs and outputs and ignoring the program. In both cases substantial understanding is possible so long as the mediating processes (the program) are simple. If our cognitive representations of environmental events are faithful reflections of the events themselves, involving little transformation or organization, then we can get quite far in our understanding by focusing exclusively on the events and ignoring the cognitive representations; and traditionally behavior theorists have assumed that cognitive representations—processes of perception, categorization, and memory— were simple. But in the last twenty years or so, evidence from a number of domains has converged to suggest that cognitive processes can no longer be ignored.

We have encountered some of this evidence in other sections of this book. In the sections on Pavlovian conditioning and operant discrimination learning we saw that conditioning involves learning to pay attention to some stimuli and ignore others. "Paying attention" means that some active evaluation and transformation of events is occurring in the cognitive representation that mediates between inputs and outputs. Merely presenting detectable stimuli to an animal does not mean they will be effective stimuli. We have seen that both Pavlovian and operant conditioning involve the learning of contingencies, between CS and US or response and reinforcer. Determining whether a contingency exists requires some computation. How is that computation accomplished? We have seen the need for appealing to expectancies in explaining some phenomena. It is hard to understand avoidance learning without acknowledging that organisms develop expectancies (p. 172), and the phenomenon of learned helplessness tells us that when organisms lack control in the present, they will expect to lack it in the future (p. 111). All of these developments point to the need for direct exploration of the cognitive processes that mediate between inputs and outputs. This is the focus of the articles in this section. The selections illustrate the abilities of rats and pigeons to learn discriminations that are far more complex than, say, red versus green. They demonstrate that animals can develop spatial representations (cognitive maps) of their environment, and sometimes solve problems through insight rather than trial and error.

A. LEARNING ABOUT RELATIONS

When an animal learns a discrimination between, say, a bright light and a dim light, with the bright light predictive of reinforcement, there are two different things it might be learning. It might be learning to respond to the bright light or it might be learning to respond to the brighter light. Stated more generally, in learning discriminations, organisms may learn to respond on the basis of absolute properties of the discriminative stimuli or on the basis of relational properties. Many years ago there was much dispute among behavior theorists about whether animals learned relations (Köhler, 1939, Spence, 1936, 1937); it is now clear that at least sometimes they do. The article by Lawrence and DeRivera is an elegant demonstration of relational learning in rats. The rats receive initial training in a brightness discrimination task that can be solved on the basis of either absolute or relational characteristics of the stimuli. Then they are given test stimuli which will induce them to make one response based on absolute properties and another based on relational ones. The rats respond to the relational cues.

What is at issue in studies of this type is how organisms perceive and organize environmental inputs. There is no dispute about whether they learn to respond to stimuli that predict reinforcement availability; the dispute is over what the effective stimuli are. Evidence that these are sometimes relations points to the need for understanding how organisms represent environmental inputs.

28 Evidence for Relational Transposition
DOUGLAS H. LAWRENCE AND JOSEPH DERIVERA

The specification of the stimulus, or more exactly the specification of those characteristics of the stimulus situation to which S reacts, has always been a difficult problem. One aspect of this problem that has attracted considerable attention is the question of whether or not S can react to the relational characteristics in a stimulus situation. The mere fact of transposition is ambiguous with respect to this question, for it can be interpreted as favoring either a relational point of view (2) or one that emphasizes reactions to the specific characteristics of the stimulus (4). The present study attempts to show that there are types of transposition behavior that clearly must be interpreted as evidence for relational responding. Theories assuming that such behaviors can be derived from reactions to the absolute values of the stimulus and the generalization of these reactions are incapable of explaining the results.

The procedure used in the present experiment differs greatly from the usual transposition test. The usual test for transposition involves a simultaneous discrimination in which S is first trained, for example, to approach a white and avoid a mid-gray. The S is then tested by means of another simultaneous discrimination involving a mid-gray and a black. If it chooses the former, it is interpreted as evidence for transposition. The procedure used in the present study is similar to this in that it uses a modified Lashley jumping stand and two cues are presented simultaneously on a given trial. But it differs from the usual procedure in that S is actually trained on a successive discrimination.

This seeming paradox is resolved in the following way. On a given trial both cards in the jumping stand are exactly alike. Each card, however, has one gray on the top half and a different gray on the bottom half. If the top gray is lighter than the bottom one, S is forced to jump to the right window to receive the reward and avoid punishment. If the top half is darker than the bottom half, S is forced to jump to the left. The advantages of this method are: (a) a sharp contrast between the two grays is always present so that their relationship should be perceptually clear regardless of which window S is oriented toward: (b) S is always rewarded or punished in the presence of both grays so that no differential reaction to their absolute characteristics is likely to develop; and (c) it is possible to train S on several such pairs of grays with varying degrees of difference between their absolute brightnesses so that it is familiarized with a wide range of such relationships.

This procedure also permits clear-cut contrasts between the predictions about transposition behavior that are derived from theories emphasizing reactions to the relational aspects of the stimulus situation and those derived from theories emphasizing reactions to specific stimulus values.

"Evidence for Relational Transposition" by Douglas H. Lawrence and Joseph DeRivera. *Journal of Comparative and Physiological Psychology*, 1954, 47, 465–471.

These contrasts were established in the present study by selecting seven grays ranging from white, no. 1, to black, no. 7. On all training trials the bottom half of each card was the mid-gray, no. 4. On any given trial the top half of both cards could be any one of the remaining six grays, 1, 2, 3, 5, 6, and 7. These occurred in a semirandom order on successive trials. Whenever the top half was lighter than the bottom half, S jumped to the right, and whenever it was darker, S jumped to the left.

In terms of a theory emphasizing reactions to the specific values of the stimuli, this should mean that no. 4 remained neutral in that the animal jumped half the time to the right and half the time to the left in its presence. Grays 1, 2, and 3, however, should have become associated with jumping right, because this was the only reaction reinforced in their presence, and grays 5, 6, and 7 should have become associated with jumping left. In terms of a relational theory, on the other hand, the specific gray values would have been of minor importance; rather, S would have learned to react to each of these six values in terms of the relationship it bore to the no. 4 gray on the bottom half of the card. "Darker than" should be associated with jumping left, and "lighter than" should be associated with jumping right. Consequently, if this reference gray, no. 4, were now shifted up or down the brightness continuum, S's reactions to the other six grays should change in accordance with the shift in relationships resulting from this change in the reference stimulus. It is in this sense that we can speak of transposition behavior in this situation.

The differential predictions made by the two theories for this type of transposition can be illustrated as follows. Suppose that during the test trials the top half of the two cards was gray no. 2 and the bottom half was gray no. 3. The specific stimulus theory would predict a jump to the right because both grays had previously been associated with such behavior. Similarly, the relational theory would predict a jump to the right in that the top half was lighter than the bottom half. Both theories would predict the same on such a test. On the other hand if the top half was gray no. 3 and the bottom half was gray no. 2, the specific stimulus theory would still predict a jump to the right for the same reasons as in the previous case, but a relational theory would predict a jump to the left because the top half was now darker than the bottom half. Thus the two theories would make directly opposing predictions on such tests.

It is apparent that several such test pairs leading to differential predictions by the two theories are possible among this set of stimuli. Consequently, this type of transposition experiment should provide a fairly clear-cut answer to the question of whether or not it is necessary to assume that relational responding is a fundamental form of behavior.

Method

Subjects

The Ss were 12 albino rats between 60 and 90 days old at the beginning of the experiment. They were tamed and then placed on a food-deprivation schedule during which they were allowed to eat all the food they wanted for 2 hr. each day. This schedule was started two weeks prior to the experiment and continued throughout the training and testing.

Apparatus

The apparatus was a modified Lashley jumping stand painted a flat black. The windows were 7 in. by 9 in. The jumping platform was 8 in. from the windows and at a height such that S's head was on the same plane as the mid-point of the two cards. The back of the platform from which Ss jumped consisted of a box, 12 by 12 by 12 in. The front wall of this box was of milk glass. A 100-w. lamp inside the box provided all the illumination for the apparatus. Because of the diffusion of the light through the milk glass, an even illumination of the two cards without shadows was obtained even though S stood in front of it.

The seven stimulus grays used were obtained by mixing various proportions of flat black and flat white paint, and then painting a large quantity of paper with each mix. In this way several cards all of a constant gray value could be obtained. An attempt was made to have equal brightness steps between adjacent grays in the series, but as the reflectance values in Table 1 indicate, this equality was not obtained. Stimulus cards were made from these gray papers by covering the top half of the card with one gray and the bottom half with a different gray.

Procedure

The Ss were adapted to the apparatus by first feeding them on it, then teaching them to jump the gap to an open window, and finally to jump the gap when the windows were closed by stimulus cards of gray. Each S was then given a "dry run" of 20 trials to these neutral cards during which either the right or left window was blocked in random order. If it jumped to the blocked one, S was placed back on the jumping stand and forced to jump again until it chose the open one. It was hoped by this method to break the animals of position preferences and to adapt them to the type of punishment involved. However, this procedure seemed to result in partial fixations for some Ss. During this adaptation period, as well as the remainder of the training and testing, S was never forced to jump by beating its tail or similar methods; S was always left on the stand until

TABLE 1. Reflectances of Seven Grays as Measured by the Illumitronic Engineering Reflectometer[a]

Gray	Reflectance	
	%	Log.
1	73.0	1.863
2	43.0	1.633
3	30.0	1.477
4	20.0	1.301
5	15.5	1.190
6	9.5	0.978
7	7.0	0.845

[a] The illumination of these when in position was 2.5 to 3.0 ft.-candles.

it had initiated its own choice. It appeared that the heat and light coming from the box behind *S* increased the motivation to jump even when a series of punishments had occurred on the preceding trials.

The training of *Ss* was in two stages. During the first stage only two different stimulus cards were used. They were 1/4, i.e., the top half was gray no. 1 and the bottom half gray no. 4, and 7/4. On a given trial both cards were exactly the same. The *Ss* were rewarded if they jumped to the right when the top half was lighter than the bottom and if they jumped to the left when the top half was darker than the bottom. Otherwise they were punished by a blocked window and fell to a platform below the apparatus. Training was by a correction method; if *S* made a mistake, it was immediately picked up and forced to jump again until it made a correct choice. A trial consisted of one rewarded response. The stimuli were so arranged that not more than two jumps to the same side occurred on consecutive trials. Half the jumps were to the right and half to the left. Five trials a day, spaced at 20- to 30-min. intervals, were given until *Ss* reached a criterion of 9 out of 10 consecutive correct responses. If upon reaching the criterion, any *S* was not jumping readily and directly at the stimulus card, it was given additional training until this condition was corrected.

During the second stage of training, all *Ss* were presented with the following set of six stimuli: 1/4, 2/4, 3/4, 5/4, 6/4, and 7/4. These stimuli were presented in six different orders with the restriction that not more than two jumps to the same side succeeded each other on consecutive trials. Again *Ss* had to jump right when the top half was lighter than the bottom half and to jump left when it was darker. Training was continued for 30 trials, with five trials per day. If by that time *S* had not reached a criterion of going twice through the sequence of six without error, training was continued until *S* did reach it. One of the 12 *Ss* showed such a strong position preference that it was discontinued before the test trials.

During the test period five trials a day were given; three were a continuation of the previous training trials and the other two were test trials. On the test trials both cards were unlocked and *S* was rewarded regardless of which way it jumped. The 24 test stimuli used are shown in Table 2. The following restrictions were imposed on the test stimuli: (a) each *S* went through the 24 stimuli in a different order; (b) on a given day 22 different stimuli were tested; (c) the two test stimuli presented to *S* on a given day were of such a nature that if the animal jumped relationally, one of the jumps would be to the right the other to the left, with the right jump occurring first on half the days and the left occurring first on the remainder; (d) the test trials were given on the third and fifth trials of each day and so interspersed with the training trials that if *S* reacted relationally to the test stimuli, it would never be rewarded more than two consecutive trials on the same side; and (e) the pair of stimuli presented on a given day always had the same number of brightness units between the two grays, e.g., 1/2 and 6/5 or 3/5 and 7/5.

Five *Ss*, picked at random, were given posttest training on a successive discrimination. It was assumed that if *Ss* had been reacting to the specific stimulus values, rather than relationally, they should be able to discriminate between grays nos. 3 and 5 even though the reference value no. 4 was absent. They had done so during the original training trials when the bottom half of each card was gray no. 4. Consequently, each of these Ss was trained for 50 trials, 5 trials a day, on a successive discrimination involving grays no. 3 and no. 5. When both cards were no. 3, they had to jump right; when both were no 5, they had to jump left. Rewards and punishment were correlated with these jumps in the same manner as during the original training.

Results

In order to reach the criterion of 9 correct out of 10 consecutive trials on stimuli 1/4 and 7/4, Ss required on the average 31.5 trials. With the overtraining given them, they averaged a total of 60.8 training trials on these stimuli. When transferred to the training stimuli 1/4, 2/4, 3/4, 5/4, 6/4, and 7/4, they required an average of 7.6 trials to reach the same criterion of 9 correct out of 10 consecutive trials. This indicates a considerable amount of transfer. Each S, however, was continued on these stimuli for at least 30 trials or until it had gone through the sequence of six stimuli two times in a row without error. As a consequence Ss averaged 48.8 training trials on these stimuli.

The Ss' reactions to the 24 test stimuli are shown in Table 2. It should be noted that in 21 of these cases, the majority of Ss chose the side predicted by the relational theory. The three exceptions are cases in which there is only one step difference in brightness between the top and bot-

TABLE 2. Frequency of Relational Responses to 24 Test Stimuli

Difference in brightness between Grays	Stimulus and response	Gray on bottom half of card						%
		No. 1	No. 2	No. 3	No. 5	No. 6	No. 7	
+1	Stimulus	2/1	3/2	4/3	6/5	7/6		
	Relational	8	7	8	10	11		80
	Nonrel.	3	4	3	1	0		20
−1	Stimulus		1/2	2/3	4/5	5/6	6/7	
	Relational		10	9	3	5	2	53
	Nonrel.		1	2	8	6	9	47
+2	Stimulus	3/1	4/2	5/3	7/5			
	Relational	9	10	10	11			91
	Nonrel.	2	1	1	0			9
−2	Stimulus			1/3	3/5	4/6	5/7	
	Relational			11	11	10	6	86
	Nonrel.			0	0	1	5	14
+3	Stimulus	4/1	5/2	6/3				
	Relational	10	10	11				94
	Nonrel.	1	1	0				6
−3	Stimulus				2/5	3/6	4/7	
	Relational				11	10	8	88
	Nonrel.				0	1	3	12
%	Relational	82	84	89	84	82	48	80
	Nonrel.	18	16	11	16	18	52	20

tom halves of the stimulus cards, i.e., stimuli 6/7, 5/6, and 4/5. Altogether, 80 per cent of the 264 test jumps are in keeping with a relational hypothesis. The extent of this accuracy can best be appreciated by noting that during this time Ss were reacting to the three training stimuli per day with only 89 per cent accuracy despite all their previous training on these. Table 2 indicates that relational responding was least evident when the two grays differed by only one unit in brightness and for the darker grays, especially no. 7, which had the same reflectance value as the flat black paint used on the jumping stand.

The first statistical test made was to determine if there was any evidence of a progressive change in relational responding as the testing continued. Each S was tested on two stimuli each day, and a different pair of stimuli was used for each S. With the stimulus sets thus balanced from day to day, no evidence was found of a progressive change in the percentage of relational choices on test stimuli during this period nor of any change in the level of accuracy on the three training stimuli per day. Thus, while the continued training during the test period may have helped to maintain the tendency toward relational choices, there is no evidence that Ss were actually learning such behavior during the test period.

In contrasting the predictions of a specific stimulus theory and a relational theory on these test stimuli, it is necessary to consider four different sets of test cards. On stimuli 1/2, 1/3, 2/3, 6/5, 7/5, and 7/6, both theories make the same prediction. For instance, on stimulus 1/2 the specific stimulus theory would predict a jump to the right because S had always been reinforced for jumping right in the presence of both these grays. Similarly, the relational theory would predict this because the top gray is lighter than the bottom one. On these six stimuli 94 per cent of the 66 test jumps were as predicted by both theories.

On the second set of stimuli, 2/1, 3/1, 3/2, 5/6, 5/7, and 6/7, the two theories make opposing predictions. For instance, on stimulus 2/1 the specific stimulus theory would predict a right jump because both grays had been associated with this response, whereas the relational theory would predict a left jump because the top gray is darker than the bottom one. On this set of six stimuli, 56 per cent of the responses were in the direction predicted by the relational theory; for six of the Ss the majority of their jumps were relationally determined, for three of them their choices were split equally between the relational and specific directions, and for two the majority of their choices were in the direction predicted by the specific stimulus hypothesis. This percentage in favor of relational responding differs from a chance split between the .10 and .20 levels of significance. It should be noted that the majority of these test' stimuli involve two grays that differ by only one step in brightness.

The third set of stimuli, 4/1, 4/2, 4/3, 4/5, 4/6, and 4/7, is that in which gray no. 4, which was always on the bottom half of the cards during training, is now on the top half. In terms of the specific stimulus theory this gray should be neutral, having been equally often associated with jumps to the right and to the left. Consequently, S's response to these test stimuli should be entirely determined by the gray on the bottom half of the card. But this would always lead to just the opposite prediction from that of a relational theory, e.g., on 4/1 the specific stimulus hypothesis would predict a right jump because the gray no. 1 had been associated with this response, whereas the relational theory would predict a left jump because the top was darker than the bottom. On these stimuli 74 per cent of the jumps were relationally determined, which is well beyond the .01 level of significance.

The fourth and final set of stimuli, 2/5, 3/5, 3/6, 5/2, 5/3, and 6/3, is that in which one gray is lighter than the neutral gray no. 4 and the other is darker. On these the predictions from the specific stimulus theory are ambiguous. Presumably the response should be determined by two factors: (a) the gray on the top half of the card should have more influence than the one on the bottom because during training this one was always the determining cue, and (b) the gray of the pair that is farthest removed in brightness from the neutral gray no. 4 should have the greater influence because of generalization. Depending on how these two factors are weighted, a wide variety of predictions can be made. If only the top half of the card is considered, the predictions are exactly the same as for the relational theory. This latter theory makes unambiguous predictions for each stimulus in this set. For this set of stimuli, 95 per cent of the responses were in keeping with the relational prediction, a value significantly different from chance well beyond the .01 level.

If the 12 stimuli of sets 2 and 3 above, for which the two theories make opposing predictions, are combined, 65 per cent of the responses are in accordance with the relational hypothesis, a value significantly different from chance at the .01 level. If, as Table 2 suggests, part of the failure to show relational behavior on some of these stimuli is due to the difficulty of the discrimination when the two grays are separated by only one unit of brightness, a clearer picture of the predominance of relational responding is shown when this type of stimulus is excluded from the comparison. Considering the 6 stimuli in the above set of 12 in which the pair of grays differs by two or three brightness units, the percentage of relational responding increases to 80.

Five animals were given posttest training on a successive discrimination involving grays no. 3 and no. 5. During the original training these Ss had shown the ability to discriminate between cards 3/4 and 5/4. If, as the specific stimulus theory seems to imply, gray no. 4 was neutral, then according to this theory Ss must have been responding in terms of grays no. 3 and no. 5. Consequently, one would expect that they would continue to respond fairly accurately even though gray no. 4 was removed from the situation. Actually all discrimination between these two grays broke down, and there was little if any sign of learning during the 50 training trials. During the first 10 of these trials, Ss chose correctly 50 per cent of the time, and during the last 10 trials they chose correctly 58 per cent of the time. This supports the idea that this discrimination is very difficult when Ss must react to the stimuli as specific values, but that it is relatively easy when they can relate each of these grays to the reference gray no. 4 on a given trial.

Discussion

In interpreting the results of this experiment, it should be borne in mind that the method of testing for transposition, and therefore the actual definition of the term transposition, in this study differs markedly from the usual method of testing. Usually S is presented during training with two stimuli and taught to approach one of these and avoid the other. Transposition is then tested by presenting S with two new stimuli. The implicit assumption is that the relationship between these new stimuli is the same as it was for the training pair. Thus, in this technique S always must select one of two simultaneously presented stimuli; in addition only the relationship, not the specific stimuli, remains constant from the training to the test situation.

In the present method the procedure is very different. While two stimuli are presented on each trial, S does not choose between them. Rather, S must react to the relationship between them by jumping either right or left. Again all the specific stimulus values that are used during the test situation have been used during the training situation; they are constant. The aspect of the situation that is varied from the training to the test trials is the relationship these specific stimuli bear to each other. The test for transposition is whether or not the behavior varies concomitantly with these changes in relationship. Because of these differences in procedure, it would seem likely that the present method should be a more sensitive test for relational responding than is the usual method. In a sense S is forced to respond relationally from the beginning of training. Furthermore, S is familiar with all the stimulus values used during the test so that these should not introduce any disruptive effect.

There would seem to be little question in terms of the present results that in most instances Ss were reacting to brightness relationships rather than to specific brightness values. A relational hypothesis is able to make a specific, unambiguous prediction about each of the 24 test stimuli used. Eighty per cent of the test responses were in keeping with these predictions, a level of transposition that is almost as great as the level of accuracy these Ss were able to maintain on the training stimuli during this period. Furthermore, it was shown that this level of accuracy was obtained on the very first day of testing and was not the result of learning or continued improvement during this period.

It is true that on the six test stimuli, 2/1, 3/1, 3/2, 5/6, 5/7, and 6/7, for which a relational hypothesis and a specific stimulus hypothesis make directly opposing predictions, only 56 per cent of the responses favor the relational predictions and 44 per cent the specific stimulus hypothesis. This small differential, however, is probably not representative of the true difference. It is especially questionable when it is noted that in the next set of test stimuli involving gray no. 4, where the two theories also make opposing predictions, the difference jumps to 74 per cent versus 26 per cent in favor of relational responding.

The lack of a significant differential in the first case seems to result from the difficulty of the discriminations involved in this set of tests. As can be seen from the logarithmic values for the reflectances in Table 1, the differences between grays no. 4 and no. 5 and between no. 6 and no. 7 are small as compared with the others. These two pairs of grays were the ones that gave results most opposed to the relational hypothesis, as shown in Table 2. This latter table also indicates two trends that lowered the percentage of relational responding. First, it indicates that when there was only one unit difference in brightness between the top and bottom half of a test stimulus, relational responding was reduced, suggesting that the grays employed were not spaced properly along the continuum for the most sensitive test of transposition. Secondly, it is evident that when the bottom half of a test card was gray no. 7, the darkest gray, relational responding was minimal. This gray has the same reflectance as the flat black used to paint the entire jumping stand. This suggests the possibility that as one of the grays on the card becomes very similar to the background gray, this similarity may dominate the response and mask the perception of the difference in brightness of the two grays on the card. In a sense the darker gray is amalgamated with the background so that relationship is obscured. If this hypothesis is correct, then this breakdown of relational responding on the dark grays should not have occurred if the background had consisted of stripes or some other distinct pattern.

Although the evidence from this experiment indicates that Ss were responding to the relational aspects of the stimulus situation, this does not imply that this mode of responding is more basic or fundamental than responding to the absolute or particular characteristics of the situation. Certainly the evidence to date indicates that the particular aspects can be the determining factor in behavior in many situations. Rather, this study indicates that when these particular aspects are minimized as reliable cues for behavior in a given training situation, and the relational properties are emphasized, S is perfectly capable of responding to the latter.

It does suggest, also, that even in situations where S is presumably reacting to an absolute characteristic, behavior may be in part determined by the relation between this characteristic and the background stimuli. For instance in the usual successive discrimination involving black and white, this discrimination presumably would be easier to learn if the apparatus were painted a neutral gray than if it were either black or white. In the former case, the differential relations of "lighter than" and "darker than" between the two stimuli and the background should facilitate learning whereas these differential relationships would be lacking if the background was either white or black. The fact that these Ss could discriminate the stimuli 3/4 and 5/4 during original training but were unable to discriminate between grays no. 3 and no. 5 during the posttest training supports this suggestion.

Acceptance of these results as evidence for the perception of, and response to, relationships suggests an alternative interpretation of those studies in which a correlation between mental age and amount of transposition behavior has been shown (1, 3). Usually these studies have been interpreted as evidence that the specific stimulus theories are correct, but that somehow the development of language responses permits more widespread transposition. The present study suggests this alternative. Children can respond relationally prior to the development of language, but do not necessarily do so in all situations. However, the very factors that lead to the development of language behavior also lead to an emphasis on relational responding as the dominant mode of behavior in the child. The result is a correlation between the rate at which language and relational responding develop.

The technique used in the present experiment should be equally applicable to studies of transposition phenomena involving size, form, or like dimensions. It would appear also to have advantages in the study of brightness thresholds. The rate of learning seems to be almost as great as on the usual simultaneous discrimination. At the same time much sharper contrasts between the two brightnesses can be obtained when both are on the same card than when they are spatially separated by the division between the two windows. Therefore, more sensitive measures of differential brightness thresholds should be obtained.

Summary

Eleven albino rats were trained in a new type of transposition situation. The procedure consisted of training Ss on a successive discrimination in which each stimulus card consisted of two grays, one brightness on the top half and a different one on the bottom half. When the top half was lighter than the bottom half, Ss jumped to the right window, and when the top half was darker than the bottom half, they jumped to the left window. When this discrimination had been mastered, Ss were tested on a set of 24 new relationships of this type. These were so selected that in 6 of them both a relational theory and a specific stimulus theory of transposition would make the same prediction, in 12 they would make opposing predictions, and in 6 the relational theory could make an unambiguous prediction whereas the specific stimulus theory could not.

1. For the entire set of 24 test stimuli, 80 per cent of the choices were as predicted by the relational theory.

2. For the set of six on which the two theories make the same prediction, 94 per cent of the choices were in agreement with them.

3. For the set of 12 on which the two theories make opposing predictions, 65 per cent of the choices were as predicted by the relational theory.

4. For the set of six on which only the relational theory could make an unambiguous prediction, 95 per cent of the choices were in this direction.

5. It is suggested that this technique should prove valuable in the study of other forms of transposition behavior and in the study of differential brightness thresholds.

Notes

[1] This study was supported in part by a research grant from the Behavioral Sciences Division of the Ford Foundation.

References

1. Alberts, Elizabeth, & Eiirenfreund, D. Transposition in children as a function of age. *J. Exp. Psychol.*, 1951, **41**, 30–38.

2. Köhler, W. *Gestalt psychology.* New York: Liveright, 1929.

3. Kuenne, Margaret R. Experimental investigation of the relation of language to transposition behavior in young children. *J. Exp. Psychol.*, 1946, **36**, 471–490.

4. Spence, K. W. The differential response in animals to stimuli varying within a single dimension. *Psychol. Rev.*, 1937, **44**, 430–444.

B. COMPLEX NATURAL CONCEPTS

When organisms learn operant discriminations, they are learning to focus on the property or properties of the discriminative stimuli that are actually predictive of reinforcement. Any stimulus has multiple properties. A red key light has a brightness, a size, a shape, and a location, as well as a color. But in learning a red–green discrimination, a pigeon learns to ignore brightness, size, and so on. We might say that because color is the predictive property of the stimulus, the stimulus comes to be defined on the basis of color.

Once this focus on color has occurred, other stimuli that are also red, but different in size, shape, and brightness from the red key, may be treated as functionally equivalent to the red key. All red stimuli might be put into a single class. This classification process is analogous to what people do when they form concepts. When we form a concept of "square," we put all objects that meet the definitional requirements of that concept into a single class and ignore a host of differences among members of that class. The possibility that operant discrimination learning might be a model of the formation of concepts has stimulated much research on human concept learning over the years (for example, Bruner et al., 1956).

But how many of our everyday concepts have definitional properties like "square" does? What defines a tool, furniture, or a game? It has been suggested in recent years that most human concepts do not have definitions; instead, these natural concepts *may be organized around a few prototypical examples or a set of properties, many of which are possessed by many of their examples (see Smith and Medin, 1981).*

Can animals learn these types of nondefinitional natural concepts in operant discrimination experiments? The answer is yes. Pigeons have been trained to respond to pictures of water, trees, and people as discriminative stimuli, though there was no single property that all such pictures shared. Not only could they learn these discriminations, but they seemed to learn them faster than presumably simpler discriminations like those between horizontal and vertical lines. And once they learned, they performed almost perfectly when presented with novel pictures of trees or water (Herrnstein, 1979; Herrnstein et al., 1976). The article by Lubow provides an example of the learning of a nondefinitional concept. Pigeons had to discriminate slides containing man-made objects from slides without such objects. They had little difficulty learning the discrimination. Think, as you read the paper, about what property or properties define man-made objects.

As in the case of the previous article, the importance of the demonstration that pigeons can acquire concepts like this is that it points to the need for understanding how organisms perceive and organize environmental inputs.

29 High-Order Concept Formation in the Pigeon

ROBERT E. LUBOW

After 30 days of operant training, with pecking responses to aerial photographs containing man-made objects reinforced with food, and no food reinforcement for pecking on photographs not containing man-made objects, a discrimination to the two classes of photographs was obtained. The discriminative response generalized to photographs with which the pigeons had no previous experience. This study demonstrates that pigeons are capable of forming relatively high-order concepts. Some possible stimulus properties controlling the discrimination are discussed.[1]

When an organism gives the same response to a set of stimuli varying on a particular dimension, but not to other stimuli that lack that stimulus dimension, that behavior is said to be an example of concept formation. It has long been recognized that animals are capable of forming simple concepts, i.e., where the stimulus dimension is easily specifiable.

As pointed out by Malott and Siddall (1972), the concepts include: size (Klüver, 1933), color (Weinstein, 1945), triangularity (Andrews and Harlow, 1948), numbers (Hicks, 1956), novelty (Brown, Overall, and Gentry, 1958; Brown, Overall, and Blodgett, 1959), patterns (Kelleher, 1958), guided missile targets (Skinner, 1960), bad parts on an assembly line (Verhave, 1966), and matching (Malott, 1969; Malott and Malott, 1970). In addition, it has been shown that dogs can be trained to respond to certain classes of explosives and tunnels (Carr-Harris and Thal, 1969).

More recently, the work on concept formation in animals has been extended to more complex stimulus dimensions, ones that the experimenter cannot specify in stimulus terms but are nevertheless highly reliable classifications on the basis of object qualities. In particular, several recent papers have reported on the ability of pigeons to form high-order abstract visual concepts (Herrnstein and Loveland, 1964; Malott and Siddall, 1972; Siegel and Honig, 1970). These studies examined the ability of the pigeon to discriminate between the class of visual images described as containing a person and another class characterized by the absence of a person.

The present study was designed to investigate the ability of pigeons to form concepts more complex than that of human *versus* nonhumans; namely, to discriminate between photographs containing man-made objects and those containing no man-made objects.

Method

The apparatus employed was similar to that described by Ludlow and Stevens (1964). The main components included a sound-attenuated com-

"High-Order Concept Formation in the Pigeon" by Robert E. Lubow. *Journal of the Experimental Analysis of Behavior*, 1974, *21*, 475–483. Copyright 1974 by the Society for the Experimental Analysis of Behavior, Inc. Reprinted by permission of the publisher and author.

partment, a food hopper, a pecking key onto which stimuli were back-projected, a sound source, a 35-mm slide projector with a circular magazine, scheduling equipment, and a numerical printout recorder. The hopper delivered grain when the pigeon made a correct key-pecking response. An auditory signal (1200 Hz, 72 dB at 2 ft) followed an incorrect key-pecking response.

The following four scheduled contingencies were in effect throughout the experiment: (1) If the subject pecked the positive slide within 2 sec from onset, the food hopper was presented. The hopper and slide remained on for a total of 1.5 sec from the time of response and were then followed by the next slide. (2) When the subject did not respond to the positive slide, the slide remained on the key for 2 sec and was then followed by the next slide. (3) If the subject pecked the negative slide within 2 sec from onset, the tone was presented. The tone and slide remained on for a total of 6 sec from the time of response and were then followed by the next slide. (4) When the subject did not respond to the negative slide, the slide remained on the key for 2 sec and was then followed by the next slide. A correct response was either pecking a positive slide or not pecking a negative slide. Conversely, an incorrect response was either pecking a negative slide or not pecking a positive slide.

The slides were of two different sets, one containing man-made objects (positive slides) and the other containing no man-made objects (negative slides). All were black and white aerial photographs. The positive slides included cities, highways, plowed fields, and orchards. The negative slides included natural terrain under various conditions, mountains, canyons, forests, and water. The photographs were obtained from several different books and varied in altitude, brightness, angle of regard, *etc.* It was assumed that the only consistent difference between these two sets of photographs was along the dimension(s) relevant to this study.

The subjects were four experimentally naive male White Carneaux pigeons, approximately 2 yr old. They were reduced to 80% of their normal baseline weight and then trained to peck at the key when it was illuminated. When this response became stable, 80 slides were introduced, 40 positive and 40 negative. The pigeon received three runs of the 80 slides each day in the same order of presentation. Acquisition training continued for 30 days.

To test for generalization, 10 new slides (five positive and five negative) replaced 10 acquisition slides on the thirty-first day. These new slides were randomly placed within the original series of 80. Each pigeon received two presentations of this series.

Since the slides were always presented in the same order during acquisition, a test for serial position effects was necessary. On the thirty-second day, the order of presentation of the original 80 acquisition slides was changed. This order continued for six days. On the thirty-eighth day, a new test for generalization was given. Again, 10 new slides replaced 10 acquisition slides, being randomly placed in the series previously presented. On the thirty-ninth day, a second test of serial position was given. This was similar to the first test except that the slides were arranged in a new order. This new order was presented for one day only.

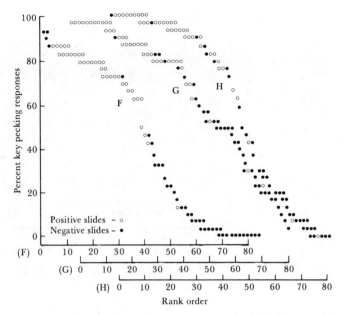

FIG 1. *Percentage of key-pecking responses to individual slides over the last 10 days of acquisition. Abscissas are displaced in order to present the data for individual subjects.*

Results

Performance of one of the four pigeons did not improve during the initial training or during any of the following tests. Data from this bird are not included in the results. However, the remaining three pigeons did discriminate between the two sets of slides. Figure I shows the percentage of key-pecking responses to each slide over the last 10 days of acquisition training. This represents the percentage of correct key-pecking responses to the positive slides and the percentage of incorrect responses to the negative slides. For example, in the case of Pigeon F, only two slides containing no man-made objects (negative) were pecked at more than 50% of the time, and five slides containing man-made objects (positive) were pecked at less than 50% of the time. For this graph and the succeeding ones, the slides were rank-ordered for number of responses. The percentage of responses was plotted as a function of the rank order. A perfect score on all 80 slides would result in two parallel lines maximally displaced, one high for the 40 positive slides and one low for the next 40 negative slides. These graphs clearly show a difference in the number of responses to the two sets of slides. A few slides were responded to incorrectly most of the time. These slides were, generally, the same slides for the three pigeons.

Figure 2 represents the percentage of responses to each slide for the combined first and second serial position tests. Only the data from the first day of the first test and the first day of the second test were used. The data show that the two sets of slides were responded to differentially,

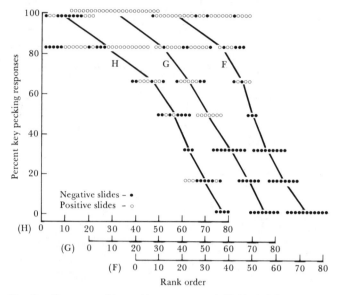

FIG. 2.   *Percentage of key-pecking responses to individual slides over both the first and second serial position tests. Abscissas are displaced in order to present the data for individual subjects.*

thus ruling out the possibility that the pigeons were learning the serial presentation of the slides. Most of the slides responded to incorrectly were again the same for all three pigeons, and the same ones that were responded to incorrectly during the initial training.

The results of the two generalization tests are shown in Fig. 3. The separation of the two sets of slides on the basis of the number of responses is not as clear as in the preceding graphs, and a statistical analysis (χ^2 test for one sample) was run on these data. The results of two of the pigeons, G and H, were significant ($p < 0.05$). The third pigeon, F, did not do as well ($p < 0.15$), although the results for its first generalization test were significant ($p < 0.05$).

All training and testing then ceased for 52 days, although the subjects remained on a food deprivation schedule. Following this period, acquisition training was resumed, followed by new tests for serial position effect and generalization. The generalization tests were performed with new stimuli. The results of this replication were comparable to that of the first experiment. The three subjects reacquired the discrimination between man-made and non-man-made stimuli, the discrimination was not based on serial position effects, and the discrimination generalized to new stimuli.

Discussion

The present results indicate that pigeons are capable of discriminating higher-order visual stimuli. They apparently discriminated successfully between photographs containing man-made objects and those containing no man-made objects. It would seem that they isolated one or more stimulus properties common to photographs of man-made objects. From quite

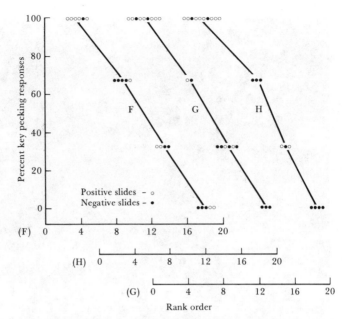

FIG. 3. *Percentage of key-pecking responses to individual slides over both the first and second generalization tests. Abscissas are displaced in order to present the data for individual subjects.*

another point of view in psychology, it may be of interest to determine the invariant stimulus properties that the bird extracted (*cf.* Gibson, 1966).

Figures 4 and 5 display some representative samples of the photographs used. Figure 4 is a selection of photographs, containing man-made objects, to which the pigeons reliably responded. Items j, k, and l were taken from the generalization tests, the remainder from acquisition. Figure 5 is a selection of photographs, containing no man-made objects, to which the pigeons reliably did not respond. Items v, w, and x were taken from the generalization tests, the remainder from acquisition.

By examining separately all those slides that the birds responded to significantly and that they avoided significantly, several hypotheses were induced to account for the stimulus basis of the discrimination. These hypotheses were:

I_p. The pigeons responded to slides containing the presence (p) of straight lines and/or approximately 90° angles.

II_p. The pigeons responded to slides that contain all of the following characteristics—light and dark areas distributed throughout the slides, high contrast between the light and dark areas, and approximately half of the total area of the slides being light, and half dark.

III_p. The pigeons operated under both Hypothesis I and Hypothesis II.

The converse of each of these hypotheses must also be considered, *e.g.*, not responding is under control of the absence (a) of straight lines and/or approximately 90° angles. To test each of the hypotheses, the 100 slides from acquisition and the two generalization tests were segregated

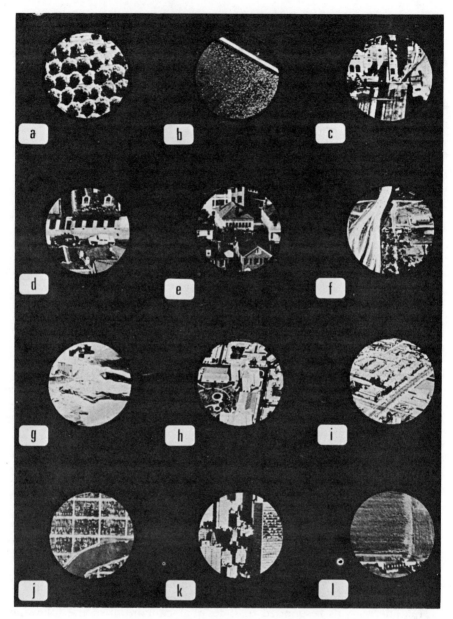

FIG. 4.   *A selection of slides with man-made objects.*

on the basis of whether or not the slide was responded to on 70% or more of the trials. This was done separately for each bird. A similar procedure was followed for not responding on 70% or more of the trials. This division was done independently of whether the slide was positive or negative. Therefore, a small number of the false positives and false negatives are included in each sample. Following this, an independent ob-

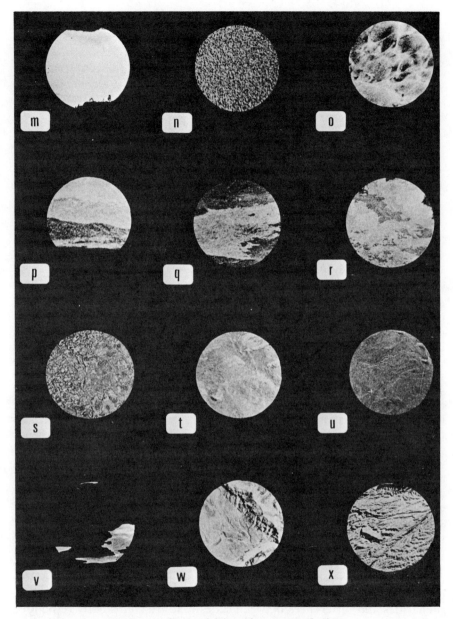

FIG. 5. *A selection of slides with no man-made objects.*

server, not knowing anything about the experiment, was given the description of the hypothetical properties to which the birds were responding, and asked to indicate the presence or absence of each property in photographs similar to Figs. 4 and 5, but ungrouped.[2] The correspondence of his judgement with that of the birds' responding is shown in Table 1.

TABLE 1. Per cent of Correspondence between Each of Six Stimulus Control Hypotheses and Responding for Three Subjects

Subject	A Number of slides responded to 70% or more	Per cent of A accounted for by hypotheses			Per cent of A unaccounted for
		I_p	II_p	III_p	
F	44	84	40	29	2
G	54	72	37	24	8
H	53	72	43	26	6
	Number of slides not responded to 70% or more	I_a	II_a	III_a	Per cent of A unaccounted for
F	37	89	97	86	0
G	17	94	100	94	0
H	31	93	100	93	0

Table 1 answers the question of what percentage of the slides that were responded to consistently had a particular stimulus characteristic. Thus, it is clear that of the two major hypotheses concerning the control of key-pecking responses, Hypothesis I_p, concerning the presence of straight lines and/or right angles, is the more potent. However, by itself, it still does not account for 16 to 28% of the slides to which the birds responded. With the addition of Hypotheses II_p, only 2% to 8% of the slides remain unaccounted. It should be noted that there is not a considerable overlap between I_p and II_p; either one may occur in the absence of the other. The figures under column III_p, fairly low, indicate that although the presence of either I_p or II_p can control behavior, the presence of both is not a necessary condition.

An analysis of the stimulus conditions controlling not responding yields a somewhat similar picture. The major difference is that the absence of either the stimulus properties of I and II are highly correlated, and that either I_a or II_a is an excellent predictor for not responding.

More work is needed to refine the hypotheses still further into more exact physicalistic terms. The approach used in the present experiment may provide a method for determining invariant properties of complex stimuli. At the very least, it provides a method for generating existence theorems for the presence of such higher-order stimuli, and at best it may provide the data for inducing what these properties are. By studying the similarities and differences between slides that are consistently responded to incorrectly and those that are consistently responded to correctly, one can construct testable hypotheses concerning the invariant stimulus properties in the complex images. Although this proposed inductive method for studying invariant properties is conceptually simple, experience has shown that the rocks of empiricism require the perseverance of Sisyphus.

Notes
[1] This work was supported by Air Force Contract 33(615)-2301 and NIH Grants MH 80731 and K3 MH 7189. Portions of this paper were presented at the 1966 Bionics Sym-

posium, Dayton, Ohio. This paper is based on work previously published but unavailable to most readers (Lubow, Siebert, & Carr-Harris, 1966).

[2] An additional two raters were used afterwards to check on the reliability of the judgments. It was found to be almost perfect.

References

Andrew, G., and Harlow, H. F. Performance of macaque monkeys on a test of generalized triangularity. *Comparative Psychology Monographs*, 1948, **19**, 1–20.

Brown, W. L., Overall, J. E., and Gentry, G. V. Conceptual discrimination in rhesus monkeys. *Journal of Comparative and Physiological Psychology*, 1958, **51**, 701–705.

Brown, W. L., Overall, J. E., and Blodgett, H. C. Novelty learning sets in rhesus monkeys. *Journal of Comparative and Physiological Psychology*, 1959, **52**, 330.

Carr-Harris, E., and Thal, R. Mine, booby-trap, trip-wire and tunnel detection dogs: final report. *U. S. Army Limited War Laboratory, Technical Report*. July, 1969, Contract No. DAAD 05-68-C-0236.

Gibson, J. J. *The senses considered as perceptual systems.* Boston: Houghton Mifflin, 1966.

Herrnstein, R. J., and Loveland, D. H. Complex visual concept in the pigeon. *Science*, 1964, **146**, 549–551.

Hicks, L. H. An analysis of number-concept formation in the rhesus monkey. *Journal of Comparative and Physiological Psychology*, 1956, **49**, 212–218.

Kelleher, R. Concept formation in chimpanzees. *Science*, 1958, **128**, 777–779.

Klüver, H. *Behavior mechanisms in monkeys.* Chicago, Ill.: University of Chicago Press, 1933.

Lubow, R. E., and Stevens, E. A technique for automatic, recycled, serial presentation of up to 80 unique visual stimuli. *Journal of the Experimental Analysis of Behavior*, 1964, **7**, 50.

Lubow, R. E., Siebert, L. E., and Carr-Harris, E. The perception of high order variables by the pigeon. *Technical Report* AFAL-TR-66-63. Air Force Avionics Laboratory, March 1966.

Malott, R. W. Perception revisited. *Perceptual and Motor Skills*, 1969, **28**, 683–693.

Malott, R. W., and Malott, M. K. Perception and stimulus generalization. In W. C. Stebbins (Ed.). *Animal psychophysics.* New York: Appleton-Century-Crofts, 1970. Pp. 363–400.

Malott, R. W., and Siddall, J. W. Acquisition of the people concept in pigeons. *Psychological Reports*, 1972, **31**, 3–13.

Siegel, R. K., and Honig, W. K. Pigeon concept formation: Successive and simultaneous acquisition. *Journal of the Experimental Analysis of Behavior*, 1970, **13**, 385–390.

Skinner, B. F. Pigeons in a pelican. *American Psychologist*, 1960, **15**, 28–37.

Verhave, T. The pigeon as a quality control inspector. In R. Ulrich, T. Stachnik, and J. Mabry (Eds.), *Control of human behavior.* Glenview: Scott Foresman, 1966. Pp. 242–246.

Weinstein, B. The evolution of intelligent behavior in rhesus monkeys. *Genetic Psychology Monographs*, 1945, **31**, 3–48.

C. COGNITIVE MAPS

When a rat is trained to navigate through a maze for food, what does it learn? Does it develop a sequence of muscle movements that lead it from the start box to the goal or does it learn the maze? Years ago behavior theorists argued about this issue, with some claiming that organisms built up cognitive maps—spatial representations of the experimental environment (for example, Tolman, 1948). Recently the issue has resurfaced, with clear evidence that in learning to run in a maze, rats build up a representation of its spatial organization (Olton, 1979; Olton and Samuelson, 1976). The article by Menzel provides a striking demonstration of the development of cognitive maps. Chimpanzees were carried in a circuitous route through the compound in which they lived, as the experimenter deposited food in various hiding places. When set free to find the food, the chimpanzees followed routes that were extremely efficient, minimizing travel time from place to place. These routes bore no relation to the routes they had traveled when the food was being deposited. The seemingly inescapable conclusion is that as the chimpanzees watched the food being hidden, "they placed little X's on their cognitive maps." When later seeking the food, they consulted these maps to determine the most efficient routes to travel.

The existence of cognitive maps is another indication of the importance of cognitive mediation. Such maps allowed the chimpanzees to impose an order or structure on the inputs they experienced, and this structure subsequently governed their behavior. We could not understand their behavior just from knowing about the inputs they experienced. Knowing how those inputs were represented is essential.

30 Chimpanzee Spatial Memory Organization

EMIL W. MENZEL

Juvenile chimpanzees, carried around an outdoor field and shown up to 18 randomly placed hidden foods, remembered most of these hiding places and the type of food that was in each. Their search pattern approximated an optimum routing, and they rarely rechecked a place they had already emptied of food.

This report describes the performance of young chimpanzees in a delayed response variation on the "traveling salesman" combinatorial problem (1, 2). In other applied sciences this problem is: Given the positions of several places on a scaled map, find the routing that will take you to all of these places with the shortest mileage. Here, the problem is: If a chimpanzee has in the past seen the locations of several hidden objects in a field, how does he manage to get to them again, and how does he organize his travel route? What does his itinerary tell us about the nature of his "cognitive mapping," his strategy, and his criteria of "efficiency" (3, 4)?

Six wild-born chimpanzees, 5 to 7 years old, were tested in the outdoor enclosure (30.5 by 122 m) in which they had lived as a group for more than a year. Their previous formal test experience (5) did not include delayed response tests involving multiple hidden goals; one animal (Bido) had had fewer than ten prior trials of any delayed response testing.

Before a trial began, all six animals were locked in a release cage on the periphery of the field. Then one experimenter took out a previously selected test animal and carried him about the field, accompanying a second experimenter who hid one piece of fruit in each of 18 randomly selected sectors of the field. Throughout this 10-minute process, the animal was not permitted to do anything other than cling to his carrier and watch the baiter; thus, primary reinforcement and locomotor practice during the information-gathering phase of a trial were eliminated (6).

After being shown the foods, the chimpanzee was returned to the group. The experimenters left the field, ascended an observation tower, and, within 2 minutes, pulled a cable that opened the release cage door. All six animals were released simultaneously and were free to roam. The five animals who had not been shown the food on a particular trial had no way to find the food other than through guesswork or cues such as odor, the behavior of the test animal, and inadvertent cues from the experimenters; thus, they served as controls for factors other than visual memory. The emotional dependence of the animals on each other precluded the possibility of testing each animal alone.

On a map that showed the location of each piece of food, the experimenters recorded the time at which each food pile was found or re-

"Chimpanzee Spatial Memory Organization" by Emil W. Menzel. *Science*, 1973, *182*, 943–945. Copyright 1973 by the American Association for the Advancement of Science. Reprinted by permission of the publisher and author.

checked, and the identity of the animal involved. In addition, qualitative notes were made on behavior related to the search. Observation continued for at least 1 hour.

One trial was given each day for 16 days. Belle, Bandit, Bido, and Gigi each served as test animals on 4 trials and as control animals on the remaining 12 trials. Shadow and Polly were controls on all trials. On each trial the experimenters followed a different path and used a different set of 18 hiding places (7).

The animal that had been shown the food found a total of 200 pieces (12.5 per trial); the animals serving as controls found a total of 17 (0.21 per animal per trial). Usually, the test animal ran unerringly and in a direct line to the exact clump of grass or leaves, tree stump, or hole in the ground where a hidden food lay, grabbed the food, stopped briefly to eat, and then ran directly to the next place, no matter how distant or obscured by visual barriers that place was (8). His pace slowed as more and more food was obtained, and eventually he lay down for long rests; but he never wandered around the field as if conducting a general search. Control animals obtained food principally by searching around the test animal or begging from him directly. Only in four instances did a test animal manually search the ground more than 2 m from a food pile, as controls did on an uncountable number of occasions. It would seem that the major cue of food location was visual memory, and that the test animal did more than merely recognize each hiding place on the basis of local cues once he chanced to pass by that place.

Figure 1 shows each test animal's performance on the trial on which he found the largest number of foods. Each animal proceeded more or less in accordance with at "least distance" principle (9, 10), and with no regard for the pathway along which the experimenters had carried him. On the average, the itinerary of a given trial was only 64 percent as long as the mean of all possible $N!$ itineraries on that trial, and none of the 16 trials exceeded its chance-expected value (11). Extensive baseline data on the animals under routine nontest conditions indicate that the routes shown in Fig. 1 would be very unlikely if no animal had been shown the food. In fact, once they were habituated to the enclosure, the animals rarely traveled across it in an hour without some special incentive.

A second experiment tested whether the chimpanzees could remember the type of hidden food as well as its location. The same test procedure and animals were used, but now 9 of the 18 food piles contained a piece of nonpreferred food, vegetable, and 9 contained a piece of preferred food, fruit. The four test animals received three trials each.

The results were similar to those of the first experiment, except that on most trials the preference for fruit and the "least distance" strategy were additive determiners of choice. For example, in the first 9 responses of her first trial, Belle took 9 fruits (F) to 0 vegetables (V); Bandit, 7F to 2V; Bido, 7F to 2V; and Gigi, 4F to 5V; most of the remaining foods were taken later. (Only Gigi's preference for fruit on trial 1 was not significant by median test; and on subsequent trials she "corrected" this.) If the itinerary to fruits and the itinerary to vegetables are considered separately, each showed a fair "least distance" pattern.

It is unlikely that all 18 places were taken into account simultaneously

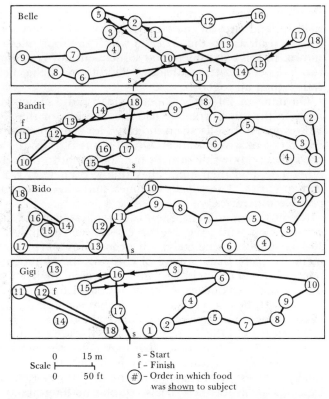

Fig. 1. *Maps showing each test animal's performance on the trial (out of four) on which he found the largest number of hidden foods in experiment 1. The connecting line gives an exact picture of the order in which the various places were searched, and a rough idea of the animal's general travel routes. (If the line touches a point, that point was searched.) Ecological details such as trees are omitted for clarity.*

at all times throughout a trial in these two experiments. On several occasions a test animal actually stepped on one pile of food on his way to another, and then, sometimes 10 minutes later, returned for it. Also, on several trials, a striking example of sudden recall occurred while an animal was apparently asleep. After having eaten many pieces of food and lain supine with his eyes closed for up to 30 minutes, the test animal suddenly jumped to his feet and ran 10 to 30 m straight to a hidden piece of food.

In only 11 instances (range 0 to 5 per animal) in these two experiments did a chimpanzee recheck a place that he had already emptied of food; thus, either memory of specific places was erased once reinforcement occurred, or the chimpanzees remembered where they had already been on trial. Places that had already been emptied by another animal were, however, often rechecked.

A third experiment examined with a less complicated procedure the relative importance of "place" cues and "response" and route cues *(3, 4, 6)*. The same test procedure and animals were used, but now only four food piles were shown on a particular trial, two on the left third of the field, 1, and two on the right third, r. The exact locations varied from trial to trial, as did the order in which the four piles (l_1, l_2, r_1, r_2,) were shown. In this experiment and subsequent ones the animals were tested in two independent trios (Shadow, Bandit, and Belle; Polly, Bido, and Gigi) rather than all together.

On none of 28 trials (7 per animal) did a chimpanzee go to the four foods in the same order we had shown them, or the reverse of that order. However, the results again indicated an acute memory of places and perception of relative distances. On all but two trials, the animals cleaned out both piles on one side of the cage, then went to the other two piles on the other side, and then quit. They followed an 1, 1, r, r sequence 14 times and an r, r, 1, 1 sequence 12 times, and often used the shortest of all 24 possible itineraries.

A fourth experiment essentially replicated these last results on travel organization while the use of cues other than distant vision were restricted almost completely. All procedures were the same as in experiment 3 except that, instead of carrying the chimpanzee about the field, one experimenter held the animal directly in front of the release cage door while a second experimenter walked from one predesignated place to the next, held a piece of fruit aloft at each place, and dropped it in the grass. (It was not covered up further and was ordinarily visible from a few meters.) On the 13 trials in which the animals went to all four places, there were only three times that they failed to follow an 1, 1, r, r or an r, r, 1, 1 sequence of travel. (The remaining 11 trials on which one or more foods was missed indicate some loss of information by comparison with experiment 3; but these trials tell one nothing about the principal question of how an itinerary between four points is organized.)

It remains possible that in the preceding tests the chimpanzees failed to take into account several places at the start of a trial, and instead recognized one of the nearest available places, went to it, looked about, recognized another goal location that was close to their present position, went to it; and so on. Therefore, we conducted a fifth experiment. It differed from experiment 3 in only one detail: two pieces of food were hidden on one third of the field, and three pieces were hidden on the opposite third of the field. On the null hypothesis, one would expect no preference for going first to the side with three pieces.

Figure 2 shows the results of each animal's first four trials. On 13 of 16 trials the chimpanzees went first to the side with the larger clustering of food. Thus, in addition to following a "least distance" strategy, they maximized the rate of food acquisition. In subsequent trials, the first-choice selection of the side with three foods declined slightly; but the overall results remain better than chance.

In summary, the chimpanzees appeared to directly perceive the relative positions of selected classes of objects and their own position in this scaled frame of reference (12). They proceeded on the strategy, Do as well as you can from wherever you are (2), taking into account the relative preference values and spatial clusterings of the foods as well as distances. If locomotor practice or primary reinforcement were necessary at all, it was before the experiments began—which renders these variables of greater

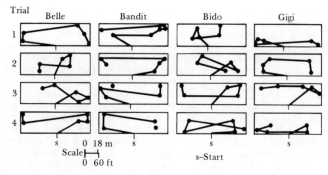

FIG. 2. *Maps showing each test animal's first four trials in experiment 5. The connecting line gives an exact picture of the order in which the various places were searched and a rough idea of the animal's general travel routes. Since the release cage was not in the center of the* X *axis, and we wished to avoid biasing right or left positions, no food was placed to the extreme end of the longer (right) side. This portion of the field is not shown on these maps.*

developmental than structural interest *(13)*. Although it is unlikely that the animals "sorted over" all *N!* possible routes before making their first move, or that "space" as they perceived it can be compared literally to a picture on a piece of paper, their achievements are a good first approximation of those at which an applied scientist would arrive from his real maps, algorithms, and a priori criteria of efficiency. Mentalistic terms such as "cognitive mapping" do not necessarily explain the above facts, but they predict them accurately and describe them succinctly. Especially in the light of other recent research *(5, 14)*, one is struck again by the parallels between chimpanzee and human behavior, the necessity for including representational processes in any adequate formulation of learning and memory, and the apparent evolutionary independence of representational ability and verbal language.

References
1. P. Haggett, *Locational Analysis in Human Geography* (St. Martin's, New York, 1966), p. 66.
2. H. A. Simon, *The Sciences of the Artificial* (M.I.T. Press, Cambridge, Mass., 1969), p. 64.
3. H. C. Tolman, *Psychol. Rev.* **55**, 189 (1948).
4. F. Restle, *ibid.* **64**, 217 (1957).
5. E. W. Menzel, in *Behavior of Nonhuman Primates,* A. M. Schrier and F. Stollnitz, Eds. (Academic Press, New York, in press), vol. 5.
6. C. H. Gleitman, *J. Comp. Physiol. Psychol.* **48**, 77 (1955).
7. To choose paths completely at random in this experiment and the next one would have meant carrying a heavy and sometimes wiggly animal many hundreds of meters. Therefore we initially used routes of the sort shown in Fig. 1, and deferred complete randomization until experiments 3 to 5, which used fewer pieces of food. The food locations for a particular trial were determined to the first approximation by three adjacent columns of a table of random permutations; the first column designated the *Y* axis (which was divided into nine units on the data maps) and the other two columns designated the *X* axis (which was divided into 39 units on the data maps). Within any one of these 351 sectors we selected the exact hiding place on the basis of available natural cover and, if possible, avoided using the same type of cover (for instance, grass clumps) more than a few times in one trial or the same exact place more than once in an experiment. The same location selection procedure

was used for experiment 2, but for experiments 3 to 5 some sectors were not used, as explained in the text.

8. If food was not located within 5 m of a distinctive landmark (such as a tree), the chimpanzees more often slowed down when they came within a few meters, and visually scanned the ground. In all of these experiments the animals' most common error was to search a grass clump, dead branch, or other features that looked (to us) almost precisely like the correct hiding place, and was within a few meters of it. I would speculate that, like human beings, the chimpanzees used a hierachy of visually perceived object-relations for determining an exact location. In the cue-giving phase of the experiment, one initially had the impression that they did not even attend to the food (unless it was held up to their mouth). Instead, they glanced once at the hiding place and then looked up toward a tree or around the field, as if to first locate the position of food relative to a local cue and then locate the position of that local cue with respect to some landmark or the field in general.

9. E. C. Tolman, *Purposive Behavior in Animals and Men* (Appleton-Century-Crofts, New York, 1932), pp. 101–142.

10. G. K. Zipf, *Human Behavior and the Principle of Least Effort* (Addison-Wesley, Cambridge, Mass., 1949).

11. Because of the labor involved in calculating the mean length of all possible itineraries on each trial with simple distances, I used mean quadratic distances instead [R. Bachi, *Reg. Sci. Assoc. Pap.* **10**, 83 (1963)].

12. These are the usual criteria of "cognitive mapping" *(3, 9)*; see also K. Z. Lorenz's "central representation of space" [in *Studies in Animal and Human Behavior* (Harvard Univ. Press, Cambridge, Mass., 1971), vol. 2, p. 217] and J. J. Gibson's "direct perception of structure" [in *The Senses Considered as Perceptual Systems* (Houghton Mifflin, Boston, 1966), pp. 266–280].

13. A. C. Catania, *Amer. Psychol.* **28**, 434 (1973).

14. R. K. Davenport and C. M. Rogers, *Science* **168**, 279 (1970); *Behavior* **39**, 318 (1971); G. G. Gallup, *Science* **167**, 86 (1970); R. A. Gardner and B. T. Gardner, *ibid.* **165**, 664 (1969); D. Premack, *ibid.* **172**, 808 (1971); P. H. Lindsay and D. A. Norman, *Human Information Processing* (Academic Press, New York, 1972).

15. Data were collected at the Delta Regional Primate Research Center, Tulane University, Covington, La, with support of grant FR-00164 from the National Institutes of Health, and written up at the State University of New York, Stony Brook, with support of grants GU 3850 and BO 38791 from the National Science Foundation. I thank Stewart Halperin and Palmer Midgett, who performed most of the testing.

D. INSIGHTFUL PROBLEM-SOLVING

Thorndike's law of effect told us that learning was a trial-and-error process. Behavior occurred in essentially random fashion, and only those responses that were successful (produced reinforcement) continued to occur. The intelligence that seemed to characterize behavior was actually the result of the selective action of the environment.

The law of effect is certainly one way for organisms to develop effective behavioral repertoires. But think how much more effective they could be if some of that trial and error occurred internally. Rather than actually expending the time and effort to make responses in attempts to secure reinforcements, organisms could imagine making a response and size up its likely consequence. By forming internal representations of responses and possible consequences and then manipulating these representations, a great deal of actual trial and error could be spared.

An early major critic of behavior theory, Wolfgang Köhler (1887–1967), argued that at least some of the time learning was like this. He demonstrated that chimpanzees could solve problems without going through a fumbling trial-and-error process. They seemed to sit back, sizing up the situation, and then arrive, by insight, at a satisfactory solution to the problem (Köhler, 1925). The article by Premack and Woodruff provides a striking example of insightful problem-solving, one that is even more remarkable than Köhler's; for in the Premack–Woodruff experiment, chimpanzees view videotapes of humans facing problems and then are able to choose pictures that represent the correct solutions to the problems. If the chimpanzees' performance involves trial and error, it is clearly of the internal variety. They demonstrate the ability to represent a problem and its possible solutions and then to manipulate these representations to arrive at the correct answer.

31 Chimpanzee Problem-Solving: A Test for Comprehension

DAVID PREMACK AND GUY WOODRUFF

An adult chimpanzee was shown videotaped scenes of a human actor struggling with one of eight problems and was then shown two photographs, one of which depicted an action or an object (or both) that could constitute a solution to the problem. On seven of the eight problems, the animal consistently chose the correct photograph. This test of problem-solving comprehension permits the animal's knowledge about problem-solving—its ability to infer the nature of problems and to recognize potential solutions to them—to be examined.

Köhler's pioneering experiments on tool use by chimpanzees provided early evidence for complex problem-solving capabilities in a nonhuman species. The chimpanzees, when faced with inaccessible food, fit sticks together for use as a rake, propped up poles or stacked boxes for use as ladders, pulled strings attached to distant goal objects, and moved aside physical obstructions blocking their paths (1). Subsequent research by other investigators has focused on behavioral mechanisms of the ape's performance. For example, many of the actions chimpanzees display in problem solution can be traced to "innate" origins in play behavior, and the behavioral progression from apparently random activity to organized, goal-directed solution behaviors may often be described in terms of trial-and-error learning (2). However, Köhler noted that some of his subjects arrived at solutions quite suddenly, after a period of intense activity and then quiescence. He proposed that such cases revealed "insight"—perceiving relationships between a problem and its solution—which organized successful goal-oriented behavior. Unfortunately, these intriguing observations have received little experimental attention in subsequent research.

To what extent does the chimpanzee comprehend the elements of a problem situation and potential solutions? Our understanding of this aspect of problem-solving in chimpanzee and other species is limited by methods that rely solely on observations of subjects, producing solutions to problems. It is essential to study not only the animal's problem-solving performance but also its knowledge about problem-solving. Accordingly, we designed a procedure which provided a chimpanzee with the opportunity to observe, rather than participate in, a problem situation. We simply showed the subject videotaped scenes of a human actor encountering one of several problems. The chimpanzee was then required to identify, rather than produce, a means for solving the actor's problem by choosing a photograph depicting a potential solution. By this technique, we examined the chimpanzee's capacity to recognize representations of problems and solutions, as well as its ability to perceive the relationship between each type of problem and its appropriate solution.

The subject was Sarah, an African-born female chimpanzee (*Pan troglodytes*) approximately 14 years old. She was obtained by the laboratory when less than 1 year old and was trained and tested on numerous cognitive tasks, including a simplified language (*3*). Although she had no formal experience with the problems investigated here, she did have extensive prior exposure to photographs and television programs broadcast over commercial networks, a factor which undoubtedly contributed to her performance with the visual test material.

The test consisted of two tests with four problems each. For each test, we staged one 30-second scene of a trainer struggling with each of four problems and videotaped each scene. In addition, we made photographs of either the trainer performing an action with an object or an object alone, which could constitute a solution to each problem. The two tests differed in the nature of the televised problems and in the content of the photographic solutions. In test 1, problems were of the standard variety used in animal testing and were based on those Köhler arranged for his chimpanzee subjects (Fig. 1) (*1*). Videotaped scenes showed the actor struggling to reach bananas made inaccessible in one of four ways. The photographic solutions depicted the actor performing an action with an object in the situation. In test 2, a new set of problems was drawn from events in the daily laboratory routine, and the photographic solutions merely showed objects which could constitute a solution to each problem. In this second test, "problem" was no longer defined simply as inaccessible food but ranged from a human actor locked inside a cage to a gas heater that had gone out (Fig. 2).

Each test consisted of several daily sessions of four trials each, with intertrial intervals of approximately 2 minutes. During each trial, Sarah was shown one black-and-white videotaped scene on a television monitor (Sony CVM-115 with an 11-inch screen). In the last 5 seconds of the scene, the videotape was put on "hold," thereby leaving an image of the problem situation on the screen like one of those shown in the left-hand columns of Figs. 1 and 2. The trainer then handed Sarah a covered box containing two of the set of four 8- by 10-inch color photographs, each mounted on a 10- by 12-inch piece of plywood. Afterward, the trainer left the room and closed the door. Sarah was required to open the box, select one photograph, and place it on a paper towel in front of the television screen. This aspect of the procedure was derived from a previous match-to-sample paradigm, in which Sarah was trained to place correct comparison stimuli on a towel and incorrect ones elsewhere. Sarah then summoned the trainer from an adjacent room by ringing a bell. Thus, the subject responded in the absence of the trainer, a procedure we use routinely for the control of social cues (*4*). When the trainer heard the bell, he returned to the test room and graded Sarah's answer, telling her either "Good Sarah, that's right," or "No Sarah, that's wrong," in a tone of voice one would use with a young child. At the end of every session she was given yogurt, fruit, or candy.

Before each test, Sarah was given a preliminary session in which she was shown the set of four videotaped scenes in order to familiarize her

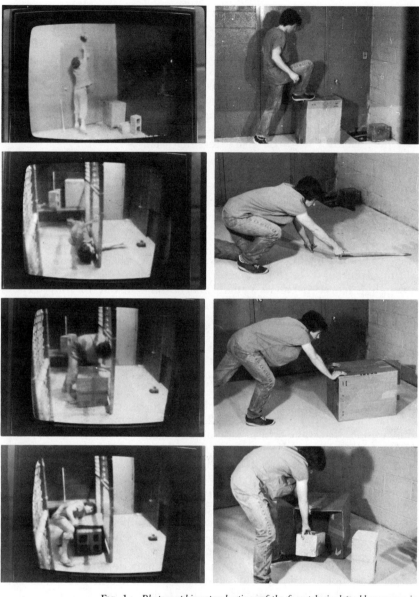

FIG. 1.   *Photographic reproductions of the four televised problem scenes in test 1 (left column) and of the color-photograph solutions (right column). Photographs of the television monitor in the left column were taken during the last 5 seconds of each 30-second videotaped scene. The correct means for solving each problem is portrayed in the photograph directly to the right of each problem scene. In problem 1, the trainer attempted to reach up toward bananas suspended by a rope from the ceiling; in problem 2, to reach under the wire mesh partition toward bananas on the floor; in problem 3, to reach around an intervening box toward bananas on the floor outside the cage; and in problem 4, to push aside a box filled with cement blocks, which obstructed his reach toward bananas on the floor outside the cage. In solution 1, the trainer stepped on a box; in solution 2, he reached out with a wooden rod; in solution 3, he pushed laterally on a box; and in solution 4, he lifted blocks out of a box.*

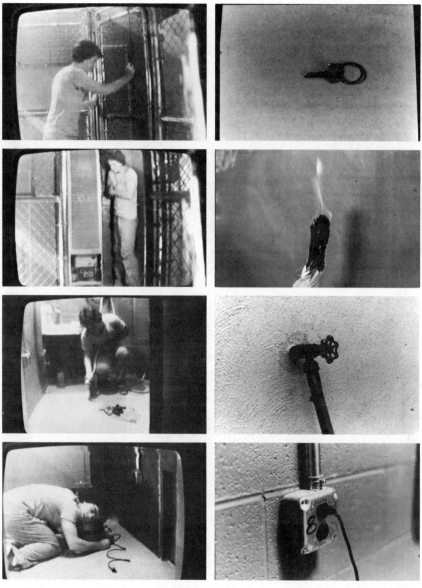

FIG. 2   *Photographic reproductions of the four televised problem scenes in test 2 (left column) and of the color-photograph solutions (right column). Photographs of the television monitor in the left column were taken during the last 5 seconds of each 30-second videotaped scene. In problem 5, the trainer struggled to escape from a locked cage, alternately grasping the bars of the cage and the padlock on the door; in problem 6, he shivered, clasped his arms to his chest, and slapped the gas heater on the wall; in problem 7, he attempted to wash down a dirty floor, but the hose was not connected to the faucet; and in problem 8, he attempted to play a phonograph record, but heard no sound because the machine was not plugged in. The photographs on the right show, for solution 5, a key ring; for solution 6, a torch in flames; for solution 7, a hose connected to a faucet; and for solution 8, a plug connected to a wall socket.*

with the test material. During subsequent sessions in each test, she was shown all four scenes, one at a time, and then asked to choose one of two photographs at the end of each scene. The order in which the scenes were presented was randomized across sessions, and the position of the correct photograph inside the box (left versus right) was counterbalanced across trials. On all trials, one photograph was correct and the other incorrect, and each correct alternative was paired equally often with every other alternative. Tests 1 and 2 consisted of six and three daily sessions, respectively.

In both tests, Sarah chose correctly on a significant proportion of the trials (21 of 24 trials correct in test 1, binomial test, $P < .001$; and 12 of 12 trials correct in test 2, $P < .001$). In the first test, she chose the correct photographic solution on all six presentations of the first three problems. Her errors were confined to problem 4, in which the trainer's access to food was hindered by a block-laden box (Fig. 1). She chose incorrectly on the first three trials with this problem and then chose correctly on the last three trials. Her incorrect choices were, in order of occurrence, reaching out with the rod, stepping on the box, and pushing the box laterally. It may be noted that Sarah's difficulty with problem 4 is in keeping with Köhler's observation that his chimpanzees solved this kind of problem only with great difficulty, if at all *(1)*. Thus, although Sarah may have learned during the course of test 1 to choose the correct photographic solution to problem 4, this would be an improbable interpretation of her overall performance. On problems 1, 2, and 3 in test 1 and in all four problems in test 2, Sarah performed without error from the outset of testing. Examining the data from her first trial with each problem (which eliminates the possibility of learning), showed that she chose correctly on a significant proportion of problems upon first exposure (seven of eight correct initial choices, binomial test, $P < .05$).

These results demonstrate that the chimpanzee was capable of bringing representations of problems and solutions into correspondence with one another. The subject's success suggests not only that she recognized that the videotaped scenes represented problems (that is, actions or conditions the human actor was unable to realize) and the photographs represented potential solutions (means by which the actor's goal could be achieved), but that she perceived the relationship between each type of problem and its appropriate solution. Quite how the chimpanzee carries out this task remains to be determined, although some alternatives can already be eliminated.

The problems could not be solved by matching videotaped scenes and photographs on the basis of physical similarity. In test 1, each video scene showed the trainer, bananas, rope, a box, a rod, and two cement blocks; and each photograph showed the trainer and either one, or in the case of the fourth problem, two of the objects. Test 2 further discounts this possibility, for there is no physical similarity whatever between, for example, a key and an actor struggling to escape from a cage, or between a flaming torch and an actor "registering" cold. Alternatively, one might suppose that not objects but the actor's posture was a basis for physical matching. In test 1 he is decidedly more upright in the first problem and its solution than in the other pairs of stimuli. Yet this would differentiate only one problem from the other three and thus would not account for the results. Posture may be one of several cues the animal uses to identify a problem, provided it is available, but the results of test 2 show that it is not a necessary cue. Although the photographs in test 1 depicted a trainer acting on an object (and thus assuming a posture), those in test 2 did not depict an actor at all but merely showed either an object that could serve as a tool (key, flaming torch) or objects in an appropriate combination (cord plugged into a socket, hose connected to a faucet). To account for Sarah's performance we must appeal to a level of analysis deeper than physical similarity of the stimuli.

Did Sarah's prior experience, either personal or observational, mediate her successful performance here? To our knowledge, she has never observed a human or conspecific encounter the types of problems investigated in test 1. However, she is almost certain to have had informal experience with some of them. It is hardly possible to prevent a chimpanzee from engaging in daily problem-solving (as Köhler noted, the "official" problem-solving he observed was not the first problem-solving in which his subjects had engaged). Sarah has obtained items lying outside her cage by reaching with a variety of objects, climbed on objects in her cage in order to grasp items on the ceiling, and even in these tests, removed the lid on the box in order to gain access to the photographic alternatives. However, the inaccessible items she reached toward were never bananas, but rather keys or articles of clothing. Her "tools" were never rods or boxes, but furniture, toys, or blankets. Physical obstructions were never boxes in her cage, but rather lids on small containers or large surfaces such as the cage walls. And, of course, the agent who participated in the problems was not the trainer, but Sarah herself. Nevertheless, her own experience differed only in detail from that represented by each of the first three problems in test 1, and this may have been the basis of her success. In contrast, we doubt whether she had any personal experience with the kind of problems depicted in problem 4. Owing to her great strength, she has probably never encountered a small object she could not move, and her failure on the fourth problem may stem from a lack of personal experience.

On the other hand, observational learning must have played an important role in Sarah's performance in test 2. Although she has used keys (problem 5) adeptly on several occasions, she has had no personal experience like that represented in problems 6, 7, or 8. She has observed trainers ignite gas heaters, attach hoses to faucets, and plug in electric cords, but she has never carried out these acts herself. Moreover, her observational experience with these activities was casual, a part of the daily routine. For example, she did not observe a trainer attempt to play the phonograph, fail, and then notice belatedly that the cord was not plugged in. None of the acts were ever staged for her benefit, the separate parts of the acts such as the plugging in of the cord or the attachment of the hose being highlighted in a didactic way.

The exact experience the subject needs in order to perform as Sarah did, the critical features of the problem scenes and photographic solutions, and how these factors for nonhuman species compare with those needed by the human child remain to be determined. Further research may answer these questions and generally enhance our knowledge about the degree to which nonhuman species and young children understand their own problem-solving behavior.

References

1. W. Köhler, *The Mentality of Apes,* (Harcourt Brace, New York, 1925).

2. P. H. Schiller, *Psychol. Rev.* **59,** 177 (1952); in *Instinctive Behavior: The Development of a Modern Concept,* C. H. Schiller, Ed. (International Universities Press, New York, 1957), pp. 264–287.

3. D. Premack, *Intelligence in Ape and Man* (Erlbaum, Hillsdale, N.J., 1976).

4. ———, G. Woodruff, K. Kennel, *Science,* in press.

5. Supported by NSF grant BMS 75–19748 and a facilities grant from the Grant Foundation. We thank Sarah's trainer, K. Kennel, for collecting the data, and A. J. Premack for helpful comments on an earlier version of the manuscript.

E. COGNITION AND THE LAW OF EFFECT

All the evidence we have reviewed for the importance of cognitive processes to behavior suggests that behavior theory may have made a mistake in placing such great emphasis on the law of effect. The law of effect focuses on the relation between behavior and consequence and ignores potential mediating processes. But if mediating processes play the prominent role they seem to, the law of effect diminishes in importance. Or does it? The article by Dennett argues that some version of the law of effect must inevitably play a part in any adequate account of behavior. In Dennett's view, to deny the significance of the law of effect is to deny the possibility of intelligent activity altogether. Since activity is so clearly intelligent, the law of effect must be operating.

But Dennett's version of the law of effect is quite different from the one we have been considering up to now. It is a cognitive law of effect. What gets generated more or less at random are ideas, and the cognitive law of effect selects the good ones. These two processes of generation and selection are the essential ingredients of creative, intelligent thinking. What Dennett's article claims is that behavior theory did not go wrong by using the law of effect as a framework for understanding behavior; its mistake was to apply it to behavior rather than to internal cognitive processes.

32 Why the Law of Effect Will Not Go Away

D. C. DENNETT

The poet Paul Valéry said: "It takes two to invent anything." He was not referring to collaborative partnerships between people but to a bifurcation in the individual inventor. "The one," he says, "makes up combinations; the other one chooses, recognizes what he wishes and what is important to him in the mass of the things which the former has imparted to him. What we call genius is much less the work of the first one than the readiness of the second one to grasp the value of what has been laid before him and to choose it."[1] This is a plausible claim. Why? Is it true? If it is, what kind of truth is it? An empirical generalization for which there is wide scale confirmation? Or a "conceptual truth" derivable from our concept of invention? Or something else?

Herbert Simon, in *The Science of the Artificial*, makes a related claim: "human problem solving, from the most blundering to the most insightful, involves nothing more than varying mixtures of trial and error and selectivity."[2] This claim is also plausible, I think, but less so. Simon presents it as if it were the conclusion of an inductive investigation, but *that*, I think, is not plausible at all. An extensive survey of human problem solving may have driven home this thesis to Simon, but its claim to our assent comes from a different quarter.

I want to show that these claims owe their plausibility to the fact that they are implications of an abstract principle whose "necessity" (such as it is) consists in this: we can know independently of empirical research in psychology that any adequate and complete psychological theory must exploit some version or other of the principle. The most familiar version of the principle I have in mind is the derided darling of the behaviorists: the Law of Effect. "The rough idea," Broadbent observes,[3] "that actions followed by reward are repeated, is one which is likely to occur to most intelligent people who think about possible explanations of behavior." This rough idea, refined, is the Law of Effect, and my claim is that it is not just part of *a* possible explanation of behavior, but of *any* possible adequate explanation of behavior.

In order to establish this condition of adequacy for psychological theories, we must first be clear about the burden of psychology. Consider the way the rest of the social sciences depend on the more basic science of psychology. Economics, or at any rate classical economics, assumes at the outset an ontology of rational, self-interested agents, and then pro-

"Why the Law of Effect Will Not Go Away" by D. C. Dennett. *Journal of the Theory of Social Behaviour*, 1975, 5, 169–187. Reprinted by permission of Basil Blackwell Publisher, Paul Secord, and the author. Read to the first meeting of the Society for the Philosophy of Psychology, October 26, 1974, at M.I.T.

poses to discover generalizations about how such agents, the "atoms" of economics will behave in the market-place. This assumption of intelligence and self-interest in agents is not idle; it is needed to ground and explain the generalizations. Consider the law of supply and demand. There is no mystery about why the law holds as reliably as it does: *people are not fools;* they want as much as they can get, they know what they want and how much they want it, and they know enough to charge what the market will bear and buy as cheap as they can. If that didn't explain why the law of supply and demand works, we would be utterly baffled or incredulous on learning that it did. Political science, sociology, anthropology and social psychology are similarly content to *assume* capacities of discrimination, perception, reason and action based on reason and then seek interesting generalizations about the exploitation of these capacities in particular circumstances. One way of alluding to this shared feature of these social sciences is to note that they are all *Intentional:* they utilize the Intentional or "mentalistic" or "cognitive" vocabulary—they speak of belief, desire, expectation, recognition, action, etc.—and they permit explanations to come to an end, at least on occasion, with the citation of a stretch of practical reasoning (usually drastically enthymematic). The voters elected the Democrat *because* they were working men and believed the Republican candidate to be anti-labour; the stock market dropped *because* investors believed other havens for their money were safer. These sciences leave to psychology the task of explaining *how there come to be* entities—organisms, human beings—that can be so usefully assumed to be self-interested, knowledgeable and rational. A fundamental task of psychology then is to explain intelligence. For the super-abstemious behaviorist who will not permit himself to speak even of intelligence (that being too "mentalistic" for him) we can say, with Hull, that a primary task of psychology "is to understand. . .why. . .behavior. . .is so generally adaptive, i.e., successful in the sense of reducing needs and facilitating survival. . . ."[4] The account of intelligence required of psychology must not of course be question-begging. It must not explain intelligence in terms of intelligence, for instance by assigning responsibility for the existence of intelligence in creatures to the munificence of an intelligent Creator, or by putting clever homunculi at the control panels of the nervous system.[5] If that were the best psychology could do, then psychology could not do the job assigned it.

We already have a model of a theory that admirably discharges just this *sort* of burden in the Darwinian theory of evolution by natural selection, and as many commentators have pointed out, the Law of Effect is closely analogous to the principle of natural selection. The Law of Effect presumes there to be a "population" of stimulus–response pairs, more or less randomly or in any case arbitrarily mated, and from this large and varied pool reinforcers *select* the well-designed, the adaptive, the fortuitously appropriate pairs in an entirely mechanical way: their recurrence is made more probable, while their maladaptive or merely neutral brethren suffer "extinction," not by being *killed* (all particular stimulus–response pairs come to swift ends), but by *failing to reproduce.* The analogy is very strong, very satisfying, and very familiar.

But there has been some misinterpretation of the nature of its appeal. Broadbent observes that

> *The attraction both of natural selection and of the Law of Effect, to certain types of mind, is that they do not call on explanatory principles of a quite separate order from those used in the physical sciences. It is not surprising therefore that the Law of Effect had been seized on, not merely as a generalization which is true of animals under certain conditions, but also as a fundamental principle which would explain all adaptive behaviour.*[6]

It is certainly true that these analogous principles appeal to physicalists or materialists because they are mechanistically explicable, but there is a more fundamental reason for favouring them: they both can provide clearly non-question-begging accounts of explicanda for which it is very hard to devise non-question-begging accounts. Darwin explains a world of final causes and teleological laws with a principle that is (to be sure) mechanistic but—more fundamentally—utterly independent of "meaning" or "purpose." It assumes a world that is *absurd* in the existentialist's sense of the term: not ludicrous but pointless, and this assumption is a necessary condition of any non-question-begging account of *purpose*. Whether we can imagine a *non*-mechanistic but also non-question-begging principle for explaining design in the biological world is doubtful; it is tempting to see the commitment to non-question-begging accounts here as tantamount to a commitment to mechanistic materialism, but the priority of these commitments is clear. It is not that one's prior prejudice in favour of materialism gives one reason to accept Darwin's principle because it is materialistic, but rather that one's prior acknowledgement of the constraint against begging the question gives one *reason to adopt materialism* once one sees that Darwin's non-question-begging account of design or purpose in nature is materialistic. One argues: Darwin's materialistic theory may not be the only non-question-begging theory of these matters, but it is one such theory, and the only one we have found, which is quite a good reason for espousing materialism.

A precisely parallel argument might occur to the psychologist trying to decide whether to throw in with the behaviourists: theories based on the Law of Effect may not be the only psychological theories that do not beg the question of intelligence, but they *are* clearly non-question-begging in this regard, and their rivals are not, which is quite a good reason for joining the austere and demanding brotherhood of behaviorists. But all is not well in that camp, and has not been for some time. Contrary to the claims of the more optimistic apologists, the Law of Effect has not been knit into any theory with anything remotely like the proven power of the theory of natural selection. The Law of Effect has appeared in several guises since Thorndike introduced it as a principle of learning; most influentially, it assumed centrality in Hull's behaviourism as the "law of primary reinforcement" and in Skinner's as the "principle of operant conditioning,"[7] but the history of these attempts is the history of ever more sophisticated failures to get the Law of Effect to *do enough work*. It may account for a *lot* of learning, but it can't seem to account for it all. Why, then, not look for another fundamental principle of more power to explain the balance? It is not just mulishness or proprietary pride that has kept behaviourists from following this suggestion, but rather something like the conviction that the Law of Effect is not just *a* good idea, but the only possible good idea for this job. There is something right in this conviction, I want to maintain, but what is wrong in it has had an ironic result: allegiance to the Law of Effect in its behaviouristic or periphera-listic versions has forced psychologists to beg small questions left and right in order to keep from begging the big question. One "saves" the Law of Effect from persistent counterinstances by the *ad hoc* postulation of reinforcers and stimulus histories for which one has not the slightest grounds except the demands of the theory. For instance one postulates that curiosity drives the reduction of which is reinforcing in order to ex-plain "latent" learning, or presumes that when one exhibits an apparently novel bit of intelligent behaviour, there *must have been* some "relevantly similar" responses in one's past for which one was reinforced. These strategies are not altogether bad; they parallel the evolutionist's specula-tive hypothetical ancestries of species, which are similarly made up out of whole cloth to begin with, but which differ usually in being clearly con-firmable or disconfirmable. These criticisms of behaviourism are not new,[8] and not universally fair in application either. I am convinced, nev-ertheless, that no behaviourism, however sophisticated, can elude all ver-sions of these familiar objections, but that is not a claim to be supported in short compass. It will be more constructive to turn to what I claim is right about the Law of Effect, and to suggest another way a version of it can be introduced to take up where behaviourism leaves off.

The first thing to note is that the Law of Effect and the principle of natural selection are not just analogues; they are designed to work to-gether. There is a kind of intelligence, or pseudo-intelligence, for which the principle of natural selection itself provides the complete explanation, and that is the "intelligence" manifest in tropistic, "instinctual" beha-viour control. The environmental appropriateness, the biological and strategic wisdom, evident in bird's-nest-building, spider-web-making and less intricate "innate" behavioural dispositions is to be explained by the same principle that explains the well-designedness of the bird's wings or the spider's eyes. We are to understand that creatures so "wired" as to exhibit useful tropistic behaviour in their environmental niches will have a survival advantage over creatures not so wired, and hence will gradually be selected by the vicissitudes of nature. Tropistic behaviour is not plastic in the individual, however, and it is evident that solely tropistically con-trolled creatures would not be evolution's final solution to the needs-versus-environment problem. *If* creatures with some plasticity in their input–output relations were to appear, *some* of them might have an ad-vantage over even the most sophisticated of their tropistic cousins. Which ones? Those that are able to distinguish good results of plasticity from bad, and preserve the good. The problem of selection reappears and points to its own solution: let some class of events in the organisms be ge-netically endowed with the capacity to increase the likelihood of the re-currence of behaviour-controlling events upon which they act. Call them reinforcers. Some mutations, we can then speculate, appeared with inap-propriate reinforcers, others with neutral reinforcers, and a lucky few with appropriate reinforcers. Those lucky few survive, of course, and their progeny are endowed genetically with a capacity to *learn*, where learning is understood to be nothing more than a change (in the environmentally appropriate direction) in stimulus–response probability relations. The obviously adaptive positive reinforcers will be events normally caused by the presence of food or water, by sexual contact, and by bodily well-being, while the normal effects of injury and deprivation will be the obvious negative reinforcers, though there could be many more than these.[9]

The picture so far is of creatures well endowed by natural selection with tropistic *hard-wiring*, including the hard-wiring of some reinforcers. These reinforcers, in turn, permit the further selection and establishment of adaptive soft-wiring, such selection to be drawn from a pool of essentially arbitrary, *undesigned* temporary interconnections. Whenever a creature is fortunate enough to have one of its interconnections be followed by an environmental effect that in turn produces a reinforcer as "feedback," that interconnection will be favoured. Skinner is quite explicit about all this. In *Science and Human Behavior* he notes that "The process of conditioning has survival value," but of course what he means is that the *capacity* to be conditioned has survival value. "Where inherited behaviour leaves off, the inherited modifiability of the process of conditioning takes over."[10] So let us use the term "Skinnerian creatures" for all creatures that are susceptible to operant conditioning, all creatures whose learning can be explained by the Law of Effect. Skinnerian creatures clearly have it over merely tropistic creatures, but it seems that there are other creatures, e.g., at least ourselves and many other mammals, that have it over merely Skinnerian creatures.

The trouble, intuitively, with Skinnerian creatures is that they can learn only by actual behavioural trial and error in the environment. A good bit of soft-wiring cannot get selected until it has had an opportunity to provoke some reinforcing feedback from the environment, and the problem seems to be that merely *potential*, as yet *unutilized* behavioural controls can *ex hypothesi* have no environmental effects which could lead to their being reinforced. And yet experience seems to show that we, and even monkeys, often think out and select an adaptive course of action without benefit of prior external feedback and reinforcement. Faced with this dilemma, we might indulge in a little wishful thinking: if only the Law of Effect could provide for the reinforcement of merely potential, unutilized bits of behaviour control wiring! If only such unutilized controls could have some subtle effect on the environment (i.e., if only merely "thinking about the solution" could have some environmental effect) and if only the environment were benign enough to bounce back the appropriate feedback in response! But that, it seems, would be miraculous.

Not so. We can have all that and more by simply positing that creatures have *two* environments, the outer environment in which they live, and an "inner" environment they carry around with them. The inner environment is just to be conceived as an input-output box for providing "feedback" for events in the brain.[11] Now we can run just the same speculative argument on Skinnerian creatures that we earlier ran on tropistic creatures. Suppose there appear among the Skinnerian creatures of the world mutations that have inner environments of the sort just mentioned. Some, we can assume, will have maladaptive inner environments (the environments will make environmentally inappropriate behaviour more likely); others will have neutral inner environments; but a lucky few will have inner environments that happen to reinforce, by and large, only adaptive *potential* behavioural controls. In a way we are turning the principle of natural selection on its head: we are talking of the evolution of (inner) environments to suit the organism, of environments that would have survival value in an organism. Mutations equipped with such benign inner environments would have a distinct survival advantage over merely Skinnerian creatures in any exiguous environment, since they could learn faster and *more safely* (for trial and error learning is not only tedious; it can be dangerous). The advantage provided by such a benign inner environment has been elegantly expressed in a phrase of Karl Popper's: it "permits our hypotheses to die in our stead."

The behaviourist, faced with the shortcomings of the Law of Effect, insisted that all we needed was more of the same (that only more of the same could explain what had to be explained), and that is what we have given him. He was just construing "the same" too narrowly. The *peripheralism* of behaviourist versions of the Law of Effect turns out to be not so essential as they had thought. For instance, our talk of an inner *environment* is merely vestigal peripheralism; the inner environment is just an inner something that selects. Ultimately of course it is environmental effects that are the measure of adaptivity and the mainspring of learning, but the environment can delegate its selective function to something in the organism (just as death had earlier delegated its selective function to pain), and if this occurs, a more intelligent, flexible, organism is the result.

It might be asked if behaviourists haven't already, in fact long ago, taken this step to inner reinforcement or selection. I think the fairest answer is that some have and some haven't, and even those that have have not been clear about what they are doing. On the one hand there are the neo-Skinnerians who have no qualms about talking about the operant conditioning that results in the subject who *imagines* courses of action followed by reinforcing results, and on the other hand you have the neo-Skinnerians that still rail against the use of such mentalistic terms as "imagine." Skinner himself falls into both camps, often within the compass of a single page.[12] "The skin," says Skinner, "is not that important as a boundary"[13] but it is hard to believe he sees the implications of this observation. In any event it will be clearer here to suppose that behaviourists are "classical" periphalists who do not envisage such a reapplication of the Law of Effect via an inner environment.

At this point it is important to ask whether this proposed principle of selection by inner environment hasn't smuggled in some incoherency or impossibility, for if it has not, we can argue that since our hypothesized mutations would clearly have the edge over merely Skinnerian creatures, there is no reason to believe that operant conditioning was evolution's final solution to the learning or intelligence problem, and we could then safely "predict" the appearance and establishment of such mutations. Here we are, we could add. We could then go on to ask how powerful our new principle was, and whether there was learning or intelligence *it* couldn't explain. And we could afford to be more open-minded about this question than the behaviourist was, since if we thought there *was* learning it couldn't handle, we'd know where to look for yet a stronger principle; yet a *fourth* incarnation of our basic principle of natural selection (or, otherwise viewed, yet a *third* incarnation of our basic psychological principle of the Law of Effect). In fact we can already see just what it will be. Nothing requires the inner environment to be entirely genetically hard-wired. A more versatile capacity would be one in which the inner environment *itself* could evolve in the individual as a result of—for starters—operant conditioning. We not only learn; we learn better how to learn, and learn better how to learn better how to learn.[14]

So is there anything incoherent about the supposition of inner environments that can select adaptive features of *potential* behaviour control systems (and favour their incorporation into *actual* behaviour controls—for that is what reinforcement amounts to in this application)? Is anything miraculous or question-begging being assumed here? The notion of an inner environment was *introduced* in explicitly non-Intentional language: the inner environment is simply any internal region that can affect and be affected by features of potential behavioural control systems. The benign and hence selected inner environments are simply those in which the result of these causal interactions is the increased conditional probability of the actualization of those potential controls that would be adaptive under the conditions in which they are probable. The way the notion is introduced is thus uncontaminated by covert appeal to intelligence, but it is still not obvious that an inner environment could "work."

What conditions must we put on features of bits of brain design to ensure that their selection by an optimally designed selector-mechanism would yield a better than chance improvement in ultimate performance? Since selection by inner environment is ultimately a mechanical sorting, which can key only on physical features of what is sorted, at the very least there would have to be a *normal* or *systematic* correlation between the physical event types selected and what we may call a *functional role* in some control program. A physically characterized type of wiring could not consist in the main of reliably adaptive tokens unless those tokens normally played a particular function.[15] This is the same condition, raised one level, that we find on operant conditioning: if physically characterized *response* classes do not produce a normally uniform environmental effect, reinforcement cannot be adaptive. So if and when this principle works, it works to establish high probabilities that particular appropriate functional roles will be filled at the appropriate times in control programs. Functional roles will be *discriminated,* and thereby control programs will become well designed.

It is hard to keep track of these purported functions and effects while speaking in the sterilized vocabulary of the behaviourist, but there is an easier way of talking: we can say that physical event tokens of a selected type have—in virtue of their normally playing a certain role in a well-designed functional organization—a *meaning* or *content.* We have many familiar examples of *adaptive potential behaviour control elements:* accurate *maps* are adaptive potential behaviour control elements, and so are true *beliefs,* warranted *expectations,* clear *concepts,* well-ordered *preferences,* sound *plans of action,* in short all the favourite tools of the cognitivist psychologist. As Popper says, it is *hypotheses*— events or states endowed with an Intentional characterization—that die in our stead. Is *cognitivist* psychology then bound ultimately to versions of the Law of Effect? That it is, I hope to show by looking at artificial intelligence (AI) research.

AI program designers work backwards on the same task behaviorists work forwards on. We have just traced the behaviourists' cautious and self-denying efforts to build from mechanistic principles towards the levels of complexity at which it becomes apt and illuminating to speak in Intentional terms about what they claim is going on. The AI researcher *starts* with an Intentionally characterized problem (e.g., how can I get a computer to *understand* questions of English?), breaks it down into sub-problems that are also Intentionally characterized (e.g., how do I get the computer to *recognize* questions, *distinguish* subjects from predicates, *ignore* irrelevant parsings?) and then breaks these problems down still further until finally he reaches problem or task descriptions that are obviously mechanistic. Here is a way of looking at the process. The AI programmer begins with an Intentionally characterized problem, and thus frankly views the computer anthropomorphically: if he *solves* the problem he will say he has designed a computer that can understand questions in English. His first and highest level of design breaks the computer down into subsystems, each of which is given Intentionally characterized tasks; he composes a flow chart of evaluators, rememberers, discriminators, overseers and the like. These are *homunculi* with a vengeance; the highest level design breaks the computer down into a committee or army of intelligent homunculi with purposes, information and strategies. Each homunculus in turn is analysed into *smaller* homunculi, but more important into *less clever* homunculi. When the level is reached where the homunculi are no more than adders and subtractors, by the time they need only the intelligence to pick the larger of two numbers when directed to, they have been reduced to functionaries "who can be replaced by a machine." The aid to comprehension of anthropomorphizing the elements just about lapses at this point, and a mechanistic view of the proceedings becomes workable and comprehensible. The AI programmer uses Intentional language fearlessly because he *knows* that if he succeeds in getting his program to run, any questions he has been begging provisionally will have been paid back. The computer is more unforgiving than any human critic; if the program works then we can be certain that all homunculi have been discharged from the theory.[16]

Working backwards in this way has proved to be a remarkably fruitful research strategy, for powerful principles of design have been developed and tested, so it is interesting to note that the overall shape of AI models is strikingly similar to the organization proposed for our post-Skinnerian mutations, and the problems encountered echo the problems faced by the behaviourist. A ubiquitous strategy in AI programming is known as *generate-and-test,* and our opening quotation of Paul Valéry perfectly describes it. The problem solver (or inventor) is broken down at some point 'or points into a generator and a tester. The generator spews up candidates for solutions or elements of solutions to the problems, and the tester accepts or rejects then on the basis of stored criteria. Simon points out the analogy, once again, to natural selection.[17]

The tester of a generate-and-test subroutine is none other than a part of the inner environment of our post-Skinnerian mutations, so if we want to know how well the principle of selection by inner environment can work, the answer is that it can work as well as generate-and-test methods can work in AI programs, which is hearteningly well.[18] Simon, as we saw at the outset, was prepared to go so far as to conclude that *all* "human problem solving, from the most blundering to the most insightful" can be captured in the net of generate-and-test programming: "varying mixtures of trial and error and selectivity." This claim is exactly analogous to the behaviorists' creed that the Law of Effect could explain all learning, and again we may ask whether this is short-sighted allegiance to an idea that is good, but not the only good idea. Generate-and-test programs can simulate, and hence account for (in one important sense)[19] a lot of problem-solving and invention; what grounds have we for supposing it is powerful enough to handle it all? The behaviourist was in no position to defend his creed, but the AI researcher is in better shape.

Some AI researchers have taken their task to be the *simulation* of particular cognitive capacities "found in nature"—even the capacities and styles of particular human individuals[20]—and such research is known as CS or "cognitive simulation" research, but others take their task to be, not simulation, but the construction of intelligent programs *by any means whatever.* The only constraint on design principles in AI thus viewed is that they should *work,* and hence any boundaries the AI programmer keeps running into are arguably boundaries that restrict *all possible* modes of intelligence and learning. Thus if AI is truly the study of all possible modes of intelligence, and if generate-and-test is truly a necessary feature of AI learning programs, then generate-and-test is a necessary feature of all modes of learning, and hence a necessary principle in any adequate psychological theory.

Both premises in that argument need further support. The first premise was proposed on the grounds that AI's guiding principle is that *anything is permitted that works,* but isn't AI really more restrictive than that principle suggests? Isn't it really that AI is the investigation of all possible *mechanistically realizable* modes of intelligence? Doesn't AI's claim to cover all possible modes beg the question against the vitalist or dualist who is looking for a non-question-begging but also non-mechanistic psychology? The AI researcher is a mechanist, to be sure, but a mechanist-*malgré-lui.* He typically does not know or care what the hardware realizations of his designs will be, and often even relinquishes control and authorship of his programs at a point where they are still replete with Intentionalistic constructions, still several levels away from machine language. He can do this because it is merely a clerical problem for compiler programs and the technicians that feed them to accomplish the ultimate "reduction" to a mechanistic level. The constraints of mechanism do not loom large for the AI researcher, for he is confident that any design he can state *clearly* can be mechanized. The operative constraint for him, then, is something like clarity, and in practice clarity is ensured for anything expressible in a programming language of some level. Anything thus expressible is clear;

what about the converse? Is anything clear thus expressible? The AI programmer believes it, but it is not something subject to proof; it is, or boils down to, some version of Church's thesis (e.g., anything computable is Turing-machine computable). But now we can see that the supposition that there might be a non-question-begging non-mechanistic psychology gets you nothing unless accompanied by the supposition that Church's thesis is false. For a non-question-begging psychology will be a psychology that makes no ultimate appeals to unexplained intelligence, and that condition can be reformulated as the condition that whatever functional parts a psychology breaks its subjects into, the smallest, or most fundamental, or least sophisticated parts must not be supposed to perform tasks or follow procedures requiring intelligence. That condition in turn is surely strong enough to ensure that any procedure admissible as an "ultimate" procedure in a psychological theory falls well within the intuitive boundaries of the "computable" or "effective" as these terms are presumed to be used in Church's thesis. The intuitively computable functions mentioned in Church's thesis are those that "any fool can do," while the admissible atomic functions of a psychological theory are those that "presuppose *no* intelligence." If Church's thesis is correct then the constraints of mechanism are no more severe than the constraint against begging the question in psychology, for any psychology that stipulated atomic tasks that were "too difficult" to fall under Church's thesis would be a theory with undischarged homunculi.[21] So our first premise, that AI is the study of all possible modes of intelligence, is supported as much as it could be, which is *not quite* total support, in two regards. The first premise depends on two unprovable but very reasonable assumptions: that Church's thesis is true, and that *there can be*, in principle, an adequate and complete psychology.

That leaves the second premise to defend: what reason is there to believe that generate-and-test is a necessary and not merely handy and ubiquitous feature of AI learning programs? First, it must be granted that many computer programs of great sophistication do not invoke any variety of generate-and-test. In these cases the correct or best steps to be taken by the computer are not selected but *given;* the program's procedures are completely designed and inflexible. These programs are the analogues of our merely tropistic creatures; their design is *fixed* by a prior design process. Sometimes there is a sequence of such programs, with the programmer making a series of changes in the program to improve its performance. Such genealogical developments do not so much represent problems solved as problems deferred, however, for the trick is to get the program to become self-designing, "to get the teacher out of the learner." As long as the programmer must, in effect, reach in and rewire the control system, the system is not *learning*. Learning can be viewed as *self-design*, and Simon suggests we "think of the design process as involving first the generation of alternatives and then the testing of these alternatives against a whole array of requirements and constraints."[22] Of course he would suggest this, and we can follow his suggestion, but are there any alternatives? Is there any way of thinking (coherently) about the design process that is incompatible with (and more powerful than) thinking of it as an evolution wrought by generate-and-test? It seems not, and here is an argument supposed to show why. I suspect this argument could be made to appear more rigorous (while also, perhaps, being revealed to be entirely unoriginal) by recasting it into the technical vocabulary of some version of "information theory" or "theory of self-organizing systems." I would be interested to learn that this was so, but am content to let the argument, which is as intuitive as it is sketchy, rest on its own merits in the meantime.

We are viewing learning as ultimately a *process* of self-design. That process is for the purposes of this argument defined only by its *product,* and the product is a *new* design. That is, as a result of the process something comes to have a design it previously did not have. This new design "must come from somewhere." That is, it takes *information* to distinguish the new design from all other designs, and that information must come from somewhere. Either all from outside the system, or all from inside, or a bit of both. If all from outside, then the system does not redesign itself; this is the case we just looked at, where the all-knowing programmer, who *has* the information, *imposes* the new design on the system from without. So the information must all come from inside, or from both inside and outside. Suppose it all comes from inside. Then either the information already exists inside or it is created inside. What I mean is this: either the new design *exists ready made* in the old design in the sense that its implementation at this time is already guaranteed by its old design, or the old design does not determine in this way what the new design will be. In the former case, the system has not really redesigned itself; it was designed all along to go into this phase at this time, and we must look to a prior design process to explain this. In the latter case, the new design is *underdetermined* by the old design. This is a feature shared with the one remaining possibility: that the information comes from both inside and outside. In both of these cases the new design is underdetermined by the old design by itself, and only in these cases is there "genuine" learning (as opposed to the merely "apparent" learning of the merely tropistic creature). In any such case of underdetermination, the new design is either underdetermined period—there is a truly random contribution here; nothing takes up all the slack left by the underdetermination of the old design—*or* the new design is determined by the combination of the old design and contributions (from either inside or outside or both) that are themselves *arbitrary,* that is, *undesigned* or *fortuitous.* But if the contribution of arbitrary elements is to yield a better than chance probability of the new design being an improvement over the old design, the old design must have the capacity to *reject* arbitrary contributions on the basis of design features—information—already present. In other words, there must be a *selection* from the fortuitous contributions, based on the old design. If the arbitrary or undesigned contribution comes from within, what we have is a non-deterministic automaton.[23] A non-deterministic automaton is one such that at some point or points its further operations must wait on the result of a procedure that is undetermined by its program and input. In other words, some tester must wait on some generator to produce a candidate for its inspection. If the undesigned contribution comes from the outside, the situation is much the same; the distinction between *input* and *random contribution* is just differently drawn. The automaton is now deterministic in that its next step is a determinate function of its program and its input, but what input it gets is a fortuitous matter. In either case the system can *protect itself* against merely fortuitous response to this merely fortuitous input only by *selecting* as a function of its old design from the fortuitous "stimulation" presented. Learning must tread the fine line between the idiocy of pre-programmed tropism on the one hand and the idiocy of an over-plastic domination by fortuitous impingements on the other. In short, every process of genuine learning (or invention, which is just a special sort of learning) must invoke, at at least one but probably many levels, the principle of generate-and-test.

The moral of this story is that cognitivist theoreticians of all stamps may proceed merrily and *fruitfully* with temporarily question-begging theoretical formulations, but if they expect AI to *pay their debts* some day (and if anything can, AI can), they must acknowledge that the *processes* invoked will inevitably bear the analogy to natural selection exemplified by the Law of Effect. The moral is *not*, of course, that behaviourism is the road to truth in psychology; even our hypothesized first-generation mutations of Skinnerian creatures were too intelligent for behaviourism to account for, and we have every reason to believe actual higher organisms are much more complicated than that. The only solace for the behaviourist in this account is that his theoretical paralysis has been suffered in a Good Cause; he has not begged the question, and if the high-flying cognitivists ever achieve his probity it will only be by relying on principles fundamentally analogous to his.

This leaves it open where these inevitable principles of selection will be invoked, and how often. Nothing requires generate-and-test formats to be simple and obviously mechanistic in any of their interesting realizations. On the contrary, *introspective* evidence, of a sort I will presently illustrate, seems to bear out the general claim that generate-and-test is a common and recognizable feature of human problem solving at the same time that it establishes that the generators and testers with which we are *introspectively* familiar are themselves highly sophisticated—highly intelligent homunculi. As Simon points out, generate-and-test is not an efficient or powerful process unless the *generator* is endowed with a high degree of selectivity (so that it generates only the most likely or most plausible candidates in a circumstance), and since, as he says, "selectivity can always be equated with some kind of feedback of information from the environment" (p. 97), we must ask, of each sort and degree of selectivity in the generator, where did *it* come from—is it learned or innate, and at the end of any successful answer to that question will be a generate-and-test process, either of natural selection if the selectivity is innate, or of some variety of learning, if it is not. A consequence of this is that we cannot tell by any simple inspection or introspection whether a particular stroke of genius we encounter is a bit of "genuine" invention at all—that is, whether the invention occurred just *now*, or is the result of much earlier processes of invention that are now playing out their effects. Did Einstein's genetic endowment guarantee his creativity, or did his genetic endowment together with his nurture, his stimulus history, guarantee his creativity or did he genuinely create (during his own thought processes), his great insights? I hope it is clear how little hinges on knowing the answer to this question.

At this point I am prepared to say that the first part of Valéry's claim stands vindicated: it takes two to invent anything: the one makes up combinations; the other one chooses. What of the second part of this claim: "What we call genius is much less the work of the first one than the readiness of the second one to grasp the value of what has been laid before him and to choose it."? We have seen a way in which this must be true, in the strained sense that the *ultimate* generators must contain an element of randomness or arbitrariness. "The original solution to a problem must lie in the category of luck."[24] But it does not seem that Valéry's second claim is true on any ordinary interpretation. For instance, it does not seem to be true of all *inter-personal* collaborations that the choosers are more the geniuses than their "idea-men" are. Some producers seldom offer poor suggestions; their choosers are virtual yes-men. Other producers are highly erratic in what they will propose, and require the censorship of severe and intelligent editors. There appears to be a trade-off here between, roughly, spontaneity or fertility of imagination on the one hand, and a critical eye on the other. A task of invention seems to require both, and it looks like a straightforwardly empirical question subject to continuous variation how much of each gets done by each collaborator.

Valéry seems to slight the contribution of the first, but perhaps that is just because he has in mind a collaboration at one end of the spectrum, where a relatively undiscriminating producer of combinations makes a lot of work for his editor. Of course, as said at the outset, Valéry is not talking about actual interpersonal collaboration, but of a bifurcation in the soul. He is perhaps thinking of his own case, which suggests that he is one of those who is *aware* of considering and rejecting many bad ideas. He does not credit *his* producer-homunculus with much genius, and is happy to identify with the *responsible* partner, the chooser. Mozart, it seems, was of the same type: "When I feel well and in a good humor, or when I am taking a drive or walking after a good meal, or in the night when I cannot sleep, thoughts crowd into my mind as easily as you would wish. Whence and how do they come? I do not know and *I have nothing to do with it*. Those which please me I keep in my head and hum them; at least others have told me that I do so."[25] In such cases the producer-chooser bifurcation lines up with the unconscious and conscious selves bifurcation. One is conscious only of the *products* of the producer, which one then consciously tests and chooses.

Poincaré, in a famous lecture of 1908, offers an "introspective" account of some mathematical inventing of his own that is more problematic: "One evening, contrary to my custom, I drank black coffee and could not sleep. Ideas rose in crowds; I felt them collide until pairs interlocked, so to speak, making a stable combination."[26] In this instance the chooser seems to have disappeared, but Poincaré has another, better interpretation of the incident. In this introspective experience he has been given a rare opportunity to glimpse the *processes* in the generator; what is normally accomplished out of sight of consciousness is witnessed on this occasion, and the ideas that form stable combinations are those few that would normally be presented to the conscious chooser for further evaluation. Poincaré supposes he has watched the selectivity within the generator at work. I am not a little sceptical about Poincaré's claimed *introspection* here (I think all introspection involves elements of rational reconstruction, and I smell a good deal of that in Poincaré's protocol), but I like his categories. In particular, Poincaré gives us, in his discussion of this experience, the key to another puzzling question.

For I have really had two burdens in this paper. The first, which I take to have discharged, is to explain why the Law of Effect is so popular in its various guises. The other is to explain why it is so *unpopular* in all its guises. There is no denying that the Law of Effect seems to be an affront to our self-esteem, and a lot of the resistance, even hatred encountered by behaviourists is surely due to this. Poincaré puts his finger on it. He was, if anyone ever has been, a creative and original thinker, and yet his own analysis of how he accomplished his inventions seemed to deny him *responsibility* for them. He saw only two alternatives, both disheartening. One was his unconscious self, the generator with whom he does not or cannot *identify* "is capable of discernment; it has tact, delicacy; it knows how to choose, to divine. What do I say? It knows better how to divine than the conscious self since it succeeds where that has failed. In a word, is not the subliminal self superior to the conscious self? I confess that, for my part, I should hate to accept this."[27] The other is that the generator is an automaton, an ultimately absurd, blind trier of all possibilities. That is of course no more a homunculus with whom to identify oneself. One does not want to be the generator, then. As Mozart says of his musical ideas: "Whence and how do they come? I do not know and I have nothing to do with it." Nor does one want to be just the tester, for then one's chances of being creative depend on the luck one has with one's collaborator, the generator. The fundamental passivity of the testing role leaves no room for the "creative self."[28] But we couldn't have hoped for any other outcome. If we are to have any adequate *analysis* of creativity, invention, intelligence, it must be one in which intelligence is analysed into something none of whose parts is intelligence, and at that level of analysis, of course, no "self" worth identifying with can survive.

The mistake in this pessimism lies in confusing explaining with explaining away. Giving a non-question-begging account of *how* creatures are intelligent can hardly prove that they aren't intelligent. If we want to catch a glimpse of a creative self, we should look, for instance, at M. Poincaré, for *he* (and not any of his proper parts) was certainly a genius.

Finally, I cannot resist passing on a wonderful bit of incidental intelligence reported by Hadamard: the Latin verb *cogito* is derived, as St. Augustine tell us, from Latin words meaning *to shake together,* while the verb *intelligo* means *to select among.* The Romans, it seems, knew what they were talking about.

Notes

[1] Quoted by Jacques Hadamard, in *The Psychology of Inventing in the Mathematical Field,* Princeton University Press, 1949, p. 30.

[2] Herbert Simon, *The Sciences of the Artificial,* M.I.T., p. 97.

[3] D. E. Broadbent, *Behaviour,* 1961 (University Paperbacks edn., p. 75).

[4] Clark Hull, *Principles of Behaviour,* 1943, p. 19.

[5] Cf. B. F. Skinner, "Behaviorism at Fifty," in T. W. Wann, ed., *Behaviorism and Phenomenology,* 1969, University of Chicago Press, p. 80; and my "Skinner Skinned" (unpublished).

[6] Broadbent, *op. cit.,* p. 56.

[7] Skinner explicitly identifies his principle with the Law of Effect in *Science and Human Behavior,* 1953, p. 87.

[8] Cf., e.g., Charles Taylor, *The Explanation of Behavior,* 1964, Chomsky's reviews of Skinner's *Verbal Behavior,* and *Beyond Freedom and Dignity,* Broadbent, *op. cit.*

[9] Cf. Skinner, *Science and Human Behavior*, p. 83. Skinner speaks of food and water *themselves* being the reinforcers, but commenting on this difference would entail entering the familiar and arid "more peripheral than thou" controversy. A point of Skinner's that is always worth reiterating, though, is that negative reinforcers are not *punishments;* they are events the cessation of which is positively reinforcing, that is, their cessation *increases* the probability of recurrence of the behaviour followed by cessation.

[10] *Science and Human Behavior*, p. 55.

[11] This is not Simon's distinction between inner and outer environment in *The Sciences of the Artificial,* but a more restrictive notion. It also has *nothing whatever* to do with any distinction between the "subjective" or "phenomenal" world and the objective, public world.

[12] See my "Skinner Skinned" for detailed support of this and similar vacillation in Skinner.

[13] "Behaviorism at Fifty," in Wann, p. 84.

[14] At a glance it seems that ultimately we want one-shot learning to change the inner environment. In ordinary perspective, we want to account for the fact that if I am trying to solve a problem, *someone can tell me,* once, what won't work and I can take this lesson to heart immediately.

[15] See Simon, *op. cit.,* p. 73, also pp. 90–2. He argues that *efficient* evolution of design also requires a hierarchical organization of design elements. My treatment of these issues is (obviously) heavily indebted to Simon's illuminating and lucid account.

[16] Cf. my "Intentional Systems," *J. Phil.,* 1971, and "Why You Can't Make a Computer Feel Pain" (unpublished). In *Content and Consciousness* (1969) I scorned theories that replaced the little man in the brain with a committee. This was a big mistake, for this is just how one gets to "pay back" the "intelligence loans" of Intentionalist theories.

[17] Simon, *op. cit.,* pp. 95–8.

[18] Hubert Dreyfus would disagree. (See *What Computers Can't Do: Critique of Artificial Reason,* Harper & Row, 1973.) But Dreyfus has not succeeded in demonstrating any *a priori* limits to generate-and-test systems hierarchically organized, so his contribution to date is salutary scepticism, not refutation.

[19] There is a tradition of overstating the import of successful AI or CS (cognitive simulation) programs (e.g., "programs are theories and successful programs are confirmed theories"). For the moment all we need accept is the minimal claim that a successful program proves a particular sort of capacity to be in principle mechanistically realizable and hence mechanistically explicable. Obviously much more can be inferred from successful programs, but it takes some detailed work to say what, where and why.

[20] See, for instance, the computer-copy of a *particular* stock-broker in E. A. Feigenbaum & J. Feldman, eds., *Computers and Thought,* 1963.

[21] Note that this does *not* commit the AI researcher to the view that "men are Turing machines." The whole point of generate-and-test strategies in program design is to *permit* computers to *hit on* solutions to problems they cannot be *guaranteed* to solve either because we can prove there is no algorithm for getting the solution or because if there is an algorithm we don't know it or couldn't use it. Is there a decision procedure ensuring checkmate in chess? Few think so, and we don't know one way or the other. If there is, it would certainly take astronomically too much time and energy to use. Hence the utility of generate-and-test and heuristics in programming.

[22] Simon, *op. cit.,* p. 74.

[23] Cf. above. Gilbert Harman points out in *Thought,* 1973, that nondeterministic automata can be physically deterministic (if what is random relative to the program is determined in the machine).

[24] Arthur Koestler, in *The Acts of Creation,* 1964, p. 559, quotes the behaviourist E. R. Guthrie to this effect, but it is a misquotation, sad to say, for had Guthrie said what Koestler says he said, he would have said something true and important. Perhaps he did say it, but not on the page, or in the book, where Koestler says he said it.

[25] Quoted in Hadamard, *op. cit.,* p. 16, italics added.

[26] Quoted in Hadamard, *op. cit.,* p. 14.

[27] Quoted in Koestler, *op. cit.,* p. 164.

[28] This passivity is curiously evoked by Koestler in his account of "underground games" in *The Act of Creation.* It is a tell-tale sign of the inescapability of the principle of selectivity discussed here that Koestler, the arch-enemy of behaviourism, can do no better, when he sets himself the task of composing a rival account of creativity, than to accept the generate-and-test format and then endow the generator with frankly mysterious effects of uncoincidental coincidence.

Part VII
Applications of Behavior Theory

We are usually impressed when developments in science provide us with a new understanding of aspects of the world around us, but our greatest appreciation of scientific progress is reserved for developments in technology. It is applications of the understanding provided by physics, chemistry, and biology—in the form of computers, television, synthetic materials, drugs, and so on—that really convince us of the power of the sciences. We expect scientific developments to result in application as well as in enlightenment.

Behavior theory has been developing effective applications of its basic principles for many years. Results from studies of Pavlovian and operant conditioning are turned into effective techniques for modifying behavior in mental hospitals, classrooms, and the workplace. This final part presents examples of a wide range of successful applications, each of which depends upon one or more of the basic principles we have encountered earlier. There are examples of the use of Pavlovian conditioning to treat addiction and phobia; there are examples of the use of operant reinforcement contingencies to modify the behavior of a severely psychotic adult and that of normal young children; there is an example of the use of operant punishment contingencies to eliminate self-destruction in disturbed children; and finally, there is an example of the use of token reinforcement in a school.

Although these applications of behavior theory are rather diverse, they have something important in common. The striking, unifying characteristic of applications of behavior theory is that they modify or eliminate target behavior without concern for how that behavior might have originated in the first place. Whatever might have been responsible for producing some pathological behavior in the past, the behavior theorist is confident that the behavior can be modified by manipulating Pavlovian and operant contingencies in the present. This characteristic of applications of behavior theory contrasts sharply with other approaches to dealing with similar problems, where great emphasis is placed on identifying the causes of the behavior to be modified.

A. PAVLOVIAN CONDITIONING

This section contains two examples of the use of Pavlovian conditioning to mod-ify behavior. Both involve a phenomenon known as counter-conditioning. In counter-conditioning, a CS that has been associated with one type of US and which is producing conditioned responses appropriate to that US is then paired with a different type of US. The new association overrides the old one, resulting in a change in behavior. In the article by Raymond, counter-conditioning is used to eliminate addiction to alcohol, drugs, and cigarettes. The ingestion of alcohol or cigarette smoke or the injection of a drug is paired with administration of apo-morphine, a drug that produces intense nausea. The result is that the taste of al-cohol and cigarettes and the drug administration ritual become intensely aversive, and the addiction is broken.

The second example, in the article by Davison, involves elimination of a patho-logical fear or phobia of snakes. Subjects are first trained in deep muscle relax-ation. Then, while relaxed, they imagine scenes involving themselves in varying degrees of contact with snakes. These imagined scenes are taken to be CSs. Whereas they had previously triggered fear, they are now paired with a state of relaxation. The relaxation overrides the fear and the phobia is eliminated. Being able to imagine being around snakes without fear makes it possible for people to have actual contact with snakes.

33 The Treatment of Addiction by Aversion Conditioning with Apomorphine

M. J. RAYMOND

An account is given of the techniques employed in using apomorphine for the treatment of chronic alcoholism, addiction to other drugs, and addiction to cigarette smoking. No evaluation is made here but each technique is illustrated by the report of a case in which the result is considered, after a reasonable follow-up period, to be highly satisfactory.

Introduction

Apomorphine is derived from morphia by the removal of a molecule of water and was first prepared in 1869 by Matthieson and Wright. It is a centrally acting emetic and, less powerfully, a hypnotic. Tolerance to it rarely if ever develops. Its value in the treatment of alcoholism was first described by Hare (1912), who was particularly concerned with its sedative and hypnotic action. Hare stated that it produced a prompt though fleeting "freedom from the dipsomaniac craving." Dent (1934) also stressed the value of the drug in the relief of the anxiety underlying addiction. Originally he produced vomiting by means of apomorphine given in conjunction with alcohol, but he subsequently modified his technique, and stated that the need for alcohol could be suppressed without nausea or vomiting, simply by the action of apomorphine on the fore-brain and the hind-brain, to correct inbalance.

Voegtlin (1947) and his collaborators began to treat alcoholics with apomorphine in 1936 but for them the essence of the treatment was the establishment of a conditioned reflex of aversion to the sight, taste, and smell of alcohol. They stressed the importance of working with the same precision as the physiologist requires when creating conditioned reflexes in laboratory animals. In subsequent work Voegtlin discarded apomorphine in favour of emetine because he regarded the hypnotic effect of apomorphine as a hindrance to conditioning.

Alcoholism

It is not our practice to treat any patient until he has accepted the fact that alcohol is for him a serious problem and that he must avoid it for the rest of his life. The treatment and its rationale are discussed with him, and he must undertake it voluntarily. We no longer consider it necessary to segregate the patient during the period of his treatment, or to subject him to the rigours of many treatments during day and night. He lives in the therapeutic community, joining in the same occupational, social, and dietary regime as the other patients. Usually he has two or three treatments during the day, but the times are varied at random. It is important to correct the idea, common among patients who have heard of the

Reprinted with permission from *Behaviour Research and Therapy,* Vol. 1, M. J. Raymond, "The Treatment of Addiction by Aversion Conditioning with Apomorphine," copyright 1964, Pergamon Press, Ltd.

treatment or who have perhaps had some experience of it, that success is going to be estimated as in direct proportion to the volume of vomitus. In fact, all that is required is a definite period of nausea, and this need not be prolonged. The dose of apomorphine is kept to a minimum: we start with 1/20 g and do not exceed 1/10 g. The dose is dissolved in 1 cm³ of normal saline and injected subcutaneously. Seven minutes after the first injection the patient is taken to the treatment room. He should on the first occasion take one small drink only, the prime object being to determine (a) the "nausea time" and (b) the "vomiting time," if in fact vomiting ensues. The patient is told to report any feeling of nausea, or queasiness he feels, and the times are noted most carefully. He must be observed for blanching, sweating, and the increased swallowing which may denote increased salivation. This must not be confused with the tongue movements of the anxious patient with a dry mouth. It may be necessary to ask the patient, perhaps repeatedly, when those signs are observed, whether he feels nauseated. It is important to realise that the nausea may be very mild and fleeting, but that once it is defined with certainty, it can be expanded quite quickly in subsequent sessions without increasing the dose. If no reaction at all is produced, the session is discontinued after half an hour. At the next session 1/10 g is employed, the procedure is repeated, and all observations carefully noted. If again no nausea is produced, then the third session will be preceded by a dose of emetine hydrochloride 1½ g. This is given in a tumblerful of weak saline ten minutes before the subcutaneous injection of apomorphine 1/20 g. The average nausea time after the emetine is twenty minutes, and the average nausea time after apomorphine is ten minutes. The time intervals recorded are measured from the time of the injection. If this manoeuvre is successful, the next session will be with apomorphine 1/10 g and if this is successful the dose may subsequently be dropped to 1/20 g. On each occasion the patient does not start to drink until just before the nausea is predicted.

The treatment room and its environs must be quiet and in addition to the obviously essential furnishings it should contain a bed or couch. An oxygen cylinder and a resuscitation tray containing syringes and Coramine should be placed within easy reach as a matter of routine. The patient is not allowed to smoke. Conversation and jocularity are discouraged. The use of "familiar bar clichés" and dramatic accoutrements such as the spotlight are impediments which have no place in the treatment. We usually insist that the patient continues to drink during the early part of the nausea period, but this does not necessitate the harsh, bullying technique one has sometimes observed. Above all, noise is to be avoided, and encouragement may be quite effectively given by gesture or by whispered instructions. It is most important that he should not be pressed or allowed to continue drinking once the nausea has passed. If alcohol is taken as the nausea subsides, the foregoing treatment will be largely vitiated, and at best aversion will take much longer to produce. It is our practice to withhold alcohol as soon as the patient's resistance to it begins to relax, and if there is any doubt about the end point, it is better to withhold alcohol as soon as nausea occurs, rather than risk "drinking through." We believe that neglect of this principle is one of the chief reasons for failures with this treatment. The amount of alcohol given should be small. If the patient becomes drunk, conditioning will not occur. It is not necessary to employ a wide range of beverages, but a variety should be available, and should of course include the patient's favourite drink. One to which he is normally somewhat averse is often most valuable in the initial stages of establishing nausea. An inferior brand of rum is very useful in this respect.

During the post nausea period the patient is usually in a drowsy state and may often be observed to yawn. It is at this stage that one can profitably discuss his revaluation of alcohol and his unique circumstances. The hazards of alcohol are repeatedly put to him, and he is repeatedly told that it will now be possible for him to live without alcohol.

The "Choice" Reaction

After nausea has been quite regularly produced for a week or ten days, and the patient is beginning to show and express distaste for alcohol, he is quite unexpectedly given a choice. Without his knowledge of the changed routine, he is given an injection of 1 cm³ of normal saline subcutaneously, and when he arrives in the treatment room seven minutes later, he finds among the alcohol various soft drinks such as tonic water, bitter lemon, tomato juice, etc. He usually comments on this immediately, but in any case is told that he may drink whatever he chooses. When he chooses a soft drink, and we have not yet had a patient who did not, the atmosphere is immediately relaxed, conversation is encouraged, and the patient, lest he remain apprehensive, is assured that he will certainly not feel in any way ill. The next two or three treatments will be with apomorphine and alcohol, with continuing careful attention to timing. Further "choice" reactions are provoked, but care is taken to avoid any regular sequence which would enable the patient to predict that a choice will be available.

Rationale Underlying the "Choice" Reaction

The ultimate aim of our therapy is to enable the patient to achieve a new, positive, and successful adaptation to the drinking situation which the average patient cannot avoid encountering recurrently in numerous and varied forms as part of the social complex. Aversion produced by classical conditioning is accompanied by considerable anxiety as may be readily observed after only a few sessions. The immediate relaxation of tension as described above strongly reinforces the conditioned aversion to alcohol and is contingent upon the patient's correct response in choosing a nonalcoholic drink. Moreover, this incorporation of free operant conditioning into the treatment establishes the patient in active control where formerly he considered himself passively controlled.

The average length of treatment is three weeks. After treatment the patient is given Antabuse and advised to take it regularly in order to guard against the possibility of the "first drink." Its action is carefully explained to him. It may be helpful if with the consent of the patient, a relative or employer is asked to see that the dose is given each morning.

Case Report

A 63-year-old man who had been a heavy drinker for many years, had for five years correctly regarded himself as an alcoholic. He had attended meetings of A.A., but was finding it increasingly difficult to manage without alcohol. He was still actively employed as a company director, but his colleagues, though they greatly valued his experience and technical advise, now anxiously sought his resignation as the only solution to an embarrassing situation. He said that he wanted treatment, and despite his age he was advised to have aversion therapy. Characteristically, he found it impossible to start for "a week or two" because of pressure of business. He and his relatives were told that it was pointless to force the issue, but were instructed exactly how to proceed when he really accepted the necessity. He arrived at the hospital ten days later, relatively sober, and declared that he was thoroughly frightened by what was probably an attempt at suicide during a period of exceptional drinking, for which he had no clear memory. Physical examination revealed hypertension, emphysema and bronchitis, multiple extra-systoles, and a fractured clavicle. Within three weeks of admission he was considered to be fit enough to start aversion therapy, though it was thought wise to start with apomorphine 1/40 g. This was subsequently increased to 1/20 g, which was the maximum dose he received throughout his treatment. The lower dose produced vomiting without appreciable nausea, but the nausea time was with the larger dose established at eight minutes, often without any vomiting at all. He received only two treatments each day, and on the 17th day was given his first "choice," to which he readily responded with the required reaction. After a further three days' treatment he was again allowed a choice, and this was repeated on the 24th and the 27th days. Treatment was concluded after 31 days. Three days later he started taking Antabuse and was discharged after a further week.

It is now almost three years since his treatment, and he reports that he has never taken alcohol since. His family confirmed this and say that he is very active and successful in his business.

Drug Addiction

Aversion conditioning may be used in the treatment of any drug addiction. The treatment is similar to that already described, and the patient administers his own drug of addiction immediately before the predicted nausea produced by an injection of apomorphine. When the drug of addiction is taken orally, it is necessary to produce vomiting in addition to nausea, and it may be necessary to use emetine hydrochloride before each session, in the manner described above. When the drug of addiction is taken by injection, part of the contents of the ampoule is discarded and replaced by normal saline, as described in the following case:

A Case of Physeptone Addiction

A 30-year-old woman (Mrs. C.) had been addicted to injections of Physeptone for six years. The drug was originally prescribed for the relief of migrainous headaches, but she now found it a necessary stimulant, without which she became anergic and deeply depressed. Her average daily dose was three ampoules (30 mg) but at times she had been known to take as many as 200 ampoules (2000 mg) in a month. There had been a striking personality change, and she was described as having become furtive and dishonest. She had been persuaded to enter hospital for treatment following a Home Office enquiry into her case.

Before the first treatment, part of the contents of an ampoule of Physeptone was withdrawn and replaced by sterile normal saline. This ampoule was placed in its box with unopened ampoules in the treatment room. Seven minutes after an injection of apomorphine 1/40 g, the patient was taken to the treatment room and told to give herself an injection of Physeptone, it being explained that she would be allowed only one ampoule, which had been already opened for her. Nausea occurred five minutes after the Physeptone injection (12 min. after the apomorphine injection). The amount of Physeptone replaced by normal saline was very gradually increased with each session. The empty ampoules were not discarded, but placed in the box so that it might be evident to the patient that a fresh ampoule was used for each session. In this way Physeptone was gradually withdrawn without the patient's knowledge. After eight days, treatment had to be discontinued because of severe depression. The patient expressed guilt and shame and thought that her family would be better without her. She was considered to be potentially suicidal and over the next three weeks was treated with E.C.T. During this period no Physeptone was given. The profuse perspiration, tremor, diarrhea, and depression which had marked the withdrawal phase had now disappeared. It thus appeared that there was no longer any autonomic dependence on the drug, but she said, however, that she still felt the craving for Physeptone. Aversion therapy was therefore resumed, and at the second session of the third day after resumption, she showed reluctance to inject herself. On the fifth day she deliberately smashed her syringe. During the post nausea period the patient was encouraged to discuss some of her problems and the family tensions in relation to her headaches. It was repeatedly suggested to her that Physeptone had simply aggravated these problems, as would be the case if she had recourse to other smilar drugs. Aversion therapy was concluded on the ninth day. She was finally discharged from hospital seven weeks later, although her headaches had returned during a ten-day period at home. She was subsequently seen regularly as an outpatient for six months.

Two and a half years after her discharge from hospital, she wrote the following: "I never get any headaches now, and have never once had the desire for Physeptone. My general health has been better than I have ever known it and I feel wonderfully well." Her general practitioner writes: "Mrs. C. is very well and not taking any medicine or drugs of any kind."

A Case of Cigarette Addiction

A fourteen-year-old boy was said by his parents to have started smoking at the age of seven and to be spending every penny of his pocket money on cigarettes. He had at one time regularly smoked 40 cigarettes per day, but now was averaging about half that number because his pocket money had been reduced. He said he wanted to give up smoking because he had a smoker's cough, was breathless on exertion, and because it was costing so much money. Physical examination and chest X-ray were normal. Treatment was given in the outpatient department. On the first occasion he was given an injection of apomorphine 1/20 g, and after seven minutes he was told to start smoking. At eleven minutes he became nauseated and vomited copiously. Four days later he came for the second treatment, and said that he still had the craving for cigarettes, but had not in fact smoked since the previous session because he felt nauseated when he tried to light one. He was given an injection of apomorphine 1/20 g, and after seven minutes he lit a cigarette reluctantly and immediately said he felt ill. He was encouraged to continue smoking, and he collapsed. He was given oxygen and an injection of Coramine. When he recovered he was very hungry and asked for food, which he ate voraciously. Four days later he was given apomorphine 1/40 g, and vomited as soon as he attempted to light a cigarette seven minutes later. When he next attended he said he no longer had any craving for cigarettes, and he made two interesting comments: "When I see an advert on T.V. for cigarettes it seems like a dead advert, like Omo." "Just smoke from my father's cigarette makes me feel ill." Two months later he left school and started working. He said he had "got a bit down" at work and wanted to "keep in with the others," so he had accepted a proffered cigarette. He immediately felt faint and hot, and was unable to smoke. It is now a year since his treatment, and his parents confirm that he no longer smokes.

References

Dent, J. Y. (1934) Apomorphine in the treatment of anxiety states with special reference to alcoholism. *Brit. J. Inebr.* **43,** 65–69; (1944) Self-treatment of anxiety and craving by apomorphine through the nose. *Brit. J. Addict.* **41,** 78–84; (1949) Apomorphine treatment of addiction. *Brit. J. Addict.* **46,** 1528; (1955) *Anxiety and its Treatment with Special Reference to Alcoholism.* Skeffington, London.

Hare F. (1912) *On Alcoholism, Its Clinical Aspects and Treatment.* Churchill, London.

Voegtlin W. (1947) The conditioned reflex treatment of alcoholism. *Arch. Neurol. Psychiat.* **57,** 514–516.

34 Systematic Desensitization as a Counter-Conditioning Process

GERALD C. DAVISON

Systematic desensitization, demonstrated in both clinical and experimental studies to reduce avoidance behavior, entails the contiguous pairing of aversive imaginal stimuli with anxiety-competing relaxation. If, as is widely assumed, the efficacy of the procedure derives from a genuine counterconditioning process, a disruption of the pairing between graded aversive stimuli and relaxation should render the technique ineffective in modifying avoidance behavior. This hypothesis was strongly confirmed: significant reduction in avoidance behavior was observed only in desensitization Ss, with none occurring either in yoked Ss for whom relaxation was paired with irrelevant stimuli or in yoked Ss who were gradually exposed to the imaginal aversive stimuli without relaxation. Other theoretical issues were raised, especially the problem of transfer from imaginal to actual stimulus situations.[1]

Recent years have witnessed increasing application of the systematic desensitization procedure, as developed by Wolpe (1958), to the modification of a wide range of neurotic disorders. In this therapeutic method the client is deeply relaxed and then instructed to imagine scenes from a hierarchy of anxiety-provoking stimuli. Initially he is asked to imagine the weakest item in the list and, if relaxation is unimpaired, is gradually presented incremental degrees of aversive stimuli until eventually he is completely desensitized to the most upsetting scene in the anxiety hierarchy.

In numerous publications, both Wolpe (e.g., 1952, 1958) and other clinical workers (e.g., Geer, 1964; Lang, 1965; Lazarus, 1963; Lazarus & Rachman, 1957; Rachman, 1959) have claimed a high degree of success in eliminating diverse forms of anxiety disorders by means of this therapeutic technique.

These clinical claims of efficacy find some support in recent laboratory investigations conducted under more controlled conditions and with more objective assessment of therapeutic outcomes (e.g., Lang and Lazovik, 1963; Lang, Lazovik, & Reynolds, 1965; Lazarus, 1961; Paul, 1966; Paul & Shannon, 1966). Although results from these experiments have confirmed the effectiveness of systematic desensitization, they do not provide direct information on the relative contributions to the observed outcomes of the different variables in the treatment procedure (e.g., relaxation, graded exposure to aversive stimuli, temporal contiguity of stimulus events). Moreover, the learning process governing the behavioral changes has not been adequately elucidated. There is some suggestive evidence from Lang et al. (1965) that extensive contact with an E, along with relaxation training, does not effect behavior change. However, one can raise questions about the suitability of their control for relaxation, inasmuch as Ss in this condition began imagining snake-aversive items, but were then led away from this theme by means of subtle manipulation of content by E. It is possible that this imaginal snake avoidance may have counteracted the nonspecific effects built into the control.

Wolpe's (1958) theoretical formulation of the desensitization process as "reciprocal inhibition" is based on Hull's (1943) drive-reduction theory of classical conditioning, a fatigue theory of extinction ("conditioned inhibition"), and Sherrington's (1906) concept of reciprocal inhibition, whereby the evocation of one reflex suppresses the evocation of other reflexes. The conditions which Wolpe (1958) specified for the occurrence of reciprocal inhibition were succinctly stated in his basic principle:

> If a response antagonistic to anxiety can be made to occur in the presence of anxiety-evoking stimuli so that it is accompanied by a complete or partial suppression of the anxiety responses, the bond between these stimuli and anxiety responses will be weakened [p. 71].

This statement appears indistinguishable from Guthrie's (1952) view of counterconditioning, according to which notion the elimination of a response can be achieved by eliciting a strong incompatible response in the presence of cues that ordinarily elicit the undesirable behavior: "Here . . . the stimulus is present, but other responses are present shutting out the former response, and the stimulus becomes a conditioner of these and an inhibitor of its former response [p. 62]." Wolpe, in fact, used the terms *reciprocal inhibition* and *counterconditioning* interchangeably, but clearly indicated a preference for the former in view of his inferences about the neurological process accounting for the observed changes in behavior. However, aside from the fact that he has as yet provided no independent evidence for the existence of reciprocal inhibition at the complex behavioral level that he is dealing with, one must be wary of basing a neurological hypothesis, albeit an ingenious one, upon a behavioral system which, itself, has been shown to have serious shortcomings (Gleitman, Nachmias, & Neisser, 1954; Kimble, 1961; Lawrence & Festinger, 1962; Mowrer, 1960; Solomon & Brush, 1956).

At the present time, it appears both unnecessary and premature to "explain" behavioral phenomena in terms of an underlying neural process whose existence is inferrable solely from the very psychological data which it is invoked to explain. It appears to this writer more fruitful to stay closer to the empirical data and to conceptualize the process of systematic desensitization in terms of counterconditioning, according to which the neutralization of aversive stimuli results from the evocation of incompatible responses which are strong enough to supersede anxiety reactions to these stimuli (cf. Bandura, in press).

Problem

In view of the fact that the behavioral outcomes associated with systematic desensitization are assumed to result from counterconditioning, evidence that such a process does in fact occur is particularly essential (cf. Breger & McGaugh, 1965). To the extent that desensitization involves counterconditioning, the contiguous association of graded anxiety-provoking stimuli and incompatible relaxation responses would constitute a necessary condition for fear reduction. It is possible, however, that the favorable outcomes produced by this method are primarily attributable to relaxation alone, to the gradual exposure to aversive stimuli, or to non-specific relationship factors. The present experiment was therefore designed to test directly the hypothesis that systematic desensitization involves a genuine counterconditioning process.

The Ss were individually matched in terms of strength of their snake-avoidance behavior and assigned to one of four conditions. For one group of Ss (desensitization), a graded series of aversive stimuli was contiguously paired in imagination with deep muscle relaxation, as in the standard clinical technique. The Ss in a second group participated in a "pseudodesensitization" treatment that was identical to the first procedure except that the content of the imaginal stimuli paired with relaxation was essentially neutral and completely irrelevant to snakes. This group provided a control for the effects of relationship factors, expectations of beneficial outcomes, and relaxation per se. A third group (exposure) was presented the same series of graded aversive items, but in the absence of deep relaxation. This condition served as a control for the effects of mere repeated exposure to the aversive stimuli. A fourth group (no treatment) participated only in the pre- and posttreatment assessments of snake avoidance.

In order to ensure comparability of stimulus events, Ss in the pseudo-desensitization and exposure groups were *yoked* to their matched partners in the desensitization group, whose progress determined the number of treatment sessions, the duration of each session, the number of stimulus exposures per session, and the duration of each exposure.

Within 3 days following the completion of treatment, all Ss were tested for snake avoidance as well as for the amount of anxiety accompanying each approach response.

On the assumption that the temporal conjunction of relaxation and anxiety-provoking stimuli is essential for change, it was predicted that only Ss in the desensitization condition would display significant decrements in avoidance behavior, and would also be superior in this respect to Ss in the three control groups.

Method

Subjects

The Ss were 28 female volunteers drawn from introductory psychology courses at a junior college. Students who reported themselves very much afraid of nonpoisonous snakes were asked to assist in a study investigating procedures for eliminating common fears. In order to minimize suggestive effects, the project was presented as an experiment, rather than as a clinical study, and no claims were made for the efficacy of the procedure to be employed. To reduce further the development of strong expectation of beneficial outcomes, which might in itself produce some positive change, E was introduced as a graduate student rather than as an experienced psychotherapist. To some extent, the result from all the experiments cited above might have been confounded by these variables.

Pre- and Posttreatment Assessments of Avoidance Behavior

These assessments were conducted by an E (E_1) who did not participate in the treatment phases of the study and had no knowledge of the conditions to which Ss were assigned. The avoidance test was similar to that employed by Lang and Lazovik (1963) except for several important changes that were introduced in order to provide a more stringent and sensitive test of the efficacy of the various treatment procedures. First, whereas Lang and Lazovik used essentially a 3-item test, the present behavioral test consisted of 13 items requiring progressively more intimate interaction with the snake (e.g., placing a gloved hand against the glass near the snake, reaching into the cage and touching the snake once, culminating with holding the snake barehanded for 30 sec.). Second, rather than obtaining a single overall estimate of felt anxiety following the entire approach test, the examiner in the present study asked S to rate herself on a 10-point scale following the successful performance of each task. Third, the examiner stood at all times not closer than 2 ft. from the cage, whereas the tester in Lang and Lazovik's study touched and held the snake before requesting an S to do so. Evidence that avoidance behavior can be reduced through observation of modeled approach responses (Bandura, Grusec, & Menlove, 1967) suggests that the behavioral changes obtained by Lang and Lazovik may reflect the effects of both vicarious extinction and counterconditioning via systematic desensitization.

Any S who, on the pretreatment assessments, succeeded in touching the snake barehanded was excluded from the study. Eligible Ss were matched individually on the basis of their approach behavior and then assigned randomly to the different treatment conditions so as to constitute "clusters" of equally avoidant Ss across groups. Initially it had been planned to include an equal number of matched Ss in the no treatment control group. However, since preliminary findings, as well as data reported by Lang and Lazovik (1963), revealed virtually no changes in nontreated controls, it was decided to enlarge the size of the three treatment conditions. Therefore, eight Ss were assigned to each of the three treatment groups, while the nontreated control group contained four cases. The experimental design is summarized in Table 1.

Treatment Procedures

The treatment sessions were conducted in a room other than the one in which the avoidance behavior was measured. The Ss in conditions em-

TABLE 1. Summary of Experimental Design

Group	Pretreatment assessment (E_1)	Treatment procedure (E_2)	Posttreatment assessment (E_1)
Desensitization[a]	Avoidance test with anxiety self-reports	Relaxation paired with graded aversive stimuli	Avoidance test with anxiety self-reports
Pseudodesensitization[a]	Same	Relaxation paired with snake-irrelevant stimuli	Same
Exposure[a]	Same	Exposure to graded aversive stimuli without relaxation	Same
No treatment[b]	Same	No treatment	Same

[a] $N = 8$.
[b] $N = 4$.

ploying relaxation training reclined in a lounger, whereas for *S*s in the exposure group the chair was set in an upright position to minimize the development of relaxed states.

Relaxation Paired with Graded Aversive Stimuli (Systematic Desensitization). During the first session, these *S*s received training in deep muscular relaxation by means of a 30-min. tape recording consisting of instructions to tense and to relax alternately the various muscle groups of the body, interspersed with suggestions of heaviness, calm, and relaxation. This procedure, used earlier by the author (Davison, 1965b), is based on Lazarus' (1963) accelerated training in Jacobsonian relaxation and is very similar to the technique used by Paul (1966).

In the second session *S*s ranked 26 cards each describing snake scenes in order of increasing aversiveness, for example, "Picking up and handling a toy snake," "Standing in front of the cage, looking down at the snake through the wire cover, and it is moving around a little," "Barehanded, picking the snake up, and it is moving around." The desensitization procedure, modeled after Lazarus (1963), Paul (1966), and Wolpe (1961), was administered in a standardized fashion, with a criterion of 15 sec. without signaling anxiety on each item. (For specifics of the procedure, see Davison, 1965a.) A maximum of nine sessions, each lasting about 45 min., was allowed for completing the anxiety hierarchy.

Relaxation Paired with Snake-Irrelevant Stimuli (Pseudodesensitization). The *S*s assigned to this group received the same type and amount of relaxation training as *S*s in the above-mentioned group. Similarly, in the second session they also ranked 26 stimulus items, except that the depicted scenes were entirely unrelated to snakes. Because of the widespread belief that exploration of childhood experiences may be important in alleviating objectively unrealistic fears, it was decided to employ descriptions of common childhood events, which *S*s were asked to rank chronologically. Some of the items were essentially neutral in content ("You are about age six, and your family is discussing where to go for a ride on Sunday afternoon, at the dinner table."), while the others had mild affective properties ("You are about five years old, and you are sitting on the floor looking sadly at a toy that you have just broken."). The use of generic content thus made it possible to use snake-irrelevant stimuli without reducing the credibility of the treatment procedure.

As in the desensitization condition, *S*s were deeply relaxed and asked to imagine vividly each scene presented by the *E* until told to discontinue the visualization. Each *S* in this condition, it will be recalled, was yoked to her matched partner in the desensitization group, whose progress defined the number of treatment sessions, the length of each session, as well as the number and duration of each imaginal exposure. Thus, *S*s undergoing pseudodesensitization received the same number and duration of pairings during each session as their desensitization mates, with the important exception that snake-irrelevant stimuli were contiguously associated with relaxation.

Exposure to Graded Aversive Stimuli without Relaxation (Exposure). The *S*s in this group were administered the same series of snake-aversive stimuli in the same order and for the same duration as determined by their respective partners in the desensitization group to whom they were yoked. However, exposure *S*s received no relaxation training (hence, had one session less with *E*), nor did they engage in anxiety-competing relaxation while visualizing the aversive situations. Because of the yoking require-ments, on those occasions when *S*s signaled anxiety, they were instructed to maintain the images until *E* asked them to discontinue. Cooperation in this obviously unpleasant task was obtained through friendly but cogent reminders that such visualization was important for the experimental de-sign.

No treatment group. The *S*s assigned to this group merely participated in the assessments of avoidance behavior at the same time as their matched partners in the desensitization condition.

Results

Table 2 presents the change scores in approach behavior for each *S* in each of the eight matched clusters.

Between-Group Differences

Because of the unequal number of *S*s in the no treatment group, these data were not included in the overall statistical analysis. Two-way analysis of variance of the change scores obtained by the three matched treatment groups yielded a highly significant treatment effect ($F = 6.84$; $p < .01$).

Further, one-tailed comparisons of pairs of treatment conditions by t tests for correlated means revealed that *S*s who had undergone systematic desensitization subsequently displayed significantly more snake-approach behavior than *S*s in either the pseudodesensitization group ($t = 2.57$; $p < .01$), the exposure group ($t = 3.60$; $p < .005$), or the no treatment control group ($t = 3.04$; $p < .01$). The pseudodesensitization and exposure groups did not differ significantly in approach behavior from the no treatment controls (t's $= .92$, $.21$, respectively), not did they differ from each other.

Within-Group Differences

Within-group changes in avoidance behavior were evaluated by t tests for correlated means. Results of this analysis likewise disclosed that only *S*s in the desensitization condition achieved a significant reduction in avoidance behavior ($t = 4.20$; $p < .005$).

TABLE 2. Changes in Snake-Approach Behavior Displayed by Subjects in Each of the Treatment Conditions

	Condition			
Matched cluster	*Desensitization*	*Pseudodesensitization*	*Exposure*	*No treatment*
1	3	2	2	0
2	3	− 1	0	—
3	6	0	− 1	− 1
4	5	1	− 5	0
5	0	1	2	—
6	6	8	1	0
7	12	0	0	—
8	7	1	1	—
M	5.25	1.50	0.0	− 0.25

Performance of the Criterion Behavior in Posttreatment Assessment

If the disensitization treatment does, in fact, involve a genuine counterconditioning process, then one would expect to find relationships between factors that are known to affect the conditioning process (e.g., number of aversive stimuli that have been neutralized) and degree of behavioral change. In this connection, of the eight Ss in the desensitization group, five completed their anxiety hierarchies within the allotted nine sessions. It is of interest to note that four of these five Ss performed the terminal behavior at the posttreatment assessment, whereas not a single S whose desensitization had to be terminated before all anxiety items had been successfully neutralized was able to hold the snake barehanded. Moreover, no S in the exposure or no treatment groups performed the terminal behavior, and only one out of the eight pseudodesensitization Ss attained the criterion performance.

Anxiety-Inhibiting Function of Relaxation

The Ss in both the disensitization and exposure conditions had been instructed to signal to E by raising their index finger whenever a particular imagined scene aroused anxiety. Since Ss in these two groups were matched for the order, number, and duration of stimulus exposures, any differences in the frequency of anxiety signaling provide suggestive evidence for the efficacy of relaxation in counteracting the development of emotional arousal during systematic desensitization (but see methodological problem raised in Discussion below).

The Ss in the desensitization group signaled anxiety on 27% of the stimulus presentations, whereas the corresponding figure for the exposure group was 61%. This highly significant difference ($t = 3.30$; $p < .01$, two-tailed test) not only furnishes an independent check on the relaxation training, but also attests to the anxiety-inhibiting capabilities of relaxation procedures.

Relationship between Anxiety Decrements and Approach Behavior

All Ss except those in the first cluster rated the degree of emotional disturbance that they experienced during the successful performance of each task in the pre- and posttreatment assessments. Since all but one S in the desensitization treatment surpassed their initial approach performance, it is possible to obtain a measure of anxiety decrement at the point at which Ss were unable to proceed any further during the pretreatment assessment. Thus, for example, an S who, on the first test, went so far as to look down at the snake with the wire cover drawn back and reported an anxiety rating of 9, but subsequently performed this same task with an anxiety rating of 2, would receive a decrement score of 7 points. These self-report data were analyzed in order to determine whether desensitization, in addition to increasing approach behavior, also reduces the degree of emotional disturbance accompanying the overt responses.

Except for one S who exhibited no behavioral change and reported a 1-point increase in anxiety, the remaining six cases all showed decreases, the mean decrement being 3.28. The t value for the correlated differences is 3.31, significant beyond the .04 level, two-tailed test.

It will be recalled that some Ss in the pseudodesensitization group showed small but nonsignificant increases in approach behavior (Table 2). These Ss also displayed some decrease in anxiety ($M = 2.67$), but not of a statistically significant magnitude ($t = 1.76$).

A within-group correlational analysis for Ss in the desensitization condition further revealed that the magnitude of anxiety decrement is highly predictive of the degree of increase exhibited by Ss in approach behavior. The product–moment correlation obtained between these two measures is $r = .81$, significant beyond the .05 level. This strong relationship indicates that Ss who experienced the greatest amount of anxiety reduction also showed the most behavioral improvement.

Anxiety Accompanying Strong Approach Responses

Although Ss who had undergone systematic desensitization exhibited highly significant improvement in overt approach to the snake, it is evident from the data that the bold approach responses performed in the posttest were accompanied by considerable anxiety, ranging from 4 to 10 on the 10-point self-report scale, with a mean of 7.75. These findings, which are consistent with results obtained by Lang and Lazovik (1963) and Lang et al. (1965), will be discussed later.

Discussion

The results of the present study provide strong support for the hypothesis that behavioral changes produced by systematic desensitization reflect a counterconditioning process. This is shown in the finding that only Ss for whom aversive stimuli were contiguously associated in imagination with the anxiety-competing response of relaxation (i.e., Ss in the desensitization group) displayed significant reduction in avoidance behavior; this reduction was also significantly greater than the nonsignificant changes observed in the pseudodesensitization, exposure, and no treatment control groups. The fact that Ss who were merely exposed to the aversive stimuli, and those for whom relaxation was paired with snake-irrelevant stimuli, showed no significant changes in snake avoidance indicates that neither graded exposure alone nor relaxation and expectations of beneficial effects were determinants of the outcomes yielded by the desensitization treatment. Moreover, the desensitization–no treatment comparison replicates Lang and Lazovik (1963), while the desensitization–pseudodesensitization comparison provides some manner of confirmation of Lang et al. (1965).

In evaluating the treatment involving mere exposure to the graded aversive stimuli, it should be noted that, in order to control for duration of visualization, Ss were often required to continue imagining a scene after they had signaled anxiety. It is possible that, had Ss been allowed to control their own exposures to the aversive items, they might have produced some extinction of fear. In a pilot study by the author (Davison, 1965b), considerable extinction was observed when Ss controlled their own exposures to aversive stimuli. In comparison, it should be pointed out that Davison's experiment, as well as the earlier observations of Grossberg (1965), Herzberg (1941), and Jones (1924), used actual rather than symbolic stimuli. Nonetheless, it would be of considerable interest and importance to determine whether self-controlled exposure to aversive stimuli in imaginal form also effects significant reduction in avoidance.

In addition, this issue of forced versus self-controlled exposure necessitates caution in interpreting the finding that desensitization Ss signaled anxiety significantly less often than their matched and yoked exposure mates. This difference may be due not only to the anxiety-competing properties of deep muscular relaxation, but also to the aversive nature of being unable to perform a response that will remove one from a fearful situation (cf. Mowrer & Viek, 1948).

Suggestive evidence was obtained indicating that the increased approach behavior of the desensitization group was due to a decrease in anxiety; that is, the actual avoidance gradient seems to have been lowered to allow for more approach. While performing on the posttreatment assessment the most difficult behavior encountered at the pretreatment assessment, desensitization Ss rated themselves as significantly less anxious; furthermore, a high positive and significant correlation was found in this group between decrements in self-reported anxiety and amount of overt behavioral improvement. These findings are consistent with the anxiety-avoidance paradigm of Mowrer (1940, 1947) and Miller (1948), as well as with theories of psychopathology based on animal learning experiments (Dollard & Miller, 1950; Mowrer, 1950)—all of which at least implicitly form the basis of Wolpian behavior therapy. According to this general view, avoidance responses are mediated by a secondary drive of fear; to the extent that a treatment method successfully reduces this fear, formerly inhibited approach responses will become manifest with the reduction of fear.

However, this anxiety-reduction analysis of the data is subject to several qualifications. First, questions can be raised as to the validity of self-report data on a numerical scale as a measure of anxiety (cf. Martin, 1961). Asking a naive S to rate herself on a scale from 1 to 10 may be making undue demands for rather fine discriminations among degrees of emotional arousal. A second problem is that Ss rates their anxiety *after* they performed a given behavior. In order to infer the role of fear in inhibiting a given behavior, a logical requirement is that such measures be taken before or during the behavior. Although Ss had been asked to rate the anxiety they were experiencing while performing the behavior, it is impossible to estimate the effect of actually performing the behavior on their self-reported ratings. A third consideration is of a theoretical nature. The experiments of Solomon and Wynne (1954) and Wynne and Solomon (1955) raise doubts about a straightforward interpretation of avoidance behavior as mediated by covert fear responses. Indeed, the data reported in the present study are amenable to at least one alternative explanation, namely, that anxiety and avoidance responses are *both* conditioned to the aversive stimuli, therefore being correlated classes of responses but not necessarily causally related. Systematic desensitization, then, may be reducing both components of avoidance behavior. Indeed, some suggestive evidence for the partial independence of anxiety and avoidance is the fact that Ss characteristically experienced high emotional arousal while successfully executing the terminal approach response, even after having completed their anxiety hierarchies. Unfortunately, these data, it will be seen below, may also be considered in support of the anxiety-avoidance hypothesis.

Limitations of Systematic Desensitization

Having confirmed that systematic desensitization significantly reduces avoidance behavior, and having provided evidence that an actual process of counterconditioning underlies these effects, it would seem valuable at this point to examine both the practical and theoretical limitations of the technique.

The practical limitations concern levels of relaxation achieved, the clarity of aversive images, and the signaling of anxiety. In the present study, as in clinical uses of the procedure, extensive reliance was placed on *Ss*' self-reports. It is clear that the outcome of any desensitization study will greatly depend on how satisfactorily these problems are dealt with.

Perhaps more intriguing are the theoretical limitations. It will be recalled that desensitization *Ss* experienced considerable anxiety while performing the terminal behavior or approach responses high in the graduated series of tasks during the posttreatment assessment. Inasmuch as five of eight *Ss* in this group had been successfully desensitized in imagination, their anxiety reactions in the posttreatment assessment situation raise an interesting theoretical question regarding transfer effects.

One would expect, on the basis of the principle of stimulus generalization (Kimble, 1961), that the degree of transfer of counterconditioning effects from one stimulus situation to another is determined by the number of common elements. According to Guthrie's (1952) notion, for example, a complex stimulus (like a snake) consists of a finite number of stimulus elements, each of which can be attached to only one molecular fear response at any given time. The desensitization procedure, as the present author has heuristically viewed it, operates in two ways to render a given molar stimulus incapable of arousing the molar response of fear. First, by beginning with the weakest items of an anxiety hierarchy one is presumably taking a very small sample of the "snake-object population of stimulus elements." Since this limited "amount of snake" elicits a limited "amount of fear," an incompatible response can be made dominant over the minimal fear response. This is why second deep muscular relaxation responses are induced prior to the introduction of the small dose of aversive stimuli. It is in this fashion that one "alienates" the small sample of fear stimuli from the limited number of molecular fear responses.

When a given anxiety item has been neutralized (defined as visualizing it for 15 sec. without signaling anxiety), another sample from the population of fear stimuli is presented, the incompatible relaxation response being set against that part of the total fear response which would ordinarily be elicited by the sample of fear stimuli. This process continues up the anxiety hierarchy until all items have been successfully desensitized.

When viewed in this fashion, the process of systematic desensitization would not be expected to effect complete transfer from the imagined to the real-life situation. For, even though an *S* succeeds in imagining the various anxiety items without becoming anxious, the facts remain that: (*a*) The visualization is unlikely to involve all the stimulus elements for the respective level of the hierarchy; and (*b*) the hierarchy itself cannot possibly provide an exhaustive sampling of the population of fear elements.

In the studies of Lang and Lazovik (1963), Lang et al. (1965), and Paul (1966), there was also a failure to find complete fearlessness on the part of successfully desensitized Ss. On the other hand, the clinical literature would lead one to expect perfect transfer, namely, "It has consistently been found that at every stage a stimulus that evokes no anxiety when imagined in a state of relaxation evokes no anxiety when encountered in reality [Wolpe, 1961, p. 191]." This discrepancy may in some measure be due to the unreliability of clinical reports. However, assuming that the clinical data are, in fact, valid, the greater generalization of counterconditioning effects in actual clinical practice may be a function of several factors which were intentionally excluded from the present experimental design. Among these would be in vivo desensitization based on differential relaxation (Davison, 1965b; Wolpe & Lazarus, 1966), the positive reinforcement of approach responses in interaction with presumed counterconditioning (Bower & Grusec, 1964; Davison, 1964; Lazarus, Davison, & Polefka, 1965), the vicarious extinction of avoidance responses by means of modeling procedures (Bandura et al., 1967; Jones, 1924), "placebo effect" (Frank, 1961; Paul, 1966), and the so-called "nonspecifics" of a therapeutic relationship (cf. Lazarus, 1963).

Etiology versus Treatment

Having furnished evidence in favor of a conditioning interpretation of a particular technique of behavior modification, it would seem appropriate to comment briefly on the implications which these findings have for the development of neurotic anxiety. An error in logic is committed if one adduces data such as these as evidence in support of a conditioning model of the *acquisition* of inappropriate anxiety: from evidence regarding efficacy in changing behavior, one cannot claim to have demonstrated that the problem evolved in an analogous fashion (cf. Rimland, 1964). Whether in the present instance neurotic disorders, modifiable via counterconditioning techniques, originate in situations conceptualized in classical conditioning terms is a very important research and preventive therapy question; it is, however, separate from the corrective therapy issue. In fact, the author has sought vainly in the experimental literature for paradigms which illustrate the acquisition of *stable* fear responses in human beings under conditions bearing even a remote resemblance to what would likely hold in real life.[2]

Notes

[1] This paper is based on the author's doctoral dissertation written at Stanford University under Albert Bandura, whose invaluable advice and direction at every stage of the research and composition he is pleased to acknowledge. For their aid and encouragement, sincere thanks are also rendered to Arnold A. Lazarus and Gordon L. Paul. The author is especially grateful to O. B. Neresen, who made available both the physical facilities and human resources at Foothill Junior College, Los Altos, California.

[2] The author is indebted to Gordon L. Paul and Bernard Rimland for first pointing out these issues.

References

Bandura, A. *Principles of behavior modification.* New York: Holt, in press.

Bandura, A., Grusec, J. E., & Menlove, F. Vicarious extinction of avoidance responses. *Journal of Personality and Social Psychology,* 1967, **5,** 16–23.

Bower, G. H., & Grusec, T. Effect of prior Pavlovian discrimination training upon learning an operant discrimination. *Journal of Experimental Analysis of Behavior*, 1964, **7**, 401–404.

Breger, L., & McGaugh, J. L. A critique and reformulation of "learning theory" approaches to psychotherapy and neurosis. *Psychological Bulletin*, 1965, **63**, 338–358.

Davison, G. C. A social learning therapy programme with an autistic child. *Behavior Research and Therapy*. 1964, **2**, 149–159.

Davison, G. C. The influence of systematic desensitization, relaxation, and graded exposure to imaginal aversive stimuli on the modification of phobic behavior. Unpublished doctoral dissertation, Stanford University, 1965. (a)

Davison, G. C. Relative contributions of differential relaxation and graded exposure to the in vivo desensitization of a neurotic fear. In, *Proceedings of the 73rd Annual Convention of the American Psychological Association, 1965*. Washington, D.C.: American Psychological Association, 1965. (b)

Dollard, J., & Miller, N. E. *Personality and psychotherapy*. New York: McGraw-Hill, 1950.

Frank, J. D. *Persuasion and healing*. Baltimore: Johns Hopkins Press, 1961.

Geer, J. Phobia treated by reciprocal inhibition. *Journal of Abnormal and Social Psychology*, 1964, **69**, 642–645.

Gleitman, H., Nachmias, J., & Neisser, U. The S–R reinforcement theory of extinction. *Psychological Review*, 1954, **61**, 23–33.

Grossberg, J. M. Successful behavior therapy in a case of speech phobia ("stage fright"). *Journal of Speech and Hearing Disorders*, 1965, **30**, 285–288.

Guthrie, E. R. *The psychology of learning*. New York: Harper, 1952.

Herzberg, A. Short treatment of neuroses by graduated tasks. *British Journal of Medical Psychology*, 1941, **19**, 36–51.

Hull, C. L. *Principles of behavior*. New York: Appleton, 1943.

Jones, M. C. The elimination of children's fears. *Journal of Experimental Psychology*, 1924, **7**, 382–390.

Kimble, G. A. *Hilgard and Marquis' conditioning and learning*. New York: Appleton-Century-Crofts, 1961.

Lang, P. J. Behavior therapy with a case of nervous anorexia. In L. P. Ullmann & L. Krasner (Eds.), *Case studies in behavior modification*. New York: Holt, 1965.

Lang, P. J., & Lazovik, A. D. Experimental desensitization of a phobia. *Journal of Abnormal and Social Psychology*, 1963, **66**, 519–525.

Lang, P. J., Lazovik, A. D., & Reynolds, D. J. Desensitization, suggestibility, and pseudotherapy. *Journal of Abnormal Psychology*, 1965, **70**, 395–402.

Lawrence, D. H., & Festinger, L. *Deterrents and reinforcement: The psychology of insufficient reward*. Stanford: Stanford University Press, 1962.

Lazarus, A. A. Group therapy of phobic disorders by systematic desensitization. *Journal of Abnormal and Social Psychology*, 1961, **63**, 504–510.

Lazarus, A. A. The results of behavior therapy in 126 cases of severe neurosis. *Behavior Research and Therapy*, 1963, **1**, 69–79.

Lazarus, A. A., & Rachman, S. The use of systematic desensitization in psychotherapy. *South African Medical Journal*, 1957, **31**, 923–937.

Lazarus, A. A., Davison, G. C., & Polefka, D. Classical and operant factors in the treatment of a school phobia. *Journal of Abnormal Psychology*, 1965, **70**, 225–229

Martin, B. The assessment of anxiety by physiological behavioral measures. *Psychological Bulletin*, 1961, **58**, 234–255.

Miller, N. E. Studies of fear as an acquirable drive: I. Fear as motivation and fear-reduction as reinforcement in the learning of new responses. *Journal of Experimental Psychology*, 1948, **38**, 89–101.

Mowrer, O. H. Anxiety-reduction and learning. *Journal of Experimental Psychology*, 1940, **27**, 497–516.

Mowrer, O. H. On the dual nature of learning—a reinterpretation of "conditioning" and "problem solving." *Harvard Education Review*, 1947, **17**, 102–148.

Mowrer, O. H. *Learning theory and personality dynamics*, New York: Ronald Press, 1950.

Mowrer, O. H. *Learning theory and behavior*. New York: Wiley, 1960.

Mowrer, O. H., & Viek, P. An experimental analogue of fear from a sense of helplessness. *Journal of Abnormal and Social Psychology*, 1948, **43**, 193–200.

Paul, G. L. *Insight versus desensitization in psychotherapy: An experiment in anxiety-reduction*, Stanford: Stanford University Press, 1966.

Paul G. L., & Shannon, D. T. Treatment of anxiety through systematic desensitization in therapy groups. *Journal of Abnormal Psychology*, 1966, **71**, 124–135.

Rachman, S. The treatment of anxiety and phobic reactions by systematic desensitization psychotherapy. *Journal of Abnormal and Social Psychology,* 1959, **58,** 259–263.

Rimland, B. *Infantile autism.* New York: Appleton-Century-Crofts, 1964.

Sherrington, C. S. *The integrative action of the central nervous system.* Cambridge: Cambridge University Press, 1906.

Solomon, R. L., & Brush, R. S. Experimentally derived conceptions of anxiety and aversion. In M. R. Jones (Ed.), *Nebraska symposium on motivation; 1956.* Lincoln: University of Nebraska Press, 1956.

Solomon, R. L., & Wynne, L. C. Traumatic avoidance learning: The principles of anxiety conservation and partial irreversibility. *Psychological Review,* 1954, **61,** 353–395.

Wolpe, J. Objective psychotherapy of the neuroses. *South African Medical Journal,* 1952, **26,** 825–829.

Wolpe, J. *Psychotherapy by reciprocal inhibition.* Stanford: Stanford University Press, 1958.

Wolpe, J. The systematic desensitization treatment of neurosis. *Journal of Nervous and Mental Disease,* 1961, **132,** 189–203.

Wolpe, J., & Lazarus, A. A. *Behavior therapy techniques.* New York: Pergamon, 1966.

Wynne, L. C., & Solomon, R. L. Traumatic avoidance learning: Acquisition and extinction in dogs deprived of normal peripheral autonomic functioning. *Genetic Psychology Monographs,* 1955, **52,** 241–284.

B. OPERANT CONDITIONING

This section contains three examples of the use of operant contingencies of reinforcement in applied settings. The first article, by Ayllon, reports a treatment program designed for a severely disturbed woman who had been hospitalized for nine years. The woman engaged in three different pathological behaviors that were targets for modification: She stole food, hoarded towels, and wore excessive amounts of clothing. Each behavior was modified with a different technique. Stealing was punished by having the meal withdrawn, towel hoarding was satiated by supplying the woman with hundreds of towels, and normal dressing was shaped using food reinforcement. Each technique was successful in eliminating the target behavior and the program as a whole had effects that went beyond these individual behaviors. Perhaps because the woman felt less "freakish" with these behaviors suppressed, she began participating in hospital social events. Where previously she had been almost completely isolated from her fellow inmates, she now slowly began to become a participating member of the hospital community.

The second article, by Williams, describes the use of extinction to eliminate a 2-year-old's bedtime tantrums. The child was accustomed to demanding and receiving extensive parental attention at bedtime; if the parents withdrew their attention prematurely, the child screamed and cried. This resulted in renewed contact with the parents; that is, the tantrums were being reinforced. The solution, to Williams, was extinction. The extinction procedure was simple. The child was simply allowed to cry himself to sleep without parental attention, however long it took. By the third night the tantrums had essentially ended.

The final article, by Homme and co-workers, is an application of the principle of reinforcer relativity that we encountered earlier (p. 123). Nursery school children engaged in a variety of very disruptive, boisterous activities that were difficult to eliminate. So rather than try to eliminate them, they were used as reinforcers, following the teacher's instructions earned the children the opportunity to engage in these boisterous activities. The result was a substantial increase in the frequency of the activities the teacher was trying to promote.

35 Intensive Treatment of Psychotic Behaviour by Stimulus Satiation and Food Reinforcement

TEODORO AYLLON

This investigation demonstrates that extensive and effective behavioural modification is feasible without costly and lengthy psychotherapeutic treatment. In addition, the often heard notion that another undesirable type of behaviour will replace the original problem behaviour is not supported by the findings to date.[1]

Introduction

Until recently, the effective control of behaviour was limited to the animal laboratory. The extension of this control to human behaviour was made when Lindsley successfully adapted the methodology of operant conditioning to the study of psychotic behaviour (Lindsley, 1956). Following Lindsley's point of departure other investigators have shown that, in its essentials, the behaviour of mental defective individuals (Orlando and Bijou, 1960), stutterers (Flanagan, Goldiamond, and Azrin, 1958), mental patients (Hutchinson and Azrin, 1961), and autistic (Ferster and DeMyer, 1961) and normal children (Bijou, 1961; Azrin and Lindsley, 1956) is subject to the same controls.

Despite the obvious implications of this research for applied settings there has been a conspicuous lag between the research findings and their application. The greatest limitation to the direct application of laboratory principles has been the absence of control over the subjects' environment. Recently, however, a series of applications in a regulated psychiatric setting has clearly demonstrated the possibilities of behavioural modification (Ayllon and Michael, 1959; Ayllon and Haughton, 1962). Some of the behaviour studied has included repetitive and highly stereotyped responses such as complaining, pacing, refusal to eat, hoarding, and many others.

What follows is a demonstration of behaviour techniques for the intensive individual treatment of psychotic behaviour. Specific pathological behaviour patterns of a single patient were treated by manipulating the patient's environment.

The Experimental Ward and Control over the Reinforcement

This investigation was conducted in a mental hospital ward, the characteristics of which have been described elsewhere (Ayllon and Haughton, 1962). Briefly, this was a female ward to which only authorized personnel were allowed access. The ward staff was made up of psychiatric nurses and untrained aides who carried out the environmental manipulations under the direction of the experimenter. Using a time-sample technique, patients were observed daily every 30 minutes from 7:00 a.m. to 11:00 p.m.

The dining room was the only place where food was available and entrance to the dining room could be regulated. Water was freely available at a drinking fountain on the ward. None of the patients had ground passes or jobs outside the ward.

Subject

The patient was a 47-year-old female patient diagnosed as a chronic schizophrenic. The patient had been hospitalized for 9 years. Upon studying the patient's behaviour on the ward, it became apparent that the nursing staff[2] spent considerable time caring for her. In particular, there were three aspects of her behaviour which seemed to defy solution. The first was stealing food. The second was the hoarding of the ward's towels in her room. The third undesirable aspect of her behaviour consisted in her wearing excessive clothing, e.g. a half-dozen dresses, several pairs of stockings, sweaters, and so on.

In order to modify the patient's behaviour systematically, each of these three types of behaviour (stealing food, hoarding, and excessive dressing) was treated separately.

Experiment I
Control of Stealing Food by Food Withdrawal

The patient had weighed over 250 pounds for many years. She ate the usual tray of food served to all patients, but, in addition, she stole food from the food counter and from other patients. Because the medical staff regarded her excessive weight as detrimental to her health, a special diet had been prescribed for her. However, the patient refused to diet and continued stealing food. In an effort to discourage the patient from stealing, the ward nurses had spent considerable time trying to persuade her to stop stealing food. As a last resort, the nurses would force her to return the stolen food.

To determine the extent of food stealing, nurses were instructed to record all behaviour associated with eating in the dining room. This record, taken for nearly a month, showed that the patient stole food during two-thirds of all meals.

Procedure

The traditional methods previously used to stop the patient from stealing food were discontinued. No longer were persuasion, coaxing, or coercion used.

The patient was assigned to a table in the dining room, and no other patients were allowed to sit with her. Nurses removed the patient from the dining room when she approached a table other than her own, or when she picked up unauthorized food from the dining room counter. In effect, this procedure resulted in the patient missing a meal whenever she attempted to steal food.

Figure 1 shows that when withdrawal of positive reinforcement (i.e. meal) was made dependent upon the patient's "stealing," this response

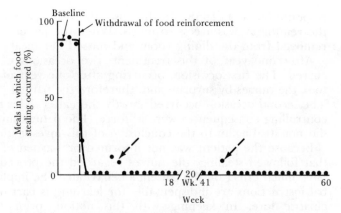

FIG. 1. *A response, food stealing, is eliminated when it results in the withdrawal of food reinforcement. The dotted arrows indicate the rare occasions when food stealing occurred. For purposes of presentation a segment comprising 20 weeks during which no stealing occurred is not included.*

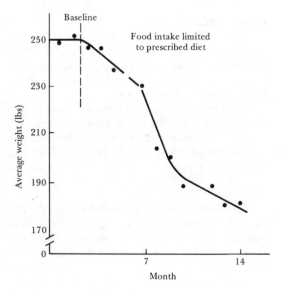

FIG. 2. *The effective control of food stealing results in a notable reduction in body weight. If the patient's food intake is limited to the prescribed diet her weight decreases gradually.*

was eliminated in two weeks. Because the patient no longer stole food, she ate only the diet prescribed for her. The effective control of the stealing response is also indicated by the gradual reduction in the patient's body weight. At no time during the patient's 9 years of hospitalization had she weighed less than 230 pounds. Figure 2 shows that at the conclusion of this treatment her weight stabilized at 180 pounds or 17 per cent loss from her original weight. At this time, the patient's physical condition was regarded as excellent.

Discussion

A principle used in the laboratory shows that the strength of a response may be weakened by the removal of positive reinforcement following the response (Ferster, 1958). In this case, the response was food-stealing and the reinforcer was access to meals. When the patient stole food she was removed from the dining room and missed her meal.

After one year of this treatment, two occasions of food stealing occurred. The first occasion, occurring after one year of not stealing food, took the nurses by surprise and, therefore the patient "got away" with it. The second occasion occurred shortly thereafter. This time, however, the controlling consequences were in force. The patient missed that meal and did not steal again to the conclusion of this investigation.

Because the patient was not informed or warned of the consequences that followed stealing, the nurses regarded the procedure as unlikely to have much effect on the patient's behaviour. The implicit belief that verbal instructions are indispensable for learning is part of present day psychiatric lore. In keeping with this notion, prior to this behaviour treatment, the nurses had tried to persuade the patient to co-operate in dieting. Because there were strong medical reasons for her losing weight, the patient's refusal to follow a prescribed diet was regarded as further evidence of her mental illness.

Experiment II
Control of One Form of Hoarding Behaviour through Stimulus Satiation

During the 9 years of hospitalization, the patient collected large numbers of towels and stored them in her room. Although many efforts had been made to discourage hoarding, this behaviour continued unaltered. The only recourse for the nursing staff was to take away the patient's towels about twice a week.

To determine the degree of hoarding behaviour, the towels in her room were counted three times a week, when the patient was not in her room. This count showed that the number of towels kept in her room ranged from 19 to 29 despite the fact that during this time the nurses continued recovering their towel supply from the patient's room.

Procedure

The routine removal of the towels from the patient's room was discontinued. Instead, a programme of stimulus satiation was carried out by the nurses. Intermittently, throughout the day, the nurses took a towel to the patient when she was in her room and simply handed it to her without any comment. The first week she was given an average of 7 towels daily, and by the third week this number was increased to 60.

Results

The technique of satiation eliminated the towel hoarding. Figure 3 shows the mean number of towels per count found in the patient's room. When the number of towels kept in her room reached the 625 mark, she started taking a few of them out. Thereafter, no more towels were given to her. During the next 12 months the mean number of towels found in her room was 1.5 per week.

Discussion

The procedure used to reduce the amount of towel hoarding bears resemblance to satiation of a reinforcer. A reinforcer loses its effect when

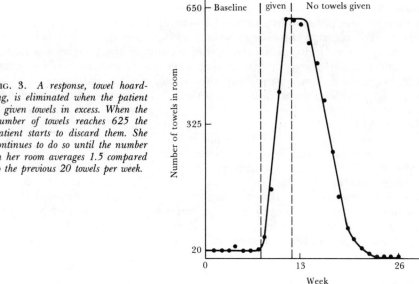

FIG. 3. *A response, towel hoarding, is eliminated when the patient is given towels in excess. When the number of towels reaches 625 the patient starts to discard them. She continues to do so until the number in her room averages 1.5 compared to the previous 20 towels per week.*

an excessive amount of that reinforcer is made available. Accordingly, the response maintained by that reinforcer is weakened. In this application, the towels constituted the reinforcing stimuli. When the number of towels in her room reached 625, continuing to give her towels seemed to make their collection aversive. The patient then proceeded to rid herself of the towels until she had virtually none.

During the first few weeks of satiation, the patient was observed patting her cheeks with a few towels, apparently enjoying them. Later, the patient was observed spending much of her time folding and stacking the approximately 600 towels in her room. A variety of remarks were made by the patient regarding receipt of towels. All verbal statements made by the patient were recorded by the nurse. The following represent typical remarks made during this experiment. First week: as the nurse entered the patient's room carrying a towel, the patient would smile and say, "Oh, you found it for me, thank you." Second week: When the number of towels given to patient increased rapidly, she told the nurses, "Don't give me no more towels. I've got enough." Third week: "Take them towels away. . . . I can't sit here all night and fold towels." Fourth and fifth weeks: "Get these dirty towels out of here." Sixth week: After she had started taking the towels out of her room, she remarked to the nurse, "I can't drag any more of these towels, I just can't do it."

The quality of these remarks suggests that the initial effect of giving towels to the patient was reinforcing. However as the towels increased they ceased to be reinforcing, and presumably became aversive.

The ward nurses, who had undergone a three year training in psychiatric nursing, found it difficult to reconcile the procedure in this experiment with their psychiatric orientation. Most nurses subscribed to the popular psychiatric view which regards hoarding behaviour as a reflection of a deep "need" for love and security. Presumably, no "real" behavioural change was possible without meeting the patient's 'needs' first. Even after the patient discontinued hoarding towels in her room, some nurses predicted that the change would not last and that worse behaviour would replace it. Using a time-sampling technique the patient was under continuous observation for over a year after the termination of the satiation programme. Not once during this period did the patient return the hoarding towels. Furthermore, no other behaviour problem replaced hoarding.

Experiment III
Control of an Additional Form of Hoarding through Food Reinforcement

Shortly after the patient had been admitted to the hospital she wore an excessive amount of clothing which included several sweaters, shawls, dresses, undergarments, and stockings. The clothing also included sheets and towels wrapped around her body, and a turban-like head-dress made up of several towels. In addition, the patient carried two to three cups on one hand while holding a bundle of miscellaneous clothing, and a large purse on the other.

To determine the amount of clothing worn by the patient, she was weighed before each meal over a period of two weeks. By subtracting her actual body weight from that recorded when she was dressed, the weight of her clothing was obtained.

Procedure

The response required for reinforcement was stepping on a scale and meeting a predetermined weight. The requirement for reinforcement consisted of meeting a single weight (i.e., her body weight plus a specified number of pounds of clothing). Initially she was given an allowance of 23 pounds over her current body weight. This allowance represented a 2 pound reduction from her usual clothing weight. When the patient exceeded the weight requirement, the nurse stated in a matter-of-fact manner, "Sorry, you weigh too much, you'll have to weigh less." Failure to meet the required weight resulted in the patient missing the meal at which she was being weighed. Sometimes, in an effort to meet the requirement, the patient discarded more clothing than she was required. When this occurred the requirement was adjusted at the next weighing-time to correspond to the limit set by the patient on the preceding occasion.

Results

When food reinforcement is made dependent upon the removal of superfluous clothing the response increases in frequency. Figure 4 shows that the patient gradually shed her clothing to meet the more demanding weight requirement until she dressed normally. At the conclusion of this experiment her clothes weighed 3 pounds compared to the 25 pounds she wore before this treatment.

Some verbal shaping was done in order to encourage the patient to leave the cups and bundles she carried with her. Nurses stopped her at the dining room and said, "Sorry, no things are allowed in the dining

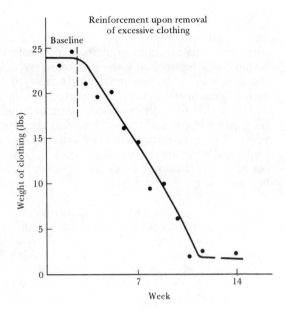

FIG. 4. *A response, excessive dressing, is eliminated when food reinforcement is made dependent upon removal of superfluous clothing. Once the weight of the clothing worn by the patient drops to 3 pounds it remains stable.*

room." No mention of clothing or specific items was made to avoid focusing undue attention upon them. Within a week, the patient typically stepped on the scale without her bundle and assorted objects. When her weight was over the limit, the patient was informed that she weighed "too much." She then proceeded to take off a few clothes, stepped on the scale again, and upon meeting the weight requirement, gained access to the dining room.

Discussion

According to the principle of reinforcement a class of responses is strengthened when it is followed by reinforcement. A reinforcer is such when it results in a response increase. In this application the removal of excessive clothing constituted the response and the reinforcer was food (i.e., access to meals). When the patient met the weight requirement she was reinforced by being given access to meals.

At the start of this experiment, the patient missed a few meals because she failed to meet the weight requirement, but soon thereafter she gradually discarded her superfluous clothing. First, she left behind odd items she had carried in her arms, such as bundles, cups, and handbags. Next she took off the elaborate headgear and assorted "capes" or shawls she had worn over her shoulders. Although she had worn 18 pairs of stockings at one time, she eventually shed these also.

During the initial part of this experiment, the patient showed some emotional behaviour, e.g., crying, shouting, and throwing chairs around. Because nurses were instructed to "ignore" this emotional behaviour, the patient obtained no sympathy or attention from them. The withholding of social reinforcement for emotional behaviour quickly led to its elimination.

At the conclusion of this behaviour treatment, the patient typically stepped on the scale wearing a dress, undergarments, a pair of stockings, and a pair of light shoes. One of the behavioural changes concomitant with the current environmental manipulation was that as the patient began dressing normally she started to participate in small social events in the hospital. This was particularly new to the patient as she had previously remained seclusive spending most of the time in her room.

About this time the patient's parents came to visit her and insisted on taking her home for a visit. This was the first time during the patient's 9 years of hospitalization that her parents had asked to take her out. They remarked that previously they had not been interested in taking her out because the patient's excessive dressing in addition to her weight made her look like a "circus freak."

Conclusions

The research presented here was conducted under nearly ideal conditions. The variables manipulated (i.e., towels and food) were under full experimental control. Using a time-sample technique the patient was observed daily every 30 minutes from 7:00 a.m. to 11:00 p.m. Nurses and aides carried out these observations which were later analyzed in terms of gross behaviour categories. These observations were in force for over a year during which time these three experiments were conducted. The results of those observations indicate that none of the three pathological behaviour patterns (i.e., food stealing, hoarding, and excessive dressing) exhibited by the patient were replaced by any undesirable behaviour.

The patient displayed some emotional behaviour in each experiment, but each time it subsided when social reinforcement (i.e., attention) was not forthcoming. The patient did not become violent or seclusive as a consequence of these experiments. Instead, she became socially more accessible to patients and staff. She did not achieve a great deal of social success but she did begin to participate actively in social functions.

A frequent problem encountered in mental hospitals is overeating. In general this problem is solved by prescribing a reduction diet. Many patients, however, refuse to take a reduction diet and continue overeating. When confronted with this behaviour, psychiatric workers generally resort to two types of explanations.

One explanation of overeating points out that only with the active and sincere cooperation of the patient can weight reduction be accomplished. When the patient refuses to co-operate he is regarded as showing more signs of mental illness and all hopes of eliminating overeating come to an end.

Another type of explanation holds that overeating is not the behaviour to be concerned with. Instead, attention is focused on the psychological "needs" of the patient. These "needs" are said to be the cause of the observable behaviour, overeating. Therefore the emphasis is on the removal of the cause and not on the symptom or behaviour itself. Whatever theoretical merit these explanations may have, it is unfortunate that they fail to suggest practical ways of treating the behaviour itself. As a consequence, the patient continues to overeat often to the detriment of his health.

The current psychiatric emphasis on the resolution of the mental conflict that is presumably at the basis of the symptoms, is perhaps misplaced. What seems to have been forgotten is that behaviour problems such as those reported here, prevent the patient from being considered for discharge not only by the hospital personnel but also by the patient's relatives. Indeed, as far as the patient's relatives are concerned, the index of improvement or deterioration is the readily observable behaviour and not a detailed account of the mechanics of the mental apparatus.

Many individuals are admitted to mental hospitals because of one or more specific behaviour difficulties and not always because of a generalized "mental" disturbance. For example, an individual may go into a mental hospital because he has refused to eat for several days or because he talks to himself incessantly. If the goal of therapy were behavioural rehabilitation, these problems would be treated and normal eating and normal talking reinstated. However, the current emphasis in psychotherapy is on "mental-conflict resolution" and little or no attention is given to dealing directly with the behavioural problems which prevent the patient from returning to the community.

Notes

[1] This report is based, in part, on a two-year research project (1959–1961), conducted by the author at the Saskatchewan Hospital, Weyburn, Saskatchewan, Canada, and supported by a grant from the Commonwealth Fund. Grateful acknowledgment is due to H. Osmond and I. Clancey of the Saskatchewan Hospital. The author also thanks E. Haughton, who assisted in the conduct of this investigation, and N. Azrin and W. Holtz for their critical reading of the manuscript.

[2] As used in this paper, *nurse* is a generic term including all those who actually work on the ward (attendants, aides, psychiatric and registered nurses).

References

Ayllon, T., and Michael, J. (1959) The psychiatric nurse as a behavioral engineer. *J. Exp. Anal. Behav.* **2**, 323–334.

Ayllon, T., and Haughton, E. (1962) Control of the behavior of schizophrenic patients by food. *J. Exp. Anal. Behav.* **5**, 343–352.

Azrin, N., and Lindsley, O. (1956) The reinforcement of cooperation between children. *J. Abnorm. (Soc.) Psychol.* **52**, 100–102.

Bijou, S. (1961) Discrimination performance as a baseline for individual analysis of young children. *Child Develpm.* **32**, 163–170.

Ferster, C. B. (1958) Control of behavior in chimpanzees and pigeons by time out from positive reinforcement. *Psychol. Monogr.* **72**, 1–38.

Ferster, C., and DeMyer, M. (1961) The development of performances in autistic children in an automatically controlled environment. *J. Chron. Dis.* **13**, 312–345.

Flanagan, B., Goldiamond, L., and Azrin, N. (1958) Operant stuttering: The control of stuttering behavior through response-contingent consequences. *J. Exp. Anal. Behav.* **56**, 49–56.

Hutchinson, R. R., and Azrin, N. H. (1961) Conditioning of mental hospital patients to fixed-ratio schedules of reinforcement. *J. Exp. Anal. Behav.* **4**, 87–95.

Lindsley, O. R. (1956) Operant conditioning methods applied to research in chronic schizophrenia. *Psychiat. Res. Rep.* **5**, 118–139.

Orlando, R., and Bijou, S. (1960) Single and multiple schedules of reinforcement in developmentally retarded children. *J. Exp. Anal. Behav.* **3**, 339–348.

36 The Elimination of Tantrum Behavior by Extinction Procedures

CARL D. WILLIAMS

This paper reports the successful treatment of tyrant-like tantrum behavior in a male child by the removal of reinforcement. The subject (S) was approximately 21 months old. He had been seriously ill much of the first 18 months of his life. His health then improved considerably, and he gained weight and vigor.

S now demanded the special care and attention that had been given him over the many critical months. He enforced some of his wishes, especially at bedtime, by unleashing tantrum behavior to control the actions of his parents.

The parents and an aunt took turns in putting him to bed both at night and for S's afternoon nap. If the parent left the bedroom after putting S in his bed, S would scream and fuss until the parent returned to the room. As a result, the parent was unable to leave the bedroom until after S went to sleep. If the parent began to read while in the bedroom, S would cry until the reading material was put down. The parents felt that S enjoyed his control over them and that he fought off going to sleep as long as he could. In any event, a parent was spending from one-half to two hours each bedtime just waiting in the bedroom until S went to sleep.

Following medical reassurance regarding S's physical condition, it was decided to remove the reinforcement of this tyrant-like tantrum behavior. Consistent with the learning principle that, in general, behavior that is not reinforced will be extinguished, a parent or the aunt put S to bed in a leisurely and relaxed fashion. After bedtime pleasantries, the parent left the bedroom and closed the door. S screamed and raged, but the parent did not re-enter the room. The duration of screaming and crying was obtained from the time the door was closed.

The result are shown in Fig. 1. It can be seen that S continued screaming for 45 min. the first time he was put to bed in the first extinction series. S did not cry at all the second time he was put to bed. This is perhaps attributable to his fatigue from the crying of Occasion 1. By the tenth occasion, S no longer whimpered, fussed, or cried when the parent left the room. Rather, he smiled as they left. The parents felt that he made happy sounds until he dropped off to sleep.

About a week later, S screamed and fussed after the aunt put him to bed, probably reflecting spontaneous recovery of the tantrum behavior. The aunt then reinforced the tantrum behavior by returning to S's bedroom and remaining there until he went to sleep. It was then necessary to extinguish this behavior a second time.

Figure 1 shows that the second extinction curve is similar to the first.

"The Elimination of Tantrum Behavior by Extinction Procedures" by Carl D. Williams. *Journal of Abnormal and Social Psychology*, 1959, 59, 269. Copyright 1959 by the American Psychological Association. Reprinted by permission of the publisher and author.

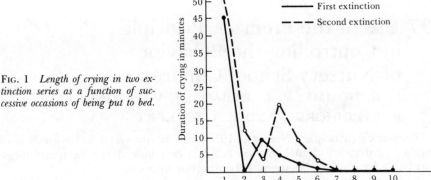

FIG. 1 *Length of crying in two extinction series as a function of successive occasions of being put to bed.*

Both curves are generally similar to extinction curves obtained with subhuman subjects. The second extinction series reached zero by the ninth occasion. No further tantrums at bedtime were reported during the next two years.

It should be emphasized that the treatment in this case did not involve aversive punishment. All that was done was to remove the reinforcement. Extinction of the tyrant-like tantrum behavior then occurred.

No unfortunate side- or aftereffects of this treatment were observed. At three and three-quarters year of age, S appeared to be a friendly, expressive, outgoing child.

37 Use of the Premack Principle in Controlling the Behavior of Nursery School Children

L. E. HOMME, P. C. DEBACA, J. V. DEVINE,

R. STEINHORST, AND E. J. RICKERT

Premack's principle (Premack, 1959) can be stated: if behavior B is of higher probability than behavior A, then behavior A can be made more probable by making behavior B contingent upon it.

In a preliminary exploration of nursery school procedures, three 3-yr-old subjects (Ss) were available three hours a day, five days a week, for about one month. On the first day, in the absence of any aversive control, verbal instructions usually had little effect on the Ss' behavior. When they were instructed to sit in their chairs, Ss would often continue what they were doing—running around the room, screaming, pushing chairs, or quietly working jigsaw puzzles. Taking Premack seriously, such behaviors were labeled as high probability behaviors and used in combination with the signals for them as reinforcers. These high probability behaviors were then made contingent on desired behaviors. For example, sitting quietly in a chair and looking at the blackboard would be intermittently followed by the sound of the bell, with the instruction: "Run and scream." The Ss would then leap to their feet and run around the room screaming. At another signal they would stop. At this time they would get another signal and an instruction to engage in some other behavior which, on a quasi-random schedule, might be one of high or low probability. At a later stage, Ss earned tokens for low probability behaviors which could later be used to "buy" the opportunity for high probability activities.

With this kind of procedure, control was virtually perfect after a few days. For example, when Ss were requested to "sit and look at the blackboard" (an activity which in the past had intermittently been interrupted by the signal for some higher probability behavior), they were under such good control that an observer, new on the scene, almost certainly would have assumed extensive aversive control was being used.

An examination of high probability behaviors quickly showed that many, if not most of them, were behaviors which ordinarily would be suppressed through punishment. Extrapolating from this we were able to predict the reinforcing properties of some behaviors which had never been emitted. For example, throwing a plastic cup across the room and kicking a waste basket had never been observed but proved to be highly reinforcing activities after they had once been evoked by instructions.

(Some unpredicted behaviors proved to be highly reinforcing, *e.g.*, pushing the experimenter around the room in his caster-equipped chair.)

In summary, even in this preliminary, unsystematic application, the Premack hypothesis proved to be an exceptionally practical principle for controlling the behavior of nursery school *S*s.

References
Premack, D. Toward empirical behavior laws: I. Positive reinforcement. *Psychol. Rev.* 1959, **66**, 219–233.

C. TOKEN REINFORCEMENT

We encountered the phenomenon of conditioned reinforcement earlier. A neutral stimulus that predicts the occurrence of an unconditioned reinforcer becomes associated with the reinforcer. As a result, it stops being neutral and behavior can be reinforced by the presentation of that stimulus. A variant of conditioned reinforcement procedures involves the use of token reinforcement. Responses produce tokens that are later exchanged for unconditioned reinforcers like food. Token reinforcement can sustain great amounts of behavior in the face of a very infrequent occurrence of the unconditioned reinforcer (p. 136).

Token reinforcement procedures have become extremely common in application. This section contains an example by O'Leary et al.

38 A Token Reinforcement Program in a Public School: A Replication and Systematic Analysis

K. D. O'LEARY, W. C. BECKER, M. B. EVANS, AND R. A. SAUDARGAS

A base rate of disruptive behavior was obtained for seven children in a second-grade class of 21 children. Rules, Educational Structure, and Praising Appropriate Behavior while Ignoring Disruptive Behavior were introduced successively; none of these procedures consistently reduced disruptive behavior. However, a combination of Rules, Educational Structure, and Praise and Ignoring nearly eliminated disruptive behavior of one child. When the Token Reinforcement Program was introduced, the frequency of disruptive behavior declined in five of the six remaining children. Withdrawal of the Token Reinforcement Program increased disruptive behavior in these five children, and reinstatement of the Token Reinforcement Program reduced disruptive behavior in four of these five. Follow-up data indicated that the teacher was able to transfer control from the token and back-up reinforcers to the reinforcers existing within the educational setting, such as stars and occasional pieces of candy. Improvements in academic achievement during the year may have been related to the Token Program, and attendance records appeared to be enhanced during the Token phases. The Token Program was utilized only in the afternoon, and the data did not indicate any generalization of appropriate behavior from the afternoon to the morning.[1]

Praise and other social stimuli connected with the teacher's behavior have been established as effective controllers of children's behavior (Allen, Hart, Buell, Harris, and Wolf, 1964; Becker, Madsen, Arnold, and Thomas, 1967; Brown and Elliot 1965; Hall, Lund, and Jackson, 1968; Harris, Johnston, Kelley, and Wolf, 1964; Harris, Wolf, and Baer, 1964; Scott, Burton, and Yarrow, 1967; Zimmerman and Zimmerman, 1962). When the teacher's use of praise and social censure is not effective, token reinforcement programs are often successful in controlling children (Birnbrauer, Wolf, Kidder, and Tague, 1965; Kuypers, Becker, and O'Leary, 1968; O'Leary and Becker, 1967; Quay, Werry, McQueen, and Sprague, 1966; Wolf, Giles, and Hall, 1968).

The token reinforcement program utilized by O'Leary and Becker (1967) in a third-grade adjustment class dramatically reduced disruptive behavior. In order to maximize the possibility of reducing the disruptive behavior of the children, O'Leary and Becker used several major variables simultaneously. The first objective of the present study was to analyze the separate effects of some of the variables utilized in the former study. More specifically, the aim was to examine the separate effects of Classroom Rules, Educational Structure, Teacher Praise, and a Token

Reinforcement Program on children's disruptive behavior. Rules consisted of a list of appropriate behaviors that were reviewed daily. Educational Structure was the organization of an academic program into specified 30-min lessons such as spelling and arithmetic. The second objective was to assess whether a Token Reinforcement Program used only in the afternoon had any effect on the children's behavior in the morning. Third, the present study sought to examine the extent to which the effects of the Token Reinforcement Program persisted when the Token Program was discontinued.

Method

Subjects

Seven members of a second-grade class of 21 children from lower-middle class homes served. At the beginning of the school year, the class had a mean age of 7 yr, 5 months, a mean IQ score of 95 (range 80 to 115) on the California Test of Mental Maturity, and a mean grade level of 1.5 on the California Achievement Test. The class was very heterogeneous with regard to social behaviors. According to the teacher, three of the children were quite well behaved but at least eight exhibited a great deal of undesirable behavior. The teacher, Mrs. A., had a master's degree in counseling but had only student teaching experience. She was invited to participate in a research project involving her class and received four graduate credits for participating in the project.

Observation

Children. Mrs. A. selected seven children for observation. All seven children were observed in the afternoon and four of the seven (S1, S2, S4, and S6) were also observed in the morning. Morning observations were made by a regular observer and a reliability checker from 9:30 to 11:30 every Monday, Wednesday, and Friday. Afternoon observations were made by two regular observers and a reliability checker from 12:30 to 2:30 every Monday, Wednesday, and Friday. Observations were made by undergraduate students who were instructed never to talk to the children or to make any differential responses to them in order to minimize the effect of the observers on the children's behavior. Before Base Period data were collected, the undergraduates were trained to observe the children over a three week period in the classroom, and attention-seeking behaviors of the children directed at the observers were effectively eliminated before the Base Period.

Each child was observed for 20 min each day. The observers watched the children in a random order. Observations were made on a 20-sec observe, 10-sec record basis; *i.e.*, the observer would watch the child for 20 sec and then take 10 sec to record the disruptive behaviors which had occurred during that 20-sec period. The categories of behavior selected for observation were identical to those used by O'Leary and Becker (1967). Briefly, the seven general categories of disruptive behavior were as follows: (1) *motor behaviors:* wandering around the room; (2) *aggressive behaviors:* hitting, kicking, striking another child with an object; (3) *disturbing another's property:* grabbing another's book, tearing up another's paper; (4) *disruptive noise:* clapping, stamping feet; (5) *turning around:*

turning to the person behind or looking to the rear of the room when Mrs. A. was in the front of the class; (6) *verbalization:* talking to others when not permitted by teacher, blurting out answers, name-calling; and (7) *inappropriate tasks:* doing arithmetic during the spelling lesson.

The present study was a systematic replication of O'Leary and Becker (1967). To facilitate comparison of the two studies, the dependent measure reported is the percentage of intervals in which one or more disruptive behaviors was recorded. Percentages rather than frequencies were used because the length of the observations varied due to unavoidable circumstances such as assemblies and snow storms. Nonetheless, most observations lasted the full 20 min, and no observation lasting less than 15 min was included.

Teacher. In order to estimate the degree to which the teacher followed the experimental instructions, Mrs. A. was observed by two undergraduates for 90 min on Tuesday and Thursday afternoons. Teacher behavior was not observed on Monday, Wednesday, and Friday when the children were observed because Mrs. A. understandably did not wish to have as many as five observers in the room at one time. Furthermore, because Mrs. A. was somewhat reluctant to have three regular observers and one or two graduate students in the room at most times, she was informed of the need for this observational intrusion and the mechanics thereof. This explanation made it impossible to assess the teacher's behavior without her knowledge, but it was felt that deception about teacher observation could have been harmful both to this project and future projects in the school. Nonetheless, frequent teacher observations by two graduate students who were often in the room the entire week ensured some uniformity of her behavior throughout the week. The graduate students frequently met with Mrs. A. to alert her to any deviations from the experimental instructions, and equally important, to reinforce her "appropriate" behavior. Observations of the teacher's behavior were made on a 20-sec observe, 10-sec record basis. The categories of teacher behavior selected for observation were as follows:

I. Comments *preceding* responses.
   A. *Academic instruction:* "Now we will do arithmetic"; "Put everything in your desk"; "Sound out the words."
   B. *Social instruction:* "I'd like you to say 'please' and 'thank you' "; "Let me see a quiet hand"; "Let's sit up."

II. Comments *following* responses.
   A. *Praise:* "Good"; "Fine"; "You're right"; "I like the way I have your attention."
   B. *Criticism:* "Don't do that"; "Be quiet"; "Sit in your seat!"
   C. *Threats:* "If you're not quiet by the time I count three. . . .": "If you don't get to work you will stay after school"; "Do you want to stay in this group?"

The teacher's praise, criticism, and threats to individual children were differentiated from praise, criticism, and threats to the class as a whole. For example, "Johnny, be quiet!" was differentiated from "Class, be quiet!" Thus, eight different classes of teacher behavior were recorded:

two classes of comments preceding responses and six classes following responses.

Procedure

The eight phases of the study were as follows: (1) Base Period, (2) Classroom Rules, (3) Educational Structure, (4) Praising Appropriate Behavior and Ignoring Disruptive Behavior, (5) Tokens and Back-up Reinforcement, (6) Praising Appropriate Behavior and Ignoring Disruptive Behavior (Withdrawal). (7) Tokens and Back-up Reinforcement, and (8) Follow-up. Three procedures, Educational Structure and both of the Token Reinforcement Phases, were instituted for a 2-hr period during the afternoon. The remainder of the procedures were in effect for the entire day. The eight procedures were in effect for all 21 children. The first four conditions were instituted in the order of hypothesized increasing effectiveness. For example, it was thought that Rules would have less effect on the children's behavior than the use of Praise. In addition, it was thought that the combination of Rules and Praise would have less effect than the Tokens and Back-up Reinforcers.

Base Period. After the initial three-week observer training period, the children were observed on eight days over a six-week Base Period to estimate the frequency of disruptive pupil behavior under usual classroom conditions.[2] The teacher was asked to handle the children in whatever way she felt appropriate. During the Base Period, Mrs. A. instructed all the children in subjects like science and arithmetic or took several students to small reading groups in the back of the room while the rest of the class engaged in independent work at their seats. Neither the particular type of activity nor the duration was the same each day. Stars and various forms of peer pressure were sporadically used as classroom control techniques, but they usually had little effect and were discontinued until experimentally reintroduced during the Follow-up Phase.

Classroom Rules. There were seven observations over a three-week period during the second phase of the study. The following rules or instructions were placed on the blackboard by the teacher: "We sit in our seats; we raise our hands to talk; we do not talk out of turn; we keep our desks clear; we face the front of the room; we will work very hard; we do not talk in the hall; we do not run; and we do not disturb reading groups." Mrs. A was asked to review the rules at least once every morning and afternoon, and frequent observations and discussions with Mrs. A. guaranteed that this was done on most occasions. The classroom activities again consisted of reading groups and independent seat work.

Educational Structure. It has been stated that a great deal of the success in token reinforcement programs may be a function of the highly structured regimen of the program and not a function of reinforcement contingencies. Since the Token Phase of the program was designed to be used during structured activities that the teacher directed, Mrs. A. was asked to reorganize her program into four 30-min sessions in the afternoon in which the whole class participated, *e.g.*, spelling, reading, arithmetic, and science. Thus, the purpose of the Educational Structure Phase was to assess the importance of structure *per se*. Mrs. A. continued to review the rules twice a day during this phase and all succeeding phases.

During this phase there were five observations over a two-week period.

Praise and Ignore. In addition to Rules and Educational Structure, Mrs. A. was asked to praise appropriate behavior and to ignore disruptive behavior as much as possible. For example, she was asked to ignore children who did not raise their hands before answering questions and to praise children who raised their hands before speaking. In addition, she was asked to discontinue her use of threats. During this phase there were five observations over a two-week period.

Token I. Classroom Rules, Educational Structure, and Praise and Ignoring remained in effect. The experimenter told the children that they would receive points or ratings four times each afternoon. The points which the children received on these four occasions ranged from 1 to 10, and the children were told that the points would reflect the extent to which they followed the rules placed on the blackboard by Mrs. A. Where possible, these points also reflected the quality of the children's participation in class discussion and the accuracy of their arithmetic or spelling. The children's behavior in the morning did not influence their ratings in the afternoon. If a child was absent, he received no points. The points or tokens were placed in small booklets on each child's desk. The points were exchangeable for back-up reinforcers such as candy, pennants, dolls, comics, barrettes, and toy trucks, ranging in value from 2 to 30 cents. The variety of prizes made it likely that at least one of the items would be a reinforcer for each child. The prizes were on display every afternoon, and the teacher asked each child to select the prize he wished to earn before the rating period started.

During the initial four days, the children were eligible for prizes just after their fourth rating at approximately 2:30. Thereafter, all prizes were distributed at the end of the day. For the first 10 school days the children could receive prizes each day. There were always two levels of prizes. During the first 10 days, a child had to receive at least 25 points to receive a 2 to 5¢ prize (level one prize) or 35 points to receive a 10¢ prize (level two prize). For the next six days, points were accumulated for two days and exchanged at the end of the second day. When children saved their points for two days, a child had to receive 55 points to receive a 10¢ prize or 70 points to receive a 20¢ prize. Then, a six-day period occurred in which points were accumulated for three days and exchanged at the end of the third day. During this period, a child had to receive 85 points to receive a 20¢ prize or 105 points to receive a 30¢ prize. Whenever the prizes were distributed, the children relinquished all their points. During Token I, there were 13 observations over a five-week period.

For the first week, the experimenter repeated the instructions to the class at the beginning of each afternoon session. Both the experimenter and Mrs. A. rated the children each day for the first week in order to teach Mrs. A. how to rate the children. The experimenter sat in the back of the room and handed his ratings to Mrs. A. in a surreptitious manner after each rating period. Mrs. A. utilized both ratings in arriving at a final rating which she put in the children's booklets at the end of each lesson period. The method of arriving at a number or rating to be placed in the child's booklet was to be based on the child's improvement in behavior. That is, if a child showed any daily improvement he could receive a rating of approximately 5 to 7 so that he could usually earn at least a small prize. Marked improvement in behavior or repeated displays of relatively good behavior usually warranted ratings from 8 to 10. Ratings from 1 to 5 were given when a child was disruptive and did not evidence any daily improvement. Although such a rating system involves much subjective judgment on the part of the teacher, it is relatively easy to implement, and a subsidiary aim of the study was to assess whether a token system could be implemented by one teacher in a class of average size. After the first week, the teacher administered the Token Program herself, and the experimenter was never present when the children were being observed. If the experimenter had been present during the Token Phases but not during Withdrawal, any effects of the Token Program would have been confounded by the experimenter's presence.

Withdrawal. To demonstrate that the token and back-up reinforcers and not other factors, such as the changes that ordinarily occur during the school year, accounted for the observed reduction in disruptive behavior, the token and back-up reinforcers were withdrawn during this phase. There were seven observations over a five-week period. When the prizes and the booklets were removed from the room, Mrs. A. told the children that she still hoped that they would behave as well as they had during the Token Period and emphasized how happy she was with their recent improvement. Rules, Educational Structure, and Praise and Ignoring remained in effect.

Token II. When the tokens and back-up reinforcers were reinstated, the children obtained a prize on the first day if they received 25 to 35 points. For the next four days there was a one-day delay between token and back-up reinforcement; the remainder of the Token Reinstatement Period involved a two-day delay of reinforcement. The prize and point system was identical to that during Token I. During this phase, there were five observations over a two-week period.

Follow-up. The token and back-up reinforcers were again withdrawn in order to see if the appropriate behavior could be maintained under more normal classroom conditions. In addition to the continued use of Praise, Rules, and Educational Structure, it was suggested that Mrs. A. initiate the use of a systematic star system. Children could receive from one to three stars for good behavior twice during the morning and once during the afternoon. In addition, the children received extra stars for better behavior during the morning restroom break and for displaying appropriate behavior upon entering the room at 9:15 and 12:30. At times, extra stars were given to the best behaved row of children. The children counted their stars at the end of the day; if they had 10 or more stars, they received a gold star that was placed on a permanent wall chart. If a child received 7 to 9 stars, he received a green star that was placed on the chart. The boys' gold stars and the girls' gold stars were counted each day; and each member of the group with the greater number of gold stars at the end of the week received a piece of candy. In addition, any child who received an entire week of gold stars received a piece of candy. All children began the day without stars so that, with the exception of the stars placed on the wall chart, everyone entered the program at the same level.

Such a procedure was a form of a token reinforcement program, but there were important procedural differences between the experimental phases designated Token and Follow-up. The back-up reinforcers used during the Token Phases were more expensive than the two pieces of candy a child could earn each week during the Follow-up Phase. In addition, four daily ratings occurred at half-hour intervals in the afternoons during the Token Phases but not during Follow-up. On the other hand, stars, peer pressure, and a very small amount of candy were used in the Follow-up Phase. As mentioned previously, both stars and peer pressure had been used sporadically in the Base Period with little effect. Most importantly, it was felt that the procedures used in the Follow-up Phase could be implemented by any teacher. During this phase there were six observations over a four-week period.

Reliability of Observations

The reliabilities of child observations were calculated according to the following procedure: an agreement was scored if both observers recorded one or more disruptive behaviors within the same 20-sec interval; a disagreement was scored if one observer recorded a disruptive behavior and the other observer recorded none. The reliability of the measure of disruptive behavior was calculated for each child each day by dividing the number of intervals in which there was agreement that one or more disruptive behaviors occurred by the total number of agreements plus disagreements. An agreement was scored if both observers recorded the same behavior within the same 20-sec interval. A disagreement was scored if one observer recorded the behavior and the other did not. The reliability of a particular class of teacher behavior on any one day was calculated by dividing the total number of agreements for that class of behaviors by the total number of agreements plus disagreements for that class of behaviors. Reliabilities were calculated differently for child behaviors and teacher behaviors because different types of dependent measures were utilized for children and the teacher, and it was felt that reliability measures should be reported for the specific dependent measures used.

At least one reliability check was made during the afternoon on every child during the Base Period, and one child had three.[3] The average reliability of the measure of disruptive behavior during the afternoons of the Base Period for each of the seven children ranged from 88 to 100%. The following figures represent the number of reliability checks and the average of those reliability checks after the Base Period through the first Token Period for each child: S1: 6, 86%; S2: 7, 94%; S3: 6, 94%; S4: 6, 93%; S5: 6, 87%; S6: 6, 84%; S7: 6, 97%. Because of the repeated high reliabilities, reliability checks were discontinued when the token and back-up reinforcers were reinstated; *i.e.*, no reliability checks were made during or after the Withdrawal Phase.

Adequate morning reliabilities were not obtained until the Rules Phase of the study. The following figures represent the number of reliability checks and the average of those reliability checks during the Rules Phase: S1: 3, 93%; S2: 4, 68%; S4: 3, 91%; S6: 3, 88%. Morning reliability checks after the Rules Phase were made approximately every three observations (approximately seven occasions) through the first Token Per-

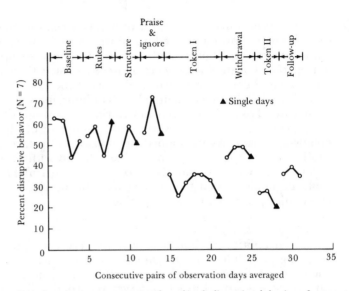

FIG. 1. *Average percentage of combined disruptive behavior of seven children during the afternoon over the eight conditions: Base, Rules, Educational Structure, Praise and Ignore, Token I, Withdrawal, Token II, Follow-up.*

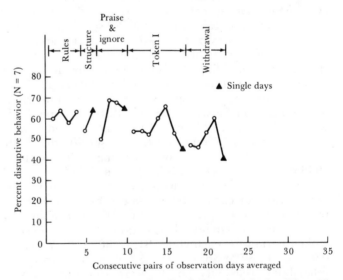

FIG. 2. *Average percentage of combined disruptive behavior of four children during the morning over five conditions: Base, Rules, Educational Structure, Praise and Ignore, Token I, Withdrawal, Token II, Follow-up.*

iod. Average reliabilities of the four children during the Rules, Educational Structure, Praise and Ignore, and Token I Phases ranged from 92 to 99%.

Eleven reliability checks for the various classes of teacher behavior before the Praise and Ignore Phase was introduced yielded average reliabi-

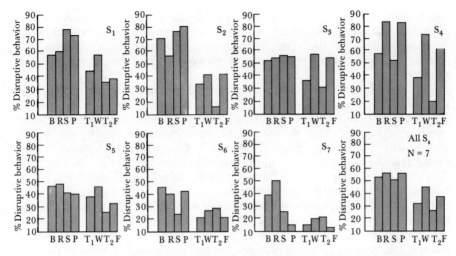

Fig. 3. *Percentage of combined disruptive behavior for each of seven children during the eight conditions: Base, Rules, Educational Structure, Praise and Ignore, Token I, Withdrawal, Token II, Follow-up.*

lities as follows: academic instruction, 75%; social instruction, 77%; praise to individuals, 77%; praise to the class, 94%; criticism to individuals, 73%; criticism to the class, 72%; threats to individuals, 83%; and threats to the class, 83%.

Results

Child Behavior

Figures 1 and 2 present morning and afternoon data; some of the variability within conditions can be seen. Figure 3 presents data of individual children as well as an average of seven children across afternoon conditions. An analysis of variance was performed on the percentages of combined disruptive behavior, averaged within the eight afternoon experimental conditions, for the seven subjects (see Fig. 3). The analysis of variance for repeated measures (Winer, 1962, p. 111) indicated differences among the eight experimental conditions ($F = 7.3$; $df = 7, 42$; $p < 0.001$). On the other hand, the percentages of combined disruptive behavior of the four children observed in the morning, averaged within conditions, did not change during Rules, Educational Structure, Praise and Ignore, or Token I ($F = 1.0$; $df = 4, 12$). Differences among afternoon conditions were assessed by *t*-tests. Significant and nonsignificant differences are grouped individually in Table 1.[4]

It should be emphasized that comparisons between Follow-up and Praise and Ignore are more meaningful than comparisons between Follow-up and Base, Rules, or Educational Structure. Praise and Follow-up were similar procedures; both included Rules, Educational Structure, and Praise and Ignore. The Base Period did not include any of these. Furthermore, after Rules and Educational Structure were initiated, Mrs. A. stated that she required more academic work from the children than during Base Period. A statistical analysis of the group data suggests that a token reinforcement program can reduce disruptive behavior and that a token reinforcement program can be replaced with a variant of a token program without an increase in disruptive behavior. However, a more detailed analysis of the data for individual children indicated that the Token Reinforcement Program was more effective for some children than others.

The introduction of Rules, Educational Structure, and Praise and Ignore did not have any consistent effects on behavior (see Fig. 3). Praising Appropriate Behavior and Ignoring Disruptive Behavior deserve special mention. Although Mrs. A. used criticism occasionally during the Praise and Ignore Phase, she generally ignored disruptive behavior and used praise frequently. Initially, a number of children responded well to Mrs. A.'s praise, but two boys (S2 and S4) who had been disruptive all year became progressively more unruly during the Praise and Ignore Phase. Other children appeared to observe these boys being disruptive, with little or no aversive consequences, and soon became disruptive themselves. Relay races and hiding under a table contributed to the pandemonium. Several children were so disruptive that the academic pursuits of the rest of the class became impossible. The situation became intolerable, and the Praise and Ignore Phase had to be discontinued much earlier than had been planned.

The disruptive behavior of S7 was reduced to a very low level of 15% by a combination of Rules, Educational Structure, and Praise and Ignore. In the previous token program (O'Leary and Becker, 1967), in which a number of variables including rules, praise, educational structure, and a token program were simultaneously introduced, disruptive behavior during the token period was reduced to a level of 10%. Thus, the present Token Reinforcement Program probably would not be expected further to reduce disruptive behavior in this child.

During Token I, there was a marked reduction ($-$18%) in the disruptive behavior of five children (S1, S2, S3, S4, and S6) and a reduction of 3% in S5. Withdrawal of the Token Program increased disruptive behavior from 5% to 45% in these six children. Reinstatement of the Token Program led to a decrease in five of these six children (S1, S2, S3, S4, S5). The disruptive behavior of five children (S1, S2, S4, S5, and S6) ranged from 8% to 39% lower during the Follow-up than during the Praise and Ignore Phase of the study. Since on no occasion did the Follow-up procedures precede Token I and/or Token II, this study did not

TABLE 1.

Significant		Non-significant	
Token I *vs.* withdrawal	$t = 3.3**$	Rules *vs.* educational structure	$t = 0.8$
Token II *vs.* withdrawal	$t = 2.9*$	Educational structure *vs.* praise	$t = 1.0$
Token I *vs.* praise	$t = 3.4**$	Base *vs.* withdrawal	$t = 1.2$
Token II *vs.* praise	$t = 3.0*$	Token I *vs.* follow-up	$t = 1.1$
Base *vs.* follow-up	$t = 3.2**$	Token II *vs.* follow-up	$t = 1.5$
Praise *vs.* follow-up	$t = 3.3**$		
Withdrawal *vs.* follow-up	$t = 3.2**$		

$**p < 0.02$, $df = 6$.
$*p < 0.05$, $df = 6$.

demonstrate that Token I and/or Token II were necessary conditions for the success of the Follow-up procedures.

In summary, Token I and Token II were definitely associated with a reduction of disruptive behavior, *and* the Follow-up procedure was effective with three of the six children (S1, S2, and S4) who had more than 15% disruptive behavior during the Praise and Ignore Phase (S7 had 15% disruptive behavior during the Praise and Ignore Phase). Token I and Token II were associated with marked reductions of disruptive behavior of S3, but the frequency of disruptive behavior during the Follow-up was not substantially lower then during the Praise and Ignore Phase. Definitive conclusions concerning the effects of the Token Program cannot be drawn for S5 and S6, although some reduction of disruptive behavior was associated with either Token I and Token II for both of these children. In addition, the disruptive behavior of S5 and S6 was 8% and 20% less respectively during Follow-up than during the Praise and Ignore Phase.

Teacher Behavior

On any one day, the percentage of each of the eight classes of teacher behavior was calculated by dividing the number of intervals in which a particular class of behavior occurred by the total number of intervals observed on that day. Percentages rather than frequencies were used because of slight variations from the usual 90-min time base.

The percentages of different classes of teacher behavior were averaged within two major conditions: (1) data before Praise and Ignore Phase, and (2) data in the Praise and Ignore and succeeding Phases. The data in Fig. 4 show that in the Praise and Ignore Phase, Mrs. A. increased use of praise to individual children from 12% to 31% and decreased use of criticism to individuals from 22% to 10%. Mrs. A. also increased use of praise to the class from 1% to 7% and decreased criticism directed to the class from 11% to 3%. Because the frequency of threats was quite low, threats to individuals and threats to the class were combined in one measure. Using this combined measure, Mrs. A.'s use of threats decreased from 5% to 1%. There were no differences in Mrs. A.'s use of academic or social instruction. Consequently, the changes in the children's disruptive behavior can probably be attributed to contingencies and not to Mrs. A.'s use of cues concerning the desired behaviors.

Discussion

Although a Token Reinforcement Program was a significant variable in reducing disruptive behavior in the present study, the results are less dramatic than those obtained by O'Leary and Becker (1967). A number of factors probably contributed to the difference in effectiveness of the programs. The average of disruptive behavior during the Base Period in the 1967 study was 76%; in the present study it was 53%. The gradual introduction of the various phases of the program was probably less effective than a simultaneous introduction of all the procedures, as in the previous study. In the earlier study, the children received more frequent ratings. Five ratings were made each day at the introduction of the 1.5-hr token program, and they were gradually reduced to three ratings per

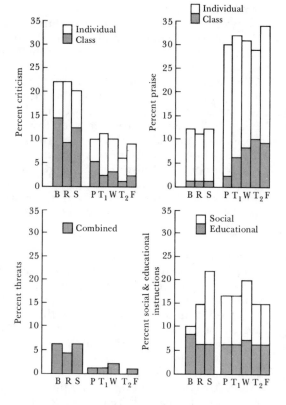

FIG. 4. *Percentage of various teacher behaviors to individuals and to the class during the eight conditions: Base, Rules, Educational Structure, Praise and Ignore, Token I, Withdrawal, Token II, Follow-up.*

day. In the present study, the children received four ratings per day during a 2-hr period. In the 1967 study, the class could earn points for popsicles by being quiet while the teacher placed ratings in the children's booklets; in the present study, group points were not incorporated into the general reinforcement program. In the 1967 study, the teacher attended a weekly psychology seminar where teachers discussed various applications of learning principles to classroom management. An *esprit de corps* was generated from that seminar that probably increased the teacher's commitment to change the children's behavior. Although Mrs. A. received graduate credits for her extensive participation in the project, she did not attend a seminar in classroom management. A number of children in the present study had an abundance of toys at home and it was difficult to obtain inexpensive prizes which would serve as reinforcers; in the earlier study, selection of reinforcers was not a difficult problem, since the children were from disadvantaged homes.

Related Gains

Academic. The 14 children for whom there were both pre- and post-measures on the California Achievement Test (including S1, S4, S5, S6, and S7) gained an average of 1.5 yr from October to June. The mean CAT score in October was 1.5 while the mean score in June was 3.0. Although there was no matched control group, such gains are greater than those usually obtained (Tiegs and Clark, 1963). While such gains are promising, conclusions about the effects of a token system on academic performance must await a more systematic analysis.

Attendance. Comparisons of the attendance records of the seven children during the observational days of the token and non-token phases yielded the following results: the average attendance percentage during the 45 observation days of Base, Rules, Educational Structure, Praise and Ignore, and Withdrawal was 86%. The average attendance percentage during the 20 observation days of Token I and Token II was 98%; the average attendance percentage during the 26 observation days of Token I, Token II, and Follow-up (a variant of a token program) was 99%. These attendance records are very encouraging, but because of the usual seasonal variations in attendance and the small sample of children, more definitive evidence is needed before conclusions about the effects of a token program on attendance can be made.

Cost of Program

The cost of the reinforcers in the present study was approximately $125.00. It is estimated that 3 hr of consulting time per week would be essential to operate a token reinforcement program effectively for one class in a public school. The cost of such a program and the amount of consulting time seem relatively small when compared to the hours psychologists spend in therapy with children, often without producing significant behavioral changes (Levitt, 1963). Furthermore, as evidenced in the present study, control of behavior may be shifted from reinforcers, such as toys, to reinforcers existing within the natural educational setting, such as stars and peer prestige.

Generalization

During the morning, the majority of the children were engaged in independent seat work, while four or five children were in a reading group with the teacher in the back of the room. Although there were rules and frequent instructions during the morning, there was little reinforcement for appropriate behavior, since Mrs. A. felt that it would be disruptive to the rest of the class to interrupt reading groups to praise children who were doing independent work at their seats. Ayllon and Azrin (1964) found that instructions without reinforcement had little effect on the behavior of mental patients. Similarly, Rules (instructions) without reinforcement did not influence the behavior of the children in this study.

Mrs. A. was instructed to praise appropriate behavior and ignore disruptive behavior in the morning as well as the afternoon. However, Mrs. A.'s criteria of appropriate behavior in the morning differed from her criteria in the afternoon. For example, in the morning she often answered questions when a child failed to raise his hand before speaking. In the afternoon, on the other hand, she generally ignored a child unless he raised his hand. In order to achive "generalization" of appropriate behavior in a Token Program such as this one, the teacher's response to disruptive behavior must remain constant throughout the day. The percentage of disruptive behavior was reduced during the morning of the first few days of Token I, but the children presumably learned to discriminate that their appropriate behavior was reinforced only in the afternoon. The differences in the children's behavior between the morning and the afternoon help to stress the point that "generalization" is no magical process, but rather a behavioral change which must be engineered like any other change.

Notes

[1] Portions of this paper were presented to the American Psychological Association, September, 1968, San Francisco, California. This research was supported primarily by Research Grant HD 00881-05 to Wesley C. Becker from the National Institutes of Health and secondarily by a Biomedical Science Grant 31-8200 to K. Daniel O'Leary from the State University of New York at Stony Brook. The authors are grateful to Nancy Brown, Connie Dockterman, Pearl Dorfmann, Jeanne Kappauf, Margery Lewy, Stanley Madsen, and Darlene Zientarski, who were the major observers in this study. Appreciation for support of this study is expressed to Dr. Lowell Johnson, Director of Instruction, Urbana Public Schools, and to Mr. Richard Sturgeon, elementary school principal. The greatest thanks goes to Mrs. Linda Alsberg, the teacher who executed the Token Reinforcement Program and tolerated the presence of observers both morning and afternoon for eight months. Her patience and self-control during the Praise and Withdrawal Phases of the program were especially appreciated.

[2] Ten of the 18 observations during the Base Period were eliminated because movies were shown on those days, and disruptive behavior on those days was significantly less than on days when movies were not shown. Although movies were seldom used after Base Period, the seven subsequent observations when movies occurred were eliminated.

[3] Before 10 of the 18 observation days during the Base Period were eliminated because movies were shown on those days, at least three reliability checks had been made during the afternoon on each child.

[4] Two-tailed tests.

References

Allen, K. Eileen, Hart, Betty M., Buell, Joan S., Harris, Florence R., and Wolf, M. M. Effects of social reinforcement on isolate behavior of a nursery school child. *Child Development,* 1964, **35**, 511–518.

Ayllon, T., and Azrin, N. H. Reinforcement and instructions with mental patients. *Journal of the Experimental Analysis of Behavior,* 1964, **7**, 327–331.

Becker, W. C., Madsen, C. H., Arnold, Carole R., and Thomas, D. R. The contingent use of teacher attention and praise in reducing classroom behavior problems. *Journal of Special Education,* 1967, **1** (3), 287–307.

Birnbrauer, J. S., Wolf, M. M., Kidder, J. D., and Tague, Celia. Classroom behavior of retarded pupils with token reinforcement. *Journal of Experimental Child Psychology,* 1965, **2**, 219–235.

Brown, P., and Elliot, R. Control of aggression in a nursery school class. *Journal of Experimental Child Psychology,* 1965, **2**, 103–107.

Hall, R. V., Lund, Diane, and Jackson, Deloris. Effects of teacher attention on study behavior. *Journal of Applied Behavior Analysis,* 1968, **1**, 1–12.

Harris, Florence R., Johnston, Margaret K., Kelley, C. Susan, and Wolf, M. M. Effects of positive social reinforcement on regressed crawling of a nursery school child. *Journal of Educational Psychology,* 1964, **55**, 35–41.

Harris, Florence R., Wolf, M. M., and Baer, D. M. Effects of social reinforcement on child behavior. *Young Children,* 1964, **20**, 8–17.

Kuypers, D. S., Becker, W. C., and O'Leary, K. D. How to make a token system fail. *Exceptional Children,* 1968, **35**, 101–109.

Levitt, E. E. Psychotherapy with children: A further evaluation, *Behaviour Research and Therapy,* 1963, **1**, 45–51.

O'Leary, K. D., and Becker, W. C. Behavior modification of an adjustment class: A token reinforcement program. *Exceptional Children,* 1967, **33**, 637–642.

Quay, H. C., Werry, J. S., McQueen, Marjorie, and Sprague, R. L. Remediation of the conduct problem child in a special class setting. *Exceptional Children,* 1966, **32**, 509–515.

Scott, Phyllis M., Burton, R. V., and Yarrow, Marian R. Social reinforcement under natural conditions. *Child Development,* 1967, **38**, 53–63.

Tiegs, E. V., and Clark, W. W. Manual, California Achievement Tests, Complete Battery. 1963 Norms. California Test Bureau, Monterey, California.

Winer, B. J. *Statistical principles in experimental design.* New York: McGraw-Hill, 1962.

Wolf, M. M., Giles, D. K., and Hall, R. V. Experiments with token reinforcement in a remedial classroom. *Behaviour Research and Therapy,* 1968, **6**, 51–64.

Zimmerman, Elaine H., and Zimmerman, J. The alteration of behavior in a special classroom situation. *Journal of the Experimental Analysis of Behavior,* 1962, **5**, 59–60.

REFERENCES TO THE INTRODUCTIONS

Allison, J., Miller, M., and Wozny, M. Conservation in behavior. *Journal of Experimental Psychology: General*, 1979, *108*, 4–34.

Barker, L. M., Best, M. R., and Domjan, M. (Eds.). *Learning Mechanisms in Food Selection*. Waco, Texas: Baylor University Press, 1977.

Bolles, R. C. *Theory of Motivation*. New York; Harper and Row, 1967 (2nd ed., 1975).

Bruner, J. S., Goodnow, J., and Austin, G. *A Study of Thinking*. New York: Wiley, 1956.

Carter, D. E., and Werner, T. J. Complex learning and information processing by pigeons: A critical analysis. *Journal of the Experimental Analysis of Behavior*, 1978, *29*, 565–601.

Charnov, E. L. Optimal foraging, the marginal value theorem. *Theoretical Population Biology*, 1976, *9*, 129–136.

deVilliers, P. A. Choice in concurrent schedules and a quantitative formulation of the law of effect. In W. K. Honig and J. E. R. Staddon (Eds.), *Handbook of Operant Behavior*. Englewood Cliffs, New Jersey: Prentice-Hall, 1977.

Ferster, C. B., and Skinner, B. F. *Schedules of Reinforcement*. New York: Appleton-Century-Crofts, 1957.

Herrnstein, R. J. Method and theory in the study of avoidance. *Psychological Review*, 1969, *76*, 49–69.

Herrnstein, R. J. On the law of effect. *Journal of the Experimental Analysis of Behavior*, 1970, *13*, 243–266.

Herrnstein, R. J. Acquisition, generalization and discrimination reversal of a natural concept. *Journal of Experimental Psychology: Animal Behavior Processes*, 1979, *5*, 116–129.

Herrnstein, R. J., Loveland, D. H., and Cable, C. Natural concepts in pigeons. *Journal of Experimental Psychology: Animal Behavior Processes*, 1976, *2*, 285–302.

Honig, W. K., and Urcuioli, P. J. The legacy of Guttman and Kalish (1956): Twenty-five years of research on stimulus generalization. *Journal of the Experimental Analysis of Behavior*, 1981, *36*, 405–445.

Köhler, W. *The Mentality of Apes*. New York: Harcourt, Brace, and World, 1925.

Köhler, W. Simple structural functions in the chimpanzee and chicken. In W. D. Ellis (Ed.), *A source book of Gestalt psychology*. New York: Harcourt, Brace, 1939.

Krebs, J. R. Optimal foraging: Decision rules for predators. In J. R. Krebs and N. B. Davies (Eds.), *Behavioral Ecology*. Sunderland, Massachusetts: Sinauer Associates, 1978.

LoLordo, V. M. Selective associations. In A. Dickenson and R. A. Boakes (Eds.), *Mechanisms of Learning and Motivation*. Hillsdale, New Jersey: Erlbaum, 1979.

Mackintosh, N. J. A theory of attention. *Psychological Review*, 1975, *82*, 276–298.

Mowrer, O. H. On the dual nature of learning—A reinterpretation of "conditioning" and "problem solving". *Harvard Educational Review*, 1947, *17*, 102–148.

Olton, D. S. Mazes, maps, and memory. *American Psychologist*, 1979, *34*, 583–596.

Olton, D. S., and Samuelson, R. J. Remembrance of places passed: Spatial memory in rats. *Journal of Experimental Psychology: Animal Behavior Processes*, 1976, *2*, 97–116.

Pavlov, I. P. *Conditioned reflexes*. Oxford: Oxford University Press, 1927.

Pearce, J. M., and Hall, G. A model for Pavlovian learning. *Psychological Review*, 1980, *87*, 532–552.

Premack, D. Reinforcement theory. In D. Levine (Ed.), *Nebraska Symposium on Motivation*. Lincoln, Nebraska: University of Nebraska Press, 1965.

Rescorla, R. A. Pavlovian conditioning and its proper control procedures. *Psychological Review*, 1967, *74*, 71–80.

Rescorla, R. A. *Pavlovian Second-Order Conditioning*. Hillsdale, New Jersey: Erlbaum, 1980.

Rescorla, R. A., and Furrow, D. R. Stimulus similarity as a determinant of Pavlovian conditioning. *Journal of Experimental Psychology: Animal Behavior Processes*, 1977, *3*, 203–215.

Rescorla, R. A., and Solomon, R. L. Two-process learning theory: Relations between Pavlovian conditioning and instrumental learning. *Psychological Review*, 1967, *74*, 151–182.

Seligman, M. E. P. *Helplessness*. San Francisco: W. H. Freeman, 1975.

Smith, E. E., and Medin, D. L. *Categories and concepts*. Cambridge, Massachusetts: Harvard University Press, 1981.

Solomon, R. L. The opponent process theory of acquired motivation. *American Psychologist*, 1980, *35*, 691–712.

Spence, K. W. The nature of discrimination learning in animals. *Psychological Review*, 1936, *43*, 427–449.

Spence, K. W. The differential response in animals to stimuli varying within a single dimension. *Psychological Review*, 1937, *44*, 430–444.

Staddon, J. E. R., and Simmelhag, V. L. The "Superstition" experiment: A reexamination of its implications for the principles of adaptive behavior. *Psychological Review*, 1971, *78*, 3–43.

Thorndike, E. L. Animal intelligence: an experimental study of the associative processes in animals. *Psychological Monographs*, 1898, *2*, whole No. 8.

Tolman, E. C. Cognitive maps in rats and man. *Psychological Review*, 1948, *55*, 189–208.